JANUA LINGUARUM

Series Maior 96

Studia Memoriae
Nicolai van Wijk Dedicata

edenda curat
C. H. van Schooneveld
Indiana University

RASMUS RASK STUDIES
IN PRAGMATIC LINGUISTICS

VOLUME 2

Conversational Routine

Explorations in Standardized Communication Situations and Prepatterned Speech

Edited by

Florian Coulmas

MOUTON PUBLISHERS · THE HAGUE · PARIS · NEW YORK

ISBN: 90-279-3098-8

Printed in the Netherlands

To whom it may concern

General Editor's Preface

During the past 10 or 15 years, it has been possible to observe an interesting development in the study of human language use. To dub this movement (maybe not unexpected by many, though unwished for by a few) the "conversational revolution" would perhaps seem a bit exaggerated. However, nobody will deny that the status of spoken language as a Distinguished Object of linguistic research has improved greately when compared to, say, the times when grammars had to be formal (or at least be dressed up formally) to be recognized by a respectable linguist.

I would like to make the point that we have to do here with a *pragmatic* development, and I will clarify my point by making a few seemingly paradoxical observations and comments.

Why, for instance, is it the case that conversation never made the grade before, although it, in the strictest sense of the word, has made the scene as long as people have been using (oral) language?

Why has there been such an unvarying and constant interest among people in the art of "conversing," be it in one's own language or in others'? And, as a complement to this popular interest, why wouldn't a serious linguist, until recent years, be caught dead doing work on "incorrect" or substandard speech? When Eva Sivertsen published her work on *Cockney* [sic] *Phonology* in 1960, it caused a mild raising of the eyebrows in many linguistic quarters. Indeed, as the author herself says, "the Cockney dialect has long fascinated the amateur linguist . . . [However], the scholar has not shared the layman's interest in this dialect," (Sivertsen 1960, flap text). So it was not only the choice of title, but the subject itself that was provocative to the scientific community.

But notwithstanding this state of affairs in professional circles, people were using "substandard" speech and kept on "conversing" at all levels, without much regard for the linguists' worries. And there is an additional, historical consideration.

With the rise of a (more or less) enlightened bourgeoisie during the first half of the 19th century in many European countries, the need arose for a new mode of conversation. It was no longer enough to be able to talk about things in a merely elegant fashion without paying too much attention to content: rather, the demand was for facts. Conversation became a way of sharing world knowledge, especially knowledge about the sciences that seemed to guarantee a world of everlasting progress. From Diderot to Meyer, from the *Encyclopédie* to the *Konversationslexikon, il n'y a qu'un cri*: "Seh mal einer nach!" (the predictable ending of any dispute in postprandial conversation at the Jesuits' house in Copenhagen, Denmark, where Meyer was second in command only to St. Thomas Aquinas and the Bible).

With the development of the tourist trade, we saw the rise of a whole new branch and mode of language teaching and learning. Rather than laboriously trying to master the intricacies of one's own or other languages' structural properties (as taught, precisely, in "grammar" schools), people were enticed to study language "without tears" (whether due to the use of the ferula or to despair), to learn to speak a foreign language without having to study any grammar at all, yet use the language with native ease within a week or a month, provided they could afford to buy a set of grammophone records or a couple of tape decks. The visual images accompanying these optimistic advertisement slogans were all in the same vein: Mr. or Ms. Would-Be-Tourist sitting in a Paris sidewalk café, or asking their way around Piccadilly Circus (no small feat), or relaxing on some Southern European beach, being engaged all the time in conversational interaction with clearly distinguishable native speakers: the Paris *maître d'*, the London bobby, the olive-skinned Papagallo. Clearly, for these tourists-*in-spe* (by contrast to their linguistic fellow-humans) conversation was the name of the game.

I would like to pursue my pragmatic bias, alluded to above, a little further, and ask: What is so important about conversation? What makes people, for instance, go through the pains of taking conversation lessons, and invest considerable amounts of money (not speaking of the time and energy involved) in acquiring skills that, after all, are not related to one's function in society or the acquisition of riches, but rather to some luxury game, or (as in the case of Eliza Doolittle) to whims and pseudo-scientific notions?

To stay with Eliza for a moment: Conversation, from her point of view, became *more* than a pointless game (although it surely remained Professor Higgins' whim to the very end). What made Eliza tick, once she got set in motion?

For Eliza, and for all of us who recognize some of her in ourselves, conversation is not just a game. In pragmatic terms, conversation is a serious and necessary occupation. It is a passport to social interaction, one could say. In Eliza's case, the least mistake in her vowel qualities would have been enough to shut the doors of "society" on her (quotes intentional). And although hers admittedly is a special case, and "society" has indeed changed (including the linguists, see above), conversation is still an important skill, just as a correct pronunciation still plays an important role for most people.

But what about the content? Does conversation have to be on serious topics to be taken seriously?

Whoever thinks so, is subject to a vocational confusion. It is typically the headmaster's, the grammarian's, the philosopher's, even the linguist's point of view. That is, it is a disorder in the mind of people who are privileged enough to be able to choose and maintain the topics of any conversation, or in general, of their interaction with their fellow humans: people, moreover, who are very much biased towards the professional view that discussions on "issues" should be the preferred form of verbal interaction.

Fortunately such (mostly implicit) assumptions have come to be questioned lately. Even linguists have begun to understand that conversational interaction has its own rules, and that these rules may be somewhat different from what the linguists used to think of when they spoke of "rules". This holds both with regard to the form and substance of the conversation, both as to its expression and its content. Eliza was perfectly aware of her own precarious conversational status, and hers is not the only case where a "faux pas" or the choice of a wrong word can mean one's final *démarche*; a terminal, not just a terminological blunder. Conversation is by no means a business to be carried on lightheartedly: neither is it a free-for-all without any rules. Daily conversation is the means for keeping people in touch, not the educated discussions of the higher kind that a minority of humans are allowed to indulge in. So what *is* involved in the art of making conversation? How does one converse?

It would be a mistake to think that the main thing is to be able to imitate the utterances of the other(s). As with any and all human interaction, conversation is not predictable. What you say depends to a great extent on what the other says: mere parroting, however, does not count as conversation. And it will not help you much to have a "native-like" command of the language when you are a foreign speaker, if all you can think about is your pronunciation. Surely Eliza's conversation was not very interesting as long as the only things she would allow herself to say were "The rain in Spain falls mainly in the plain," and similar profundities.

But how about the rules of conversation? And where do conversational routines come in? Contrary to the conception of grammar held by many naïve linguists, the conversational rules are rules in their own right. They should not be confused with, or patterned upon, the kind of rules that are found e.g., in a generative grammar of the Chomskyan kind. The fact that their existence, or maybe just their importance, has been overlooked by professional linguists for a long time can be explained by the official biases of linguistics, allowing rules of a particular form only. Clearly, conversational rules cannot be dealt with on the basis of a syntax-oriented rule concept (and this includes syntax-based semantics as well). Conversational rules and routines purport to structure and make possible both the predictable and the non-predictable aspects of conversation. As such, they are an important part of any serious descriptive work in the area of one of the commonest forms of human verbal interaction.

What I have been stressing here is, of course, the *pragmatic* point of view, which allows us to incorporate other aspects in our analysis of conversation than are usually accounted for in strictly syntax-oriented descriptions. In this larger framework we are able to ask more interesting questions about what is going on when people "make conversation" than we could in "older" models of description. Among these questions are those such as:

- Who decides on when and where to begin or end a conversation (opening and closing routines)?
- Who decides on the topic, respectively a change of topic, for a conversation?
- Whose belief system and world view are borne out and reinforced by conversational routines and rules? (For instance in parent-child interaction: certain matters are at the bottom of the conversational pool, and bringing them up would muddle the waters. Certain topical and turn-taking rules exclude the child from freely interacting with his/her parents, whose general concept of conversation with children often seems to be of the "talk-to" rather than "talk-with" kind).
- Whose positions are justified and fortified by the use of particular routines (modes of address, reverential and referential "strokes," etc.)?

The list is far from complete, but it serves to point out the importance of the matters Coulmas' authors are discussing in the present volume, and why I think it is an interesting addition to our *Studies* and to the study of its subject: the pragmatic knowledge and understanding of the oldest linguistic trade.

Mullsjö, Sweden, 24 August 1979

Jacob Mey
General Editor

Contents

FLORIAN COULMAS

Introduction: Conversational Routine

After many years of intensive research in sociolinguistics, speech act theory, and conversational analysis there is no need whatsoever, to *defend* the claim that conversation is a structured activity. The pragmatic dimension of speech is generally recognized, and the organizational machinery of conversational interaction is given its proper place in the study of languages, largely thanks to the pioneer work of scholars with a sociological background such as Sacks and Schegloff. That conversation is not an arbitrary array of utterances, and that there is, indeed, structure in speech beyond the internal structure of decontextualized sentences is a fact now commonly accepted among linguists as well as ethnographers of communication. Yet, some discourse phenomena are still waiting for proper treatment.

Our knowledge of verbal routines, of how they are performed, what part they play in the "speech economy" (Hymes, 1974:447) of a community, and how they affect its linguistic system is still largely confined to the ancedotal, and to individual studies of isolated cases. Perhaps this is so, because it often proves necessary to enter the psycho-socio-cultural domain in order to account for the dynamics of routinized speech. And in recent times, this has not been something linguists have dwelled upon.

Theoretical linguists, in the last two decades, have been trained to investigate the generative capacity of language. The relations between the generative system and the socio-linguistic habits regulating how this system is put to use were dismissed, as a "problem of performance," from linguistics proper. As a side effect, the study of prefabricated linguistic expressions was almost completely neglected. So prevailing was the study of the undoubtedly essential property of language to allow the production of ever new sentences that the assumption that almost every sentence has an occurrence probability of close to zero was never questioned, much less put to a rigorous test. This assumption may have obscured the fact for many that much of what is actually said in everyday interaction is by no means unique. Rather, a great deal of communicative activity consists of enacting routines making use of prefabricated linguistic units in a well-known and generally accepted manner. We greet and bid farewell to one another, introduce ourselves and others, apologize and express gratitude, buy groceries and order meals, exchange wishes, make requests, ask for advice or information, report on what we did, and announce what we are about to do, etc. As similar speech situations recur, speakers make use of similar and sometimes identical expressions, which have proved to be functionally appropriate. Thus, competent language use is always characterized by an equilibrium between the novel and the familiar. In every society there are standardized communication situations in which its members react in an automatic manner. Routines reflect, in a sense a conception of a social system (cf., Coulmas 1979 for details), and their importance for socialization as well as secondary acculturation is quite obvious, because routines are tools which individuals employ in order to relate to others in an accepted way.

It is not surprising, therefore, that child discourse is one of the domains of research where routines have been given the attention they deserve lately. It was argued, for instance, by Bates (1976:292) that children acquire a repertoire of performative or pragmatic idioms "without having the flexible, conscious control over form-function relations." Idioms of this sort enable children to perform a number of communicative functions before they are capable of forming similar free expressions of equal complexity. Ervin-Tripp (1977:168) has pointed out that a number of highly frequent directive markers, such as *why don't you, wouldja, canya* or *couldja* have acquired lexical status: "high frequency forms can be interpreted by storage in the lexical unit, and by identifying as wholes." They are learned *en bloc,* and, as Garvey (1977:43) observes, are available at an early age. It is not only that children learn how to perform individual speech acts in this way; they also gain control of a device for guiding the sequencing of moves in conversation. Typically, speech acts are not only internally structured, they are also elements of larger structures. Their sequential character is part of what normal speakers know about language. To some extent, the sequential organization of conversation is routinized. It is only natural that children should acquire sequencing routines – such as, e.g., summons-answer (Schegloff, 1968); greeting-greeting (Firth, 1972; Goody, 1972) etc. – at a developmentally early stage.

It would be a mistake to infer from these observations that conversational routine is only a problem of language acquisition and language use. Rather, a proper account of routines will have to analyze the intricate relations between language use as a kind of rule governed behaviour and language as a system, the relations which are involved in prepatterned speech.

It will have to account, on the one hand, for the delicate double analyzability of many routine formulae, abounding in everyday conversation. To avoid preconceived definitions of routine formulae that may prove arbitrary, we will simply regard them as highly conventionalized prepatterned expressions whose occurrence is tied to more or less standardized communication situations. We have at our disposal a large stock of these expressions, for all kinds of occasions, and the dilemma they present to the analyst is this: While most of them, except for one-word formulae such as *hi, hello, yes, no, right, well,* etc., display grammatical structure, a great many of them are simultaneously either on the brink of lexicalization or have turned into fixed idiomatic units of the lexicon already.

On the other hand, a proper treatment will have to account for routine in discourse organization. The recurrence of communicative goals in everyday life has led to the evolution of standardized strategies for their accomplishment. Many speech events are very similar, and essentially of the same kind. The wording may not be identical from one performance to the next, but the sequential organization is more or less constant. Considerable range is shown here. In some cases, strategies have turned into full rituals with little or no tolerance of variation; examples are certain parts of religious services or childrens' verses. In other cases, only the order is fixed and the wording is flexible (cf., Goffman, 1971:92ff.). Ritual is not restricted to the sacred sphere of social organization. In his minute analyses of face-to-face interaction in everyday life Goffman (esp., 1967, 1971) has freed this notion from its exclusively religious context. He has convincingly demonstrated that the social function of ritual is not only to uphold authority, but that it serves an important function in giving men confidence and behavioral certainty. Successful co-ordination of social intercourse heavily depends on standardized ways of organizing interpersonal encounters. These standardized ways are what Goffman calls "interaction rituals".

Interaction in everyday life involves ritual, convention, and routine. Conventions in the sense of Lewis (1969) and Schiffer (1972) could be considered as profane rituals; and routines as "empty" conventions. These, however, are only rough-and-ready differentiations. No keen distinction can be drawn between these three notions. According to the authors just mentioned, conventions are standardized solutions to co-ordination problems. By the same token, routines are kinds of interactions where no "negotiations" (cf. Cicourel, 1972:81) is necessary between individuals. In the enactment of verbal routines the creativity of language is socially canalized according to successful solutions of recurring verbal tasks, fixed by functional appropriateness and tradition.

The Oxford English Dictionary defines routine as "a regular course of procedure; a more or less mechanical or unvarying performance of certain acts or duties." Clearly, according to this definition, routine can be found in a great variety of human practices. Wherever repetition leads to automatization, we could call a performance a routine. For our purpose, we have to make some qualifications on this definition. First, the focus of this book is on routine in *conversation.* Hence, we will not consider here each and every routinized way in which socially recognized functions are carried out, but only communicative functions. Secondly, as a direct consequence of the afore-mentioned restriction of our attention, we will not consider idiosyncratic routines evolving in the biography of individuals, because conversation is, by its very nature, a co-operative practice. Conversational routines are tacit agreements, which the members of a community presume to be shared by every reasonable co-member. In embodying societal knowledge they are essential in the handling of day-to-day situations.

Even if idiosyncratic and non-communicative routines are left unconsidered, we have to account for a wide range of phenomena under the heading of "conversational routine". As early as 1962, Hymes pointed out that an immense portion of verbal behavior consists of linguistic routines, and that the speech habits of a community cannot be fully described without a thorough account of routines. The analysis of routines, he maintains, "includes identification of idiomatic units, not only greeting formulas and the like, but the full range of utterances which acquire conventional significance, for an individual, group or whole culture" (Hymes, 1962:38f.). As indicated above, linguistic conventions and routines are essentially a social phenomenon. Thus, I feel, the "*conventional* significance" of a lexical unit, phrase, or pattern *for an individual* is not a very happy notion. Apart from this, however, I find myself in perfect agreement with Hymes, particularly as regards the relationship of routine and idiomaticity.

Not all routines are idioms, in the sense that their meanings are unpredictable (cf., Chafe, 1973; Makkai, 1972, 1975). But routine usage of expressions can, and often does have an effect on the meanings and the meaningfulness of these expressions. Excessive currency corrupts expressiveness and diminishes meaningfulness. Investigation of what is called the contact or phatic function of speech (Malinowski, 1923; Laver, 1975) revealed a high recurrence of stereotyped patterns of behavior of which stereotyped phrases are internal ingredients. Phrases such as, *Good to see you! How are you? Take care! I haven't seen you for ages! Nice to meet you. I'm afraid I must . . ., I'm sorry, I have to . . ., Be seeing you, Cheerio, See you, Many thanks! Good Lord* etc., etc., (for some further English examples see e.g., Quirk et al., 1972:411ff.) are often perceived as hackneyed expressions having lost their expressiveness. They don't lack meaning in a strict sense altogether, as Malinowski (op. cit.) seems to have assumed; but it is common knowledge in semantics – or rather information theory – that frequency of occurrence and meaningfulness are inversely related; thus, as they are used more and more they mean less and less (cf. Chao, 1968:73). Relative frequency of occurrence – a factor completely ignored in competence linguistics – can therefore be considered an intrinsic feature of linguistic units. Obviously, it is closely related to the usefulness of expressions to speakers in recurrent situations.

Erosion of its literal meaning is one way in which an expression can turn into an idiom. The relations between function and meaning, and the difference between them, as well as the dependence of the latter on the former, becomes patently apparent in this connection. In Wittgenstein's (1968) terms, it is well-known, meaning is a function of use. Linguistic routines, idiomatized or not, furnish the most powerful testimony of the cogency of this view. Their meanings often are quite different from the sums of their parts, and cannot be properly explained without reference to the conditions of their use (cf. also Hockett, 1956 and Pike, 1967:602ff. on this point). This is one of the basic assumptions, common to the articles of this book.

It is important to note, however, that relative frequency of occurrence and conditions of use are not equally and invariably important dimensions of the semantic description of all linguistic units. Fillmore has advanced a very important theoretical point on this in a recent paper. He claims "that semantic theory must reject the suggestion that all meanings need to be described in the same terms" (1978:18). For example, in the case of a formulaic expression such as *help yourself!*, a specification of the conditions of its use is more important than with a lexical items such as *butterfly* whose meaning is best described in terms of a categorial definition or class membership. There are different kinds of semantic information that combine to form lexical items, fixed phrases, clichés, routine formulae, etc. More often than not, lexical items seem to have the capacity of realizing more than one kind of meaning, which is not only a question of polysemy (cf. Makkai, 1978). They occur as independent units in their own right and for their own meaning, and they enter into larger units where their "regular" semantic and syntactic properties are often suspended. Hence, semantic theory, Fillmore concludes, "needs to recognize 'idioms,' having non-compositional semantic structure, 'phraseological units,' phrasal units that are partly arbitrary and partly motivated, as well as non-idiomatic 'formulas,' expressions whose frequency or popularity, rather than meaning, is conventional" (op. cit., 23). Even if routinely employed expressions are not idiomatic in a grammatical sense, they thus have a special status in the language, owing to the frequent and situation-bound use that the speech community makes of them.

It was repeatedly stressed by many scholars – especially Chafe, 1968; Makkai, 1972, 1975; Bolinger, 1976 – that any linguistic description which is meant to account for what the members of a speech community (implicitly) know about their language, and what they do with their language, must take into consideration these and similar properties of expressions. Idiomaticity, routine, and collocatability are psychologically real and salient characteristics of expressions, and hence, relevant categories of linguistic descriptions.

It may be noted in passing, that recognition of these features as features of language implies the breakdown of a number of sacred distinctions of modern linguistic theory. Frequency of occurrence and routine are allegedly performance phenomena. Yet, it was noted above, they have an impact on the meaning and meaningfulness of expressions; and meaning, it is commonly assumed, belongs to competence. Idiomaticity – and this was demonstrated most strikingly by Chafe (1970) – is a major linguistic device of semantic innovation, and, as such, does not allow a strictly synchronic treatment. Metaphor is clearly a property of utterances, or rather, a mechanism by which the speaker conveys his intended meaning. Successful metaphors turn into idioms, and many idioms are metaphorically transparent. Hence, idioms range on a continuum between productive and petrified metaphors. Some are units of the language, others are on the brink of turning into such units. Finally, the restricted collocatability of many lexical items cannot be explained on grammatical grounds. Again, we have to refer to diachronic considerations as well as norms of usage if we want to come to a proper understanding of why **My good wishes* or **Several thanks* are deviant while *My best wishes* and *Many thanks* are not. Similarly, the items which can be used to fill the blank in *Have a good* . . . are not only determined syntactically and semantically, but also by rules of usage. As with idioms, no straight line can be drawn between the freely collocatable, the restrictedly collocatable and the completely frozen.

What is generally seen as linguistic creativity – the innovative capacity of grammatical rules – is not only restricted by these rules themselves (Hymes has emphasized this point repeatedly; cf., e.g., 1974). Rather, creativity in language is to be regarded as an intricate interplay of grammatical rules, functional adequacy, situational appropriateness, stylistic preferences, and norms of use. The ability to communicate in a socially acceptable manner implies a knowledge of this interplay, whose significance becomes particularly obvious in connection with the creation and performance of routines. Potentially, therefore, the study of conversational routine and, more generally, conventionality in language could shed important new light on the relation of language system and language use. With linguistic routine in focus, traditional boundaries within linguistics are shifting: the old dichotomies between language and speech, synchronic and diachronic analyses, competence and performance, can no longer be taken as absolute. Their value as analytic distinctions is severely relativized in a context of research where structure and function are not seen as independent dimensions of language, but where the interaction between both is considered the most important and interesting issue.

Routines are a means of guiding a person's normal participation in social interaction. Viewed from the interpretative side, they constitute standardized links between what people actually say and what sort of communicative functions their utterances serve to perform. Literal meanings and functions of utterances – i.e., the verbal acts that they accomplish – are not bi-uniquely mapped on each other. This is a very general and important characteristic of language, which has been discussed in detail under the suggestive heading of "indirect speech acts" (cf., e.g., Davison, 1975; Fraser, 1975; Searle, 1975, 1975a; Brown/Levinson, 1978). Discrepancies between meaning and function, or, to use Searle's terms: between propositional content and illocutionary force of an utterance can be observed frequently and regularly in conversational etiquette. Much discussed examples are modalized expressions of the kind quoted above, i.e., *can you . . .*, *would you . . .*, *could you . . .* etc. They have been described as questioning certain felicity conditions of the speech act in whose place they are uttered (Searle, 1975). Superficially, expressions such as these are questions, but they are intended and normally function as requests. That they are correctly interpreted – so the argument goes – is due to the fact that the conditions for the performance of the action in question are obviously fulfilled, and that the speaker is not assumed to question the obvious. Therefore, his intended illocutionary point is most likely not the one of a question, but something else: a request or command.

The process in operation here was dubbed "implicature" by Grice (1968). According to his theory, the key to a proper understanding of human conversation is the "Cooperative Principle"; the mutual assumption of participants that they contribute to the common verbal exchange in a sensible way. The interpretation of implicatures is a process of closing inferential gaps which need to be filled in order to preserve the assumption that the Cooperative Principle is being observed, in spite of outward indications to the contrary. Grice makes an important distinction between *conversational* implicatures, which have to be calculated in the course of conversation, and *conventional* implicatures that have become automatic. Many routines can be regarded as implicatures of the latter kind. That is, they originate in conversational implicatures, but the calculation of the implicatures having turned into a routine is no longer actually carried out.

Some routines of this kind can be subsumed under general rules of usage. As an illustration consider a rule formulated by Sinclair et al., (1972) as a result of their observation of classroom discourse: Any interrogative containing one of the modal auxiliaries *can, could, will, would,* with the addressee as subject and the predicate describing an action that is feasible for the addressee to perform, is to be interpreted as a command. In keeping with this rule, certain lexical items are routinely interpreted in a derived, or non-literal sense. Similarly, no inferential reasoning is necessary in order to find out that the speaker is not actually gripped by fear or physically ailing when he says *I'm afraid . . .* or *I'm sick of. . . .* These expressions have acquired conventionalized readings which may have evolved out of implicatures or metaphors. The calculation of a conventional implicature is a form of problem solving. The enactment (and interpretation) of a conversational routine, by contrast, can be described as a resort to a successful solution of a recurrent problem.

For a non-native speaker there is often no difference between conversational implicatures and conventional ones (routines): In either case, he has to try to interpret their meanings by inference, unless he happens to have learned the conventional implicature in question. However, many routines, especially politeness routines, defy interpretation by inference on the basis of word meanings alone and without knowledge of cultural habits, customs, values, attitudes, etc. A striking example for this is reported by Doi, a Japanese scholar who describes the adaption difficulties he experienced during his stay in the USA:

> The "please help yourself" that Americans use so often had a rather unpleasant ring in my ears before I became used to English conversation. The meaning, of course, is simply "please take what you want without hesitation", but literally translated it has somehow a flavor of "nobody else will help you", and I could not see how it came to be an expression of good will. (Doi, 1973:13)

The non-native speaker who has learned the meanings of the words *please help yourself* has only mastered one part of the routine that these words are used to perform in a culturally sanctioned way. Conversely, a proper understanding of a routine does not necessarily depend on an understanding of the individual words. Rather, foreign language learners tend to acquire a repertoire of routine formulae, that is, linguistic expressions whose occurrence is triggered or required by standardized situational circumstances, much sooner than they see through their internal structure, thus ensuring their ability to master recurrent communicative tasks. Evidence for this assumption is presented by Hakuta who investigated second language learning of infants through rote memorization of "prefabricated patterns". He concludes that this is a very important strategy, because it enables the learner to employ regular, patterned segments of speech "without knowledge of their underlying structure, but with the knowledge as to which particular situations call for what patterns" (Hakuta, 1974:288). The meaning of the whole phrase is experienced by the learner as part of habitual action and situational context. Thus, the meanings of the constituent parts of a routine often do not suffice to guarantee proper understanding, and by the same token, routines may be learned before and independent of their individual word meanings and internal structures.

In addition to the fact that routines make the fullest use of cultural knowledge common to the members of a community, they are of vital importance to the foreign speaker for the following reason. In the course of learning a foreign language, there are a number of recurrent communication problems.

For example, the learner will often be in a situation where he wants to learn something rather specific about the language, where he wants his partner to repeat or paraphrase what he has said, where he wants to say that he did not understand, or that his partner should please speak slowly, etc. These are important learning strategies whose routinization can greatly accelerate the learning process. It is therefore important for the learner to acquire or develop routines allowing him to carry out these strategies at minimal effort and maximal effect. *I don't understand. Please, speak slowly. Please, say it again. What does ... mean? What's the opposite of ...? How do you say ... in English? Can I say ...?* are stock phrases which foreign speakers may use as chunks repeatedly without variation. Fixed as they are, their use involves no combinatorial difficulties, and they prove very useful in reaching the intended communicative goals.

The same holds true for regular language use in day-to-day interaction. For the foreigner it is important to master the use of everyday routines, because they are what provides speech with a "natural" and proficient flavor. Owing to the general lack of attention to this phenomenon, we do not have at our disposal many data or measurements as to the ratio of prepatterned and newly invented phrases in extemporaneous speech. However, some observations indicate that prepatterned speech units are vastly more pervasive than our generatively programmed mind might lead us to assume. Sorhus (1977) studied a corpus of over 130.000 words of spontaneous Canadian speech, and she came to the startling result that in daily conversational exchanges an average of a fixed expression every five words is a normal rate. In other words, her count has yielded a frequency as high as 20 per cent of the words uttered. To be sure, a careful evaluation of this material is necessary, and it cannot be considered unquestioningly as representative. Yet it is very impressive. Sorhus' explanation for such a high rate is also quite persuasive. The focus of her investigation was on hesitation phenomena, and it was in this context that her attention was drawn to prepatterned phrases. She realized that one of the functions of many of these phrases is "to give the speaker time to find words for his ideas" (Sorhus, 1972:214) and became convinced that they "act as fillers, too" (212).

Undoubtedly, speakers often need time to arrange their thoughts and to prepare consecutive conversational moves. That routinized speech serves an important function here is a plausible hypothesis, which is much in keeping with what Ladefoged has to say on the interaction of memory and combinational manipulation in speech from a neurophysiological point of view: "The central nervous system is like a special kind of computer which has rapid access to items in a very large memory, but comparatively little ability to process these items when they have been taken out of memory" (quoted from Bolinger, 1976:2). Thus routine formulae can be drawn from the memory without much effort, and, at the same time, they give us time for conversational planning.

So far, our discussion has shown that routines embody instructions for executing certain verbal functions involving more complicated different processes than the computation of elementary meanings. It is important to note that they operate on different levels of everyday discourse. If approached under a "form-centered" perspective, routines figure as conventionalized, prepatterned speech units to be analyzed with regard to the communicative functions they are suited to perform. On the other hand, routines can also be detected on the more abstract level of strategies and action patterns or procedures. This approach could be called "function-centered". The focus of the former approach is on lexical material, whereas the latter concentrates on principles of conversational organization. These approaches should not be regarded as alternative, but rather as mutually supplementary and correlative. In practice, neither of them is carried through in its pure form, and the division of this book into two parts only very roughly reflects a preference of the respective authors for one or the other.

In the first part of the book, a number of articles discuss routine formulae from a contrastive viewpoint in various different languages. As Ferguson points out in the first chapter, routines are a universal phenomenon of human languages, which in some cases – notably greeting formulae – can be linked to animal behavior. However, there is considerable variation between different cultures, which often do not agree in having equivalent formulae for similar situations. Ferguson examines examples from Syrian Arabic and American English. In discussing problems of variation, use, and acquisition as well as diachronic characteristics of routines, he argues that they constitute "a set of facts about human language" which are not only of cardinal interest to the ethnographer of communication, but also need to be accommodated in linguistic theory.

A similar approach is taken by Tannen and Öztek who present Turkish and Greek "combinations of words which have become associated in everyone's mind and are often repeated in sequence." Their comparative investigation is a contribution to the study of speech in culturally specific settings, uncovering cross-cultural differences as well as similarities. Through commonly accepted routines the individual affirms his belongingness to a socio-cultural group. Hence, routine formulae are heavily loaded with social meaning and closely linked with rules of conduct. It is not only in this regard, however, that verbal stereotypes differ from one language to another. Apparently, there is also a wide span of variation as to the total number of commonly used formulae: "Greek has fewer fixed formulas than Turkish but many more than English." In order to remedy the almost complete lack of data in this area a list of over 200 fixed expressions is appended to Tannen and Öztek's paper.

In Lithuanian routine formulae are found to be even less frequent than in English. In her paper Drazdauskiene discusses the problem of stereotypes in conversation from the perspective of foreign language education. By and large, the same functions are manifested by stereotypes in English and Lithuanian, but differences in routinized speech are equally apparent. These differences are found to be owing not so much to the differing socio-cultural contexts of the two languages as to structural distinctions regarding the expressions of meaning: analytical in English and synthetical in Lithuanian. This sheds interesting light on the relationship of structure and function in language. The question as to how structural properties of languages affect pecularities of language behavior in different speech communities opens an intriguing field of future research. Drazdauskiene's findings point to a different degree of straightforwardness and courtesy in the two languages, which is paralleled, if not occasioned, by structural differences.

Generally, frequency and distribution of routine formulae are determined by two factors: the social organization of the speech community, and the structural make-up of its language. As regards the first factor, the more tradition-oriented a society is, the more its members seem to make use of situational formulae. The rich repertoire of Japanese routine formulae underpins the validity of this hypothesis. A sub-set of Japanese routines is investigated in Coulmas' paper on thanks and apologies. Japanese etiquette calls for the expression of gratitude or apology on many different occasions, and the language provides a great variety of suitable formulae. Coulmas shows that the distribution of Japanese gratitude and apology formulae differ characteristically from European languages in such a way as to suggest a close relation between the respective speech acts they serve to perform. He then goes on to demonstrate some general structural similarities of thanks and apologies, which are both second elements of tripartite interaction patterns. A conspicuous feature of their distributional structure is their frequent occurrence at the initial position of conversations, thus serving as "openers". Japanese politeness requires the sense of obligation toward another person to be expressed not only at the time when he actually carries out a favorable act but also when one sees him again the next time. Again the interrelation of form and function is very interesting here, because apology formulae in many instances are used for expressing gratitude, and both apology and gratitude formulae often serve to perform greetings. Thus, there is a decisive difference between using apology or gratitude expressions and making apologies or thanks. Furthermore, standards as to what calls for an apology or for thanks vary considerably from one society to another. Yet, in spite of the polyfunctionality of gratitude and apology formulae in Japanese, their occurrence is characterized by a high degree of predictability, which is typical of routine formulae of various kinds, and without which a rational ordering of verbal interaction would be impossible.

Many routines have a function in sustaining orderlines in conversation and in securing a smooth flow of interaction, but particularly salient in this regard are what Keller calls "gambits". Gambits are sentence openings serving as conversational strategy signals. They introduce what the speaker is about to say, and, at the same time, provide him with a means of evaluating his conversational contribution (is it a statement of opinion or a suggestion, an expansion of the subject or the introduction of a new topic, a reinforcing argument or a conflicting view?). Moreover, they serve an important function in conversational role negotiation, as for example, when a participant establishes his partner's permission to take or keep a turn (e.g., *Do you know what I think . . ., Listen to me . . ., Wait a second . . .*), or when he indicates his readiness to pass the turn to the next speaker (e.g., *So, what do you think of that?*). For every strategic function in conversation there are gambits whose proper usage greatly facilitate the progression from one state of the game to the next. An eloquent speaker has at his disposal a great variety of these "communicative control signals," and quite obviously, they are invaluable for the foreign speaker who learns to use them at the right instant in conversation. They not only impart a skillful and adroit impression to his speech, but also give him some time to think of what to say next. It may be noted in passing that Keller is in line here with the findings of Sorhus (1977) reported above. His interest in this particular kind of conversational routines, like Drazdauskiene's, originally arose out of a research program in English as a Second Language which resulted in a series of three textbooks for the Language Bureau of the Federal Government of Canada. Gambits are only very rarely made teaching objects in foreign language classes. This neglect, however, is in radical disproportion with the pervasiveness of these expressions in everyday conversation. Many foreign language teachers may find them too unimportant to pay much attention to them. Like anybody else they are not consciously aware of every aspect of their own native language usage and fail to realize how important a role they play in the way conversation is organized and assembled in a socially meaningful manner.

Manes and Wolfson investigate another set of expressions whose formulaic character is not immediately obvious, yet are highly routinized and regular: Compliments in American English are, as they convincingly show, formulaic in nature. Their analysis is based on a great deal of systematic observation of actual behavior, and highlights some interesting points that would not be likely to be accessible to intuition or self-report. In contrast to several institution-bound speech acts, compliments do not seem to be a genre whose performance is severely restricted by social conditions. There is no apparent restriction on the speaker's imagination other than that something positive should be said of the addressee. Obviously, there are innumerable ways of doing that. Yet, a thorough analysis of the vocabulary used in a large set of compliments as well as their syntactic make-up testifies "the almost total lack of originality" as the most conspicuous feature of compliments. Structural variation and lexical choice are found to be extremely limited. If this is somewhat counter-expectational, the authors show that, in ethnographic terms, both the routine character of compliment formulae and its latency are functional. Compliments are often embedded in "framing remarks". What Manes and Wolfson have to say on this point accords very well with Keller's observations about gambits. Apparently, it is the formulaic character of these framings which often obscures the fact that the compliments around which they are arranged are themselves formulae. The major communicative function of compliments is phatic. It is not unlikely that this is, in fact, the ulterior reason for their formulaic nature.

Like the other chapters of the first part of the book, Verschueren's paper focusses on lexical material, and like most of them, his method is comparative. Yet, his investigation of conversational routines in English and Dutch takes a different approach. While Ferguson, Tannen and Öztek, Drazdauskiene, Coulmas, Keller and Manes and Wolfson concentrate on sets of lexical items which are being used for the *enactment* of routines, Verschueren is concerned with lexical items for the *description* of routines. The approach that he advances is somewhat reminiscent of ethno-semantic studies, his main hypothesis being that the lexical items which a language provides for the description or naming of speech acts, can be viewed as indices of the importance of these speech acts for the members of its speech community. In this regard, he is particularly interested in finding out why some routines, for example greetings, farewells, thanks, apologies, introductions, congratulations, or compliments, etc. have lexicalized labels for their description while others have none. How can we explain these "lexical gaps," and what conclusions can we draw from interlinguistic differences in this regard? It was pointed out repeatedly that routines carry a great deal of social meaning. The notions that get lexicalized in a language for their description represent typifications of routines and action patterns. Therefore, it is not unreasonable to assume that lexical patterns of vocabulary items for the description of rotines can be correlated with the cognitive status of these routines as well as with other aspects of verbal behavior in the respective culture. In short, lexical descriptions of routines embody knowledge. Hence, they offer a promising starting point for the ethnography of communication. However, a comprehensive assessment of their analytic significance in this regard would seem to require an interdisciplinary approach.

A discussion of conversational routine touches upon many aspects of verbal behavior and inevitably leads beyond the realm of lexical items, however indicative they may be. Thus, in the second part of this book, a number of problems in regard to routine strategies and action patterns are investigated.

A topic of major importance is the presentation of respect and verbal politeness. A detailed analysis of politeness strategies as well as the verbal means for their execution is carried out by House and Kasper. The general assumption that different communities sustain different politeness standards together with the observation that the performance of German students of English "is often considered impolite by native speakers" had motivated a contrastive analysis of politeness phenomena. A comparative study of complaints and requests reveals interesting differences as to the "directness level" of these speech acts when performed by English and German speakers. In a sense, the notion of *directness level* is an elaboration of Grice's *implicature* (see above p. 7) in that the relative complexity of the calculation of an implicature corresponds to the directness level of the utterance. From the data that House and Kasper examine, significant differences emerge in the directness levels of German and English requests and complaints. Thus, an unexpected and very stimulating result of their analysis is that implicature turns out to be a dimension of ethnolinguistic variation. Among the lexical items that serve as "politeness markers," modalized expressions are again found to play an important role. A variety of sub-classes is distinguished ("upgraders," "downgraders," "hedgers," etc.) some of which closely correspond to Keller's classification of gambits. Apparently, expressions of this kind exist in all languages, but their strategic functions for communicating politeness and respect differ greatly in accordance with social norms and rules of conduct.

Implicature as a routinely employed strategy for the expression of meaning is a point which is also discussed by Griffin and Mehan. One of the questions they address in their study is in how far implicatures become routinized in teacher-pupil interaction. As a general strategy they seem to play an important role in teachers' evaluations of pupils' responses: if a minor part of an answer is expressly mentioned by the teacher as being correct, he often thereby implicates that the rest is false. Utterances of this sort simultaneously serve two or more functions. Accordingly, implicatures are seen by Griffing and Mehan, above all, as evidence of the "polyfunctional nature of language" without which the multiform accomplishments of linguistic acts would be impossible. In the picture they sketch of the sociolinguistic complexities of lessons it occupies a central position. It is this ability to produce utterances that serve a variety of functions at once which prevents the course of action in the classroom to turn into an automatic and repetitious ritual. While many aspects are predetermined, not everything is fixed once and for all in classroom interaction. It is, in other words, not completely without negotiation. Rather, classroom interaction is characterized by spontaneous improvisations on basic patterns making use of routinized elements. In order to account for this "fine play between ritual and spontaneous motifs" Griffin and Mehan develop a very dynamic notion of routine and ritual, suggesting that rules are "spontaneous rituals and negotiated conventions." Routines can be changed, and conventions can be renegotiated. Given the role relations in the classroom, this is, however, often done by announcements of the teacher.

Announcements are what Rehbein is concerned with in his article. While the focus of most of the papers in the first part of the book is on all sorts of strategy markers, he gives a detailed account of the internal structure of a particular type of routine strategy. More accurately, he scrutinizes those segments of discourse where conversational aims are verbalized thus exteriorating the planning phase of verbal action. Announcing, in Rehbein's sense, is an important part of conversational organization. It is a pattern of communicative action routinely employed as an organizational tool whenever the participants of a speech event want to co-ordinate their communicative plans. In many instances, the message of such announcements is framed by routine formulae, such as *by the way . . ., listen . . ., o.k. then . . .,* etc. "Speaking implies hearing, and hearing implies engaging the speaker in an unfolding spiral of meaning, not the transmission and reception of information as separate and distinct acts," as Griffing and Mehan put it. Announcing anticipated activities is an important means of directing the hearer's attention, and thus a vital prerequisite for the realization of language as a mode of interaction. How important it is becomes intelligible on the basis of Rehbein's minute analysis of the initial phase of conversational moves which is shown to encompass a plan, an announcement, a beginning, and an opening.

Announcing is a partially routinized strategy of discourse organization which speakers frequently employ when they "fall out of a routine," that is, when they want the discourse to turn into a direction which does not conform with routine expectations. Clearly, there are different kinds of routines involved here, one of which may supersede the other. In "On saying you're sorry," Edmondson sketches a discourse model in which different senses of conversational routine are distinguished and accommodated. Like Coulmas and Fraser he investigates some problems of apologizing, concentrating on the ritualized aspects of this speech act and on their intergration in a discourse-analytic framework. On the basis of his empirical observations he arrives at a holistic notion of conversational routine which resembles that of Griffin and Mehan. Routine in conversation he suggests, involves "the links between a communicative act and a situation, a communicative act and some other communicative act, a locutionary and an illocutionary act, or an illocutionary act and an interactional act."

The routine links between situational circumstances and linguistic expressions seem to be strongly developed in all societies at interaction boundaries. Many scholars (notably Eibl-Eibesfeld, 1968; Firth, 1972; Goffman, 1972;

Goody, 1972) have pointed out the universality of ritual in greeting and parting behavior, which is also refered to in some of the chapters of this book (Ferguson, Tannen/Öztek, Coulmas). Laver singles out the problem of politeness in salutations in his treatment of conversational routine. Greeting formulae are the paradigm case of linguistic expressions whose referential meanings are functionally dominated, if not superseded, by their affective qualities. Insignificant as they are in terms of communicating information, they are an important instrument of what was called "phatic communion" by Malinowski. In Laver's analysis the framework for expressing politeness in language, which has been laid out by Brown and Levinson (1978), is applied to linguistic tokens used in greeting and parting salutations. Like many other routines, these formulae have often been put away indiscriminately in a file labeled "expressive function". However, as has been noted repeatedly, routines serve a variety of functions, and their situational conditions of use are accordingly complicated. Those occurring at interaction boundaries are crucially important for setting the stage of evolving social relationships. Like other "politeness markers" they define as well as indicate solidarity and respect, thus serving as a means of maintaining the delicate balance of mutual face wants.

The contributions of this volume are concerned with the clarification of the role of routinized, highly conventionalized, and to some extent, ritualized aspects of human conversation. Routine is a linguistic feature which is localized at the interface of language and speaking. It is a property of utterances; i.e., a property of instantiations of expressions; but it has an effect on language. Its penetration forces us to go beyond the reductionist limitations of solely structural analyses. Every normal member of a speech community can distinguish routine utterances from idiosyncratic ones. Furthermore, he knows that routine usage affects the meaningfulness of expressions, and he knows whether or not an utterance is to be assigned the full force of its literal meaning. Hence, this feature is worth explaining in a comprehensive theory of language. In such a theory, language is conceptualized as discourse. Context cannot be ignored here, and neither can the communicative functions that routinized discourse units are capable of serving. In other words, conversational routine requires a sociolinguistically informed pragmatic investigation, because a routine is not an expression or strategy, but rather an expression which is appropriate to a situation of a certain kind or a strategy which is appropriate relative to certain communicative ends. Hence, routines must be accounted for together with a description of situational or institutional contexts within which they could be produced. To a greater or lesser extent routines are routines by virtue of their being associated with typical circumstances. If a conventional situation is not matched by conventional speech, or, if a routinized discourse unit is removed from its conventional context, conversational routine is transformed into productive, sometimes original speech:

The old man is writing his autobiography. He begins it with words which my late Uncle Alex told me one time should be used by religious skeptics as a prelude to their nightly prayers. These are the words: "To whom it may concern." (Vonnegut, 1977:25).

PART ONE

Prepatterned Speech

CHARLES A. FERGUSON

The Structure and Use of Politeness Formulas*

ABSTRACT

The use of interpersonal verbal routines such as greetings and thanks is examined as a universal phenomenon of human languages, related in some way to the widespread "greeting" behavior of other animals. Examples from Syrian Arabic, American English, and other languages are used to show differing patterns of structure and use, susceptible of grammatical and sociolinguistic analysis. Features of diachronic change and children's acquisition are briefly treated. Call is made for better description and analysis of politeness formulas in grammars of languages and in ethnographies of communication. (Ritual, politeness, language change, language acquisition.)

THE STRUCTURE AND USE OF POLITENESS FORMULAS

The purpose of this paper[1] is to examine with some care the little snippets of ritual used in everyday encounters between people, expressions like *good morning,* or *thank you,* or *God bless you* said when someone sneezes, or *bye-bye* said to an infant by a departing guest. All human speech communities have such formulas, although their character and the incidence of their use may vary enormously from one society to another. Stragely enough this universal phenomenon has been very little studied by linguists or anthropologists or other students of human behavior. These politeness formulas (as I call them) are, in the words of Erving Goffman, "among the most conventionalized and perfunctory doings we engage in and traditionally have been treated by students of modern society as part of the dust of social activity, empty and trivial" (Goffman, 1971:90). Goffman, in his intentionally irritating way, seems to attribute our failure to study these interpersonal rituals to the general decline of religion in modern times. He says: "Only our secular view of society prevents us from appreciating the ubiquitousness and strategy of their location, and, in turn, their role in social organization" (89). Without

*Reprinted by permission of the author and Cambridge University Press from *Language in Society,* vol. 5, 1976, pp. 137–151.

in any way accepting his explanation for the dearth of systematic study of politeness formulas, I join him in bewailing it, and find in his works some of the most insightful treatments of them.[2]

Given the present popularity of the kind of investigation of animal behavior which goes under the name of "ethology" and the propensity on the part of a number of reputable scientists and sometimes less reputable popularizers of ethology to explain human behavior by reference to the activities of geese, stickleback fish, chacma baboons, and so on, it is even more surprising that no one has attempted to spell out in detail the biological substrate of the universal human exchange of politeness formulas. I say this because it seems to me fairly plausible that this human phenomenon *is* related phyletically to the bowings and touchings and well-described display phenomena of other species.[3] Yet the tendency has been to point to "greeting" behavior of numerous animal species and then jump to interpretations of human religion, esthetics, and philosophy rather than proceed to a systematic study of apparently simpler and more obviously related human behavior. I am thinking, in particular, of the stimulating and instructive discussion on the Ritualization of Behavior in Animals and Men conducted by Julian Huxley under the auspices of the Royal Society of London ten years ago (Huxley, 1966). The biologists provided excellent accounts of ritualization and its presumed evolutionary advantages, and the social scientists discussed topics ranging from mother-child interaction to the ritualization of international relations, but there was a noticeable gap in that no one provided accounts of observed interpersonal rituals of the politeness formula sort. It is surely a matter of interest that just as all human societies apparently use ritualized, non-verbal signals, they also have verbal ones, politeness formulas, which are used in conjunction with the non-verbal ones but are yet related in linguistic structure to the language as a whole which is used by the community.

Coming from another direction, it is also surprising that the intense interest among linguists and psychologists in the innate aspects of human linguistic competence, innate devices for acquiring language, and the like, has not led toward consideration of possible innate predispositions to the use of interjections and ritualized exchanges in which a given formula triggers an automatic response. Interest has focused more on innate grammatical relations, innate grammar evaluation mechanisms, innate representation of the principles of universal grammar. Little interest has been shown in how such a complex and delicate capacity could have evolved in our hominid or prehominid predecessors. One place to look might well be the universally operative phenomenon of politeness formulas. For those neurolinguists who are interested in localization of brain functions, it is worth noting the evidence that aphasics with lesions in the left hemisphere who have trouble with speech in general may use ritualized politeness formulas, like the related hesitation forms, non-referential introducers and conventionalized interjections with impressive fluency. I am not, of course, seriously suggesting that human language had its origin in politeness formulas[4] – although that would be no sillier than other hypotheses that have been taken seriously – but I would like to persuade reluctant students of language, of whatever disciplinary or theoretical orientations, that politeness formulas deserve their attention.

At present most accounts of politeness formulas are probably appendices of short chapters in grammars, although accounts may also be found in ethnographies and in guidebooks for travellers, officials, and missionaries. The accounts in grammars are usually limited to lists of formulas, with the briefest indication of their use and a sentence or two which says how important the formulas are in dealing with the 'natives'. As a typical example let me cite Banfield and Macintyre's *Grammar of the Nupe Language.* It contains lists of over 50 formulas and appropriate replies (108-13), and its 'sentence of importance' reads: "It is a very important subject, as salutations, etc., play a very large part in native life and customs, and the foreigner who can make the customary polite inquiries and return the proper answers to such inquiries, will hold a high position in the estimation of the people with whom he comes in contact" (108). Social scientists are only now beginning to recognize the importance and complexity of the use of politeness formulas in modern Western conversation and their usefulness to foreigners learning them, as ethnomethodologists and others subject American and English patterns to close scrutiny (e.g., Schegloff 1968, Schegloff & Sacks 1973). Very rarely do we have a straightforward account 'of native customs' which gives exact texts of the formulas and appropriate conditions of response (an example is Mercier's study of Moroccan politeness). Even rarer is a formal analysis such as Irvine's grammar of Wolof greetings (Irvine 1974) or a discursive sociolinguistic analysis such as Apte's description of expressions of gratitude in Marathi and Hindi (Apte 1974).

Studies which attempt comparative and general theoretical treatment of politeness formulas are usually limited to discussion of greetings, and I find it of some passing interest that four of the five important studies I am familiar with are themselves examples of ritualization. J. Huxley, R. Firth, E. Goody, and E. Goffman all are constrained to explain greetings in terms of a three-fold function, or three-fold condition of occurrence. I doubt that these authors are Trinitarian in their theology, but they all seem resolutely trinitarian in scholarly explanation, even though their respective trinities do not match very well. Huxley says that the three functions of ritualization are to improve the signal and therefore communication, to reduce intra-specific damage, and to strengthen sexual and social bonding. Firth sees three 'major social themes' of greetings and farewells: attention-production, identification, and reduction of anxiety in social contact. Goody finds three 'general functions' attached to greeting: to open a sequence of communicative acts, to define and affirm identity and rank, and to manipulate a relationship to achieve a specific result. Goffman claims that there are three 'general circumstances' in which supportive interchanges, as he calls them, take place: business, accident and ceremony, i.e., people are in contact because of other things they have to do, or by change being in the same area, or deliberately for the purpose of one or both of the individuals to perform a supportive riual. The fifth, less ritualized, study by Hilary Callen (Callen 1970, Chapter 7) is perhaps closest to the viewpoint adopted here, but without the focus on language analysis.

USE OF FORMULAS

Let me introduce the topic by two personal experiences, one which convinced me of the importance of politeness formulas and one which demonstrated that at least some of the dependencies among adjacent formulas have the nature of productive syntactic rules familiar from elsewhere in grammars. The first was an informal experiment – if I dare use that word – which I conducted many years ago with my secretary at that time. To see what the result would be, I simply did not reply verbally to her *good morning.* Instead I smiled in a friendly way and through the rest of the day behaved as usual. The next morning I did the same thing. That second day was full of tension. I got strange looks not only from the secretary but from several others on the staff, and there was a definite air of "What's the matter with Ferguson?" I abandoned the experiment on the third day because I was afraid of the explosion and possible lasting consequences. Of course it might not have been as serious as for the distracted night heron that Lorenz reports forgot to make his bow of greeting at the nest and was attacked by his own young (Lorenz 1937), or an unfortunate female gentoo penguin who neglects to bow in greeting to her mate when he is defending their territory (Roberts 1940). But it *was* serious. The importance of our trivial, muttered, more-or-less automatic polite phrases becomes clear when they are omitted or not acknowledged.[5]

The other experience was more complicated. I have recorded it elsewhere (Ferguson 1973), but it is worth repeating in this context. I was buying an article of clothing in an Arab market in Jerusalem years ago at a time when I was beginning my study of the Arabic spoken in that area. A passerby stopped to watch and enjoy the bargaining process, and when the purchase was completed he said to me *mabrūk*. I did not know that formula, which is normally addressed to the owner of a new possession such as clothing, car, or house, but clearly some response was in order. Now Arabic has a sizeable number of what have been called 'root-echo responses' (Ferguson 1967) formulas, each of which is an appropriate response to the occurrence of a particular triconsonantal root such as *√slm* or *√ʕfw* in the preceding formula. In my limited experience with Syrian Arabic, I had learned that an appropriate response to *ʕid mbārak* 'happy holiday' (lit., 'blessed holiday') was *'aḷḷa ybārik fık* 'God bless you' and I had also heard this response to the expression *ħallit lbarake* said about someone whose fruit trees were producing well. Probably *'aḷḷa ybārik fīk* was the root-echo response to *√brk.* I tried it, and the smile showed I had given the right reply. The whole analysis took only a split second, and was just like getting an instance of grammatical concord or case government right. It is a good example of the kinds of 'rules' which govern the use of politeness formulas, although in detail it may be quite unlike any 'rules' for formulas for English.

The greeting *good morning* is an excellent, uncomplicated example of a politeness formula. It is highly stereotyped and can be altered only with the definite recognition on the part of the speaker and hearer that it is being altered for some special effect. The adjective must be *good,* just as with *birthday* it is *happy* or with *Christmas* it is *merry* in American English. Substitutions of one of these adjectives for another in such formulas would mark intended humorous effect, or recongizable attempt to avoid a cliché, or the dialect of another part of the English-speaking world. Incidentally, *good morning* is in origin not an 'affirmation,' as Firth identifies it, but a 'welfare-wish' *may you have a good morning,* but it can be treated as an affirmation and given a facetious response such as *what's good about it?* The formula *good morning* is one of a small closed set with *good afternoon, good evening,* and *good night* in structure, although the uses do not match exactly. It is interesting to watch the process of re-emergence of the formula *good day* which had almost completely vanished from American English. In the last decade it has become normal under certain conditions, such as picking up a hitch hiker, for the two persons in an encounter to use as their farewell exchange *have a good day* followed by *you too.*

The occasions for use of *good morning* seem simple and obvious to the native speaker of English, but in fact they are fairly complicated. It is said at a certain time of day; English is one of the languages which have salutations for different periods of the day such as Arabic or Gonja, not one of the languages without this temporal variation, such as Bengali or Wolof. The appropriate time of day for *good morning* varies regionally (although not as much as for *good evening* which differs sharply in different parts of the United States) but generally is between waking up in the morning and the midday meal. It is said only on the first encounter of two people in the morning and is not repeated at subsequent encounters (as *hi* or *hello* can be, sometimes with the addition of *again* or a comment). Its use implies a certain degree of formality in the occasion, and hence it is not normally appropriate for two university students seeing each other for the first time that morning, walking from one class to another. And, of course, it can be used metaphorically, or by displacement, on a wrong occasion to point up a particular aspect of the encounter. So we can say *good morning* sarcastically to someone who oversleeps and wakes up in the middle of the afternoon, or to someone who comes home at 2 a.m. when expected the previous evening. All these appropriateness conditions must somehow be acquired by the native speaker of English and are correspondingly problems for the foreign learner of English. The corresponding Syrian Arabic formula *ṣabāħ lxēr* is used roughly the same way as English *good morning* but with many differences in detail, especially in kinds of response. Let us, however, examine briefly an Arabic salutation whose occasions for use are highly problematic for the English speaker.

In the general Syrian dialect area the formula *naʕiman* is part of the stock of polite salutations and its expected reply is the root echo *'aḷḷa yinʕam ʕalēk.* Careful observation of its use would show that it is addressed to someone who has just had a bath, a haircut, or a shave, or has just awakened from a nap. The ordinary adult speaker of the language uses these formulas without conscious rule-appreciation, and upon being asked usually cannot give right away the full list of appropriate occasions. Like *good morning, naʕiman* can be used metaphorically. For example, to a student who asks a question in class which has just been answered, the instructor might say *naʕiman* implying that the student was napping during the previous discussion, and the class would immediately appreciate the joke. The social anthropologist or culture historian who might want to find a link connecting the various occasions of use of *naʕiman* would probably find it in the institution of the public bath, and indeed the isogloss which marks the distribution of this formula and its counterparts in the Arabic-speaking world and other Middle Eastern speech communities probably reflects the wide distribution and popularity of that institution. In Morocco the corresponding formula *bṣaħħtək* or *bəṣṣāħħa urāħa* 'by your health' or 'by your health and relaxation' is apparently still used after another scene of the bath, blood letting (Mercier 1957). The point to be made here is the old, familiar anthropological and linguistic one that although a particular phenomenon is universal in human societies – in this instance the phenomenon of exchange of politeness formulas – the structures and incidence of use are so culture specific and tied to the cultural history of the particular society or group that the structural or functional universals must be sought at other levels.

PATTERNS OF RESPONSE

In both English and Syrian Arabic an appropriate response to *good morning* is an exact copy, with sometimes a slight change in intonation. This kind of full echo response is so common in formula exchanges that one is tempted to claim its universality, or at least the high probability that every speech community has at least some politeness formulas which have this kind of response. Another widespread form of response is the simple acknowledgement by an affirmative or interrogative word which says in effect 'formula noted, your turn now' without repeating or modifying the initiating formula. An English example is the *yes?* response to the summons use of *hello* (Goffman 1971: 104). Of greater interest to the linguist are modified echo responses, in which there is addition or deletion or permutation or the ringing of paradigmatic changes of some kind. The Arabic root-echo response already mentioned is an example. A simpler one is the well-known response to *'assalāmu ʕalaykum* 'peace be on you' which is *waʕalaykumu ssalām* 'and on you be peace.' Finally, many speech communities have one or more generalized or 'general purpose' responses appropriate for a number of different initiating formulas with or without an echo component. Thus, apparently, any of the numerous topical salutations of Gonja may have the response *awo* 'it is cool' and for many of them the response *alanfia* 'good health' is appropriate. Syrian Arabic has a general purpose response *'aḷḷa yiħfaẓak* 'God keep you' which seems to be appropriate whenever there is no particular specified response, or as an addition to or further response to another welfare-wish with God as the subject. (This formula does, however, also have its own realm of specific appropriateness. For example, if someone's children are mentioned and the appropriate formula is used *'aḷḷa yxallilak* (or – *lo,* etc.) *yāhun* 'God keep them for you' (or 'for him,' etc.) the use of *'aḷḷa yiħfaẓak* seems to be the prescribed response rather than a generalized use.) The Nupe salutations and greetings as reported by Banfield & Macintyre illustrate all these types of response: some formulas take just simple acknowledgement of 'yes' (*hin, eba* or *to*); others are echoed, e.g., formulas consisting of or beginning with *oka* 'I greet you (for)' have *oku* in the response; and there is a general purpose reply to all welfare wishes involving God, namely *ami* 'amen' (op. cit.).

Many Arabic exchanges of greetings follow the simple principle of 'the same or more so.' Thus the common informal 'hello' of Syrian Arabic is *marħaba* (original meaning 'welcome'), and the responses most often heard are, in descending order of frequency *marħaba, marħabtēn, mīt marħaba,* and *marāħib,* i.e., 'hello, two hellos, a hundred hellos, hellos.' This principle of response received endorsement in the Holy Koran itself, which says, in effect, (Surah IV, verse 86) 'If someone greets you, either return the greeting or greet him better, for God takes everything into account.' We must, of course, remind ourselves that responses according to this principle are just as conventionalized as other formulas. My occasional attempts to reply with '10 hellos' or '200 hellos' or '1000 hellos' were met with amused smiles or irritation. Unlike our English *good morning,* the Syrian Arabic *good morning* has an array of responses exemplifying the 'same or more so' principle. Two fairly common responses are *mīt ṣsbāh* '100 mornings' (sc., 'good') and *ṣabāḥ lxērāt,* the plural of the formula. Other *good mornings* which are appropriate as responses but not as initiators and are presumably felt to be stronger include: *ṣabāḥ nnūr* 'morning of light' which is one of the commonest of all responses, and mornings of flowers of various kinds, used between familiars as expressions of good will and humor, e.g., *ṣabāḥ lward* 'morning of roses' and *ṣabāḥ lfull* 'morning of jasmine.' Incidentally, the 'same or more so' principle is just as evident among Christian Arabs as Muslims, and many people are not aware of the Koranic reference. It seems likely that this greeting principle was already in existence in Semitic languages at the time of Muhammad, but it would be interesting to trace its spread in relation to the spread of Islam and the Arabic language. The 'same or more so' principle is distinct from the 'you-too' kind of response which is familiar to us and used in many speech communities. Syrian Arabic examples[6] are ℣ *sallim idēk* '(God) keep your hands,' ℟ *w'idēk* 'and your hands' which are thanks and response in connection with a favor or act of service done with the hands, and the salutation and response used at several annual festivals such as New Year's or Christian Easter ℣ *kull sane w'inte sālim* ℟ *w'inte sālim* 'all year and you in sound health' - 'and you in sound health.'

VARIATION

The kinds of variation within languages and across languages which have been illustrated raise the fundamental question of the general conditions and general types of variation found. A great deal of variation is in the nature of fuller forms vs. shorter forms, and Goffman has suggested the concept of 'attenuation rules' for analysis of this dimension of variation. He talks about the abbreviated forms of 'passing greetings' and other kinds of reduced exchanges. This concept, picked up by others such as Irvine, is useful but it is misleading to the extent that it implies a norm of full forms and various kinds of attenuation depending on specifiable conditions. A conceptual framework which allows both elaboration and reduction from the norm seems more productive. The familiar Arabic (Islamic) greeting *'assalāmu ʕalaykum* has as its normal response, as we have seen, *waʕalaykumu ssalām.* In some instances, however, a fuller form may be used such as *waʕalaykumu ssalām waraḥmutuḷḷāh* 'and on you peace and the mercy of God' but this is recognized as being an elaboration. And in Morocco, at least, an attenuated reply *waʕalaykum* 'and on you' is attested, for example in reply to a non-Muslim who has (either in ignorance or deliberately) used *'assalāmu ʕalaykum* in greeting (Mercier 1957).

In general the structure of politeness formulas varies in constituency and intensity in correlation with a number of social dimensions. At least four of these dimensions are operative also in 'greeting' behavior of other animals, especially birds and primates and seem likely to be universal in human societies (cf. Callan 1970, 117-22; Goodal 1971, 239-40; Irvine 1974, 168-70).

(1) length of time elapsed since previous encounter
(2) distance between communicators
(3) number of individuals in the relevant groups
(4) relative social status of the communicators

The nature and amount of the variation is not predictable in any universal sense. For example, in some human societies the superior initiates the greeting (e.g., Moroccan Arabic), in others the inferior does so (e.g., Gonja), and in still others the social dominance differentiation is more complex (e.g., American English), but what is universal is the correlation between the structure of formula and the social (or sociotemporal, sociospatial) dimension. The relationship between formulas and social status may, of course, be viewed in either direction – that the social status is naturally reflected in the use of politeness formulas or that the function of the formulas is to mark the social status; certainly in some accounts of animal behavior the 'greeting' behavior seems to be the chief defining characteristic of the social hierarchy which is attributed to the group.

Goffman and Firth in their somewhat different ways both feel that greetings and farewells constitute a natural unit and should be considered together. Firth defines greeting and parting behavior in their social sense as "recognition of an encounter . . . as socially acceptable" and the "recognition that the encounter has been acceptable" respectively (Firth 1972, 1). Goffman expresses the view that "greetings mark the transition to a condition of increased access and farewells to a state of decreased access" and is able to include them both in his definition of 'access rituals' which "mark a change in degree of access" (Goffman 1971:107). If the focus of the investigation is on the encounter itself it is certainly legitimate to investigate the behavioral brackets around it as similar and related phenomena, but this intended natural classification obscures the relation which is sometimes even closer between one or the other of these and other politeness formulas which are used in the course of encounters or even as expressive elements in monologs. Goody's study of Gonja gives ample testimony to this. In Gonja the same word *choro* must be translated as both 'greet' and 'thank' and includes verbal greetings, visits and other physical activities, and prestations. Certainly some of the structural features of formula exchange (internal as well as patterns of response and turn taking) are equally evident in greetings and thank yous, apologies, pardons, wishes for health, condolences, topical blessings, curses, and a host of other usages. It is true that of all these it is greeting behavior that has the clearest counterpart in animal behavior – even farewells are less well attested and problematic – and it would probably be a fruitful hypothesis to explore that all politeness formulas use originated in 'greeting behavior' of some kind. The truth remains that we are too ignorant of the behavioral, specifically the linguistic, facts in this whole area to make an early claim about natural units. We need much more patient and careful description of the structure and use of politeness formulas in different communities and different languages.

Before leaving this essentially synchronic, descriptive section I would like to mention the linguistic phenomena of embedding and replacement in formula constructions. What happens when one exchange must fit inside another by the nature of the occasion? Or when two responses are both appropriate for different reasons? The phenomena are reminiscent of similar ones in sentence grammars and discourse analysis. If we took seriously the suggestion that human speech started with formulaic exchanges, we could see in these constructions the forerunners of substantial parts of syntax. The notion of embedding in politeness formulas is discussed by Goffman in connection with such occasions as taking one's leave at the end of a farewell party, where the exchange has to terminate the immediate occasion and also refer to the expected long-term absence, or parting after an encounter which includes an introduction, where the farewell must be preceded by an acknowledgement of the introduction. A nice example of embedding and the deletion or replacement of one formula by another that 'outranks' it may be seen in Syrian Arabic farewells which include wishes for recovery from sickness.

The normal farewell exchange in Syrian Arabic is a triad of formulas A:B:C such that if A is said first, the addressee must reply with B, and the original speaker may (optionally) reply with C. If B is said first then C is normally obligatory. A is *(b)xāṭrak* 'by your leave,' said by the person who is leaving; B is *maʕ ssalame* 'with peace,' said by the one who is staying; C *'aḷḷa ysallmak* 'God keep you,' a root-echo response to *√slm.*[7] The normal exchange about recovery of health is ℣ *mʕafa nšaḷḷa* '(may you be) strengthened, God-willing' ℟ *'aḷḷa yʕāfik* 'God strengthen you,' the root-echo response to *√ʕfw.* At a farewell where the recovery exchange is also appropriate, there are several ways of continuing the exchanges. Here are two examples:

(1) Patient (leaving the office after receiving a prescription)	mitšakkir ya daktōr xāṭrak	Thank you doctor. By your leave.
Doctor	mʕāfa nšaḷḷa maʕ ssalāme	Strengthened, God willing. With peace.

(2)	Visitor	nšaḷḷa bitkūn ṣah̄h̄ēt	God willing you will have recovered.
	Patient	mamnūnak ktīr	Thank you much.
	Visitor	mʕāfa xāṭrak	Strengthened! By your leave.
	Patient	'aḷḷa yʕāfīk wyih̄fazak	God strengthen you and keep you.

In the first exchange the farewell sequence is complete A:B, but the recovery wish goes without response; in the second exchange it is the farewell which is incomplete and the recovery wish which has its response. When the recovery wish is embedded within a farewell exchange, *maʕ ssalāme* normally provides full closure and the response to the recovery wish is not said, as in (1). In (2), however, the patient apparently wants to express special appreciation of his friend's coming to see him, and he takes the option of replying to the recovery wish and adding the general purpose response *'aḷḷa yih̄faẓak,* which here has the effect of closing the farewell in place of the *maʕ ssalāme* which is normally required. Such patterns of embedding and deletion can be represented by rules similar to those of intra-sentence syntactic patterns, with the usual inclusion of optional rules whose selection is conditioned by social factors and communicative intent.

DIACHRONIC CONSIDERATIONS

Like any other special subsystem in language, politeness formulas should be examined diachronically to see whether they behave in special ways different from the main body of the language. The baby talk register, for example, which is a special subsystem in language, turns out to be unexpectedly conservative – key items may remain in use for millennia – and it shows specific features of diffusion and serves as a source for certain kinds of lexical items in the matrix language (Ferguson 1964, 1975; Bynon 1968; Crawford 1970; Oswalt 1975). Politeness formulas have at least three diachronic characteristics of interest: weakening, archaism, and areal diffusion.

Politeness formulas, in so far as they are non-referential in meaning and important for their presence or absence on the appropriate occasion rather than for the exact meaning carried by their constituent parts, are subject to the special weakenings (aphesis, contraction, erosion) which expressions of that type such as titles, asseverative particles and the like undergo. (cf. Jespersen 1922:266-8, 273, for discussion of 'extreme weakening' of greetings, etc., which he relates to weakenings in non-verbal greeting gestures.) In the past forty years it has been possible to observe the weakening from *How are you* to *Hi!* in American English. At the first stage the full form alternated with such shortenings as [haway^{ə}] [hay^{ə}] until the second of these became the commonest form, represented in writing as *Hiya!*, and began to lose its connection with the original *How are you.* In the next stage *Hiya!* alternated with *Hi!* until the latter attained its present dominance and for most speakers has no relation to *How are you,* which is now used in different functions from its shortened form.

On the other hand, politeness formulas, in so far as they constitute a folk-literature genre similar to proverbs, riddles, and nursery rhymes, tend to include archaic forms and constructions which have disappeared from ordinary conversational speech. Many Syrian Arabic politeness formulas are wholly or partially Classical Arabic in form, just as a considerable proportion (possibly 40 per cent) of current Syrian Arabic proverbs are Classical. It must be noted that the contradiction between the tendency to extreme weakening and the tendency to archaism is only apparent. For example Classical Arabic *'in šā'a ḷḷāhu* 'if God wills' is continued as a Syrian Arabic formula preserving the conditional particle *'in* which is rare in many varieties of Syrian Arabic and the verb *šā'a* 'wish' which is similarly marginal, yet the whole formula has been weakened to *nšaḷḷa* or *nšāḷḷa.* A parellel instance in English would be *goodbye,* said to come from an earlier form of *God be with you*; it preserves an archaic construction but is phonetically modified and eroded.

The third feature of diachrony to be noted is the strong tendency for the structure and use of politeness formulas to diffuse with other elements of culture across language boundaries. Thus, for example, a striking number of Arabic greetings and thank you formulas have spread along with Islam to speech communities which have not shifted to Arabic. In South Asia, where patterns of politeness formulas are quite different from those in the Arab world, Muslim populations use Perso-Arabic formulas quite at variance with the usage of Hindu speakers of the same language. The best known example of such an Islamic formula is undoubtedly *'assalāmu ʕalaykum,* which in one form or another has gone wherever Islam has gone. In the Middle East the diffusion of use as opposed to structure of politeness formulas is particularly clear. In Arabic, Persian, and Turkish there are often close counterparts in formula use even when the forms themselves are not borrowed. For example, European languages generally have one common expression for 'please' which may be used either for requesting a favor or offering a service, but Middle Eastern languages generally have two sharply different expressions corresponding to these two 'meanings'. In teaching Arabic to a European this distinction requires explanation, but in teaching Arabic to a non-Arabic-speaking Middle Easterner it is necessary only to give equivalents, e.g., Arabic *tfaḍḍal* = Persian *befœrma'd* = Turkish *buyrunuz,* all 'please' in the sense of offering service or special consideration to the addressee.

The archaism and cross-language diffusion of politeness formulas may result in long persistence of a formula in a community despite substantial change in language or religion. Thus, for example, the exchange of blessing formulas in connection with good harvests (cf., p. 25 above) has probably persisted for well over two millenia in the Middle East, as attested by the final verse of Psalm 129, which says in reference to the wicked who will have no harvest, "no one passing them will say, 'The Lord's blessing on you!' – 'We bless you in the name of the Lord'."

ACQUISITION

Any discussion of language structure and use is incomplete if it does not include some account of acquisition both for the indirect evidence which ontogenesis offers on the structure itself and for the clues it may give to the understanding of diachronic processes leading to or from the patterns in question. Accordingly, let us ask how children, as they grow up, learn politeness formulas and how to use them. The recent study of Gleason and Weintraub (1976) on the acquisition of 'routines' offers an excellent start toward an answer to this question. The authors are interested in the general question of how politeness formulas and other ritualized routines are acquired, although the behavior they observed in detail was limited chiefly to the *Trick or treat* sequence used by American children at Hallowe'en as they go from house to house in costumes to collect gifts of candy and fruit. Gleason and Weintraub claim that routines are acquired differently from the rest of language in that they are explicitly taught by parents, who prompt their use with the markers *Say* and later *What do you say?* and who ask after the occasion *What did you say?* (cf. also the conversation recorded in Sacks 1972, where a mother prompts her child to reply to a greeting). They point out that *bye-bye*, which is the earliest routine to be learned, may even be marked by *Say* when the child is too young to speak and is only expected to open and close its fist in a primitive motion of waving.[8] Firth refers to similar observations of Baganda children being drilled in the movements and gestures which accompany greetings and farewells even before they could speak (Firth 1972, 33).

Gleason and Weintraub note another feature of the acquisition of formulas, "the general failure of adults to provide expatiations of expansions based upon them. An adult teaching a lexical item and a concept embeds it in a number of forms: *See the doggie? That's a doggie. The doggie is eating his dinner.* But *bye-bye* and other early routines, including politeness formulas (*Thank you* in particular) and greetings, do not spark any explanatory discussions." (Gleason & Weintraub1976.) Their point is that such routines have little internal structure or variability and little in the way of underlying cognitive structure compared with less ritualized speech and are to be learned as appropriate for a situation rather than to express a referential message. The point is doubtless well taken for such expressions as *bye-bye* or *thank you*, but one wonders how the patterns of the more complex interchanges of formulas are acquired. It is clear that only a beginning has been made in the developmental study of the structure and use of politeness formulas.

The acquisition of politeness formulas is related to the general question of the role of unanalyzed units in language development, 'prefabricated routines' as Roger Brown has called them. Linguists and psycholinguists, in their concern to understand the astonishingly rapid acquisition of the complexities of phonological and grammatical systems and the creative aspects of language, have tended to neglect the role of phonologically or semanticosyntactically unanalyzed chunks which the child learns and uses in a kind of interim strategy until he gradually decomposes them into their constituents and frees these constituents for 'creative' recombination and extension. Kenji Hakuta in his study of a Japanese child acquiring English demonstrates the importance of this strategy in second language acquisition (Hakuta 1975:19–50), but insufficient attention has been given to it in first language acquisition. Adult use of unanalyzed routines such as politeness formulas is evidence that for some parts of language this strategy remains available throughout the lifetime of the language user.[9]

SUMMARY

This paper has claimed that the use of politeness formulas is universal in human societies and has documented the highly patterned nature of such formulas and their use in particular speech communities. It has also considered the way they change through time and the way they are acquired in the language socialization of the individual. It has not, however, attempted to construct a theory of politeness formulas or to find a place for them within some larger theory. In fact, theories of quite different kinds may draw upon the data of politeness formulas or serve as a framework for their description. Some observers relate them to general theories of ritual (e.g., Firth 1971), others to a general theory of politeness (e.g., Brown and Levinson 1978) or to universals of encounters and greetings (Youssouf, Grimshaw & Bird 1975); Goffman uses them to find the ground rules of his social order of public encounter. In particular, politeness formulas pose problems for linguists and ethnographers of communication. They constitute another set of facts about human language which the linguists must somehow fit into their theories of grammar or turn over to others who are better able to deal with them, and they constitute one more of the seemingly endless array of patterned uses of language which the ethnographers must describe, analyze and explain.

NOTES

1. This paper was written while the author was a Visiting Fellow in the Department of Phonetics and Linguistics of the School of Oriental and African Studies, and I wish to thank the staff and students of SOAS who gave me the opportunity to conduct a seminar on the topic and discussed the paper itself critically and constructively; the short-comings in the paper remain in spite of their efforts.
2. The term 'politeness formula' is not a fully satisfactory designation, since the expressions included in the category may be neutral as to politeness or even rude, and the term suggests politeness as the basic dimension of analysis instead of ritualized interpersonal exchanges. The term is taken from Jespersen 1923:266, where it is used in roughly the sense intended here.
3. Cf. Goffman 1971, 100 fn., "there could hardly be a better argument for there being common ground between animal and human studies than that provided by greeting behavior." Ethological accounts of human greeting behavior, however, pay no attention to the verbal component (Eibl-Eibesfeld 1968; Kendon and Ferber 1974).
4. Even Desmond Morris, one of the most extensive and explicit interpreters of human behavior in terms of animal instinct, claims only that human 'grooming talk' while homologous to animal greeting behaviors, arose later as a secondary modification of 'information talking' and is of lower rank than 'mood talking' and 'explanatory talking' (Morris 1967:177–80). Morris' discussion of the emergence and varied functions of language is certainly interesting and suggestive, but it seems to be completely undocumented speculation.
5. On the non-returning of greetings in American English, cf. Goffman 1971:102–3; on failing to express thanks in American English, cf. Apte 1974:85.
6. As convenient abbreviations for initiator formula and response formula the symbols ℣ and ℟ are used here; they are taken from liturgical usage in which they indicate 'versicle' and 'response' respectively.
7. Syrian Arabic has other triadic exchanges of the A:B:(C); B:C sort, such as *tfaḍḍal* 'please;' *sahhtēn* 'two healths;' *ʕala 'albak* 'on your heart' used in connection with eating or mention of food.
8. The observation of the American researchers that *bye-bye* is the earliest routine to be acquired is confirmed by the British researcher in child language, Natalie Waterson, who has also recorded early teaching of *please* and *thank you* (personal communication). Apte 1974 comments (85) on the very early teaching of *please* and *thank you* in America.
9. Discussions of phonologically unanalyzed word-shapes, their critical role in early speech development, and their apparent persistence in adult phonology may be found in Ferguson & Farwell 1975 and Ingram, forthcoming, Chapter 2.

DEBORAH TANNEN and PIYALE CÖMERT ÖZTEK

Health to Our Mouths*†
Formulaic Expressions in Turkish and Greek

In the film "A Thousand Clowns" Jason Robards Jr. for a lark walks up to a series of strangers in the street and says emphatically, "I'm sorry," "I'm so sorry." The surprised strangers promptly forgive him: "That's quite all right."[1] These people respond automatically, as they have learned, to a formulaic ritual. David Olson (1976) asserts that meaning in conversation is deduced from what is known about context and from "conventionalized interpretation" rather than from an analysis of the semantics of the words spoken. That is why it makes little difference whether you say, "I couldn't care less' or "I could care less," even though the latter "means" quite the opposite of what it intends. Since the speaker's intention is clear, it doesn't matter what the words say literally. Most obvious is the formulaic nature of such expressions as "How are you," and the inappropriateness of a literal response. Foreign speakers of any language get into trouble when they decipher a formula for its literal meaning.

While it is likely that our understanding of any utterance in conversation is firstly contextual and only secondarily literal,[2] there are many phrases which are more "formulaic" than others. Fillmore has been gathering such phrases in English, and he has so far isolated at least 2500, including idioms, cliches, stock phrases, aphorisms and proverbs – that is, combinations of words which have become associated in everyone's mind and are often repeated in sequence.

Although English has so many of these formulaic expressions, yet Americans seem to have a feeling that it is somehow in poor taste to use them at crucial times, as Zimmer and Fillmore have noted. Thus one often hears disclaimers

*Reprinted by permission of the authors from *Proceedings of the Third Annual Meeting of the Berkeley Linguistic Society*, pp. 516–34.
†We would like to thank C. Fillmore and K. Zimmer for their support and encouragement as well as their helpful comments on the first draft. In addition, Deborah thanks her many Greek informants, too numerous to name, but especially Rouli Ghemeni and Cleo Helidonis for helping to assemble the initial list of Greek formulas, then distributing questionnaires in Greece, and answering followup questions promptly and in detail.

such as, "I know this is a cliche, but . . ." or "Everyone must say this, but . . . ." Furthermore, there are many situations in which Americans feel that something must be said, but they don't know what would be appropriate. Fillmore reports that the most frequently heard comment at a funeral was, "There's really nothing to say at a time like this."

Turkish and Modern Greek (and presumably many other languages) have fixed formulas which supply something to say "at a time like this." The paradigm of a "formula" in this sense is one which is invariable in form (except of course for tense, number and person changes), and is very limited if not invariable in applicability. The same expression is used by everyone in that culture in the appropriate situation, no one in that culture would use any other expression, and the failure to use it is socially marked.[3] Formulas in Turkish and Greek, as in English, fall along a continuum with regard to how often they are used, and how obligatory they are considered to be. Turkish has many formulas which cluster at the obligatory end of the continuum, while formulas in English tend towards the optinal end. Greek has fewer fixed formulas than Turkish but many more than English. (The formulas listed in the appendix are ranked according to obligatoriness.)

The closest thing in English to obligatory situational formulas are expressions like "Happy Birthday," "Merry Christmas," "Happy New Year," and "Goodnight." The pair of English expressions referred to earlier ("I'm sorry," "That's quite all right"), while formulaic in nature, are not fixed in form and function. For one thing, the English expressions can be varied in form: "I'm so sorry," "I'm really sorry," 'Gee, I'm sorry," "I'm terribly sorry," and it would be possible for someone to substitute any of a number of other expressions, such as "Excuse me," or "Please forgive me," and "Never mind," or "It doesn't matter," and so on. However, it is generally considered necessary to say something in a situation where you have, for example, stepped on someone's foot. In contrast, when an American sneezes, some people say "Bless you," and some say "Gesundheit," and some people say nothing, and few people mind if they sneeze and nothing is said. This formula, therefore, would be further towards the optional end of our proposed continuum. For those who *always* say "Gesundheit," however, it may be possible to grasp the compulsive aspect of situation formulas in Turkish and Greek. When such a person hears someone sneeze in an exam or on the street, s/he feels compelled to say the formula even though s/he realizes that it is inappropriate to speak in those settings. Yet s/he will often prefer to behave inappropriately rather than resist uttering the formula. Similarly, people who come from cultures in which formulas are part of their habitual speech, find it extremely difficult to get along without them. The Turkish author of this paper constantly feels the discomfort of not being able to utter formulas in English. In fact, formulas are so pleasurable, they are addictive. When the American author returned from a trip to Greece and was told "Welcome back" (something of a formula for Americans), she could not help replying, "Well I found you," which of course elicited puzzled looks and necessitated a brief explanation of the Greek formula. Zimmer (1958) points out that Germans living in Turkey inserted Turkish formulas at the appropriate times in otherwise monolingual German conversations.

Many of the Turkish formulas are closely related to the "psycho-ostensives" in Yiddish which Matisoff (1979) has brilliantly catalogued and illuminated. As the name implies, psycho-ostensives express the speaker's attitude toward what s/he is talking about. However, Yiddish psycho-ostensives, God bless them, are more often sentence-interruptors, and there is a priority in Yiddish culture on verbal inventiveness, so that these emotive expressions are productive. In contrast, Greek and Turkish formulas are fixed set and are more often than not complete utterances in themselves, although some of them do come in the middle of sentences.

Psycho-ostensives focus on the relationship between the speaker and his/her subject matter. "Situational formulas" (to borrow Zimmer's term) form part of a social interaction and focus on the relationship between the interlocutors. The ritualistic nature of these expressions is especially clear in paired formulas, where the use of one by one speaker necessitates that the other speaker respond with the other member of the pair, as in the English example, "I'm sorry," and "That's quite all right,"[4] or the fixed pairs in Turkish and Greek,

(1) Turkish: hoş geldin, hoş bulduk,
(2) Greek: *kalos orises, kalos se vrika.*[5]

What Matisoff says about Yiddish psycho-ostensives applies to our material as well: "Often it is not so much that the speaker is using an emotive formula that actually belies his true feelings, as that the formula has become a surrogate for the true feeling, an almost automatic linguistic feature that constant usage has rendered as predictable and redundant as the concord in number between subject and verb." (p. 6) While many formulas are uttered automatically in daily interactions, still in crucial situations, these cultures have agreed to accept the surrogate as evidence of the true feeling, so formulas are not judged insincere by Greeks and Turks. They accept the assumption that the emotions are fresh each time they are experienced, and the formulas are simply the best way to express them.

If we consider the functions of formulaic expressions, we can see something about the relationship of people to their world. Formulas in both Greek and Turkish fall into three main categories: *anxiety-provoking events, happy events* and *rapport establishment.*[6]

Anxiety-provoking events seem to occasion formulas for the purpose of creating a sense of control over forces that otherwise seem uncontrollable and threatening. They fall into two categories: *health* and *loss*. For example, If someone appears to be choking on food, one feels the need to do something to save her/him. An American might slap him/her on the back; a Turk would say

(3) helâl, "it is lawful, legitimate."

Originally, this formula probably implied that one chokes from eating something that does not belong to her/him, without asking permission. The speaker then breaks the "magic" by giving permission to eat the food. The same formula, by extension, is used even if there is no food involved. Similarly, if someone is ill, others say to him/her

(4) geçiş olsun, "may it be past,"
(5) *perastika* "Passingly."

In Turkish this can also be said to someone who has recently recovered. In Greek there is a different expression for this situation: *sidherenios,* "of iron."

Formulas under the broad category *loss* can be further classified as referring to *departure* or *death.* There are many formulas used when the speaker, the addressee, or a third person goes away, either for a trip (6), (7), or to go to sleep (8), (9).

(6) iyi yolculuklar, "Good trip"
(7) *kalo taxidi,* "Good journey"
(8) *oneira glyka,* "Sweet dreams" or
(9) *kalo ximeroma,* "Good dawning."

Leave-taking occasions the greatest number of formulas we have gathered: about 15 per cent in Turkish and about 20 per cent in Greek. For example, the Turkish

(10) Allah kavuştursun, "may God reunite,"

said after someone close to the addressee has left to go on a trip is similar to the Greek

(11) *kali andamosi,* "Good meeting"

spoken by both the person who is leaving for a trip and those who stay behind.

When someone dies, the pairs of formulas used are,

(12) başın sağolsun, "may your head be alive"
sen sağol, "you be alive"
(13) *syllypitiria,* "Condolences"
zoi se sas, "Life to you."

These formulas recognize the fact that a death reminds everyone of their own mortality; hence, the reassuring wish of life to those remaining.

Happy events are always occasions for formulas which acknowledge good fortune, although there is also an awareness that luck may change, so there are formulas to protect the good from evil forces. Happy events fall into the general categories *occasions* and *gain.* Occasions include general occasions such as holidays as well as personal occasions such as birthdays, weddings, baptisms (for Greeks). Gain includes *arrivals* and *new possessions.* For example, a good wish is in order when a new article of clothing is acquired:

(14) güle güle giy, "wear it laughingly"
(15) *me gheia*, "with health."

If someone has the good fortune to enjoy a visit from a loved one, his/her friends will remark,

(16) gözünüz aydın, "your eye sparkling"
(17) *kalos edhechtikes,* "Well you received."

The spirit is the same, if the Turkish metaphor is more charming. If someone buys a new house, the response will be:

(18) güle güle oturun, "stay laughingly,"
(19) *kaloriziko,* "Good fate."[7]

Any social interaction is an occasion for establishing rapport between participants. There are two strategies for building rapport: putting oneself down and building the other up. This can be seen especially in Turkish formulas, where relative status is a key factor. Thus one may say to guests as to a social superior,

(20) buyurun, "condescend yourself ." . . to sit, talk.

The close connection between depricating oneself and elevating the other can be seen in the common expression,

(21) efendim, "my lord"

which can be the response when someone calls your name. The Greek expression

(21) *oriste*

functions like these two and comes from the verb "dominate."

A fascinating example of a situation in which rapport establishment is called for is the common experience of speaking favorably about one friend in the presence of another. We all know the slight twinge of jealousy that can be triggered by such a remark. In Turkish, this instinctive response is recognized, and the speaker reassures the other,

(22) sizden iyi olmasın, "may s/he not be better than you"

employing the strategy of building the other up.

Any interaction can trigger such formulas, either by the action of the addressee or the intentions or the actions of the speaker. For example, if someone puts herself/himself down verbally or by gesture, you can build her/him back up by uttering

(23) estağfurullah, "I ask pardon of God"

one of the most frequently used formulas in Turkish.

We have been looking at the situations that require formulas, and indeed they seem to be situations which are emotionally loaded for people in many cultures. As we said before, there are also formulas which are not so much situation-specific as psycho-ostensive, that is, showing the speaker's attitude toward what s/he has said. Events which trigger these sorts of formulas are roughly either past or future, and either good or bad. The attitudes towards these events correlate with Matisoff's categories for Yiddish: bono-petition, or wishing for good, and malo-fugition, or warding off evil. More specifically, one can wish that a past good will not be destroyed or wish that it be increased, or that it be diffused to others. The concept of the evil eye is very powerful in both Turkey and Greece; that is the process by which good fortune is "jinxed." Thus mention of a good event or state almost never passes without the use of some accompanying formula, for example,

(24) Allah nazardan saklasın, "may God protect from the evil eye"
(25) *Na mi vaskathis,* "May you not be touched by the evil eye."[8]

(26) Allah beterinden saklasın, "God protect from worse"
(27) *mi cheirotera,* "Not worse"

or one can express the wish that it may improve or not diffuse to those one loves. A similar attitude can be seen toward future good and bad events. Possible good can be wished for oneself or others, for example,

(28) Allah gönlüne göre versin, "may God give according to your heart"
(29) *Oti epythimeite,* "Whatever you long for."

Possible bad can be warded off or, in Turkish at least, can be wished for one's enemies:

(30) düşman başına, "to enemy's head."

All these formulas dealing with good and bad events strive to overcome human powerlessness. Two sources of power are appealed to: God and the magical power of words. The good will of God can be invoked in two ways: by expressing an awareness of his power,

(31) evel Allah, "God first"
(32) *Prota o Theos,* "God first"

or by asking for his aid,

(33) Allah kolaylık versin, "may God give ease,"
(34) *O Theos voithos,* "God the helper."

In reference to bad fortune, one can plead for God's mercy:

(35) Allah muhtaç etmesin, "may God not make needy,"
(36) *Theos fylaxi,* "God protect."

If words can have the power to bring about desired events, this power can also be involuntarily activated, so the mention of a bad event must be followed by words to erase the effect, such as,

(37) agzından yel alsın, "may the wind take it from your mouth,"
(38) *Vhangase tin glossa sou,* "Bite your tongue."

In the case of the latter expression in Greek, one must actually close the teeth visibly on the tongue before the conversation can proceed. What is striking about these formulas is the concrete substance given to the utterance of words.

A number of expressions that exist in Turkish and not in Greek curiously have to do with the telling or announcing of events. Again, these seem to refer to the perceived power of the utterance. So if someone shows the intention of relating a piece of news, the addressee will pave the way with,

(39) hayrola, "may it be good."

Similarly, in Turkish, you can say to someone who is about to recount a dream

(40) hayirdir inşallah, "God grant it be good."

Formulaic expressions perform a social function and thus are part of the social institutions of the cultures in which they function. They both reflect and reinforce the institutions and attitudes of those cultures. For example, in the villages of Greece, a man may respond to the question, "How many children do you have?" with the answer, "I have two children, and, I beg your pardon, one daughter." Now there is clearly something going on in the fact that "daughter" is not seen to be included in the category "children." But one notices as well that the formula,

(41) *me to sympatheio,* "with your indulgence," or "I beg your pardon"

is also uttered when one has spoken an off-color word in conversation. This seems to say something about the place of women in the culture and at the same time must contribute to the enculturation of women if little girls hear their fathers speak this formula about them.

Similarly, a formula that is sometimes used for a good wish when one is saying goodbye to a pregnant woman is

(42) *me to ghio,* "with the son."

This can be used even if she is not yet pregnant, in which case the assumption is that she wants to be. Either "son" is synonymous with "child," or the assumption is that a male child is preferable. It should be noted that these formulas are heard in the villages but rarely in Athens.

Although both Turkish and Greek cultures place much emphasis on marriage and child-bearing, there are many formulas in Greek concerning pregnancy, as for example (43), but none in Turkish.

(43) *kali lefteria,* "good freedom"

There seems to be a feeling among Turks that it is indelicate to mention this subject. There are formulaic expressions in Turkish said to a couple after they get married, but formulas uttered to wish good luck to people who are not yet married appear to be general good wishes rather than specifically related to marriage. In Greece, however, young people are always being wished luck in marriage. Thus at a wedding people often say to unmarried guests, especially women,

(44) *kai sta dhika sou,* "and at yours."[9]

Again in the villages, if an unmarried young woman offers someone (especially older men and women) a glass of water, that person will say, as a toast,

(45) *stis chares sou,* "to your joys"

which is understood to mean, "your wedding."

Matisoff has noted that Yiddish psycho-ostensives are concerned with certain key desiderata, in the order of desirability: long life, good health, a good living, and children. These are very close to what is wished for in Greek and Turkish expressions. Interestingly, while Greek formulas value long life first and good health second, and, to some extent, the blessing of children, they do not seem to be concerned with "a good living." The Turkish expressions, while also valuing long life and health, have many formulas in which happiness is invoked, in the charming set of expressions of the paradigm *güle güle,* "Laughingly, laughingly," where the Greek equivalents wish for health or simply "good."

(46) güle güle (git), "(go) laughingly"
(47) güle güle büyütün, "raise laughingly"
(48) güle güle giy, "wear laughingly"
(49) güle güle oturun, "stay laughingly"

(50) *(na pas) sto kalo,* "(go) to the good"
(51) *kali anatrofi,* "good upbringing"
(52) *me gheia,* [wear it] "with health"
(53) *kaloriziko,* "good fate"

Another difference is that Turkish expressions are concerned with status roles, and therefore certain formulas are uttered only by people of high status to their inferiors or vice versa. Greek does not evidence this phenomenon. We are not in a position to explain the reasons for these differences; that would be an interesting area for future investigation.

The world view that emerges from these expressions in Turkish and Greek is characterized by the capriciousness of fortune – a preoccupation with the precariousness of good fortune and the imminence of bad. Thus much energy is devoted to performing proper verbal rituals and to not offending God with complacency or pride. Understandably, therefore, many formulas have religious overtones; hence the frequency of references to *Allah* (Turkish) and *Theos* (Greek). Since, however, the Greek formulas which mention God are used less frequently than those which do not, the use of specifically religious formulas can identify a speaker as a religious person. This is related to the more general function of formulas to establish the person who uses them correctly, as a group member. This suggests another area for future research: who uses formulas, and to whom? It is likely that relative power and other social factors are reflected and solidified in the use of certain formulas.

Again, there are more fixed formulas in Turkish which are used uniformly and are considered obligatory by many people than there are in Greek. In both countries, older people tend to use formulas more than younger ones, and in Greece formulas are far more widely used in the villages than in Athens.

Insofar as the culture approves their use, formulas serve the felicitous purpose of furnishing the "right" thing to say in a situation in which it is felt that something should be said. The net effect is a very pleasant feeling of harmony. Anthropologist E. Colson (1973) explains that Americans feel much anxiety about decision-making because the responsibility resides with them personally. Natives of Gwembe in Zambia feel no anxiety about decision-making, for the appropriate procedure, divination, is formulated and agreed upon in their culture. Colson explains, "Whether the decision-making process gives rise to stress appears to relate to the difficulty of making a responsible choice that will be acknowledged as such by the actor and his critics . . . It is when people cannot agree on what is the right choice or when they cannot agree on what are the appropriate procedures for legitimating choice that decision-making becomes charged with emotion." (p. 55) Similarly, we feel anxious when someone tells us, for example, of a death in their family; we fear that what we say may not be quite right. Cultures that have set formulas afford their members the tranquility of knowing that what they say will be interpreted by the addressee in the same way that it is intended, and that, after all, is the ultimate purpose of communication.

APPENDIX

The following formulas in Modern Greek are ranked according to obligatoriness, according to the judgments of 25 Greeks of varying ages, sex and geographical origins, all now living in Athens.

1. *chronia polla,* "many years;" holidays, namedays, birthdays.
2. *kalinychta,* "goodnight;" leaving at night, going to sleep.
3. *kali epitychia,* "good success;" operation.
4. *syllypitiria,* "condolences;" to one bereaved.
5. *stin ygheia sas,* "to your health;" toast.
6. *perastika,* "passingly;" to one who is ill.
7. *kalos orises,* 'welcome," familiar; to one arriving.
8. *na tous chairesai,* "enjoy them" [your loved ones] ; general wish.
9. *kali orexi,* "good appetite;" before a meal or to one eating.
10. *kalo taxidi,* "good trip;" to one leaving for a trip.
11. *Kali stadhiodhromia,* "good racecourse;" start of new career.
12. *kalo proodo,* "good progress;" graduation.
13. *kalos politis,* "good citizen;" to a man discharged from army.
14. *kaloriziko,* "good fate;" to one who has acquired a new item.
15. *kali tychi,* "good luck;" whenever someone needs it.
16. *kali dhiaskedhasi,* "good enjoyment;" to one leaving.
17. *na ta ekatastiseis,* "hundred them;" on someone's birthday.
18. *kalos sas vrika,* "well I found you," formal; response to (7).
19. *me gheia,* "with health;" to someone who has got new clothing.
20. *(na pas) sto kalo,* "(go) to the good;" to someone leaving.
21. *kala stefana,* "good wreaths;" on an engagement.
22. *kalos na ton dhechteis,* "receive him well;" to someone who will have a loved one visit.
23. *kali lefteria,* "good freedom;" to a pregnant woman.
24. *Theos schores' ton,* "God forgive him;" mention of dead person.
25. *i ora i kali,* "the good hour;" mention of good event.
26. *kali andamosi,* "good meeting;" leaving for a long time (both leaver and stayer say).
27. *me to kalo,* "with the good;" to someone leaving.
28. *oti epythimeite,* "whatever you long for;" to someone leaving.
29. *kalo ximeroma,* "good dawning;" going to sleep.
30. *na chairesai ton andhra sou,* "enjoy your husband [children, etc.] "; general good wish.
31. *na ta chiliasis,* "thousand them;" on someone's birthday.
32. *O Theos voithos,* "God the Helper;" mention of future event.
33. *ora kali,* "good hour;" variant of (25).
34. *i Panaghia mazi sou,* "the Virgin with you;" to someone leaving.
35. *se kali meria,* "in a good place;" when giving someone money.
36. *na zisete,* "may you [pl.] live;" marriage.
37. *kali chonepsi,* "good digestion;" after a meal.
38. *oneira glyka,* "sweet dreams;" to someone going to sleep.
39. *na sou zisi,* "may [he/she] live to you;" occasion celebrated by someone's child. The formula is said to parent.
40. *gheia sta cheria sou,* "health to your hands;" to someone who has shown something they made.
41. *o Theos mazi sou,* "God with you;" to someone leaving.
42. *kala saranda,* "good forty;" to woman who has given birth.
43. *o makaritis,* "the forgiven one;" mention of deceased person.
44. *kaloforemeno,* "Well-worn;" new clothing.
45. *me to sympatheio,* "with the indulgence," or "I beg your pardon;" at the mention of an off-color word.

46. *sidherenios*, "of iron;" to someone who has recovered from illness.
47. *me to ghio* (*me ena ghio*), "with the son" (with son); to a pregnant woman.

Other Formulas

The following are not presented in any particular order.

48. *chtypa xylo*, "knock wood;" mention of fortunate event or state.
49. *kali evdhomadha*, "good week;" greeting on Monday.
50. *kalo mina*, "good month;" greeting, 1st day of the month.
51. *alloimono*, "woe;" at the mention of something terrible.
52. *gheia sou*, "your health;" used like 'hi!'
53. *chairete*, "hello;" slightly more formal than (52).
54. *kalimera*, "good morning" or "good day;" greating until 6PM.
55. *kalispera*, "good evening;" greeting after 6 PM.
56. *chairo poly*, "I am very pleased;" on being introduced.
57. *charika poly*, "I was very pleased;" goodbye to new acquaintance.
58. *ti kaneis?* "how are You?" greeting.
59. *kala, esy?* "well, you?" response to (58).
60. *gheia mas*, "our health;" toast.
61. *na'sai kala*, "may you be well;" acceptance of an apology.
62. *mi cheirotera*, "not worse;" mention of bad event.
63. *na mi vaskathis*, "may you not be touched by evil eye;" mention of something good.

The following Turkish formulas are in order of obligatoriness according to the judgments of 23 Turks with varying ages, sex and geographical origins, all now graduate students at University of California, Berkeley, University of California, Los Angeles or Stanford University.

1. hoş geldin(iz), hoş bulduk, "welcome, well we found you;" arrival.
2. Allah's ısmarladık, güle güle, "goodbye, (go) laughingly;" leaving.
3. günaydın, "good morning."
4. geçmiş olsun, "may it be past,;" to the person who is sick or has recently recovered from illness.
5. tebrik ederim, "I congratulate;" congratulation.
6. buyurun, "condescend yourself" . . . to sit, speak, come in etc.; to a social superior or to a person with whom the speaker is on relatively formal terms.
7. tebrikler, "congratulations."
8. teşekkür ederim, birşey değil, "thank you, (it is) nothing;" thanking.
9. iyi geceler, "good night."
10. iyi/hayırlı yolculuklar, "good trip;" leaving on a trip.
11. eline sağlık, afiyet olsun, "health to your hand, bon appetit;" to the person who has done the cooking and the response.
12. kursura bakmayın, rica ederim, "(overlook) forgive (my) faults, I plead;" asking (the guests) forgiveness for your faults and the response.
13. özür dilerim, rica ederim, "I am sorry, I plead;" asking forgiveness and the response.
14. Allah rahatlık versin, sana da, "may God give you comfort, to you, too;" exchange before going to bed.

15. sağol, "be alive;" thanking.
16. iyi günler, "good day;" short term leaving.
17. tanıstığımıza memnun oldum, ben de, "I am pleased to have met you, me, too;" parting with someone you have just been introduced to.
18. Allah rahmet eylesin, "may God have mercy on (him/her);" referring to a dead person (a muslim).
19. iyi akşamlar, "good evening;" greeting.
20. memnun oldum, ben de (memnun oldum), "I am pleased, I am (pleased), too;" after being introduced to someone.
21. afedersiniz, "pardon me."
22. bayramınız kutlu olsun, sağol, "may your feast be merry, be alive (see 15 above);" wish of 'good feast' (national feast) to a group (e.g. by the mayor), and group response.
23. merhaba, "hello."
24. bayramınız kutlu olsun (same as 22), "may your feast be merry;" at a national feast day (individual greeting).
25. lütfen, "please."
26. nasılsınız?, teşekkür ederim, siz nasılsınız? "How are you?, Thank you, how are you?".
27. kolay gelsin/gele, "may it be easy;" to a hard working person (mental or physical work).
28. yine buyurun, bize de buyurun, "condescend yourself (to visit us) again, you condescend yourself (to visit us), too;" guest leaving.
29. sağol, sen de sağol, "be alive, you be alive, too;" thanking and response.
30. afiyet olsun, buyurun, "bon appetit, condescend yourself (to join me/us with my/our meal);" starting a conversation with someone who is eating.
31. rica ederim, "I plead;" to someone who puts him/herself down verbally or by gesture (similar to 78).
32. güle güle giy, "wear laughingly;" new article of clothing.
33. güle güle git, güle güle gel, "go and come laughingly;" leaving on a trip.
34. başınız sağolsun, sen sağol, "may your head be alive, you be alive;" death.
35. güle güle kullan, "use laughingly;" something new to be used.
36. Allah gönlüne göre versin, "may God give according to your heart;" when someone expresses her/his high hopes of the future.
37. şerefe, "cheers;" toast.
38. aferin, "well done;" to a child who has been obedient or has done what s/he should.
39. sıhhatler olsun, "may (it) be healthy;" after a bath or (to a man only) after a haircut.
40. yolun(uz) açık olsun, "may your way be open;" trip.
41. Allah mesut etsin, "may God make happy;" marriage.
42. bayramınız mübarek olsun, sizin de, "may your feast be merry;" wish of 'good feast' at a religious feast, and the response.
43. nazar değmesin, "may the evil eye not touch you;" at the mention of something/someone good, beautiful etc.
44. Allah sakladı/korudu, "God hid/protected from danger;" after an accident in which no one is hurt.
45. iyi şanslar, "good luck."
46. selâm söyle, "say goodbye (to someone);" to someone leaving.
47. maşallah, "what (wonders) God hath willed;" at the mention of a person (or a state) who is healthy, talented or beautiful etc.

48. gözün(üz) aydın, "your eye sparkling;" to a person whose friend (relative) has arrived.
49. iyi uykular, "good sleeping;" to the person who is going to bed.
50. Allah şeytana uydurmasın, "may God not make (you/him/her follow the devil;" at the mention of a good person.
51. hayırlı uğurlu olsun, "may it be good (bring luck;" in reference to something newly acquired.
52. güle güle otur(un), "live (sit, stay) laughingly;" new home.
53. sağlık olsun, "may it be healthy;" when something is lost, broken etc.
54. Allah korusun, "God forbid, God protect;" at the mention of a possible bad event.
55. inşallah, "may it please God (I hope);" good wish.
56. hoşçakal, "remain pleasant;" goodbye.
57. nice/cok senelere, "to many years;" anniversary, new year.
58. Allah kolayık versin, "may God give ease;" hard work (physical).
59. hayırdır inşallah, "I hope it is good (see 55 for 'inşallah');" to or by someone who is about to tell a dream.
60. canın sağ olsun, "may your soul be alive;" when someone breaks/loses something.
61. bereket versin, "may (God give plenty);" said by the person who has received money (e.g. a beggar) or charity.
62. Allah kabul etsin, "may God accept;" about a day's fasting or prayer.
63. iyi isler/yıllar, "good work(s)/years;" good wish about work, happy new year.
64. çok yaşa, sen de gör, "live long, you see (me live) too;" sneezing.
65. birşey rica edeceğim, estağfurullahh, "I will plead (ask you) for a favor, not at all (see 78 for 'estağfurullah');" asking for a favor and the response.
66. Allah'ın izni (peygamberin kavli) ile kızınızı istiyoruz, "we want your daughter's hand with the permission of God (and the word of the prophet);" parents of the groom asking the parents of the bride to give their consent to the marriage.
67. (çocukların) gözlerinden öperim, "I kiss the eyes (of the children);" to someone (who has children) leaving.
68. (dedenin) ellerinden öperim, "I kiss the hands (of your grandfather);" to someone (who lives with his/her grandfather) leaving.
69. Allah kavuşturşun, "may God reunite;" departure of someone close to the addressee.
70. Amin, "Amen"; response to a good wish *or* after a prayer.
71. Allah razı olsun, "may God approve;" to someone who did (you) a favor.
72. memnuniyetle, "with pleasure;" response to a request.
73. eksik olmayın, "may you not be absent;" thanking an offer or favor.
74. ziyade olsun, afiyet olsun, "may it be plenty, bon appetit;" exchange by the host/ess and the guests after a meal.
75. uğurlar ola, "may (your way) be lucky;" to someone leaving or passing by.
76. zahmet olacak, rica ederim, "it will be trouble (for you), I plead (see 31 for 'rica ederim');" asking for a favor and the reassurance of the other person that s/he will do it willingly.
77. Allah başka keder vermesin, "may God not give other grief;" after a bad, unlucky event.
78. estağfurullah, "I ask pardon of God (not at all);" to someone who puts her/himself down verbally or by gesture.
79. Allah zihin açıklığı versin, "may God give openness of mind;" hard work (mental).
80. hayırlı isler/yillar/sabahlar, "good work(s)/years/morning;" general good wish about work/happy new year/good morning.

81. bir zahmet . . . , "a trouble;" asking for a small favor.
82. Allah beterinden saklasın. "God protect from worse;" after an accident.
83. eyvallah, "so be it;" okey *or* thank you *or* goodbye.
84. başımızın üstünde yeri var, "(it) has a place on our head;" reassuring the person asking for a favor that it is no trouble.
85. ağzına sağlık, "health to your mouth;" to the person who has told (your) fortune from coffee grounds *or* to someone who has said something very much to the point.
86. kısmetse/kısmet olursa, "if it is (my, our) destiny;" at the mention of future intentions.
87. ellerin dert görmesin, "may your hands never know trouble;" thanking for something done with the hands.
88. darısı başına, "the corn to your head (may you follow suit);" any happy event.
89. güle güle büyütün, "raise laughingly;" to the parents of a new baby.
90. Allah bozmasın, "may God not destroy;" at the mention of a happily married couple or a general good state.
91. Allah günahlarını/taksiratını affetsin, "may God forgive his/her sins;" referring to a dead person.
92. iyi günlerde giy, "wear (it) in good days;" new article of clothing.
93. Allah sabır(lar) versin, "may God give patience (pl.);" for something that requires patience.
94. cümlemize/zi/zin, "to/acc./of us all;" at the mention of a good wish.
95. başüstüne, "upon my head;" polite answer to a request or order.
96. Allah ne muradın varsa versin, "may God grant you all your wishes;" way of expressing gratitude for a favor.
97. nur içinde yatsın, "may he rest in holy light;" referring to a dead person (whose death is not recent).
98. uğurlar olsun, "may (your way) be lucky;" to someone who is leaving or passing by (similar to 75).
99. kesen(iz)e bereket, "plenty to your wallet;" thanking the host/ess after a meal.
100. helâl, "(it is) lawful, legitimate;" to someone who chokes.
101. Allah'ın izniyle, "with God's permission;" at the mention of a future intention.
102. Allah izin verirse, "God allowing/permitting;" at the mention of a future intention.
103. toprağı bol olsun, "may his earth be plenty;" referring to a dead person (whose death is not recent).
104. Allah analı babalı büyütsün, "may God raise (the baby) with her/his mother and father;" about a baby or children.
105. apıptır soylesmesi . . ., "it is a shameful thing to say (but) . . .;" before uttering something one is not supposed to say.
106. Allah versin, "may God give;" polite refusal of a beggar asking for money *or* at the mention of someone rich or happy.
107. Allah nazardan saklasın, "may God protect from the evil eye;" at the mention of a person (or state) who is talented, healthy, beautiful etc.
108. evel Allah, "God first;" showing faith in God.
109. Allah nasip ederse, "if God gives (me my) share;" at the mention of a future intention.
110. tatlı rüyalar, "sweet dreams;" to someone going to bed.
111. Allah'a emanet, "left in the care of God;" (same as 107).
112. hayrola, "may it be good;" wish that the news one is about to hear are good.
113. rastgele, "may you come across (them);" to the person going fishing or hunting.

114. Allah dert göstermesin, "may God not show grief;" general good wish.
115. sağolsun(lar) . . . ,' "may s/he (they) be alive . . .;" complaining about a family member.
116. sizden iyi olmasın, "may s/he not be better than you (but) . . .;" talking to a friend about a close friend.
117. Allah ziyade etsin, "may God make better/more;" to the host/ess after a meal.
118. üzerinize afiyet, "health onto you;" talking about illness.
119. hamdolsun, "thank God;" expressing thanks to God and as an answer to the question: "how are you?."
120. Allah düşürmesin, "may God not make fall;" talking about doctors, hospitals or an institution that gives one a hard time.
121. Allah düşmanıma vermesin, "may God not give (even) to my enemy;" at the mention of something very bad.
122. hayırlı ise olsun, "may it be if it is good;" good wish about something the consequences of which are unknown (generally about a marriage).
123. bir yastıkta kocayın, "grow old on the same pillow;" marriage.
124. sağlıcakla kal, "remain with health;" by someone who is leaving.
125. Allah daim etsin, "may God make (it) permanent;" wish for the continuation of a good state.
126. Allah muhtaç etmesin, "may God not make (one) needy;" talking about old age or a stage when one may have to be dependent on others.
127. sözüm meclisten dışarı, "my word out of the group;" mentioning something bad, dirty, tabu that should not be mentioned in the presence of the group addressed.
128. el öpenlerin çok olsun, "may you have a lot of people kiss your hand;" by the person whose hand is kissed.
129. Allah affetsin, "may God forgive;" at the mention of a sinful person dead or alive.
130. Allah daha iyi etsin, "may God make better;" at the mention of a good state.
131. tövbe de, "say: 'I repent';" to the person who talks about something sinful.
132. tövbeler olsun, "may it be repentance;" by the person who talks about something sinful.
133. tövbe tövbe, "(I) repent;" same as 132.
134. kurban olsun, "may (it) be a sacrifice to you;" asking someone you love to do something good for her/himself. (Erzurum dialect).
135. görüşmek üzere, "(with the intention of) meeting again;" parting with someone.
136. Allah'ın gücüne gider, "God may be offended;" when someone complains about something that is considered God's gift.
137. ağzından yel alsın, "may the wind take it from your mouth;" at the mention of a possible bad event.
138. Allah şaşırtmasın, "may God not mislead;" at the mention of a good person.
139. düsman kulağına kurşun, "lead(/led/) to the enemy's ear;" at the mention of a possible bad event.
140. düşman başına, "to the enemy's head;" at the mention of something very bad.
141. kurban olsun, "may (it) be a sacrifice to you;" affirmative answer to a request from someone you love (a different use of the same expression in 134).
142. tünaydın, "good afternoon."
143. dilini isir, "bite your tongue;" at the mention of a possible bad event.

Other Formulas

144. rahatzız olmayın, "don't be uncomfortable;" guest to other guests in the room who stand up to greet him/her as s/he comes in.
145. selâmünaleyküm, aleykümselâm, "peace be on you, peace be to you;" greeting a group of people and the response.
146. (iki oğlum) kusura bakmayın (bir de kızım var), "(I have two sons and) excuse me (one daughter);" telling how many children one has. (Erzurum dialect.)
147. efendim, "my lord;" answering when one's name is called or when one has not quite heard something that was addressed to one.
148. (annenize)hürmetler ederim, "I (send) respect (to your mother);" to someone (who has a mother) leaving.
149. bayramınız mübarek olsun, "may your feast be merry;" at a religious feast day.
150. iyi eğlenceler, "good enjoyment;" to someone going to a party, celebration etc.
151. Allah şifa versin, "may God give recovery;" to or about someone who has been sick for some time.

The parentheses in formulas 1, 40, 48, 52, 93, 99 and 115 indicate plural.

NOTES

1. Thanks to Hector Javkin for this example.
2. See Tannen (1978). The guiding structure may be expectation: what we expect an utterance to "mean." It would take an enormous amount of energy and concentration to decipher every utterance for its literal meaning.
3. Turkish and Greek suggested themselves for comparison because they exhibit great similarity both in the situations which require formulas and in the semantic content of those formulas. The reason for this similarity may be the close historical connection and geographical proximity of these two cultures. It would be interesting to investigate whether other cultures which have formulas exhibit the same patterns. We have some information suggesting that Arabic and Mediterranean cultures at least do.
4. Eve Sweetser points out that, at one time and in a certain subculture, "See you later, alligator" obligatorily triggered the paired response, "In a while, crocodile."
5. Transliteration will reflect Modern Greek spelling as much as possible. The following correspondences are employed: γ *-gh*, δ *-dh*, ντ*-d*, ξ *-x*, χ *-ch*. ου *-ou* is prounounced /u/. The following five Greek spellings are all pronounced /i/: οι *-oi*, ει *-ei*, υ *- y*, η *- i*, ι *-i*. Both αι *-ai* and ϵ *-e* are pronounced /ϵ/. Both *o* and ω are transliterated as *o* and pronounced /o/.
6. This classification is similar to Matisoff's for psycho-ostensives, except that he does not have the category "rapport establishment," not surprisingly, since the latter is associated most closely with situational formulas.
7. The Turkish expression is specific to house-acquisition. The Greek formula is the same one used for any new item except clothing.
8. As in Yiddish *keyn ayn-hore* (Matisoff p. 51). This is an excellent example of the primacy of function as opposed to semantics. The American author, as well as every second or third generation Jewish American she questioned, is quite familiar with this expression and knows just how it is used but was thoroughly shocked to learn that it means "no evil eye." Similarly, the Turkish author had to look up the literal definitions of some formulas she uses very frequently.

9. The American author knows an unmarried Greek woman who has given up going to weddings because she has tired of hearing this emotionally loaded formulaic "good wish." Laura Nader points out some women might start to worry when they stop hearing it.

MARIA-LIUDVIKA DRAZDAUSKIENE

On Stereotypes in Conversation, Their Meaning and Significance

ABSTRACT

"Stereotypes in Conversation, Their Meaning and Significance" is a first attempt at the contrastive analysis of conversational routine in English and Lithuanian, two Indo-european languages which have been most indispensable in linguistic research for different reasons: the most widely used and the most studied language of the world and one of the least spoken (in the Lithuanian SSR less than three million), yet one of the most important languages for historical linguistics. Though the general law of conversational routine is found to hold true for both languages, a number of differences are revealed in them as to the quantity of stereotypes, their emotive coloring and frequency.

INTRODUCTION

The question concerning stereotypes[1] in speech is neither new nor original in contemporary linguistic research. Contrary to the known concepts of the novelty of utterances[2] and still more to those of the generation of utterances,[3] the recurrence of stereotypes in speech has been confirmed by a number of authors[4] and backed up by a considerable amount of evidence. Learning a foreign language through the acquisition of stereotypes has been considered as a possible methodological approach.[5] Moreover, a number of oral courses have appeared putting this idea into practice.[6] Linguistic routine, however, may still conceal the many intricacies of man's verbal behavior and its study is sure to be of value both in practice and theory. Before considering the material of research under review and the clues it gives, one particularly interesting point in arguments on stereotypes should be mentioned. It has been noticed that native speakers and even some linguists are rather sensitive when the recurrence of stereotypes in speech is raised. It is an interesting phenomenon. If stereotypes really do recur in speech, they must be a result of some subconscious process because, otherwise, speakers who, in theory, find it offensive to their sense of pride would try to and, indeed, probably succeed in avoiding them. Furthermore, if the recurrence of stereotypes in speech is a subconscious act, then this points to some regularities, or, rather, peculiarities in the process of speaking.

The present paper is based on the material rendered by spontaneous dialog and polylog in English and Lithuanian. Contrastive research has been undertaken to be able to draw at least a tentative conclusion of what is or may be a general trait in the process of speaking and what is a specific feature of a particular language. The only drawback is that the material is somewhat limited in size. Less than five thousand cards, some containing very long unsegmented utterances, have been used to register the basic material of both languages in addition to the material of earlier research which was also made use of.

However agreeable or disagreeable the idea of stereotypes in speech may be, it is a fact that some functional varieties of English are so typical in this respect that stereotypes are found to be the most distinct differential feature in them. This applies first and foremost to small talk. A considerable amount of stereotypes is also recurrent in prefaces, introductions and acknowledgements. In other words, stereotypes are typical in those texts in which the phatic function is dominant. The phatic function, as is well known, serves the expression of contact establishment, sharing and involvement in communication. Thus, stereotype expression in the phatic function is a result of the demands of the recurrent context of situation[7] realized as a habitual need to express the meaning of sharing and involvement known as a standard of civil behavior.

It has also been found[8] that stereotypes are fairly recurrent in the speech of one individual in the communicative (or: referential) function in English. The analysis of the individual's speech led to some general observations and suppositions concerning speaking. To be able to assert anything valid or at least credible of the process of speaking in general, one has to consider the recurrence of stereotypes in other forms of speech in the referential function. Furthermore, the material of stereotypes, if discovered in the referential function, might also contribute to discourse organization.

The identification of stereotypes in actual linguistic material in the referential function is a fairly demanding, but rewarding task. It is more strenuous, however, than the identification of stereotypes in the phatic function. My own study of the phatic function[9] was carried out in identical contexts in which texts matched even topically. The material of the present investigation was not specified as to the topics or context of the situation and therefore was much more difficult to broach. It may also be of interest to mention that the dialog and polylog was more difficult to analyse than the monolog in the referential function.

OPENERS

Though stereotypes were found recurrent in spontaneous dialogues both in

English and Lithuanian, it was the material of the English conversations that had an overwhelming majority of stereotypes proper. The most characteristically stereotype and numerous were the parenthetic and opening parts of most utterances in English. For example: *I think, I suppose, I believe, I mean, you mean, do you mean*; rarer: *I presume, I imagine, I wonder*; quite rare: *you see* (parenthetic); and very frequent: *in fact* and *as a matter of fact* (opening and parenthetic). These were the most straightforward and they did not exhaust the material. Other frequent opening stereotypes included: *I don't think, I don't know, I'm not sure, I'm afraid, I would say, I must say, you must admit, you must have been surprised, the fact is, the thing that, the first thing that, the next thing, it is/was the point, but the whole point, one of the ways that, on the matter of (detail), etc. etc.*

Taken as objects in isolation, *I think, I suppose* or *I believe* do not seem to deserve much consideration. Their frequency, however, makes an analyst consider their meaning and functional value. There was not perhaps a single utterance in several thousands of the total in English in which *I think* was used in the meaning to form opinion and to come to conclusions.[10] In all the cases of their occurence in the material under analysis, *I think, I suppose* and *I believe* were used meaning that the speaker considers the idea and is personally involved, yet not willing to put it bluntly and considerate not to be too abrupt, matter-of-fact or quarrelsome. For example: *I think I like the idea. I think they're absolutely feeble. Erm I think the front goes down first. I think this is because most students haven't got the confidence to show the work they do. I think I like Polish, etc.*, not to mention the cases in which *I think* was only one segment of an utterance all of which was nothing more than a general agreement. For example: *Well, I think that on the whole this is true in this country, too.*

In addition to the meaning of both personal involvement and courteous detachment very typical of *I think* as the opening part of the utterance, *I suppose* and *I believe* were frequently used to express a kind of probing or fitting manner of the speaker's words and his tentative approach. For example: *I suppose a business course isn't particularly academic, if you like, but . . . I suppose we can't call that justice, can we? I believe you have to go through some sort of test when you first become a taxi-driver . . .*

Similarly, *I mean*, for example, was frequent in the sense of the intention to specify what has been said (*well, that's just what I mean*) as well as in the meaning of explanation both when the speaker agrees or disagrees or is concerned to be quite subtle and precise in his expression. For example: *Yes, that's right, I mean, I have done that before. When I say short term, I mean any period up to ten years, etc.*

A similar degree of personal involvement, diminished assurance and therefore courteous detachment and optional treatment of the subject matter may be said to be peculiar to the other stereotypes enumerated on p. 57 above, especially of *I don't think* in disagreements. For example: *I don't think I do. I don't think I would be able to wear them, etc.*; cf. also: *I'm afraid I don't know. I don't know if this is a pattern in England, but . . .*

As has been evident, introductory use of the above mentioned stereotypes may be said to achieve moderate or diminished straightforwardness of the utterance in English or simply provide an introductory filled-in pause, as in *I must say I wondered.* It is important to notice here, too, how stable the fusion of the opening stereotype and the nucleus of the utterance is in English, both semantically and structurally.

Stereotype English parenthesis, especially personal, increases the familiar tone of the utterance. For example: *She impressed me, I think, To get drunk, I suppose.* Impersonal parenthesis (*by the way, in fact, as a matter of fact, etc.*) also adds up to familiarity. For example: *Have you ever ridden a camel, in fact? They are quite numerous, as a matter of fact.* Finally, it might be relevant to see how opening stereotypes in English may extend gradually to take up the best part of the utterance:

I think I know him.
I think this may be a myth.
Well, I think this is a matter of indifference.
I think that probably is the case in England.
I think one of the most remarkable things about Owen is really how early he is.

Stereotypes among parenthetic and especially opening uses in Lithuanian have been found much less in number and far less stable structurally than in English. Opening stereotypes are very few and more or less established in formal usage. For example: *Dristu manyti, kad jie pasiteisina* (= *I dare think . . .*). *Turiu pasakyti, kad ne viskas buvo atlikta be priekaistu* (= *I have to say . . .*). These regularly occur in formal tentative statements or reproaches.

Lithuanian stereotypes which are flexible in the structure of the utterance are a little more numerous. For example: *man atrodo* and *man rodos* (syn.) (both principal and parenthetic), *taip sakant* (parenthetic), *tarp kitko, kiek man zinoma, kiek as zinau* (generally opening, also parenthetic), *jeigu taip galima pasakyti, ko gero* (generally parenthetic) and others. These stereotypes are analogous in meaning with the above mentioned English stereotypes (cf.: *man atrodo/man rodos* = *it seems to me; that is to say, by the way, as far as it is known to me, as far as I know, if it is possible to put it this way, still it's more likely*, accordingly) and also express personal attitude, involvement, moderate assurance and familiarity. For example: *Bet kaipo toks dalykas, man atrodo, kad gali, labai gali buti. . . . tai pasitaiko labai daznai, man rodos.*

Mat, cia as neieskau, taip sakant, kritikos, bet . . . Tark kitko, siandien V. vardadienis. Kiek man zinoma, tai ivyks. . . . bet, kiek as zinau, musu studentia, kai raso, tai daznai pasirenka citatas is kritikos. Ekonomika – humanitarinis mosklas, jeigu taip galima pasakyti. Aciu, bet, ko gero, negalesiu ateiti.

It would not be out of place to mention here that the meaning of the first person singular which is important in these stereotypes qualitatively and quantitatively, is expressed covertly or synthetically in Lithuanian. *I*, as a word, is very rarely present, if at all, in the utterance in Lithuanian.[11] *Man* being the Dativ of the first person singular pronoun, *man atrodo* and *man rodos* are treated as impersonal sentences in Lithuanian grammars, for the pronoun is indeed indirectly expressed here. *Dristu manyti* and *turiu pasakyti* have the meaning of the first person singular built in in the first person singular flexion *-u* of the Present Tense verb. The meaning of the person being always expressed by the flexion of the verb, the personal pronoun in the function of the subject is generally omitted in familiar and even in formal uses in Lithuanian (cf. *manyciau*[1] *I would think; noritu tiketis*[2] *I'd like to hope* [formal]; *manau*[3] *I think; zinai*[4] = *you know* [familiar]).

This is one of the reasons why opening and parenthetic stereotypes are less numerous in Lithuanian because what in English is a two-word combination which occurs stereotyped (*I think, I don't know,* etc.) is only one word in Lithuanian (*manau, nezinau,* etc.). Indeed, there are numerous one-word parenthetic uses in Lithuanian, owing to the omission of the subject expressed by the personal pronoun. For example: *manau* =*I think; manyciau* = *I would think; matai* = *you see; supranti* = *you*(sg) *know/see; suprantat* = *you*(pl) *know/see; zinai*[1] *you*(sg) *now; zinot*[2] *you*(pl) *know; tiesa*[3] = *it's true/by the by* and others. Even though this kind of parenthesis is frequent in Lithuanian, the concept of the stereotype is irrelevant in respect to one word. However, common extracontextual attitudes being the implied meaning, it may very well be that it is owing to their brevity that these parenthetic uses in Lithuanian become obtrusive and come to be treated as parasitic.

Still more numerous are one-word impersonal parenthetic uses in Lithuanian. For example: *resiskia, vadinasi, zodziu, kazkurtai, atseit, zinok* and others, meaning *it means, thus/so, in a word, somewhat/somewhere, as it were, you(sg) know(imp.),* accordingly. Most of these are mere fillers-in and may preferably be avoided altogether, for they are often found obstrusive by sensitive native speakers as well as by the supporters of the doctrine of the norm.

However, stereotype opening and parenthetic uses are entirely optional in Lithuanian. Whilst these stereotypes in Lithuanian mainly affect the tone of the utterance and are not at all established structurally and traditionally, except formal uses, the meaning (or, perhaps, literal presence) of the opening and parenthetic stereotypes in English is so essential that English loses its genuine character without them. (The volume of the opening stereotypes in an utterance in English has been shown on p. 57 above.)

In Lithuanian the function of opening and parenthetic stereotypes is so nonobligatory that intensive oral discourse tends to be void of them altogether.[12] The more familiar the discourse actually is, the less refinement and courteous parentheses there are in Lithuanian. And this is the other extreme that may be observed in Lithuanian as compared with the English way of expression (cf. p. 57 above). For example:

> "*Ir turbut patekai i epigonu kategorija . .*"
> "*Visi pradedam kuo nors sekdami.*"
> "*Ar tau menusibodo disonansas?*"
> "*As dar tik ieskau tikro disonanso.*"

The above said does not mean that courtesy is not verbally expressed in Lithuanian. The use of the second person plural *jus* alone in contrast to the second person singular *tu* expresses courtesy. For example: *Palikit ir man* (= *Leave, 2nd prs pl, some for me*). Courtesy is also expressed to a certain degree in the above utterances quoted to illustrate the straightforwardness in Lithuanian. The built-in negative particle of the verb form *menusibodo* makes the question somewhat courteous because the negative question in Lithuanian expresses diminished assurance or supposition (for detailed treatment of this point see below pp. 62f.). What was meant by straightforwardness is not typical of Lithuanian as a means of the expression of courteous or tentative approach, whereas there are numerous other ways of expressing courtesy in Lithuanian. It may be expressed by a verb of favorable connotation in the past tense with the infinitive forming the complex predicate (*O kai buvai jaunas, kaip meginai reikstis muzikoje? = When you were young, how did you try your success in music?*), the past passive verb expressing supposition (*Bet tarp siu punktu buta ir akademinio periodo. = Yet, in between, there had been an academic period, hadn't there?*),[13] the subjunctive expressing tentative approach (*Juk galetum papasakoti. = Why, you could give your impressions.*), by a number of idiomatic phrases or specific clichés (*Gal del to, kad labai velai pradejau mokytis muzikos. = Perhaps because I started practising music very late.*) and other means. Familiar courtesy may also be expressed by one-word parenthesis (*isties, zinai, supranti, vienok, etc.*, meaning *in fact, you know, you see* and *however,* accordingly), most of which, if excessive, make speech affected by individual idiosyncrasis or mark the habits of a social group.

This leads to a conclusion of the principal differential feature of English and Lithuanian which is that in the familiar register English is verbally more courteous and less straightforward than Lithuanian. It is mainly because of the neglect of this feature in learning English as a foreign language that some Lithuanian speakers of English are said to sound rude to native speakers of English. It may well be the case when a Lithuanian speaker purges of *I think, I suppose, I would say, I don't think, I don't known, I mean, the fact is* and other stereotypes which are essential in English conversational routine. Though, in addition to the above mentioned means, courtesy in Lithuanian may also be expressed by a variety of suprasegmental and extralinguistic means, they do not seem to work effectively in foreigner's English. Finally, owing to the differences of the expression of courtesy in English and Lithuanian, it comes to be limited to an apologetic smile on the part of the inefficient Lithuanian speaker of English.

Yet, the curious thing is that opening and parenthetic uses that reduce straightforwardness in English cannot be taught as a thing *per se* even on semantic basis because it involves a complicated set of meanings which may be too difficult to be grasped by the young and as difficult for anyone, if the stereotypes that reduce straightforwardness were to be matched by conscious judgement when learnt in isolation. Moreover, no foreign language may ever be learnt by recommendations. A student has to experience the flow of a foreign language to sense and memorize the typical recurrent units (not words) in the context and reproduce them alike. This is exactly what is offered to a foreigner in a number of modern courses of English[14] which provide the material with its typical stereotype routine. It is only in ultimate contexts that the typical English stereotypes may be learnt and used with confidence.

CONCLUDING PHRASES

Other stereotypes in the investigated material included a number of typical word combinations in typical syntactical relations. These were the phrases concluding an enumeration or an utterance. For example: *I'm not familiar with that song but it sounds* **something like that**. . . . *where you get little trout streams* **and things like this** (also: **things like that**). *Clothing, perhaps education, er,* **and this sort of thing.**

Analogously, similar stereotypes were registered in Lithuanian. For example: *Uztruski, kol surasi, o paskui vienu prisedimu padarei, ir viskas. Apskritai tai jo, eina laikas, neatsigaunam, zinai, nuo tu darbų, gruodžio galo* **ir visko**. *Pažiurek, gal knygą* **ar ką nors tokio**. *Pasikviesiu seseri, Laimą* **ir dar ką nors**. However very similar in meaning (*something like that* = *ką nors tokio, etc.*) these utterance finishing stereotypes in Lithuanian are not as frequent and established as those in English. *Ir viskas/visko* (*Gen*) is the only stereotype end of an utterance in Lithuanian which is highly recurrent and which has no meaning equivalent in English. It is an abrupt end of an utterance meaning *and that's all.* The known English *and all* does not seem to be its meaning of English may be noticed.

RESPONDERS

It goes without saying that typically stereotypes were brief response utterances (agreements and disagreements) as well as some questions and exclamations in English and Lithuanian. However, the material of brief response utterances as well as stereotypes characteristic of the *phatic function* have not been taken for detailed analysis in the present paper.[15] As regards stereotype questions, *How about you, (John) What about (a drink)? Do you really? How do you mean* . . . ? and others were found recurrent in English, whereas *Čia tikrai jo? Gal žinai, ar yra? Gal žinai, kaip surasti? Gal kartais matei? Tikrai?* and others were found recurrent in Lithuanian. Concerning the tone and straightforwardness of stereotype questions, they were more or less analogous in both languages. The English stereotype questions were far more general than the Lithuanian ones (cf.: *Čia tikrai jo/Marcinkevičiaus? = Is it really his/M's? Gal žinai, ar yra? = Perhaps you know if they have it? Gal kartais matei? = Perhaps you happened to see?*), except one Lithuanian one-word question *Tikrai?* which is fairly familiar and very general. It is, rather, an interrogatory comment and may have at least four stereotype English questions as its meaning equivalents: *Is that so? Do you really? Is it really? Is that what you mean?* It is not, however, the expression of meaning by synthetic forms in Lithuanian that matters here. *Tikrai?* functions like an idiom and not an abbreviated utterance because of the synthesized lexical and grammatical meaning in the verb form that is so typical of Lithuanian. On the other hand, English stereotype *disjunctive questions* appear to be unique in contrast with stereotype questions in Lithuanian. There is a kind of the stereotype question (*Matei, ar ne? Sakiau, ar ne?*) in Lithuanian which are somewhat analogous to the *disjunctive question* in English. They are far rarer and far less stereotype than the disjunctive *It is, isn't it?* and others in English.

In contrast with English, however, there are two types of courteous questions in Lithuanian, often stereotype and used as polite requests and inquiries. For example: *Gal pasakytum/pasakytumet, kas/kur/kaip . . . ? Gal žinai, kaip ten surasti/kaip vadinasi . . . ?* meaning *Could you tell who/where/how . . . ? Perhaps you know how one can find/how it is called . . .?*, accordingly. The other type is *Ar nepasakytum, kada/kur . . . ?*, meaning *Could you tell when/where . . .?* The verb may naturally vary as a lexeme and synthesize the meaning of the 2nd person (sg and pl) in the flexion of the verb in the present or future tense or the subjunctive. These questions are extremely frequent and courteous in Lithuanian, the only difference being that the *Gal*-question is in the positive form, whereas the *Ar*-question is in the negative form, as a rule. The latter question is a source of tremendous interference into the English of Lithuanian speakers. The meaning of courteous attitude in the negative *Ar*-question which is grammatically an equivalent of the general question in English is so rooted in the consciousness of a Lithuanian that the negative general question in English (for example: *Haven't I left my umbrella here?*) happens to be the first choice in translation and even spontaneous speech of Lithuanian learners. This is a typical instance of how universally shared civil human attitudes and intentions interfere with the normal linguistic routine in a foreign language when there is but slight literal disagreement between the languages in question.

In summarizing on stereotype questions in English and Lithuanian, we find that stereotype questions in English are more general and more numerous than those in Lithuanian. Besides, questions being the stimulating factor in communication, the use of some stereotypes reveal the role of meaning, even conventional, in stereotype linguistic expression in a foreign language. It is the need to express the socially significant meaning that violates the routinized norm of English among Lithuanian speakers.

Typical stereotype exclamations in English were: *Good heavens! Now, wait a moment! Look here! You don't say so! How lovely! How awful! Isn't it lovely! What an armful!* and others, as the material under analysis had it. Most frequent stereotype exclamations in Lithuanian were found to be *Klausyk! Palauk! Ką tu sakai! Negali buti! Kaip įdomu! Nieko 'sau! Kažkas baisaus! Siaubas!* and others. It must be said that stereotype exclamations are more frequent in English than in Lithuanian. English stereotype exclamations seem also to be more emotive, especially in the expression of positive evaluation. The difference is especially evident when the purport of exclamations is considered. Most frequent Lithuanian stereotype exclamations are imperatives (*Klausyk! = Look here! Palauk! = Wait a moment!*), responses, expressing moderate surprise (*Ką tu sakai! Eik tu! = You don't say so! Nieko 'sau! = See!/Here you are!* etc.) or essentially negative hyperboles (*Kažkas baisaus! = Something awful! Baisu! = How awful! Siaubas! = Terrible!* etc.). Positive hyperboles which are so frequent in English (*How lovely! Isn't it lovely! That sounds lovely! What a treat!* etc.) are very rare in Lithuanian. *Įdomu! Kaip įdomu! Kaip gražu!*, meaning *Interesting! How interesting! How beautiful,* accordingly may be said to be the peak of positive emotive expression in stereotype exclamations in Lithuanian. Some banal positive hyperboles (*Žavinga! = Splendid! Pasaka! = A wonderland!*/literal/etc.) come from the speech of young people and make Lithuanian socially marked. Most of the above material bears this mark of the sophistication of the educated in urban environment in Lithuanian. It has actually been derived from the speech of students and employees of the capital of the Republic. It must also be noticed that stereotype exclamations in Lithuanian are briefer than analogous exclamations in English because of the expression of meaning synthetically in Lithuanian.

EMOTIVE EVALUATORS

Stereotype uses also include emotive evaluative utterances which were ever so typical in English. For example: *It sounds lovely. It sounds marvellous. That is marvellous really. That sounds a bit stupid . . . I think it's nice (to ask him). It's fantastic memory. The ostrich looks marvellous . . . It was very amusing. That would be lovely. That sounds certainly an interesting idea. These (homes) are in general excellent places. (Some people) are terribly careless. It was an extraordinary story* and many others.

Stereotype evaluative statements were extremely rare in Lithuanian. It must be reiterated that Lithuanian has a very moderate emotive coloring in evaluative utterances. For example: *Gražiai atrodo, tiesa. Geras apsakymas. 'Nieko sau* and a few others, meaning *Looks beautiful, doesn't she. A good story. Not bad/She isn't bad looking,* accordingly. Most typical evaluative utterances in Lithuanian contain *labai* (= *very*) as a degree word. For example: *Jie bus labai laimingi. Jis man labai reikalingas. Busiu labai dekingas.* Very emotive and superlative evaluations (for example: *Žavingas kudikis. Nuostabi daina. Didžiausias turtas. Žveriškas noras. Baisus dalykas. Baisus darbas, etc.*), especially positive, sound affected and alien in Lithuanian. Again, negative hyperbolization may be noted dominant as more natural in Lithuanian.

RECURRENT SYNTACTIC PATTERNS

Finally, the material of both languages revealed a number of favorite, i.e., recurrent syntactical patterns which were either fully identical or had one variant member. For example: *I've never heard of this before. I've never thought of them . . . (as being alien). I have always been fascinated by (the way they live). I'd always imagined they were extremely (timid). It's very difficult to say. Well, it's a difficult question to answer. I'm rather happy about that. I'm happy to say . . . I'm (particularly) interested in . . .* and a number of others.

It must be noticed at once that the above mentioned stereotype patterns in English contain evident emotive hyperbolization, whereas this kind of stereotype patterns in Lithuanian are characterized by a more moderate emotive, generally negative evaluation. For example: *Niekaip negalėjau tau prisiskambint. Niekaip nevyksta sklandus darbas. Darbar jau nieko nepakeisi. . . . bet vis tiek verta pamėginti. . . . bet vis tiek bus smagu. . . . bet taip ir neradau. Gal ir ne, aš nežinau. Man būtų labai įdomu(naudinga). Aš esu visiškai pasimetus. Aš tiesiog neįsivaizduoju dabar. Aš tiesiog nežinau* (. . .). *Aš tiesiog neprisimenu. Tai mes jums (paskambinsim). Tai nesvarbu (kada). Tai aš tave trukdau. Tai reikia padaryt. Reikės (paklaust). Reikia (pagalvot). Tai būtų (smagu). Kaip dabar vadina. Kaip dabar nešioja. Taigi nieko čia baisaus. Taigi nieko čia tokio* and others.

Some stereotypes in this group have an anlogous degree of overstatement in both languages. For example: *I've never . . . I've always . . .* ~ *(Aš) niekaip negaliu . . . Aš niekada nesitikėjau . . . Tiesiog nežinau,* etc. These overstatemets are quite specific in Lithuanian in the sense that they are typical of urban environment and thus are socially marked.

It should be noted that, owing to the expression of meaning synthetically in Lithuanian, some stereotype syntactical patterns have alternative forms and increase the general number of stereotypes in this language. Cf.: *(Man) reikia* (pres.) *paklaust*; *Reikės* (fut) *paklaust. Reikia/Reikės padaryt,* etc.

It may also be of interest to point out that this group of English stereotypes included the known hyperbole *It's ages since I had one/saw you/you* which has a proper meaning equivalent in Lithuanian only for the animate. This is the idiom *Šimtas metų!* (= *A hundred years!*). What is used as its meaning equivalents in respect to the inanimate in Lithuanian is the emphatic negative. For example: *Nežinau/Neatmenu, kada mačiau/turejau . . .*

DISCUSSION

To conclude, linguistic analysis of spontaneous discourse in English and Lithuanian in respect to stereotypes reveals that, since meaning is expressed synthetically in Lithuanian (cf. the section on Openers), stereotypes are more numerous in English than in Lithuanian. Several examples of stereotypes, as mentioned in the section on Recurrent Syntactic Patterns, do not reach quantitative balance in the use of stereotypes in English and Lithuanian. Since no statistical analysis has been carried out, it is impossible to estimate exactly the quantitative distribution of stereotypes in both languages. Judging by the material under review, stereotype uses in English exceed those in Lithuanian.

Though there exist structural peculiarities which somewhat reduce the number of stereotypes in Lithuanian, it has to be admitted that stereotypes are regular in spontaneous discourse both in English and Lithuanian. A typical feature of Lithuanian stereotypes is that nearly all of them are socially marked. Most of the above Lithuanian stereotypes are typical of the speech of the educated person in urban environment. Indeed, it is not quite likely that such stereotypes as *As tiesiog neprisimenu. (Man) butų labai įdomu. Tai butų malonu* and others may occur in the speech of a peasant. It is also true that Lithuanian in rural environment may be and often is far more original than the Lithuanian of townsmen. It is not likely, however, that it may be void of stereotypes. It is quite possible that stereotypes may differ, as is evident from the material used for this paper, but they are nonetheless there.[16] However socially marked, stereotypes seem to be a regular feature of spontaneous and even edited speech.

The different degree and quality of emotive coloring in English and Lithuanian stereotypes has to be taken into consideration in conclusion. As has been pointed out, English evaluative stereotypes (section on Responses and Emotive Evaluators) were found more emotive in positive evaluation than Lithuanian ones, though it used to be considered that understatement is typical of linguistic expression in English.[17] If we were to judge a people by their language, it might be possible to assume that Lithuanian speech testifies to the reserved nature and extreme reticence of its speakers. Judging by the dominant minor key in Lithuanian folk songs and actual reticence of the people in some ethnographic areas in Lithuania, this might be the case. However, to draw conclusions from the linguistic material here rather than reach them by speculation, is to assume that, in case of identical reticence of native speakers of English and Lithuanian, native speakers of Lithuanian do not make the most of the expressive potential of their language.

Most of the stereotypes in English and Lithuanian may have been seen to share more than formal identity. They share meaning, too. The meaning of personal concern and courteous detachment is functionally typical of nearly all stereotypes in the section on Openers, whereas the meaning of positive and negative evaluation is typical of stereotypes in the section on Responders and Emotive Evaluators.

The uniform meaning of the above stereotypes makes them very much related to the uses in the phatic function which materializes a highly generalized meaning of sharing, involvement, gratitude and concern without much referential significance (consider meaning in small talk). At this point it is possible to venture explanations of the causes of the occurrence of stereotypes in speech in different functions. Doubtless, stereotypes occur in the phatic function under the stimulus of situational demands and are produced automatically. Automatic reproduction is relevant in the use of stereotypes reviewed in the sections on Openers and Concluding Phrases. However, the material of the present paper which basically comes from the referential function (cf. stereotypes in the sections in Responders and Emotive Evaluators) seems to suggest a question whether stereotype usage in the referential function may be due to the likeness of individual intentions and concepts which might render identical linguistic expression, finally identified as stereotyped. This supposition remains to be confirmed or overruled by factual evidence.

As to their meaning, some stereotypes (cf. section on Concluding Phrases) fall out of the above considered semantic categories. Though their meaning is not personal involvement or emotive evaluation, they are unified by their meaning of the organization of the utterance or the projection of the general background of speech. The organizing meaning, like the meaning of syncategorematic vocabulary, is functional. Functional meaning, i.e., the meaning of relations and organization, is shared by the community at a definite level of its development and education and renders identical linguistic expression in individual and group speech, both spoken and written. This is a source of the recurrence of parenthetical stereotypes (cf. the material in the section on Concluding Phrases and partly in the section on Openers). It might also be added that *in other words, in terms of* and other word combinations are among the most frequent unmentioned stereotypes of this category, recurring in spoken and written English, both in monolog and polylog. It does not need to be added that in language with a developed cultural tradition some stereotypes come to be produced automatically like words in usage and by habit (this is especially relevant to the stereotypes reviewed in the sections on Openers and Concluding Phrases).

Even though we may not mean exactly the same thing twice (therefore all utterances differ as pure phenomena, cf. note 4, p. 55), we do say the same thing twice and many more times, as has been shown by the material of the present paper. To rehabilitate the speaker, it remains to be said that man says the same thing a number of times not because he is a tedious bore. It happens because man has socially shared intentions stimulated to a great extent by contexts of situation which recur and so does linguistic expression because it is economical, functionally required and satisfactory.

NOTES

1. Stereotypes or clichés are segments of speech identical to or larger than a word combination which recur syntactically and even lexically unchanged generally in identical contexts of situation. *Cliché*, as a synonym of the stereotype, does not imply here the tasteless use of trite figures of speech. Strictly speaking, the use of the term *cliché* might be avoided in such cases so as not to overuse the term. The stereotype, as a term, has no evaluative aspects of meaning whatsoever. Stereotypes, as seen in this paper, have nothing to do with the speaker's taste, efficiency or resourcefulness. They are, rather, routinized discourse units caused by standardized conditions of communication and identical contexts of situation. It is quite important to make this point here at the start so that conclusions should evoke no unnecessary or unwanted disappointment or offense in the reader.

2. Cf. for example, P. Farb 1974:222; M. Bloomfield and E. Haugen 1974:5.
3. Cf.: N. Chomsky (1965).
4. Cf.: Шведова (1960), 367; Драздаускене (1974), 56–64; Формановская (1977), 8ff. It may be pointed out here that leading linguists of the present century were aware of the phenomenon of stereotypes in speech and generally took a broad point of view in theory. Cf.: "Within a speech community some utterances are the same, though they differ as pure phenomena. Nobody says quite the same thing twice" (L. Bloomfield, quoted from M. Bloomfield and E. Haugen 1974:82).
   "The content of the message is slight and highly stereotyped" (D. Bolinger 1968:2).
   "If, in a particular speech situation, only one analogy plays any part in determining what is said, then what is said is an exact repetition of something the speaker has heard or said before" (C. Hockett 1975:118).
   "Frequent and thoroughly expected collocations (like 'freezing cold') are most apt to strike us as clichés when they are used on occasions which lead us to expect relatively high precision and relatively low redundancy. As so often in matters of language, it is not usually a question of whether a given expression out of context is or is not a cliché" (R. Quirk 1968:149).
5. Cf.: Халеева; *O. Akhmanova, R. Idzelis; L. Brazdauskiene* (1979).
6. Cf.: L. G. Alexander and others.
7. Cf. in this respect: N. Denison 1975:6–7 and F. Coulmas (1979b).
8. See: L. Drazdauskiene (1979).
9. See: драздаускене (1970).
10. *Think* in the meaning of forming opinion was fairly frequent in *The White House Transcripts,* for example. American texts were not used as the material of the present paper.
11. It is an interesting accidental contrast that Lithuanian *as* (= *I*) which is frequently omitted in the utterance is not capitalized. It is *Jus* and *Tu* (= you) that are capitalized in writing when addressed to someone in person.
12. This observation may not reflect as extreme a contrast as it implies between the use of opening and parenthetic stereotypes in English and Lithuanian because the author of the present paper has always remained a foreigner in the English context, actual or textual, and therefore may have failed to register the actual frequency of stereotype opening and parenthetic uses in thoroughly casual and intimate communication in English, whereas, in case of Lithuanian, it is based on a genuine knowledge of the native speaker. It is only an empirical generalization of a linguist.
13. Semantically, there is meaning equivalence between the Lithuanian *buta* and the English *had been, hadn't there?*
14. Cf.: *L. Dickinson, R. Mackin* 1969; *M. Coles, B. Lord* 1970; *B. Abbs, V. Cook* 1970; *Mary Underwood* 1975, and other textbooks.
15. See: драздаускене (1970).
16. Concerning the material of the present paper, it is very important to bear in mind that modern Lithuanian usage is far less studied than modern English usage. There are no works yet published on conversational Lithuanian in general or Lithuanian conversational routine. Therefore this investigation has no background support and lacks exhaustion. As to the English material, it can never be claimed to be complete, either. It has also to be borne in mind that the aim of the present paper has not been the presentation of the system of conversational routine in both languages for it is impossible in one article. The paper brings forward a number of evident peculiarities of stereotype usage in conversation in English and Lithuanian.
17. Cf.: *M. Schlauch* 1945:121–122; *E. Esar* 1961:261–263; *G. Stone* 1961:106–107; *H. Spitzbardt* 1962:126–136; *A. Warner* 1964:46–52 and other authors.

FLORIAN COULMAS

"Poison to Your Soul"
Thanks and Apologies Contrastively Viewed*

ABSTRACT

I want to consider here two kinds of highly recurrent and routinized speech acts, thanks and apologies, and to argue that a contrastively informed analysis can belp to reveal certain typological relationships between them. Several kinds of both thanks and apologies are distinguished, and it is demonstrated that the values and norms of a given speech community have a bearing on whether or not they are to be considered as being related activities.

Theoretically this study is grounded in contrastive pragmatics. It draws on materials of some European languages as well as Japanese. From the discussion of gratitude and apology expressions it emerges that a contrastive analysis of routine formulae requires a careful account of communicative functions as defined and exercised in different sociocultural systems.

INTRODUCTION

The purpose of this paper is twofold. First I want to discuss some conspicuous similarities of thanks and apologies. Secondly, an analysis of these kinds of speech acts in Japanese is presented, and some general issues of contrastive linguistics are raised.

One of the central problems in contrastive analysis is the relation between form and function in language. If we know *how* to say, *I'm sorry,* in another language we still don't know *when* and *to whom* we should say it according to the norms of interaction of the respective community. Our knowledge of the corresponding form may indeed lead us to ignore or not recognize functional restrictions on its use that inhere in the communicative pattern of the culture. With regard to prepatterned phrases the risk is particularly high that

*In view of the subject of this work, my indebtedness to Dieter Wunderlich should not be left unnoted. Were it not for his critical remarks, comments and helpful suggestions, this paper would be considerably worse than it is.

The research on which this study is based was supported by the Deutsche Forschungsgemeinschaft (DFG), grant no. Wu 86/4.

the foreign language user sticks to the underlying rules governing the usage of the corresponding phrases of his mother tongue. This kind of transfer of pragmatic rules from one linguistic system to another may lead to interferential mistakes just as any other transfer (for details cf. Coulmas 1979a). Hence an apparent correspondence of routine formulae between languages often coincides with significant differences regarding their appropriateness to various contexts. It cannot be taken for granted that interactional routines are defined in an identical manner in different cultures. The consequences for the analysis of linguistic acts are clear. The question of how a given communicative function is verbally realized in another speech community must always be conjoined with the question of how this function itself is defined by the members of the community in question, and what status it has in the framework of its overall communicative pattern. It is one thing to state the semantic equivalence of linguistic expressions of two given languages. An assessment of their equivalence in terms of communicative functions is quite another thing. The difficulty boils down to the general question of how speech acts can be crossculturally compared and "translated". To treat speech acts such as thanks and apologies as invariable abstract categories is surely a premature stance. What we can do without too much or too little naivety is hence to start out with kinds of speech acts as defined in a given socio-cultural and linguistic system, and then proceed to look for similar or equivalent linguistic acts in another culture. A number of careful analyses of this kind can eventually contribute to a better understanding of a kind of speech act as a generic type.

THANKS AND APOLOGIES: TYPOLOGICAL SIMILARITIES

When I mentioned the plan of writing a paper on thanks and apologies to a colleague, his first question was: "What have these two got to do with each other?" This seems to be a typical reaction. Europeans do not normally conceive of thanks and apologies as related activities. On closer inspection, however, some typological similarities become apparent.

Thanks and apologies are speech acts that are relatively frequently performed in daily encounters. In terms of exchange of information, they may not seem to be very important. Obviously, their significance lies on the interpersonal level of rapport. Every society and every socio-cultural group seems to have its norms and values with regard to what kinds of deeds and omissions require apologies and thanks, and how these obligations can be met verbally. It is not surprising, then, that the verbal means employed on such occasions are often found to exhibit a high degree of routinization. Not only do the members of a group know when a speech act of either kind is in place, they also have an understanding of what is the appropriate thing to say, in other words, how these speech acts are carried out in a situationally adequate way. Again, there is some variation regarding the rigidity of norms, but it is quite clear that there *are* cultural norms about the appropriate usage of the phrases in question. They are part of what defines polite behavior in a society. As the "ceremonial idiom" – to use Goffman's (1956) term – varies from one socio-cultural group to another, it should be plain that the requirements to be fulfilled in order for uses of apology and gratitude expressions to constitute apologies and thanks, respectively, may also differ between societies. That they both play a vital role in verbal politeness is obvious.

Sequentiality

This section describes the positioning of thanks and apologies in conversational interaction. My basic claim is that certain sequential conditions are typical of both of them, thus pointing toward a structural complementarity of these speech acts.

That in language form and function are not bi-uniquely mapped in each other, i.e., that a given linguistic form can often serve a variety of functions, and that a given communicative function can in most cases be fulfilled by a variety of forms, is a commonplace hardly worth dwelling on. What kind of speech act is constituted by a given utterance often cannot be determined by looking at the utterance alone. An important feature of speech acts is their sequential character (cf. Wunderlich, 1976:300f.). When we attempt to analyze the internal logic of apologies and thanks, it is hence important to notice their sequential nature as *reactive* speech acts. They are always preceded (or accompanied) by a certain intervention in the course of events calling for an acknowledgement. Putting it in terms of presuppositions, we can also say that thanks and apologies presuppose some intervention in the course of events as a rationale of their performance. This view may, indeed, be more correct, because the sincere performance of thanks[1] and apologies does not imply the factual but rather the assumed existence of such an intervention. The point is the assessment of an interactional interchange by the speaker. Correspondingly, thanks and apologies can be met by reactions that presuppose or explicitly express an opposing or concurrent assessment. In sum, both kinds of speech acts under consideration here occupy, as a rule, the second position in a three-place pattern. It should be noted that, as opposed to the second and third, the first element of the pattern needn't be verbal.

In many cases, only the sequential environment of an utterance can tell us what kind of speech act has been performed. The conditions of sequential positioning of a given expression are accordingly very telling as regards its functional potential. Let us take a look now at some standardized sequences of gratitude and apology expressions and the appropriate routine responders:

(a_1)	A: *Thank you so much* B: *That's all right.*	(b_1)	A: *Excuse me please.* B: *That's all right.*
(a_2)	A: *Thanks a lot.* B: *Not at all.*	(b_2)	A: *I'm sorry.* B: *Not at all.*
(a_3)	A: *Merci Monsieur.* B: *De rien.*	(b_3)	A: *Excusez moi.* B: *De rien.*
(a_4)	A: *Merci beaucoup.* B: *Pas de quoi.*	(b_4)	A: *Pardon.* B: *Pas de quoi.*
(a_5)	A: *Danke schön.* B: *Bitte.*	(b_5)	A: *Verzeihung.* B: *Bitte.*
(a_6)	A: *Recht herzlichen Dank.* B: *Aber ich bitte Sie.*	(b_6)	A: *Ich bitte vielmals um Entschuldigung.* B: *Aber ich bitte Sie.*
(a_7)	A: *Danke.* B: *Schon gut.*	(b_7)	A: *Entschuldige.* B: *Schon gut.*
(a_8)	A: *Efcharisto.* B: *Tipote.*	(b_8)	A: *Me sichorite.* B: *Tipote.*

The English, French, German, and Greek examples exhibit a common property. In all of the (a)-(b) pairs the reactive phrase (B's part) is the same in (a) and (b), although in the (a) sequences a verbalization of gratitude is the initiating phrase, whereas it is an apology expression in the (b) sequences. This can, of course, by no means prove that apologies and thanks are more or less the same thing. However, it is a strong hint that they have certain features in common. They both require an appreciative reaction. It should be noted once again that both thanks and apologies involve the speaker's interpretation of the way in which the course of events was influenced, and that the response in turn takes account of this interpretation. What stands out in the above examples is that the B-expressions, i.e., the third-position elements of the pattern, all have a bifunctional character serving as reactive routine formulae in the sequel of either apologies or thanks. *Keine Ursache, don't mention it, prego, then iparchun logos* are other formulae of the same kind, equally situable for appreciating thanks or apologies.

By contrast, there are also formulae not designed for bifunctional usage but restricted to contexts of either thanks, such as e.g., *gern geschehen, you're welcome, avec plaisir,* or apologies, such as e.g., *macht nichts, then pirasi, never mind.* A sequence such as (a_9) would be quite odd.

(a_9) A: *Schönen Dank!*
B: *Macht nichts.*

As a matter of fact, if irony is excluded, B's utterance can only be understood here as a deliberate violation of a rule of conversational conduct, namely that the utterer of a gratitude expression is entitled to an appreciative response, for instance *bitte* or *gern geschehen* (or some non-verbal equivalent). Instead, what B actually does in (a_9) is this: By using a formula which is an appropriate response to an apology, he reinterprets the event which led to A's expressing his gratitude in the first place as something which the latter should rather have apologized than thanked for. This, of course, amounts to an implicit reproach. Conversely, formulas such as *you'r welcome* or *'pleasure* would be very much out of place as a response to someone's expressing her or his regret. Again, they may be employed purposely in a deviating manner as a means to reinterpret a communicative situation. Suppose a student has his toe stepped on by a beautiful girl. She apologizes, and he replies *'pleasure* or *you're entirely welcome!* Implicitly declining her definition of the situation he reinterprets her mistake as a kind of favor that he was glad to do for her, thus taking the chance to indicate his willingness to establish a relationship with the delinquent instead of just forgiving her her false step. Intonation is very important here. A mocking undertone turns the same device into an instrument for ironically pointing out the malefactor's clumsiness.

It is thus a common characteristic of thanks and apologies that they occur in second position functioning as a means to convey a certain interpretation of the respective first-position element. As a consequence, very minor linguistic means are enough to change the character of the whole episode and, potentially, the subsequent interaction. my guess is that this is partly a result of the similar nature of thanks and apologies and of their being experienced as such in Western cultures as well as in others. That the conditions for thanking someone or apologizing are often seen as similar becomes also obvious from speech acts best described as apologetic thanks.

(a_{10}) *I'm so grateful, how can I ever repay you.*

(a_{10}) is not at all an unusual reaction to a major favor. Sometimes we may even find it difficult to decide whether we should express gratitude or apology; for instance, after having intruded upon someone because of some urgent affair. Doing both is often the proper solution, and, clearly, apologies and thanks are not incompatible then.

It should not be overlooked, however, that the variety of situations where thanks or apologies are called for do not coincide. Just as the occurrences of some responsive phrases are restricted to one or the other, there are also of course mutually incompatible thanks and apologies. We have, in other words, to reckon with different kinds of thanks as well as apologies. Hence, what we are looking for is not so much a common denominator; rather the link between them will most likely prove to be an intersection of the ranges of the respective application where both are not incompatible. Before we proceed to the analysis of this intersection let us quickly examine how different kinds of thanks and apologies can be distinguished. No exhaustive account can be given here. Some regrettably sketchy remarks must suffice to indicate that a miscellany of events is subsumed under apologies and thanks.

Thanks

If we inspect the occurrence of gratitude expressions, a number of criteria suggest themselves for keeping different kinds of thanks distinct; that is, there are different kinds of properties that enable us to make distinctions. Let us return in this connection to the first position of the communicative pattern of verbal gratitude. Every verbalization of gratitude, or, rather I should say, every sincere verbalization of gratitude is directed to some action (or actions) of a "benefactor" or to a result of this action. May this be called *the object of gratitude.* The object of gratitude can differ in kind on a very wide scale. Among the dimensions in which thanks can differ from one another the following four seem to be particularly important:

I – thanks *ex ante* (for a promise, offer, invitation)
– thanks *ex post* (for a favor, invitation (afterwards))

II – thanks for material goods (gifts, services)
– thanks for immaterial goods (wishes, compliments, congratulations, information)

III – thanks for some action initiated by the benefactor
– thanks for some action resulting from a request/wish/order by the beneficiary

IV – thanks that imply indebtedness
– thanks that do not imply indebtedness

Obviously, these four criteria do not define eight distinct classes of thanks, and they are certainly no definitive taxonomy. Other criteria are conceivable, and the ones listed here are not mutually exclusive. According to this quadrochotomy the object of gratitude can be described in terms of different properties. It can be real *vs* potential; material *vs* immaterial; requested *vs* not requested; indebting *vs* not indebting. Obviously, the object of gratitude varies also on a scale of weightiness. Different objects of gratitude require different strategies for thanks and the appropriate responders, as will be seen presently (section on Responders).

A further complication is that the nature of the object of gratitude is not the only factor that determines the choice of a gratitude expression. The quality of the interpersonal relation between the participants is equally important. Whether the interaction takes place between close friends, family members, strangers, or employer and employee, etc. in a way affects the assessment of the object of gratitude, and hence the choice of a gratitude expression. Thus the social relation of the participants and the inherent properties of the object of gratitude work together to determine the degree of gratefulness that should be expressed in a given situation. Differences in this respect are obviously subject to cultural variation.

Apologies

Let us turn back now to apologies. We find similar conditions here. Like thanks, apologies are reactive. They make reference to the first element of the three-place apology pattern. As such they are directed towards some action or event or a consequence thereof. This part of the course of events is considered negative and unwanted for the recipient of the apology. His interlocutor sees a reason for regret in it. Let us call it, then, *the object of regret*.

Again, the object of regret can differ in various dimensions from one apology to another. It can be described as a kind of damage, annoyance or inconvenience which is predictable *vs* unpredictable; indebting *vs* not indebting. Accordingly, there are different kinds of apologies as well as responses.

Predictable intervention into the normal course of events calls for anticipatory apologies (*ex ante*) if conditions allow. Sometimes apology and object of regret occur simultaneously. If an interaction is initiated in a way or under conditions that the initiator knows or assumes to be undesired by his interlocutor he will often start off with an apology. The following words were what Patty Keene first said when she approached Mr Hoover:

> Excuse me for calling you by name, Mr. Hoover, but I can't help knowing who you are, with your picture in all your ads and everything. (*Breakfast of Champions*, p. 132).

Patty apologizes for what she is about to do and immediately offers a justification.[2]

Similarly, to intrude upon someone often is regarded as an object of regret. The problem here is that we cannot ask a person permission to intrude upon him without doing just that. Hence the derived usage of apology expressions as attention getters. There is always the possibility that someone I want to ask for directions does feel very much disturbed. To take account of this possibility, I had therefore best begin with an apology. There are, of course, standards with regard to what can be requested and expected of others, and they are reflected in the nuances and kinds of apologies which are felt to be appropriate relative to a given case of intruding upon someone, invasion of privacy, etc.

The same is true of *ex post* apologies. It depends on the nature and gravity of the object of regret (i) what kind of formula we choose (*sorry, I'm sorry, I'm awfully sorry, I'm really terribly sorry, I apologize, please forgive me,* etc.); and (ii) whether or not our apologies will be accepted. *Sorry, I'm late* may be acceptable when I come late to a party, but not when I made somebody else miss his airplane.

It is a conspicuous feature of some apologies that they are produced in spite of the unavoidability of the object of regret or its being beyond the control of the speaker. These cases are particularly frequent in institutionalized contexts, e.g., if a representative of an organization has to apologize for a delay which he had no means to prevent. Of course, he identifies with the organization and speaks on its behalf, but in addition he may also express his regret for an event which is obviously unpleasant for his interlocutor.

Such an interaction does not allow a response that imposes responsibility on him who proferred the apology. Interestingly we do make apologies, on occasion, without thereby recognizing any real responsibility. The object of regret, in these cases, is not indebting. The occurrence of apologies of this kind clearly shows that regret, not necessarily responsibility for an unwelcome change of the course of events, is the point of making apologies.[3] Apologies with no responsibility for the object of regret on the side of the speaker have a strong resemblance to expressions of sympathy. Neither of them require or allow pardoning, and it is no coincidence that similar or identical linguistic means are used for either purpose. *I'm sorry, das tut mir leid, je suis desolé,* and many other variants can be employed to express regret about something that one has or has not occasioned. The object of regret does not have to be indebting for the speaker. In other words, at one end, apologies border and gradually merge into expressions of sympathy.

At the other end of the total range of apologies, where responsibility is admitted, a number of similarities with certain kinds of thanks become visible. The latter emerge most patently if we consider the response strategies appropriate for thanks and apologies.

Responders

Recall that some formulae were seen to serve as responders to apologies as well as thanks. The strategies underlying their usage are also the same. In principle, there are two options: recognizing the object of gratitude or regret and relieving the interlocutor of its burden, or, alternatively, denying the existence of such an object or playing it down. Which of these strategies is opted for in a given situation depends on the role relationship of the participants and on the nature of the object of gratitude or regret, respectively. Of particular importance is the degree to which the speaker who verbalizes gratitude or apology is responsible or held responsible for its coming into existence. Whether a benefit was asked for or voluntarily offered, whether or not one is involved or assumed to be involved in some mishap thus has a bearing on the way thanks and apologies are reciprocated.

For instance, ex ante thanks are, in a way, advance thanks directed towards a declaration of the intention to do something for the benefit of someone else. In response, we do not normally use phrases implying that we did perform an act for the benefit of our interlocutor, such as e.g., German *gern geschehen*. Formulae like this are more appropriate following ex post thanks, because by using them we implicitly recognize the existence of the object of gratitude.

The above mentioned general distinction between two kinds of response strategies is lurking here: (i) recognizing the object of gratitude and indicating that whatever one has done to bring about its existence was gladly done (*you're welcome, that's quite all right, gern geschehen*); (ii) denying the existence of the object of gratitude or playing it down (*not at all, don't mention it, pas de quoi, de rien, keine Ursache, nicht der Rede wert*).

Recognizing the existence of the object of gratitude is not always permissible. If, for example, thanks are directed to an immaterial object of gratitude such as a compliment[4] *you're welcome* is surely no appropriate reaction. The flatterer cannot admit flattery.

By the same token, wishes generally do not seem to count as objects of gratitude for which the speaker can implicitly claim credit. Consider the following episode from Kurt Vonnegut's "*Breakfast of Champions*":

> Trout . . . sneezed.
> 'God bless you', said the manager. This was a fully automatic response many Americans had to hearing a person sneeze.
> 'Thank you', said Trout. Thus a temporary friendship was formed. (1974:74)

Trout's *thank you* is a "fully automatic response" here too. There is not very much actually that the manager did to put Trout under an obligation to feel grateful. Hence *you're welcome* would be somewhat overbearing as a reply.

Actually, it would be a breach of conduct, because *God bless you – thank you* is a conventionalized two-place sequence. It is interesting to note, in passing, how pointedly the author directs our attention to the superordinate communicative function of the exchange on the interpersonal level: "Thus a temporary friendship was formed." Another reason why a responder that indicates the benefactor's satisfaction at having done something for the benefit of his interlocutor may be barred is that the occasion for the whole episode was unpleasant for the latter. Thus *'pleasure* is rather an unseemly response to thanks for consolence.

Similarly, responders of this kind are unlikely if the object of gratitude is not indebting. An object of gratitude is not indebting if it is being payed for. If we buy our groceries we may very well say *thank you* to the salesclerk, just as the cashier may say *thank you* upon receiving the money. But neither shopkeeper nor customer are likely to reply *'pleasure.* German *gern geschehen* is positively impossible in such a setting. This formula seems to presuppose a free decision of the benefactor. In the context of buying and selling, however, the course of events is largely predesigned. By contrast, *bitte* is a natural completition of the pattern in this setting. It does not necessarily imply recognition of a benefit for which the interlocutor had good reason to express his appreciation.

Bitte is one of the responders for thanks and apologies. While its main function in contexts of verbal gratitude is to acknowledge receit, the situation is slightly different with apologies. Here it conveys more of a sense of acceptance. *Bitte* or *ja bitte* (with rising intonation) is, for instance, an apt response to an introductory apology. It signals permission to intrude and at the same time a request for the intruder to disclose his desire. Notice that a negative response is quite unlikely in cases like this, because the apologetic tone places the addressee under a strong obligation to comply. Yet there are of course standards as to the circumstances under which we can legitimate our intruding upon others by means of an apologetic opener.

Similarly as with thanks, responders to apologies differ as regards the extent of recognition of the object of regret that they imply. If I say, *for this last time I'll forgive you,* I accept the apology while indicating that there *is* something to forgive. By contrast, *why, no, that's quite all right,* is more like playing down the existence of an object of regret or denying it altogether.

Not infrequently we make apologies that do not call for any reaction at all. For example, when leaving a restaurant table thus terminating or temporarily interrupting an interaction we "excuse" ourselves. The same device may also be used, in formal settings, to ask for permission or consent. If this is not the case, it is simply a polite way to inform our partner of our intentions. Obviously, the truck driver does not ask for permission:

'Excuse me,' said the truck driver to Trout, 'I've got to take a leak.' (*Breakfast of Champions,* p. 88.)

The choice of apologetic formulae in contexts of this kind indicates, however, that the situation is conventionally interpreted as a negative – negative for the addressee, that is – intervention in the course of events. Yet, this intervention is not regarded as an unseemly exaction, and responders that implicitly recognize the speaker's right to pardon are out of place.

Thanks and apologies can be viewed in the light of many other distinctions. An investigation in terms of possible responders is important for two different reasons. One is that the responders provide an interpretation of object of regret and object of gratitude which is a correlate of the interpretation of the course of events underlying verbal apology and gratitude respectively. The other is that the conditions of their application reveal a structural complementarity of thanks and apologies.

The Pattern

Reviewing the above discussion, we are now in a position to draw some general conclusions. Two key concepts have emerged from the analysis of thanks and apologies: the object of gratitude and the object of regret. It was argued that they can be characterized as varying along several dimensions some of which are pertinent to both of them. There is a common domain where thanks and apologies are both appropriate. This is where it becomes difficult to keep object of gratitude and object of regret distinct from each other. Only a slight shift in the interpretation of the situation may turn a favor (calling for verbal gratitude) into an exaction (calling for verbal apology). The link between object of gratitude and object of regret is the concept of *indebtedness*. Thanks implying the indebtedness of the recipient of the benefit closely resemble apologies where the speaker actually recognizes his indebtedness to his interlocutor.

Apologies are offered to acknowledge and express regret for a fault or offence, by way of reparation of the negatively affected interaction. The speaker may explicitly recognize his debt, for example, when he says, *it was my fault, I'm terribly sorry.* The same is true for contexts of verbal gratitude where the concept of indebtedness is also made explicit on occasion. Introductions to books or initial footnotes to articles are a typical case in point. Gratitude for helpful comments and suggestions is customarily expressed by phrases such as, *I am greatly/deeply/equally indebted to . . .; for much of XYZ I am indebted to N.N.; the author holds a debt of gratitude to many,* etc.

Clearly, expression of indebtedness of the speaker is not obligatory for every individual instance of verbal gratitude or apology. Nor is recognition of indebtedness a characteristic feature of all thanks and apologies. It should be plain, however, that it is this concept that accounts for the similarities of certain kinds of thanks and apologies discussed above.

The internal patterns of thanks and apologies and the relations between them is roughly representable in the following scheme:[5]

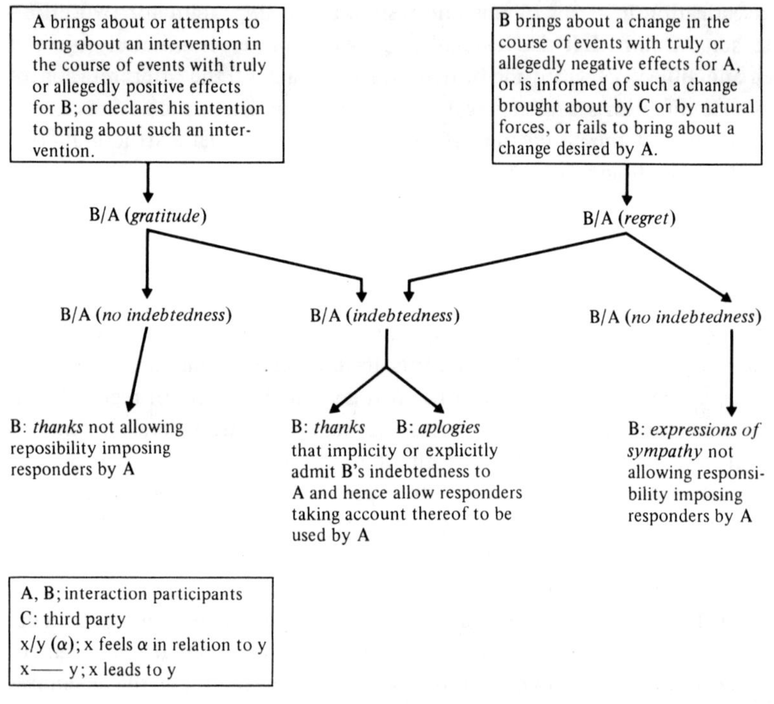

Figure 1

THE JAPANESE SCENE

To start this section, let me quote a statement from a recent review of the image of Japanese culture as represented in Western books on Japan (Ono, 1976:26):

> Each Western word is loaded with cultural and historical meanings, associations. . . . Thus Western words as such are not appropriate for describing non-Western reality.

How much of this is true, and how much is just an offspring of relativistic mysticism? Whatever the answer to this question, it is, no doubt, of major importance to the analysis of verbal activity. After all, "thanks" and "apology" are Western words, and clearly, the above discussion of these two kinds of speech acts was informed by an Occidental understanding of thanks and apologies throughout. I do not mean to imply that patterns of linguistic activity characteristic of a particular speech community defy an external analysis that draws on categories which were not developed within the community in question. But the applicability of such categories should not be taken for granted. In particular, we should not assume that names of speech acts of individual languages define universal types of speech acts. With this in mind we can now approach the problem of the cross-cultural comparability of thanks and apologies.

Apologies and thanks are strategic devices whose most important function is to balance politeness relations between interlocutors. It has been convincingly argued by R. Lakoff (1973) among others that politeness is a universal linguistic variable. As regards apologies and thanks, it seems to be a reasonable assumption that they exist as generic speech acts in every speech community. I would even go so far as to venture the hypothesis that every language provides a stock of conventionalized means for fulfilling these functions. However, the way in which a cultural context imposes restrictions on a kind of linguistic activity can often be seen to vary in a specific way from one socio-cultural system to another.

Hymes (1971), for instance, observed that British *thank you* is different from American *thank you.* While in American English it is still mainly a formula for the expression of gratitude, "British 'thank you' seems on its way to marking formally the segments of certain interactions, with only residual attachment to 'thanking' in some cases" (1971:69).[6] From a study on verbalization of gratitude in South Asian languages (Apte, 1974) we know how differently gratitude expressions are used by Marathi and Hindi speakers as compared to Europeans. Gratitude and indebtedness seem to be more closely linked. Indeed, there is no such thing as verbal gratitude that does not imply the speaker's indebtedness towards the listener. Hence "in situations involving exchanges of goods, no verbalization of gratitude takes place, Neither the customer nor the shopkeeper will therefore exchange phrases equivalent to 'thank you' " (1974:69). Similarly, to help each other among family members is only to comply with one's duties, and, therefore "any verbalization of gratitude is considered taboo, and it is insulting or looked down upon when family members or close friends interact with each other" (ibidem 79). It follows then that we have to consult the values of a society in order to determine when verbal gratitude is considered proper payment for an action, accomplishment, or gift, and when it isn't. The same holds true for apologies.

Face

In a society which is so highly conscious of 'face' as the Japanese (cf. Sugiyama Lebra, 1976) it is not surprising to find many predetermined patterns of interaction behavior providing the participants with the appropriate means to prevent embarrassing suprises. The large set of Japanese routine formulae plays an essential role in this respect. Among them apology expressions are a conspicuously large group.

There is a great variety of very general apology formulae whose range of application is not very specific. They are used on occasions where European speakers may find it difficult to see any object of regret. The fact of the matter is that, in many cases, 'apologizing' is not the sole function which their utterance serves. Rather they are used to line other speech acts such as greetings, offers, thanks with an apologetic undertone.

In this regard we have to account for two complementary observations. Among Japanese students of English, German, or other European languages, it is a common mistake to make apologies where no such acts are expected or anticipated in the respective speech community. While this may be a result of the general behavioral insecurity due to the language barrier, other causes come to light on closer inspection.

Notice that, correspondingly, a Western student who has been taught Japanese experiences the extensive usage of apology expressions as a striking feature of everyday communication when he first comes to Japan. Even if he has learned the most common expressions of apology, he finds out very soon that he lacks the necessary knowledge of speech situations which would allow him to predict and use them in an appropriate way. Apology expressions seem to be used much more frequently than in Western cultures, and, in many cases, the Western student will be unable to see any reason at all for apologizing.

For instance, a formula such as *sumimasen* or its variants *sumimasen dōmo, dōmo sumimasen deshita,* etc., can be used as general conversation opener; attention getter; leave taking formula; *ex ante* or *ex post* apology; and, notably, gratitude formula. In Japanese text books *arigato* ('thanks') is usually described as the most general and commonly used gratitude expression. The Japanese, however, seem to use *sumimasen* more often than *arigato* where Europeans would say "thank you." Upon receiving a gift, we would not normally say *excuse me* or *I'm sorry.* In such a situation *sumimasen* is, by contrast, quite appropriate. We can translate it, according to context, either as "thank you" or as "I'm sorry." That the Japanese language has such a polyfunctional word is, however, clearly not the end of the analysis.

It is quite apparent that the underlying conception of object of gratitude and object of regret does not concur completely with its European counterpart. The literal meaning of *sumimasen* is, 'this is not the end' or 'it is not finished.' In other words, when the Japanese express appreciation, what they are saying is that the respective matter is not over until the benefactor has been somehow repaid. The speaker of *sumimasen* acknowledges his indebtedness toward his interlocutor. The Japanese conception of gifts and favors focusses on the trouble they have caused the benefactor rather than the aspects which are pleasing to the recipient. When leaving after a dinner invitation we might say, *thank you so much for the wonderful evening.* Under similar circumstances, one of the things the Japanese guest could and frequently does say is *o-jama itashimashita* ('I have intruded on you'). Literally this formula means, 'disturbance have done to you.'[7] A typical response of the host to this is, *iie, iie, dō itashimashite* ('no, no, don't mention it'). And this is also an apt response to an (unapologetic) verbalization of gratitude (if there is such a thing in Japanese). Hence (a_{11}) and (b_{11}) are both perfectly natural sequences.

(a_{11}) A: *Arigato gozaimashita*
('Thank you very much')
B: *Iie, dō itashimashite*

(b_{11}) A: *Gomeiwaku wo kakemashita*
('I caused you trouble')
B: *Iie, dō itashimashite*

Dō itashimashite or *iie, dō itashimashite* is a responder for both apologies and thanks. *Iie* is the morphological unbound negative. While A acknowledges the existence of some object of gratitude or regret and hence his indebtedness, B denies it. This is a typical pattern in the use of Japanese gratitude and apology expressions.

Apologies have been described by Goffman as gestures "through which an individual splits himself into two parts, the part that is guilty of an offence and the part that dissociates itself from the delict and affirms a belief in the offended rule" (1971:143). If we apply this conception to verbal apology in Japanese society, we are forced to the conclusion that the socially controled part of the individual has a firm grip on its offensive counterpart. To the Japanese, breach of conduct, violation of a social rule, etc. involve first of all loss of face. Face-conscious behavior is characterized by two correlative attitudes: not embarrassing others and protecting one's own face. Maintenance of face is one of the central values governing interaction in Japan. It is most important in the domain of ritual behavior in a very wide sense, as defined by Sugiyama Lebra:

> The ritual situation that elicits ritual behavior ranges widely, from the extremely structured situation, such as a ceremony, to the undefined, accidental situation, such as an unexpected encounter with an acquaintance on the street, from play scenes to work scenes.

What links them all is that Ego defines Alter or a third person (or both) as an outsider whose opinion he cares for (1976:120).

In this domain, face-saving behavior is mandatory. Among the many mechanisms for defending face of which the Japanese dispose apologies for actual, anticipated or only assumed violations of etiquette or conventional rules play an important part. Apologies indicate the speaker's willingness to conform to conventional rules and social expectations. Not infrequently this seems to be their sole purpose. Verbal apology occurs even if there was no serious or real offence as a precaution against inadvertant misconduct or unanticipated negative interpretation of one's performance. If a situation is actually impaired by a violation of a social rule blaming oneself for the violation is an essential part of the repair. One of the mechanisms for defending face is to use apologies not only as a part of repair work but also as a means to forestall the need for repair. Hence apology expressions are often used in Japan where Occidentals cannot perceive any object of regret. Most conspicuous in this regard are apologies that are performed in reaction to a favor. The reverse side of the benefit of a favor is the strain that it cost the benefactor to carry out. For this strain the one who benefited is held responsible, and thus an apology is appropriate.

In Japanese, many gratitude expressions can be replaced by apology expressions, but not all. *Sumimasen* is seldom inappropriate and can be heard on all sorts of different occasions. On the other hand, the Japanese are very particular about using the appropriate form in the appropriate context. There is not so much demand for originality as in Western cultures, and no fear of repeating the same formula others have just used. In many situations the choice of possible locutions is very limited. At the beginning of a meal, for instance, a guest will invariably say, *itadakimasu* ('I receive'), a completely fixed i.e., morphologically unalterable gratitude formula. In this context any other expression would sound unnatural, although a *sumimasen* could be added by a very polite (most likely female) speaker. *Go-chisō-sama* is an equally standardized gratitude expression used at the end of the meal. There is no need to coin an original expression on the spot to sound sincere. According to the interpersonal and role relationships between participants the relative politeness of the formula can be varied. The degree of politeness increases with the length of the phrase:

go-chisō-sama
go-chisō-sama deshita
go-chisō-sama de-gozaimashita

Chisō means 'delicious food'. The other elements are honorific filligree. *Go-*

and *-sama* are honorific prefix and suffix, respectively. To dispense with the latter is possible in a very intimate setting. The former, however, cannot be omitted in an after meal context. As with many other routine formulae, polite *go-* (and *o-*) is no longer an optional element but has become an integral part of the formula. *Deshita* and *de-gozaimashita* are polite and very polite forms of the copula. The grammatical form of the formula is thus a declarative sentence, a statement: 'This was delicious food.' Functionally, verbalization of gratitude is the prime aspect. Typically this formula is used after one has been treated to a meal, not if the meal is being payed for, i.e, to a restaurant owner.

Formal Properties

In this section I want to consider some formal properties of Japanese routine formulae for apologies and thanks. The declarative sentence pattern is very common among Japanese routine formulae. In most cases various forms of the copula or of the verb *suru* ('to do') furnish the grammatical frame providing functional slots for different arguments to be filled in as the occasion demands. Hence we find identical patterns in many apology and gratitude formulae:

– This/that is/was X. *Go-X-(sama) desu*
Go-X-(sama) deshita (past)
Go-X-(sama) (de-)gozaimashita (past)

and
– I do/did X *X shimasu/itashimasu*
X shimashita/itashimashita (past)

These patterns occur frequently with both thanks and apologies. In most cases the content of the declarative sentence is an evaluative interpretation of a state of affairs, a preceding action, or an inner state of one of the participants. Typical examples are, *go-chisō-sama deshita* (gratitude) and *go-meiwaku-sama deshita* (apology; meiwaku = 'trouble'). As a result of their high frequency and familiarity these and similar formulae can also be used elliptically such that copula or verb are omitted. If this is not the case they are marked for tense. Whether the object of gratitude or regret is anticipated or retrospectively appreciated can thus be reflected in the morphological structure. E.g.,

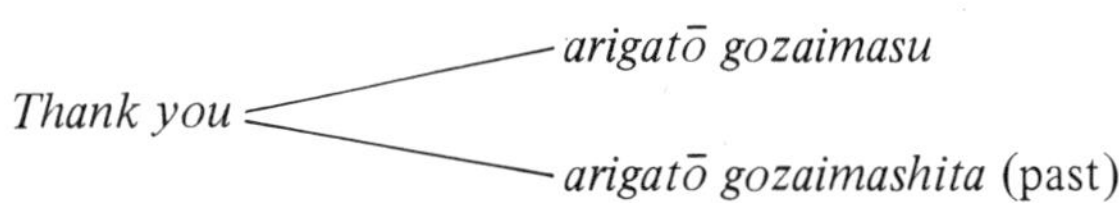

It should, however, be noted that the past tense form does not always mean past, and that the present tense form is occasionally used where the subject of gratitude is clearly in the past. Restaurant owners can be heard to say, '*mai do dōmo arigatō gozaimashita* to departing guests. Hence a past tense form is used side by side with the adverbial *mai do* which means 'always' (literally 'every time'). The speaker extends his thanks to every time the guest has visited his place in the past, but the present time is of course not excluded. If a favor was performed in the past, the Japanese speaker is more likely to choose a past tense form, yet he may want to stress the persistence of his gratitude and rather use a present tense form.

Another noticeable feature of many gratitude and apology formulae is that they are, in a sense, self-contained discourse units. They constitute a complete segment of a speech event and do not necessarily require a response. In the form of a declarative sentence the speaker indicates his awareness of the existence of an object of gratitude or regret without any further commet and without expecting any response. This kind of single-unit-pattern is frequently followed in various everyday interactions where no actual wrongdoing calling for an apology is involved. Formulae such as *gomen nasai, sumimasen (deshita), shitsurei shimasu/shimashita* (*shitsurei* = literally 'lack of manners') are in permanent use where people interact with each other. Again, they may be delivered at different levels of politeness, and serve a variety of functions in addition to verbal gratitude and apology. *Sumimasen* is commonly used as attention getter and also as a leave-taking formula. If it is used in the latter function, it serves as a direct repair of an intervention in the course of events which is interpreted as affecting the partner in a negative way. Similarly, *shitsurei shimasu* is typically used at interaction boundaries, e.g., upon entering somebody's office or leaving a restaurant table, one's place of work, etc. Rather than voicing a serious apology, where an explicit offer of repair must be matched by accepting it, the speaker indicates his awareness of the social norms of behavior as well as his readiness to comply with them. Hence no reply is necessary to sustain a smooth course of interaction.

Another common function of these and similar formulae is as conventionalized greetings. Thus a guest meeting his host some time after he has been invited will again express his appreciation:

Kono mae wa dōmo shitsurei shimashita.
('As for last time, I was very rude.')
or
Senjitsu wa dōmo sumimasen deshita.
('As for the other day, thank you very much.)

These are appropriate formulae to express the speaker's obligation to his benefactor. However, there needn't be any specific incident such as an invitation to occasion a greeting formula of this kind. They may also be used to indicate a general feeling of gratefulness and obligation without there being any specific object of gratitude or regret. Thus formulae of this sort can be exchanged in symmetric sequences such as (a_{12}).

(a_{12}) A: *Kono mae wa dōmo.*
("As for last time, thanks.")
B: *Kono mae wa dōmo.*

The referential indeterminacy is very obvious in the following formula which is used either as a salutation or at the time of departure by the one who leaves: *Iroiro- to dōmo,* which means, 'thanks for various different things' or 'thanks for whatever you have done for me.' As (a_{12}), this formula may be followed by *arigatō gozaimashita,* making the appreciative aspect of the salutation more explicit. But used by itself it is also a common greeting. Obviously, the referential indeterminacy is an interactional precondition for this kind of usage. What is being expressed here is not so much gratitude referring to any particular object, but rather recognition of a certain type of social relationship, where one party admits a general feeling of indebtedness to the other. Yet the three-place-pattern is not suspended here, because some however vaguely defined object of regret or gratitude is assumed, that is called to mind by a salutation of this kind.

Greeting behavior is expected to convey the social relationship that the speaker assumes or tries to establish. The speaker-addressee relationship is clearly reflected in Japanese discourse most of the time, and this holds certainly true for such ritualized discourse units as greetings.[8] In Japanese, apology or gratitude expressions often are the customary verbal forms for fulfilling this function.

These examples could lead us to the conclusion that our initial observation about the high frequency of apologies in Japanese verbal behavior was only a result of our failure to distinguish form from function; that most of the apologies observed in everyday interaction are in fact desubstantialized routines with no semantic content, merely functioning as means of 'phatic communion'. However, the situation seems to be more complex. It is not chance that, rather than other idioms, apology or gratitude expressions are often used as greetings. To be sure, other forms of salutation (referring for example to the weather or the time of day) are available, and they are used. Still, the functionally similar employment of apology and gratitude expressions must be seen as a significant reflection of social values and attitudes prevailing in Japanese culture.

There is a further point to be made about this. As I have mentioned above, in Japanese culture the need for original expressions is not strong. Frequent repetition does not necessarily result in loss of content. Apologies and thanks used in salutation contexts may well be termed 'ritualistic' since they are part of socially defined routines. But even if these salutations are not expected to yield any significant information, they carry a major social theme. They set the tone of interaction between members of a hierarchically structured society adhering to an ethics of indebtedness. In Japan, the smallest favor makes the receiver a debtor. Social relations can be regarded, to a large extent, as forming a reticulum of mutual responsibilities and debts. Not every favor can be repaid, and if circumstances do not allow proper repayment, Japanese tend to apologize. They acknowledge the burden of the debt and their own internal discomfort about it. It is in this context that one must view the many words the Japaneses have to express obligation. Apologies, used in innumerable circumstances, and serving a variety of functions beyond the imagination of an Occidental, are not merely degenerate clichés with no substantial message associated with them. Rather they serve to balance debt and credit between parties, and, at the same time, they convey a sense of the omnipresent moral indebtedness so characteristic of social relationships in Japan.

It should not be overlooked that, although using standardized expressions is not regarded as diminishing the force of an apology, there is, of course, a great variety of formulae enabling the speaker to adjust the apology to the seriousness of the object of regret. For instance, *gomen ne* is a very casual apology used in an intimate setting. *Sumimasen* and *shitsurei shimasu* are often used on the most insignificant occasions (insignificant in terms of misconduct, that is). By contrast, *o-yurushi kudasai* ('I beg your pardon,' in the literal sense), *o-wabi itashimasu* ('I offer my apologies') or *mōshiwake arimasen* ('there is no excuse,' 'this is unpardonable') are expressions that communicate a more dramatic sense of apology, and they are reserved for occasions where something wrong has happened. *O-kinodoku-sama (degozaimashita)* ('I'm terribly sorry,' literally, 'this must have been poison to your soul') is a very strong expression of regret too, used when one is sympathizing with another's misfortune. Stripped of the honorifics *o-* and *-sama,* this formula formerly served as a polite expression of thanks: *Kinodoku desu (yo),* 'poison to the speaker's soul' in this case, because of the debt placed upon him by the favor that he had received. If somewhat old-fashioned, it seems to testify nevertheless that gratitude was traditionally experienced as an unpleasant sensation, which is easier to bear if verbally acknowledged. This formula is also used as an apology in the sense that the speaker recognizes his responsibility for having caused a *kinodoku* of the listener. *O-kinodoku deshita* or *o-kinodoku shimashita, sumimasen* are slightly casual variants of the proper form *o-kinodokuna koto o shite shimaemashita (mōshiwake arimasen)* ('there is no excuse for my having brought poison to your soul'). Another formula of current usage is similar in this regard: *sore-wa kyōshuku desu.* Its literal meaning is, 'I feel ashamed,' but 'thank you' would be the most apt translation. That generosity can make one feel ashamed is not unfamiliar to the Occidental mind. However, the distinction between shame and gratefulness is clearly marked. This is not so in Japanese culture. Hence the boundary between apologies and thanks is blurred. This is not to say that there are no clear cases. Quite the contrary is true. While some of the formulae discussed above have a very wide range of application, others are tied to quite special circumstances. For example, *o-matase shimashita* is a conventionalized apology to be used upon arriving late at an appointment: 'I made you wait.' Obviously, no gratitude is involved here. On the other hand, solely appreciative formulae such as *o-kage-sama de* ('thanks to you') do not necessarily carry any apologetic connotations. Yet in many cases sincere gratitude seems to require the Japanese speaker to express regret. More often than not both thanks and apologies stress obligation and interpersonal commitment.

Concluding Remarks

In this brief discussion I have not been able to treat fully all aspects of thanks and apologies in Japanese, and the general account of these two kinds of linguistic acts is bound to remain fragmentary as well. Yet there are a number of conclusions to be drawn from the above considerations.

What stands out most prominently is this: apologies and thanks as defined against the background of a given socio-cultural system are not the same thing as when seen in another cultural context. While thanks and apologies may exist as generic types of activities across cultures, it is obvious that the pragmatic considerations of their implementation are culturally defined. It has emerged from the observations of the Japanese scene that one social organization may stress different aspects than others do.

Among the linguistic tools of ready-made routine behaviors in Japan apologies occupy a prominent position. Under the effect of an ethics of indebtedness, the Japanese tend to equate gratitude with a feeling of guilt. Apology expressions seem to be the most appropriate means to meet the resultant requirements. Accordingly, Japanese verbal behavior exhibits an exquisite sensitivity to mutual obligations, responsibilities, and moral indebtedness, drawing on the large range of routine formulae provided by the Japanese language. That Japanese students tend to make overfrequent usage of apology expressions in Western languages is hence readily explained as an instance of pragmatic interference.

Two further points about the rich stock of Japanese standardized expressions follow. The first one is that many of them can function as self-contained discourse units. Thus thanks and apologies are typically delivered in the form of declarative sentences. As a part of a highly conventionalized communicative pattern they do not necessarily call for a response. Leaving an expression of apology unanswered does hence not imply agreement with the statement expressed therewith; that is, that the other party is being rude, or that something is deplorable, unpardonable, etc. If there is no real issue between the parties, apology expressions can pass unacknowledged. A major function of their usage is to make communication unoffensive. In other cases, however, a response is felt to be appropriate, and the most common strategy then is to deny the guilt implicit in the apology.

The other point is that formulaic utterances are not considered as hackneyed expressions lacking in any real content, as is often the case in Western cultures. More important than originality of expression is to say the right thing in the right place. The use of routine formulae is not discrediting to the speaker, and apologies and thanks do not sound insincere if they follow conventionalized patterns. Indeed, linguistic etiquette requires the speaker of Japanese to make extensive usage of routines, often leaving little room for variation.

NOTES

1. For the concept of sincerity in speech acts see Searle, 1969.
2. For a philosophical treatment of events calling for excuse or justification see Austin's renowned paper, *A Plea for Excuses* (1956). A minute analysis of the sequential conditions is presented in Rehbein, 1972.
3. This paper was completed before I was able to read Edmondsons's contribution to this volume. His analysis of apologies is compatible with mine, although we seem to have approached some of the problems from opposite angles. Hence Edmondson's concept of the *Complainable* is clearly not equivalent with my *object of regret* but rather its correlate as viewed from the side of the receiver of an apology.
4. On the routinized character of compliments in American English, see Manes & Wolfson, this volume.
5. This chart does not capture any corrupt uses of gratitude and apology expressions. By that I mean employment of the respective linguistic material in the service of communicative functions other than the verbalization of gratitude and apology. Prevalent among them is the polite camouflage of impolite actions. *Thank you,* for instance, is used in certain settings as a means to terminate a conversational exchange regardless of the interlocutor's consent (cf. Schegloff/Sacks, 1973). Similarly, *excuse me* or *excuse me but* can often be observed to function as speech act frames (not quite the same as Keller's (this volume) 'semantic frames') enabling the speaker to forward an argument regardless of the completion of his interlocutor's turn.

   I cannot go into the manifold problems of corrupt usage of gratitude and apology expressions here. They seem to warrant more detailed attention in a separate paper.

6. In Australian English *thank you* can also be used as a kind of verbalized punctuation mark of interaction. It can thus occur three times in succession, if, for instance, a ticket is sold on a train:

   Conductor (handing over the ticket): 'Thank you.'
   Passenger: 'Thank you.'
   Conductor: 'Thank you.'

   I owe this observation to Michael Clyne (personal communication).
7. The honorific prefix *o-* is often translated as 'honorable'. Hence *o-jama itashimashita* is translated as "honorable-disturbance have done." This treatment of *o-* is quite misleading, because it gives rise to the impression that conversation in Japanese must be quite a cumbersome affair. It seems more plausible to describe *o-* as a deictic device indicating that an action is directed to the interlocutor.
8. I cannot go here into the intricacies of Japanese honorifics. It must suffice to emphasize that honorific usage in Japanese is not an extravagant supplement of ordinary verbal behavior but an indispensable component of the entire linguistic system. For details see Harada, 1976.

ERIC KELLER

Gambits: Conversational Strategy Signals*

ABSTRACT

A psycholonguistic analysis of conversational discourse is concerned with the strategies used by speakers to structure their content and their conversational procedure. Some of these strategies have an overt and verbal representation in the form of semi-fixed expressions that are here called 'gambits'. Typical examples are "The main point is," "I have something to add to that," or "What I really said is this." Such expressions serve a variety of functions, such as introducing a topic, structuring turn-taking, or indicating a speaker's readiness to receive some information. On the basis of some 500 such gambits, an initial subdivision is performed which distinguishes four main functions: semantic framing, social signalling, state-of-consciousness signalling, and communicative signalling. These functions are illustrated with a stretch of discourse recorded from a television talk show.

INTRODUCTION

Conversational speech can be viewed from a number of different perspectives. It can be viewed as text originating from a number of different sources. Or it can be viewed as the outward manifestation of a sociological structure in constant realignment. But here, I will approach it from yet a third perspective, from that of the psycholinguistic strategies used by the participant in a conversation. I hope to show that by viewing conversational discourse in this manner, we can identify special signals used by speakers as part of their conversational strategies, and can discover in this fashion much of the underlying structure of this type of discourse.

The polished conversationalist is a familiar figure. He breaks smoothly into conversations, picks up the thread effortlessly, holds his listeners enthralled as he develops his point, and then elegantly bows out of the conversation. How does he do it? No doubt the answer is complex, involving personality factors,

*This article was first published in The Journal of Pragmatics. Henrietta Cedergren's helpful comments on an earlier version of this paper are gratefully acknowledged.

group dynamics, and degree of familiarity between the speaker and the other conversational participants. But from a purely linguistic point of view, it is also possible to identify a further factor for facilitating conversational discourse, the presence or absence of a certain set of signals in the conversationalist's speech, used to introduce level shifts within the conversation, or to prepare listeners for the next turn in the logical argument. This set of signals will here be called "gambits".[1]

Generally, gambits serve to introduce what the speaker is about to say. When introducing an opinion, he might for instance use the gambit "The way I look at it" or "In my opinion. . . . When leading into an unpleasant topic, he might say, "Whether we like it or not, . . ." or "To be realistic, . . ."; and to bow out of a conversation, he might attempt to break the conversational bond by saying, "Well, it was nice talking to you, but. . . ." Not all gambits have to be multiple word units. A generalization, for instance, can be equally well introduced by such terms as "Generally" or "Ordinarily" as with the expression "In general."

In discourse analysis from a psycholinguistic angle, these expressions are *verbal signals* used at a number of levels of conversational strategy. First and most important, gambits act as *semantic introducers*. They indicate the general frame of the topic which is about to be broached in the conversation. A topic can for instance be framed in terms of a personal opinion or as a piece of unpleasant realism, as we have seen in the examples of the preceding paragraph. Second, they signal the participant's *social context* in the conversation. Gambits may be used to signal a wish to take a turn in the conversation, to get another participant to answer, or to express a wish to end the conversation. Furthermore, they may signal a person's *state of consciousness*. As an example, a person's readiness to receive information can be indicated by saying "Yes, I'm listening" or simply "Yes?." By contrast, the expressions "I'm not really interested in that," or "Why don't you just leave me alone" signal the opposite state. And finally, gambits have a *communication control* function. With hesitations such as "you know" and "you see," gambits sometimes share the purpose of filling in time, or "holding the line," to look for a word or for an adequate syntactic structure. In addition, there are special gambits used for the purpose of assuring that the communication lines are open, such as "Are you with me" or "Is that clear?." Gambits can either serve one of these four functions alone (e.g., "Is that clear?"), or can fulfill several of these functions at the same time; so for instance the gambit "I'd like to add something to that" signals that the speaker wants to take a turn (i.e., signal a desired social context), at the same time as it indicates that semantically, his message will fall into the category of subject-expansion.

These various levels can all be inferred by a consideration of gambits within their original contexts, or within contexts specifically produced to illustrate their use. In fact, a sufficiently large collection of gambits, sorted according to these criteria, can form the basis of an inventory of semantic, social, psychological, and communicative control signals used by speakers of a language. With this rationale, a fairly large set of gambits was assembled, initially to serve as documentation for the writing of a series of textbooks on conversational strategies in English as a second language (Keller and Taba-Warner, 1976, 1977 and 1978). In the present paper, this material will be further analysed, and the key roles played by gambits within conversational discourse will be illustrated.

The argument will be presented in the following sequence. After introducing the corpus, each of the discourse functions mentioned above will be illustrated in some detail. Some of the salient features of this type of conversational signal will be taken up next, and finally a framework for the analysis of conversational discourse will be suggested on the basis of a piece of spontaneous text analyzed in terms of the gambits it contains.

THE ORIGINAL CORPUS

A collection of some 500 gambits commonly used in North American English was collected from two sources. Slightly over half of the expressions were derived from a recorded and transcribed corpus of formal and informal spoken English. This corpus consists of over 10,000 sentences of Canadian English speech (131,536 words), collected from boardroom-type discussions, and from media discussions or interviews. Twenty-eight people were involved in the boardroom-type discussions which form sixty percent of the corpus, while 275 participants taped from radio and television discussions contributed the remaining forty percent (Barker, Adams and Sorhus, 1974). The corpus was assembled by members of the Research Group of the Studies Division of the Public Service Commission in the Canadian Federal Government, and a list of fixed expressions deriving from the study was kindly made available to me for the writing of didactic materials while I was a member of the Program Development and Consultation Unit, English Program at the Language Training Branch of the Federal Government of Canada.

These fixed expressions received an initial sorting for gambit-like structures using some of the sociolinguistic and semantic criteria mentioned above; on the basis of the categories thus derived, the second half of the corpus was collected by consulting the various linguists associated with the Program Development and Consultation Unit concerning gambits they would use themselves, or would know to be used in similar circumstances.[2] Each purported gambit thus solicited was embedded in a suitable linguistic context and was only accepted into the final list if at least three of the consulted linguists considered it to be part of everyday North American English speech. As gambits were added to the lists, the criteria were refined and expanded so as to suggest further possible contexts in which gambits could occur.

Expressions, consisting of a single or several habitually co-occurring lexemes, were classified as gambits if they met the following criteria:

1. They would have to be used to introduce a semantic frame, signal social context or a person's state of consciousness, serve an explicit communication control function, or assume any combination of these functions.
2. They could be used, under usual circumstances, in initial position within a sentence, or form a complete utterance. This second criterion was based on the notion that like in chess, gambits represented a move initiating a natural series of events, i.e., a turn in the conversation or a set of phrases or sentences developing a single topic, and are thus likely to occur at the beginning of utterances. Moreover, because of the uncertainty, and thus linguistic difficulty, surrounding the initial phase of any turn in the conversation, these expressions were of primary didactic interest to us.
3. They would have to have been in common use by a wide range of speakers in North America, and especially in English Canada, for an extended period of time. Gambits existing exclusively in modish or underground use (e.g., "That's cool, man," "Like I said, man, . . .") were thus not included in the list because of their basic instability and lack of breadth in language use.

These criteria thus excluded expressions from the restricted set of standard formulas of conversational initiation and leave-taking and the like, such as "Hello," "Thank you," or "Good luck." Such formulas are not used, as gambits are, to introduce a subject, and their capacity for social, psychological, or communicative signalling is very limited and standardized. By means of these criteria, gambits were also distinguished from idioms, such as "It's a young man's game," or "It's just sour grapes." Such expressions obviously do not satisfy criterion 1.

During data collection, it became evident that it is impossible to have a complete list of gambits. This is because these expressions often consist of verbal or nominal elements that allow of morphological and syntactic manipulation. For instance, the gambit "I think so" can easily be permuted into "I thought so," "I would think so," or "I might think so," or the expression "The surprising thing is" can under suitable circumstances assume the form "What surprised me most was," or even, given the right context, "The surprising element (e.g., in his story) was . . . ." Or someone wanting to create his own gambits can easily do so by picking a set of (usually fairly common) words to correspond to his intended social context signal and semantic content. So it is for instance possible to acknowledge another person's opinion and introduce one's own by saying "I won't refute what you're saying there, but I think that . . . ." This gambit might find its more fixed counterpart in the expression "Not that I disagree with you, but . . . ." This line of reasoning suggests that criteria 1 and 2 (purpose and placement of gambit) may be more incisive criteria for defining gambits in the absolute than criterion 3 (fixedness of use), a point which will be discussed more extensively below. For the purposes of the didactic corpus, it was decided to list just the main uses of a particular construction. The final inventory of gambits used for our didactic materials is listed in Keller and Taba-Warner, 1978. In addition to the gambits listed there, I will add a few more gambits in this article to illustrate certain points, and I will leave out others because of a refinement in the criteria used in defining these expressions.

SEMANTIC FRAMING

Most commonly and most overtly, gambits refer to semantic information. They serve to signal that the stretch of utterance to follow is to be taken in a particular manner, for instance as an opinion, or as a piece of unpleasant realism. Gambits thus do not signal specific meaning, as propositions or idioms do, but a general frame within which such meaning can be conveyed. For instance, the statement "In my opinion, he's a fool" contains the specific meaning "He is a fool," a meaning which is qualified by the gambit as an opinion. This function of gambits has here been named "semantic framing."

This aspect of gambits makes them unusually fertile objects of discourse analysis, since an inventory of typically used semantic frames can form the rudiments of a semantic frame map used by speakers as they structure their discourse. If it can be demonstrated that speakers habitually structure their speech in terms of these frames, it becomes imperative to consider these signals as part of the (overt or implicit) signalling inventory used at time of speaking.

With this in mind, the list of semantic frames abstracted from the described corpus of gambits is presented here. Since this is only an initial analysis of gambits, it is not suggested that this inventory is complete. For each type of introducer, I will list about three examples. This is not meant to, and hardly ever does, exhaust the list of commonly used gambits under that heading, but provides an indication of the variety of ways the same basic frame can be conveyed. The expressions ending in three dots need a specific complement to make them full-fledged gambits; for instance the expression "To get back to . . ." is usually found in the form "To get back to what we were talking about," which is a gambit to bring the conversation back to the main topic.

(1) Major semantic field indicators

(a) Congruent major semantic field: "I have a question on that," "We'll first take up the questions," "One answer to that would be . . . ."

(b) Incongruent major semantic field (a digression):
Initiation: "This reminds me . . .," "Speaking of . . .," "Before I forget."
Return to main topic: "In any case," "To get back to . . .," "Going back to . . . ."

(2) Various aspects of a topic

(a) A list:
Beginning: "First," "To begin with," "First of all."
Middle: "Second," "Another thing is," "Next."
End: "And finally," "As the last thing."

(b) A main aspect: "The main thing is," "Most of all," "The real problem is."

(c) A surprising aspect: "Believe it or not," "Strangely enough," "You may not believe this, but . . . ."

(d) An unpleasant aspect: "To be realistic," "Let's face it," "The catch is."

(e) An emphasized aspect: "The main thing is," "It bears emphasizing," "The most important thing is."

(3) Opinion

(a) Guessing: "My guess is."

(b) An opinion: "I'm pretty sure that," "I have reason to believe."

(c) A conviction: "I honestly feel," "I'm positive," "Without a doubt."

(d) A personal viewpoint: "In my (personal) estimation," "I personally believe," "To my mind," "The way I look at it."

(e) A personal evaluation: "As far as I can tell," "As I see it," "It appears to me," "To the best of my knowledge."

(f) Personal circumstances: "In my case," "What I'm concerned," "For my own part."

(g) Confidential information: "Just between you and me," "Rumour has it," "I hear from the grapevine."

(4) Action strategy

(a) A suggestion: "Why don't you do the following," "Here's what you can do."
(b) A plan: "What we have in mind is," "Here's what we'll do."

(5) Subject-expansion

(a) Expanding a point: "When it comes to . . .," "As far as that is concerned," "In a case like this."
(b) Adding items: "And another thing," "What's more," "I might add," "And furthermore."
(c) Giving a reason: "The reason why," "Seeing as how . . .," "On account of this," "For this reason."
(d) Explain a result: "As a result," "Consequently."
(e) Positive contigency: "In case of . . .," "If and when . . .," "As soon as . . .," "By the time . . . ."
(f) Negative contingency: "Barring the possibility . . .," "Unless . . .."
(g) Restatement: "What you're saying is," "If I read you right," "What I mean is," "What I meant to say is."
(h) Appearance and reality: "You may think . . . but in fact," "It may seem . . . but actually," "On the surface it appears as if . . . but the truth of the matter is."

(6) Subject-evaluation

(a) Reservations: "Yes, but consider," "Yes, but don't forget," "That's fine, but," "But the problem is."
(b) Taking into account: "Seeing as how . . .," "Keeping in mind . . .," "Allowing for the fact . . . "
(c) Seeing the other side: "All the same," "Yet on the other hand," "Mind you, though," "But then again."

(7) Argumentation

(a) Generalization:
High frequency: "Most of the time," "Again and again," "Time and again."
As a rule: "In general," "Ordinarily," "As a rule."
Low frequency: "Once in a while," "Every so often," "Every now and then."
(b) Exceptions: "As an exception."
(c) Examples: "As an example," "For one thing," "To give you an idea."

(d) Summarizing: "Summing up," "In short," "To make a long story short," "In a nutshell."

It is evident from the presentation chosen for this analysis that it is useful to distinguish between at least three levels of frame to be signalled. By using gambits of section (1), the speaker delimits the type of discourse he is choosing: questions, answers, exposition, digression, etc. Within one of these types of discourse, say, the expository or the answer type, he may enter into various aspects of a given topic, may present an opinion, may expose an action strategy, may expand a subject already under discussion, may evaluate it, or may offer arguments concerning it. Each of these categories have been broken down into subcategories, with some of these requiring even further subdivision. What is the limit of this process of subdivision? For the present purposes, the test chosen was one of 'loose substitutability'. If one gambit could be substituted for another within a sentence without drastically changing the meaning of its frame, the two were considered to belong to the same category. So for instance "*Believe it or not,* I got the best mark in that course" is not drastically different from "*Strangely enough,* I got the best mark in that course," but it is rather different from "*Let's face it,* I got the best mark in that course." It is this criterion that forced a further subdivision for some semantic introducers, such as those leading into a generalization, or those implying a list.

There is a further subdivision to be noted for these semantic introducers. Some of them, particularly those of sections (1) to (4), can be used to open a new topic or subtopic without overt reference to the previous topic. These gambits have been named "Openers" (Keller, 1977). The remaining ones by contrast are likely to be used for linking a topic under discussion into a topic or subtopic to be opened up, and were thus called "Links". For discourse analysis, this is probably a distinction of some consequence since it is likely that these expressions will be used at different levels within the topic hierarchy.

THE SIGNALLING OF SOCIAL CONTEXT

In addition to gambits that introduce or link semantic frames, there are some others that signal a speaker's wish to place himself and his listeners into certain social structural formations. When a speaker uses the gambit "Pardon me for interrupting, but," it is clear that he wishes to assume an active participant role within the group of people contributing to the conversation. On the other hand, when he says "Well, what do *you* think of it," he very probably wants to exchange his active participant role for a passive one, at least for a short while.

I have been able to identify two main types of sociological signals. On the one hand there are several types of signals for turn-taking, and on the other, there is a set of signals that can only be used by a speaker if he occupies, or claims to occupy, a particular social role. Through this exclusiveness of use, they signal the speaker's special social status, or his claim to such a status.

In the enumeration of these two types of signals, I have again given the examples in quotation marks, but I have put the basic signalling functions into brackets, formulated in normal English. This is not to suggest that gambits must necessarily exist *in that form* as an "underlying structure" or as a "subconscious wish". But it is certain that no matter what form these expressions are in, they do exist somewhere in the speaker's consciousness as he formulates his utterance, because they do serve very definite communicative functions. Since we are lacking unequivocal knowledge concerning the true internal representation of these signals, I shall proceed on the assumption that the present square bracket convention is adequate for the expository purposes desired here.

Among the turn-taking signals, the following were identified:

(1) [I want to have a turn]: "May I interrupt you for a moment," "Can you spare a minute," "I'd like to say something," "I have something to say on that too."
(2) [I want to keep my turn]: "Wait a second," "Well, let's see now," "What I would say is . . . ."
(3) [I want to abandon my turn]: "That's about all I have to say on that," "That's about it."
(4) [I don't want to take a turn]'I have nothing to say on that," "I'll pass on that."
(5) [Why don't you take a turn]: "So, what do you think of that?," "And what about you?," "What have you got to say on that?."
(6) [I want to leave the conversational group]: "It's been nice talking to you," "I'd better not take up any more of your time."

Since conversational discourse is often defined in terms of several speakers taking turns (Schegloff and Sacks, 1973; Wells, Montgomery and MacLure, 1978; Dore, 1978), it is not surprising that some special expressions exist in the language to signal intentions and wishes concerning the participants' turns in the conversation. Such overt turn-taking signals are of varying frequency. In informal discourse involving just two speakers they appear to be quite rare, since the intention to take a turn is usually signalled non-verbally, by facial signs or by clearing one's throat. In more formal discussion on the other hand, especially among many participants, a special restricted set of signals may be in use ("Our next speaker is . . .," "It's Peter's turn now").

In addition to the turn-taking signals, there are the expressions that are marked as to a speaker's social role. The general "underlying structure" of these expressions is something like [By virtue of my special role, I say the following]. In the case of a teacher or tester, this role signal would for instance be implied in examples such as "That's correct," "You're nearly right," "No, that's not it, I'm afraid." Or gambits like "Why don't you do the following" or "Here's what you can do" fulfill a function of suggesting an action, and thus are at least slightly marked for a counselling role. A leader role, again, is implied in such expressions as "Here's what we'll do," "I'll tell you what we'll do," or "Keep me posted, will you."

Some interesting systematic relations exist between the basic social signalling functions (in square brackets) and their surface forms (in quotation marks). The most obvious fact is that that there are relatively few surface gambits that directly reflect a basic social signalling function. Only very seldom does one hear an overt turn-taking expression, such as "Well, I've had my say now, why don't you say something about this," or a special-role signal such as "Well, after all, I'm the teacher around here, so I say what goes and what doesn't." Much more commonly, such signals are not overt, but implied. The reason for this seems to be at least two-fold. First of all, directly expressed social role or turn-taking signals are considered to be quite rude in our society, somewhat akin to pointing a finger at people. Secondly, it is much more efficient to combine the social-role or turn-taking signals with a semantic function. "Here's what we'll do" signals a plan for action, as well as it implies that the speaker is the leader of the group. This follows the general rule typical for discourse in our society, that except in formal circumstances, social roles are rarely overtly defined, but usually remain at the subliminal level. Even when the true topic of conversation is in fact the speakers' respective social roles, semantic information tends to predominate. For instance, two vice presidents wrangling about the succession to the presidency of a company will prefer to throw detailed information at each other about mismanagement in their respective domains, rather than overtly state their social aspirations.

STATE-OF-CONSCIOUSNESS SIGNALS

More overt than many of the social context signals are those that indicate a person's state of consciousness concerning information, opinions, or emotions. Typical of this function are gambits indicating a person's readiness to receive or provide new information, opinions, or emotions, or gambits suggesting that some knowledge or concern is being shared. Gambits that indicate readiness to engage in some action or to accept other people's opinions also seem to belong into this category of signals.

Under this general heading, eleven different states were identified on the basis of the material immediately available; yet here too it is likely that a number of additional states could be identified:

(1) [I am ready to receive information]: "I'd like to hear all about it," "I'd like to know some more about . . . ."

(2) [I am not ready to receive information]: "I'm not really interested in that," "I have no use for that," "I'm not concerned with that," "Why don't you just leave me alone."

(3) [I am ready to provide information or an opinion]: "I've got something to tell you," "Wouldn't you know, but," "Well, here's what I think about that."

(4) [I am not ready to provide information or an opinion]: "I don't want to get into that," "That's really none of your business."

(5) [I am sharing some knowledge/an opinion/an emotion with you]:
Knowledge: "I knew that," "No doubt about that."
An opinion: "You said it," "That's for sure," "That's what I was going to say," "I know what you mean."
An emotion: "That must have been just awful," "What a shame," "I feel with you."

(6) [I am not sharing your knowledge/opinion/emotion]:
Knowledge: "I didn't know that," "That's news to me."
Opinion: "I don't think so at all," "I couldn't agree less."
Emotion: "Serves you right," "It's your own fault."

(7) [I am not (entirely) sharing your opinion]: "I don't think so," "Do you really think," "I don't quite see that."

(8) [I would like you to share my opinion]: "Wouldn't it be a good idea, if . . .," "What do you say about that."

(9) [I yield to your opinion]: "When you put it that way," "Now that I think about it," "On second thought."

(10) [I am ready for some particular action]: "I'd love to," "I wouldn't mind," "Why don't we."

(11) [I am not ready for some particular action]: "I'd rather not," "I don't think it would be a good idea," "No way."

Here, we seem to be dealing with signals of a clearly different type. These indicate the speaker's state of consciousness with respect to what he is ready to do, to listen to, to say, or to empathize with. For some of these gambits, the communicative function is easily identified; by signalling his readiness to receive or provide information, a speaker communicates to the listener what "mode" he is in, and thus permits the establishment of a communication link. Obviously it is necessary to have at least one person in "receive mode" and another in "transmit mode" for a message to pass from one to the other. By using gambits of this type, the speaker facilitates the establishment of the right combination of modes in the speaker and the hearer. Other gambits are somewhat more complex. Indicating the sharing or non-sharing of knowledge and emotions, as well as expressing one's intended actions, in other words, the advertising of the speaker's state of consciousness, probably serves to facilitate comprehension of discourse or actions which are to follow.

COMMUNICATION CONTROL SIGNALS

Somewhat related to the state-of-consciousness signals just described are the communication control signals. The focus of state-of-consciousness signals is what the speaker is ready to do, say, think, and the like; communication control signals on the other hand serve to assure that the listener is in a state of consciousness permitting the reception of the message. Four types of signals were distinguished in this category:

(1) [Do you understand/hear me?]: "Are you following me?," "Can you hear me?," "Is that clear?," "Right?."
(2) [I understood/heard you]: "Okay," "Sure," "And so?."
(3) [I did not understand/hear you]: "Pardon me?," "Would you mind repeating that?," "Sorry, I didn't get that last part."
(4) [You must have misunderstood me/not heard me right]: "That's not what I said," "What I really said is this," "What I've been telling you all along is . . . ."

"Hearing" and "understanding" clearly denote different segments of the communication channel. Yet it is interesting to note that such gambits as those of section (3) are not marked for this distinction. The reason for this is not difficult to surmise; no one enjoys admitting not having understood something since such an admission could reflect negatively upon oneself. To save face, unmarked verbs like "to get" (something) may be used, or the issue may be evaded altogether through the use of direct requests for repetitions. Similarly, a speaker who is checking to see that his listener has understood, or who realizes that the message has in fact not been understood correctly, may use an evasive device to save his listener some embarrassment. For instance, by saying "Is that clear?" or "What I really mean" he opens up the possibility that he himself may be responsible for any lack of understanding.

LINGUISTIC FEATURES OF GAMBITS

We have seen that gambits can be expressive of a large variety of semantic, social, psychological, and communicative information. In this section, we will examine some of the rules that appear to govern the precise surface structure that gambits can take. For instance, we have seen that a desire to take a turn in the conversation can be expressed in various different ways ("May I interrupt for a moment," "Can you spare a minute," etc.). Why will speakers at times choose one, and at other times another surface form?

The main variable governing this type of choice seems to be *appropriateness*. Obviously, it is inappropriate to use the word "interrupt" when there is a natural pause in the conversation. Or the expression "Can you spare a minute" becomes ironic if the person addressed is evidently enjoying a break from his work. The exact lexemic selections leading to the construction of a gambit will thus be guided not only by the underlying (social, psychological, etc.) information, but also by the perceived real-world situation. An adequately chosen gambit will have to be congruent with both types of information.

One specific aspect of the perceived real world concerns the speaker's familiarity with his audience, and his social rank occupied within the group. These factors control the *degree of politeness* that is used in choosing a particular surface form of a gambit. For instance, it is likely that one would choose a gambit like "Excuse me for interrupting" in a situation where politeness is appropriate, while "Hold it" and "Wait a minute" would be reserved for more informal and familiar contexts.

Along these lines, it was observed throughout the corpus that gambits tended to be structured to express politeness. This may be due to two factors. On the one hand, it may reflect one basic reason for using these expressions in the first place. Topics, turns in the conversation, and states of consciousness are in a constant state of flux in conversational discourse. These changes are disturbing to the participants when they occur too abruptly, and it is thus polite to guard one's listeners against the abruptness of the transition by using gambits. Moreover, there are strong social forces in society that favor the preservation of form and politeness as an expression of mutual respect. "Watered down" gambits such as "You're close" for "You're wrong," or "Personally, I wouldn't say that" for "You're talking nonsense" exemplify this tendency.

The second reason for the typically high degree of politeness in gambits may be the source of the original corpus. It was assembled essentially on the basis of the speech of Canadian government employees, a group of people naturally reticent about using impolite or even offensive gambits. It may be that discourse recorded from different sources might yield a somewhat different set of gambits.

Another stylistic adjustment made when choosing surface forms concerns the *size of the audience.* Several gambits are marked for use with a single listener; for example a suggestion offered to an audience of one could take the form "If I were you," while with a larger audience, the unmarked form "Why not . . ." might be used. Or to indicate disagreement with a single listener, one might say "I don't see it the way you do," while with more than one, one might choose "I don't see it that way."

A comparison of a large number of gambits from the same category also revealed that at least for some gambits, some of the lexemes making up the expression may be more substitutable than others. It is for instance possible to identify the gambits "Not that I disagree with you, but," "Not that I want to contradict you, but," "Not that this proves you wrong, but," or even "Not that this is all nonsense, but," all containing the same "Not that . . ., but" construction. Since this construction is generally used in the context of attempting to set the listener at ease by not condemning his opinion (altogether), it suggests that this construction by itself contains some social and semantic information, only to be completed and refined by the specific content words selected to "fill the slot." This becomes poignantly clear when considering the gambit "Not that I *agree* with you, but," as used for instance by a slightly ironic debater. The structure "Not that . . ., but" suggests the usual placating introduction to the listener, but the semantically opposed (because negated) content word "agree' gives the gambit its unexpected ironic twist.

Evidence of this sort indicates that the function word frame is more fixed in usage than the content words used with it; yet even with this distinction, gambits consisting of several semantically coherent lexemes are not as immutable as other so-called fixed expressions (such as idioms), since they can still undergo syntactic and morphological manipulation. It is thus possible to find the syntactic variants "Not *to* disagree with you, but," and "I *won't* disagree with you, but," as well as the above-mentioned standard form "Not *that* I disagree with you, but." Given this variability in degree of fixedness, it is probable that fixedness of structure is not a crucial identifying feature of gambits.

This reasoning removes one of the criteria that were originally used to define gambits. The remaining two criteria (various types of signalling, initial position within the sentence) are not adequate to the task of separating gambits from other types of utterances, since a great many possible utterances can fulfill these criteria without intrinsically seeming to belong to the present group of expressions. There must thus be a further typical feature of gambits which has up to now escaped our attention.

In reading over the set of gambits listed above, it will be noticed that the end of gambits may typically be marked by a drop in the intonational contour. For instance, the sentence "In my opinion, he's a fool" may be marked by a drop in the intonation between "opinion" and "he," a transition that is generally marked by a comma in the written version. This suggests that gambits may in some manner be syntactically independent from the utterances they introduce.

In many cases, this syntactic independence is easy to identify. Gambits such as "Wait a second" or "I'd love to" are independent utterances, and others such as "As a rule," "Again and again" are adverbial phrases that precede the main part of a sentence. The problem arises with gambits such as "Wouldn't it be a good idea, if . . ." or "What do you say about . . . ." Such expressions are often in clear syntactic relation to their succeeding utterances ("Wouldn't it be a good idea if we all *went* skiing," "What do you say about Tarzan marry*ing* Jane?"). In these cases we have essentially three choices. We can postulate syntactic independence at an underlying level, we can postulate that the entire utterance represents a gambit, or we can rule this type of expression out of bounds. None of these alternatives is very attractive. The first would open the door to such expressions as "I think," "I promise," "I say," and other illocutionary acts in the sense of Searle (1969), expressions that do not generally allow a falling intonation to mark their separation from the utterance they qualify. The second alternative conflicts with the rule established above that gambits provide only a semantic frame, but do not convey specific meaning, and the third alternative would eliminate some structures that intuitively fall into the category of gambits, i.e., those that are marked for one of the signalling functions and whose end can be accompanied by a drop in the intonational contour.

It may be that this will remain a somewhat fuzzy area for some time. For the time being, a strong marking for one or several of the four functions, accompanied by a drop in the intonational contour at the end of the expression, may have to do as identifying features. An analysis of gambits in the context of recorded discourse will hopefully lead us to a clearer definition in the future.

GAMBITS IN DISCOURSE ANALYSIS

It was noted above that gambits could play a useful part in a discourse analysis by indicating the general frame of the topic to be taken up, as well as the various social, psychological, and communicative signals used in discourse. These functions will now be illustrated with a stretch of discourse taken from a television talk show. The criteria for selecting the segment present here were that the topic be of general interest, but fully developed within a short time, and that it involve a fair number of turns in the conversation.

The analysis is presented in three sections. The text itself appears at the left. The topic or subtopic under discussion is delimited in the text by square brackets, and is summarized in the middle section. Gambits appearing in the text are given in boldface, and are analyzed in the section at the right. In the immediately preceding portion of the talk show, the host and guest discussed rote learning, taking as an example the memorization of Newton's three laws of gravity.

TEXT	TOPICS	GAMBITS
Guest: [That's the point, YOU SEE, they . . . they, they, they make us learn this stuff, and we don't know what the hell it means, and they don't know what the hell it means, and it is only ——] [I —— . . . you know, I came to realize what you are really taught in school is that, that uh . . .]	Learning without knowing what one is learning (Topic abandoned)	**That's the point;** Semantic: emphasized point (2e) **You see;** Consciousness: share my opinion (8), Communication: Do you understand? (1)
[ah-eh, you know, **First of all,** **I must preface this** with where I came to realize it, I was in a factory, doing an industrial film for the manufacture of, you know, Hogdoodoo's T-Tissue, or something, I don't know, and at five minutes of ten, a bell rang, and about fity uh workers came in, salivating for coffee. They dra- . . . they sat down, they drank their coffee, and about ten minutes after ten, another bell rang, and they all put their styrofoam cups in the trash can, went back to work,]	Story about factory workers living only for their coffee breaks	**First of all;** Semantic: list (2a) **I must preface this;** Semantic: insertion
[**And I said,** wow, the bell is what we heard for all those twelve years in school, and that was the message . . . **Host: Uhuhm . . .** Guest: . . . the medium . . . **Host: Uhuhm . . .** **Guest:** . . . as McLuhan says, is the message. The stuff that came between the bells	The bell is more important than the class →	**And I said;** Semantic: Direct quotation (of one's own thoughts) **Uhuhm** (or similar); Consciousness: I'm sharing your opinion (5), Communication: I understand you (2)

is irrelevant, such as your three laws of uh . . .	"The medium is the message"	
Host: That's right, that's right . . .		**That's right;** Consciousness: I'm sharing your opinion (5), Communication: I understand you
Guest: . . . gravity. Or Hannibal crossed the Alps on 37 elephants, or 4100 elephants, who cares "Charles Martell at the Battle of Tours" and brtt . . . brtt . . . "defeated the Moor." I'll – I remember the poem, except for the date. The poem was invented for the purpose of getting me to the —— remember the date when Charles Martell defeated the Moor, and the poem is emblazoned on my mind forever, but I can't remember the date, that's the one thing in the middle of it.]		
[**So the point is** that the medium is the message, and what we are taught in school for twelve years is to learn to tolerate boredom, so that when it gets five minutes of ten, it's important not simply that we go to the cafeteria for coffee, but that we want to go . . .	We learn to tolerate boredom	**So the point is;** Semantic: emphasized point (2e), summarizing (7d)
Host: Uhhum . . .		**Uhhum:** See above
Guest: . . . to the cafeteria for coffee.		
Chuckle in the audience		
Otherwise there would be disruption in the factory.		
Host: Uhhum . . .		
Guest: If you became thirsty for coffee at twenty minutes past ten, just everybody else h-had come back, that could really make big trouble, wild-cat strikes, and terrible things.		
Host: [Have you ever experimented with . . . with . . . with . . .	(Host starts new topic while guest is not quite ready to abandon his)	
Guest: This is all good stuff, folks!]		
Host: That's right. Now this		**That's right;** see

is impor – Have you ever experimented with Pavlovian theory?		above
with . . . **Guest:** Not . . . **Host:** Have you – do you have any pets?	Experimentation with salivating to a bell	**Now this is impor** – Semantic: emphasized point (2e), Social: I want to have a turn, Consciousness: I am ready to give an opinion (3)
. . .		

There are a number of interesting relationships to note between gambits and the structuring of discourse. We can see, for instance, that the gambits which are heavily marked for semantic frame ("That's the point," line 1, "First of all," line 11, "I must preface this," line 12, "And I said," line 29, "So the point is," line 60, and "Now this is impor ——" [presumably "important"], line 88) all appear in relationship to interfaces between various topics or subtopics. Some relationships are fairly straightforward, such as the placing of "And I said," line 29, or "So the point is," line 60, while others are a bit more complex. "I must preface this," line 12, for instance appears between a stretch of discourse representing an abandoned topic (to be taken up again in line 62) and one that is fully developed. This is not surprising, since the semantic frame suggested by this gambit is "insertion." in other words, "what is to follow should actually precede what I've already said." Another interesting transition from one topic to another is found in line 85. There the host finds that he has started his new topic a bit before the guest was willing to relinquish his; he quickly agrees with the guest concerning the value of what has just been said ("That's right"), but actively seeks his turn in the conversation by continuing with "This is important." In addition to being marked for the social turn-taking level, it is also marked semantically for emphasis; we may assume that the host used this doubly marked gambit to explain or excuse his somewhat abrupt transition from one topic to another and to attract the listeners' attention to the topic he is about to broach.

In contrast to the semantically marked gambits, the gambits marked for state of consciousness and communication control are not constrained by the topic or subtopic boundaries. For instance, "That's right" appears both during the development of a topic in line 41 and at the interface between two topics in line 88.

Some other expressions that could be taken for gambits, such as the heavily used term "you know" (lines 8, 11, and 16) were not identified as such since they were not marked for any of the four variables usually signalled by gambits. They act predominantly as fillers for time presumably spent searching for the right word or for an adequate means of structuring discourse. This emerges both from individual examples (consider for instance the uses in lines

8 and 16), as from the fact that the three instances of the term occur at the beginning of the topic to develop, at a time when the guest is still searching for ways of structuring his discourse. Even though I have chosen not to call these expressions gambits, it is evident that they signal some noteworthy aspects of topic development within discourse.

Finally, we note again that the lists presented above are by no means complete. The gambits "I must preface this" and "And I said" suggest topic frames that were not included in our analysis. This is hardly worrisome, since the first gambit could be called an insertion gambit and could appear under a new heading (lc) in the listing of semantic indicators, and the second gambit could appear under the heading (7) Argumentation as a direct quotation gambit. Much more important than these predictable gaps in the system is the fact that quite evidently, gambits play an important role in structuring discourse, and that the four levels of signalling isolated above appear to be well supported by an examination of a stretch of discourse taken nearly randomly from spontaneous speech.

CONCLUSION

In the preceding pages, an analysis of an initial corpus of expressions marked for definable semantic, social, psychological and communicative signalling functions has been presented. These so-called gambits are evidently used by speakers to structure their presentation of topics and their taking of turns in the conversation, to indicate their state of consciousness with respect to some information, opinion, knowledge, emotion or planned action, and to check whether communication is being passed on to the listener. Various systematic aspects of gambits were discussed, such as factors influencing the exact surface realization that various underlying signals may take, and degree of fixedness within the language of these expressions. Finally, the present analysis of gambits was applied to a stretch of discourse, where it was shown that this type of expression seems to be implicated in some key roles in structuring the flow of discourse.

This role of gambits promises some interesting possible developments in the analysis of discourse. Since gambits say much more about text that is to follow than they say about themselves, it follows that these expressions are valuable clues to the overall structuring of discourse. It thus appears that gambits force us to look at discourse "from the top down," or to use a term common in computer programming, to perform a "top-down analysis." In this type of analysis, a problem is not approached from its constituent parts, but from the point of view of its overall structure. Once the central problem, or the main structure of a problem, has been defined, the full analysis of its parts will be much more accessible than if each individual part is analyzed by itself and is later reconciled into an overall structure. This type of analysis has not been traditional in linguistics, since the history of this field has been marked by a succession of relatively limited interests in ever larger parts of discourse, such as the phoneme, the syntactic structure of the sentence, and the semantic analysis of parts of the sentence. Only recently has there been an increased interest in discourse as a whole. From the perspective of the analyses presented here, it would seem that only now, the time is ripe for a development of top-down analysis, involving among other features the key role played by gambits.

In view of the development of linguistics, it is not surprising that as far as I can tell, two of the functions of gambits described here have not had extensive treatment in the literature. The first is the "semantic frame" function. It has been common to proceed in semantic analysis in terms of "actor", "action", "object" and other atomic elements of meaning. These are all valuable clues to the specific meaning of an utterance; the analysis of gambits, however, has revealed that a set of typical semantic frames is signalled to the listener to advise him of the general nature of the semantic information conveyed. Secondly, we have been able to identify a "state-of-consciousness" signal. Discourse between various individuals is evidently facilitated if the various participants are advised of the psychological "mode" the speaker is in, with respect to the opinion, plans, etc. of the other participants in the conversation. If the speaker is not in a receptive mode, further discourse is pointless, a situation which may explain a premature abortion of a topic, or a particular change in topic within discourse.

All the same, top-down analysis involving gambits has for the present not yet been subjected to an extensive test. Longer stretches of discourse from a variety of sources are needed to assess the pervasiveness of these expressions, and the validity of the analyses presented here. But from early indications, including some work being conducted on psychotic speech here in Montreal, I am almost certain that this type of analysis bears a great potential for linking and explaining some haunting aspects of normal, as well as of abnormal types of discourse.

NOTES

1. This paper contains relatively few references to previous research in the domain. This is in large measure due to the fact that it reports research and cogitation conducted some time before the recent development of insightful frameworks for the discourse analysis of conversational speech (Dore, 1978; Shields, 1978; Wells, Montgomery and MacLure, 1978). Even if a closer connection between this material and the mentioned discourse analysis frameworks had been desired, it would have been difficult

to establish because gambits seem to highlight aspects of discourse that are either different or cut across the structures differentiated by these authors.

2. They are, in alphabetical order, Cornelius von Baeyer, Jim Fox, Anne Greenwood, Heidemarie Maclean, Vera McLay, Sylvia Taba-Warner and Howard Woods. Their conscientious and time-consuming participation in this project is gratefully acknowledged.

JOAN MANES and NESSA WOLFSON

The Compliment Formula

ABSTRACT

An analysis of six hundred and eighty-six compliments gathered through observation of everyday interactions reveals that compliments in American English are formulaic in nature. The semantic, syntactic and discourse features of the compliment formula are examined, as well as the fact that the formulaic nature of compliments is not explicitly recognized by native speakers. A consideration of the role of compliments in interactions shows that both the existence of a formula and its lack of recognition are, in fact, functional.

One of the most striking features of compliments in American English is their almost total lack of originality. An initial examination of a large corpus reveals a surprising repetetiveness in both the object of the compliments and the lexical items used to describe them. Closer investigation, however, is required to discover the regularities that exist on all levels, the syntactic, discourse and social as well as the semantic. Compliments are, in fact, formulas, although this is not immediately obvious, partly because their patterning occurs on so many interacting levels and partly because formulaic compliments serve a number of different discourse functions and may occur at almost any point within an interaction. Nevertheless, as we will show, both the formulaic nature of compliments and the fact that their formulaic nature is not immediately obvious are intimately connected to their functions within interactions.

THE DATA

It is our conviction that an ethnographic approach is the only reliable method for collecting data about the way compliments, or indeed, any other speech act functions[1] in everyday interactions. Secondary sources such as novels and plays, because they are mediated by the stylistic requirements of the artist, cannot be depended upon to reflect exactly the complexity of actual speech use. Intuitions about speech usage are notoriously unreliable, as speakers tend to be aware of the societal norms and are under the mistaken impression that these norms represent the actual speech patterns of the community (cf. Blom and Gumperz 1972, Labov 1972). Our own past research (Manes 1976, Wolfson 1976, Wolfson and Manes in press) has borne out the necessity for participant observation in the collection of data on everyday speech forms.

The data upon which this analysis is based consist of six hundred and eighty-six compliments collected during the academic year 1977–78 in Charlottesville, Virginia and Philadelphia, Pennsylvania. Although a large portion of these compliments were collected by the authors, a considerable number were also collected by students both at the University of Virginia and at the University of Pennsylvania as part of seminars in sociolinguistics conducted by the authors.[2] Since the aim was to collect as varied a sample as possible, it was enormously helpful to have data collected by such a large number of people. The compliments which make up the corpus were gathered in everyday interactions which the researchers observed or in which they participated. Every effort was made to sample as large a variety of speech situations as possible. The speakers and addressees were men and women of all ages and from a range of occupational and educational backgrounds. In addition to collecting the compliments and the responses to them, the observers were careful to take note of the sex, approximate age and occupation of both speaker and addressee, as well as their relationship to one another, wherever such information was available.

The data include compliments given and received by waitresses, cashiers and customers, employers and employees, clergymen, landlords and salesmen, colleagues, friends, neighbors and family members. The objects complimented range from hairdos and fingernails to cars and furniture, from jewelry and clothing to photographs and academic papers, from chalk and bulletin boards to children and pets. The resulting corpus thus contains compliments given in a far greater range of speech situations than would have been possible if the authors had been limited to data which they themselves collected.

THE SEMANTIC FORMULA

It is obvious that since compliments are expression of positive evaluation, every compliment must include at least one term which carried positive semantic load.[3] What is interesting is that, despite the almost unlimited number of terms which may be chosen, the overwhelming majority of compliments contain one of a highly restricted set of adjectives and verbs.

The range of adjectives which can be used in compliments is enormous. In our data alone we find no fewer than seventy-two different adjectives. Some are topic specific (*delicious, curly*) while others are extremely general (*nice, beautiful, fantastic*); some are quite strong in their expression of positive evaluation (*fantastic, gorgeous, stupendous*) while others carry a much weaker semantic load (*nice, good*). Out of this wide variety of terms, however, only a very few occur with any degree of regularity. Not surprisingly, *nice* and *good*, with their weak semantic load, are by far the most common. Of the six hundred and eighty-six compliments in our data there are five hundred and forty-six in which the positive semantic load is carried by an adjective. Of these, one hundred and twenty-five, or 22.9 per cent, make use of *nice* and another one hundred and seven, or 19.6 per cent, use *good*. Thus we find numerous compliments of the following sort:

(1) Your apartment's nice.
(2) Oh, new shoes? They are really nice.
(3) Bill, you look so nice today.[4]
(4) This is good. It tastes like fresh orange juice.
(5) Your moustache looks good.
(6) You did a good job.

Only three other adjectives, *beautiful, pretty* and *great*, appear in more than 5 per cent of adjectival compliments. *Pretty* and *beautiful* occur in 9.7 per cent and 9.2 per cent of such compliments respectively, while *great* occurs in 6.2 per cent.

(7) That's such a pretty sweater.
(8) You did a beautiful job of explaining that.
(9) That book you lent me was great. It was great. What an ending!

Thus two thirds of all adjectival compliments make use of **only five adjectives.** In the other one third (one hundred and fifty-six compliments) we find a total of sixty-seven different adjectives, most occurring only once or twice.

The fact that we find only seventy-two different positive adjectives in our corpus does not, by any means, imply that these are the only adjectives which occur in compliments. Indeed, we are certain that further research would uncover a much greater variety of adjectives than that so far collected. What the figures presented here suggest is that, although the possible choice of complimentary adjectives is very great, speakers prefer to use one of a very restricted set of semantically vague adjectives. The compliments thus created are, to all intents and purposes, semantic formulas.

Although 80 per cent of all compliments in our data are of the adjectival type just discussed, compliments which make use of verbs to carry the positive semantic load do occur:

(10) I like your haircut.
(11) I love your glasses.
(12) I really enjoyed your class.

In contrast to the wide range of semantically positive adjectives found, only a very few semantically positive verbs appear in compliments. The only such verbs which occur in our corpus are *like, love, admire, enjoy* and *be impressed by*. This limited set of verbs, moreover, forms a pattern of usage similar to but even more striking than that of adjectives: just two verbs, *like* and *love,* occur in 86 per cent of all compliments which contain a semantically positive verb. As with adjectives, most other positive verbs occur only once or twice in our data. Here again we find speakers making use of what amounts to a semantic formula: *I like/love NP.*

Although 96 per cent of the data consist of compliments using semantically positive adjectives and verbs, other forms which are clearly intended and interpreted as compliments do occur. There are some verbs which are not inherently positive but which, when used in the correct context, usually with an intensifier such as *really,* function as compliments. Thus we find:

(13) You've really fixed this place up since the last people were here.
(14) Your talk was the one that really went over.

There are also compliments in which the positive term is an adverb or a noun:

(15) You really handled that situation well.
(16) You've really fixed up this room nicely.
(17) You do this kind of writing so well.
(18) You're just a whiz at sewing.

Compliments of this sort are surprisingly rare. Only one adverb, *well,* occurs more than twice, and even it is found no more than fourteen times. Clearly, speakers strongly prefer to make use of one of the semantic formulas just described: a positive adjective or a verb of liking.

Another semantic pattern which deserves notice is the use of intensifiers. As can be seen from the example so far cited, *really* and other intensifiers are quite common in compliments, occurring in over one third of our data. We have noted above that verbs which are not verbs of liking normally occur with intensifiers (see examples 13 and 14). Furthermore, *quite a* and *some* appear in compliments in what would normally be the adjective position:

(19) That's quite a record collection you've got.
(20) That's some birthday cake.

This suggests that intensifiers, perhaps because of their frequent association with clearly complimentary terms, can themselves function as semantically positive items. Although they are by no means a necessary part of the compliment formula, intensifiers occur frequently enough to be considered a typical feature of compliments.

Another typical feature of compliments is the use of certain deictic elements, specifically second person pronouns and demonstratives:

(21) That's a sharp suit and tie you're wearing.
(22) I love your skirt and your blouse.
(23) That's a nice piece of work.
(24) Wow, you've got a great apartment.
(25) This is pretty.

The use of these elements is related to the fact, discussed below, that compliments are typically independent of the utterances which precede them. If a compliment appears as an aside in the middle of a conversation or, as is frequently the case, begins the conversation, the listener may well be confused as to the intended object of the compliment. The purpose of deixis in compliments, then, is to identify clearly the person or object to be complimented. The reason deictic elements are not invariably part of compliments is that identification may be accomplished through other means. We have many examples in our data in which the object of the compliment is identified by the verbal or nonverbal context. However, second person pronouns and demonstratives occur in 75 per cent of all compliments in our data. Furthermore, in 40 per cent of the cases in which there is no deixis, the compliment is preceded by another compliment which does include such an element, or the object of the compliment is actually named:

(26) Mary, I like that coat on you. It looks just super.
(27) I love your skirt, Betty. It's very attractive.
(28) Mmm. The chocolate sauce is good.

Thus deixis in compliments, in the form of second person pronouns and demonstratives, may be seen to serve an extremely important discourse function.

The above analysis indicates that although there is seemingly no limit to the possible forms a compliment may take in English, a very few semantic items occur with extraordinary frequency. They include a small set of adjectives and verbs, a few intensifiers, and certain deictic elements. What this means is that, in giving compliments, most speakers of American English make use of what can only be called semantic formulas.

THE SYNTACTIC FORMULA

There seems, on the surface, to be no reason for any specific syntactic pattern to occur in compliments. An analysis of their syntax, however, reveals that compliment structure is even more severely restricted on the syntactic level than on the semantic. To be precise, **53.6 per cent of the compliments in our data make use of a single syntactic pattern**:

$$\text{(29)}\quad \text{NP} \left\{ \begin{matrix} \text{is} \\ \text{looks} \end{matrix} \right\} \text{(really) ADJ}^{5}$$

(e.g., 'Your hair looks nice'; 'That shirt is so nice. It looks so comfortable'; 'This is really good'). Two other syntactic patterns:

$$\text{(30)}\quad \text{I (really)} \left\{ \begin{matrix} \text{like} \\ \text{love} \end{matrix} \right\} \text{NP}$$

(e.g., 'I love your hair'; 'I really like those shoes') and:

(31) PRO is (really) (a) ADJ NP

(e.g., 'That a nice piece of work'; 'This was really a great meal') account for an additional 16.1 per cent and 14.9 per cent of the data respectively. Thus only three patterns are required to describe 85 per cent of the compliments found. Indeed, only nine patterns occur with any regularity and these nine account for 97.2 per cent of our data. In addition to the three major patterns already described, we find the following six:

(32) You V (a) (really) ADJ NP (3.3 per cent)

(e.g., 'You did a good job')

(33) You V (NP) (really) ADV (2.7 per cent)

(e.g., 'You really handled that situation well')

(34) You have (a) (really) ADJ NP[6] (2.4 per cent)

(e.g., 'You have such beautiful hair')

(35) What (a) ADJ NP ! (1.6 per cent)

(e.g., "What a lovely baby you have!')

(36) ADJ NP ! (1.6 per cent)

(e.g., 'Nice game!)

(37) Isn't NP ADJ ![7] (1.0 per cent)

(e.g., 'Isn't your ring beautiful! Isn't it pretty!).
No pattern other than those listed above occurs more than twice in our data. The distribution of syntactic patterns in compliments is shown in Figure 1.

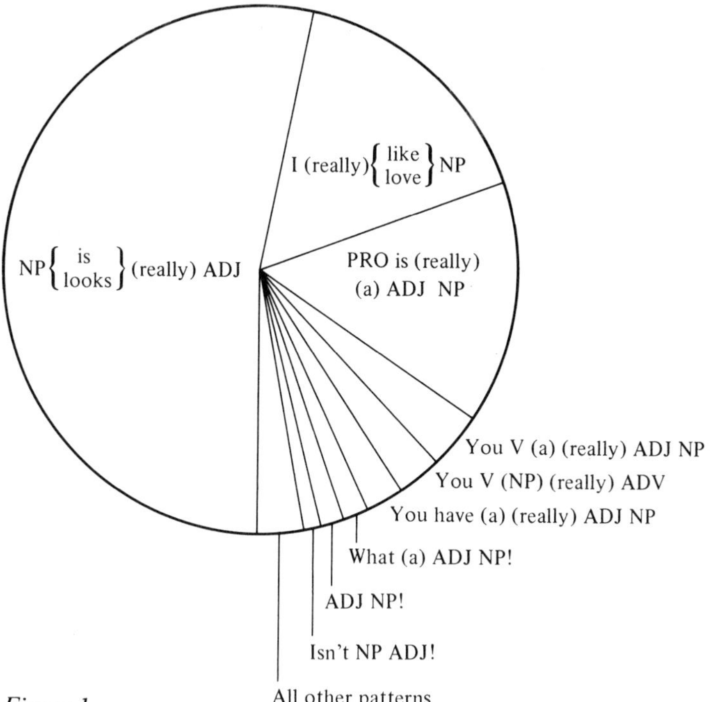

Figure 1

Any of the patterns described above may, of course, be embedded within a larger syntactic frame. Speakers sometimes introduce compliments with a phrase such as 'I think' or 'I wanted to tell you.' We find, for example:

(38) I think your hair looks good this way.
(39) By the way, I have to tell you how professional I thought your magazine looked.
(40) Why don't you just accept the fact that you did a good job?

Such embedding does not change the structure of the actual compliment. In addition to embedding, we frequently find compliments preceded and/or followed by related remarks. As already noted, compliments may occur in sequence. Questions or comments which are not themselves compliments may also occur in conjunction with compliments, as discussed below.

In the previous section we discussed the adjectives and verbs which bring positive semantic value to the compliment. It must be noted, however, that there are morphological as well as semantic constraints on these elements. Adjectives in compliments almost uniformly occur in their base forms. Rarely do we find instances of comparatives or superlatives, although these can occur:

(41) Your accent is charming. Much nicer than ours.
(42) Hank, that's some of the best banjo picking I've ever heard.

Just as adjectives are found almost exclusively in their base forms, so verbs seldom occur in compliments except in the simple present or past form. There appears to be a strong constraint on the use of the future tense in compliments, so strong, in fact, that our own corpus contains not a single example. The constraint concerning aspect is somewhat weaker. We do find occasional examples of progressives, present perfects and even conditionals used in compliments:

(43) Jane, you're looking great as usual.
(44) I've always loved that shirt.
(45) I think you'd be good in law school.

Forms such as these, however, are extremely rare. It seems clear that compliments typically use only verbs which are not marked for aspect.

Another typical feature of compliments, one which reflects an interactional rather than a syntactic constraint, concerns the addressee: compliments are almost always addressed to the person who owns the object being complimented or who is himself being complimented. We do find a few indirect compliments, which are overtly addressed to one person but actually compliment another party who is present. It is interesting to note that in such cases it is frequently the person complimented rather than the addressee who responds to the compliment:

(46) S: Look what a pretty sweater she has.
C: My mother gave it to me.

(47) S: He's the best player around.
C: I'm not. You've beaten me many times.

Indirect compliments, however, make up less than 5 per cent of our data. Compliments in our society are typically addressed **directly** to the person being complimented.

Our examination of the semantic and syntactic patterns to be found in compliments reveals an extraordinary degree of regularity. Most impressive, perhaps, is the fact that 85 per cent of all compliments in the data fall into one of only three syntactic patterns. Almost equally striking is the tendency on the part of speakers to use one of only seven adjectives and verbs to convey their positive evaluation. Adjectives occur almost exclusively in their base forms and verbs in the simple present or past. In addition to these syntactic and semantic constraints, compliments are subject to interactional and discourse constraints. To be specific, compliments are typically addressed directly to the person being complimented, and deixis is nearly always present to provide unambiguous identification of the object of the compliment.

Regularity of this magnitude cannot merely be noted; it calls for explanation. The combination of a restricted semantic set and an even more highly restricted set of syntactic structures makes it clear that what we are dealing with here is not simply a matter of frequency. Rather, we are forced to recognize that **compliments are formulas**, as much so as thanks and greetings. The speech act of complimenting is, in fact, characterized by the formulaic nature of its syntactic and semantic composition. Compliments are not merely sentences which remark on a particularly attractive item or attribute; they are highly structured formulas which can be adapted with minimal effort to a wide variety of situations in which a favorable comment is required or desired. By substituting the correct noun phrase, *I really like NP* or *NP looks nice* can be appropriately applied to haircuts, homemade bread, shirts, new cars or a job well done.

THE FUNCTION OF THE FORMULA

The fact that compliments are formulaic in nature, is, in itself, an important and interesting linguistic finding. But recognizing the formulaic nature of compliments is only the first step in explaining their extraordinary semantic and syntactic regularity. There is no question but that native speakers are perfectly capable of making use of a wide variety of syntactic and semantic choices. Why, therefore, do they so consistantly select one of three syntactic structures and one of only seven lexical items to express their positive evaluations of another's property, attribute or accomplishment? The answer to this question can only be uncovered through a consideration of the function of complimenting in an interaction.

Put simply, the question is: what is a person doing when he offers a compliment? The immediate answer is that he is stating a favorable judgment or opinion, saying something nice to another individual. In doing so, the speaker expresses a commonality of taste or interest with the addressee, thus reinforcing, or in the case of strangers, creating at least a minimal amount of solidarity. This reinforcement and/or creation of solidarity appears to be a basic function of compliments in our society. It is the recognition of this function which allows us to understand why it is that speakers seem to prefer conventional patterns in compliments. If anything in the compliment or the way it is worded creates social distance, the expression of solidarity which is the raison d'etre of the compliment may be vitiated. The use of a formula helps avoid this potential difficulty.

It is a sociolinguistic truism that members of a speech community are quick to pigeonhole one another on the basis of speech forms. Speakers who are engaging in pleasantries with one another in order to establish rapport need to minimize differences in their speech use which might undermine their efforts. For example, the use of a syntactic structure which is strongly marked as uneducated may cause the addressee to regard the speaker as beneath him. On the other hand, a word which another speaker feels to be perfectly appropriate may be heard as affected or as condescending by the addressee. Negative judgments of this type would interfere with the solidarity-creating function of the compliment. Use of a formulaic adjective or verb in a precoded syntactic structure makes the speaker much less vulnerable to such judgments and enhances the possibility that the compliment will fulfill its function.

Similarly, the use of certain forms might identify the speaker as a member of a different social group. Indeed, in some cases, the semantically positive term used in the compliment may have different, even negative, connotations for the listener. An erudite expression addressed to the wrong person could even result in total lack of comprehension. Certain colloquial expressions may be equally unintelligible if they are addressed to a member of a different age or ethnic group, for example. By using one of a set of very general lexical items the speaker lessens the possibility of inadvertently emphasizing differences in group membership.

This is not to say that compliments exchanged by members of the same group may not make use of marked forms such as specific lexical items which may easily fit into one of the slots in the formula. In fact, such usage does occur and often serves to further affirm solidarity. For example, an elderly Jewish woman who works as cashier in a sandwich shop frequented by one of the researchers, made use of a Yiddish expression in offering the following compliment:

(48) S: Is that your son? Kinehura, he's adorable.
C: Thanks.

The use of the expression *kinehura,* which is intended to ward off the evil eye, is traditional among Yiddish speakers when speaking well of children, or in fact, of anyone or anything potentially vulnerable which is dear to the addressee.[8] It is, therefore, a clear compliment marker in Yiddish and carries a heavy cultural load. Adding this expression to a compliment in English serves to intensify the effect of solidarity created by the compliment.

An incorrect assumption that a listener is, or wishes to be identified as, a member of a specific group may lead to correspondingly negative results. In telling a story or a joke, for example, the speaker must have an audience who share his background and cultural assumptions well enough to not only understand but sympathize with the point of view presented (cf. Wolfson 1978). If compliments are to be used to **establish** solidarity where there is little or no similarity of background, only the most general of cultural values can be assumed to be shared. A preliminary analysis by the authors suggests that, parallel to the semantic and syntactic patterns found in compliments, there also exist a set of general cultural assumptions which underlie them.[9] From our data it seems clear that members of the wider speech community agree in placing positive value, for example, upon objects which are new and people who look young or thin:

(49) Š: That outfit's nice. Is it new?

(50) S: John, you look so different from the last time I saw you, banging away on the drums in our living room.
A: A little older maybe.
S: No, you look much younger. You look wonderful.

(51) S: Hey, Joe, you really look good. You've lost weight.

The use of a formulaic compliment invoking one of these assumptions and using an adjective or verb which is semantically positive but nonspecific, serves to level out differences in social role or in group membership which might otherwise interfere with the communicative function of the compliment.

In addition to minimizing potential interference with the expression of solidarity, the formulaic composition of compliments serves a second important function in making compliments readily identifiable in any context. Not only do compliments occur in a wide range of speech situations, but they are frequently independent of the speech event which precedes them. During the course of a conversation at a dinner table or a party, on a shopping trip or in an office, it is perfectly appropriate for any of the participants to interrupt the conversation to give a compliment. This compliment may very well have no particular relevance to the topic under discussion although it may be triggered by some word or phrase used:

(52) A: Anyway, I've been working pretty hard . . .
S: What a pretty outfit!
A: Thanks. I've accomplished . . .

(53) A: I heard somebody walking around downstairs and I just assumed it was Jane. I went into her room to look in the mirror 'cause I'd never worn this sweater before . . .
S: That's a really nice sweater.
A: So, anyway, I went downstairs and nobody was there.

Compliments often serve to initiate a conversation and, in fact, not infrequently the compliment/response exchange itself constitutes an entire speech event. A typical situation occurred when one of the researchers passed a colleague in the hall. No greeting was given. Rather, the following exchange took place:

(54) S: That's a really nice skirt you're wearing.
A: Oh, and I had so much trouble trying to decide what to wear this morning.

Whether compliments occur at the beginning of a conversation, in isolation, or during an interaction of which they are not an integral part, their independence from what precedes makes it imperative that they somehow be readily identifiable as compliments. This is pointed up by cases in which an atypical semantic or syntactic choice results in an intended compliment's not being recognized as such:

(55) S: That's an interesting dress.
A: Gee, is that a compliment, John?
S: (embarrassed) Well, sure. I didn't say it was dull, did I?

(56) S: You keep wearing such elegant clothes. Don't you know we're supposed to be poor?
A: What is that supposed to mean?
S: It didn't come out right. It was supposed to be a compliment. I mean you look very nice.
A: Thanks.

Ambiguity and confusion of this sort is avoided by the use of a compliment formula.

The collection of data itself provided strong evidence of the identifiability of formulaic compliments. As part of a seminar in sociolinguistics, students who had little or no background in this discipline were asked to contribute to our data by collecting compliments in everyday speech situations. It is noteworthy that the students, naive native speakers, did not ask that compliments be described or defined for them and indicated no confusion concerning what was expected of them. The data which they collected, with almost no exceptions, were unambiguously identifiable as compliments.

Once their data were collected and shared, however, many of the students expressed great surprise and consternation about the fact that compliments appeared to be so unoriginal. (This reaction may be likened to the 'tertiary response' to language described by Bloomfield (1944), although in this case there was less hostility than shock. The lack of hostility was undoubtedly due to the fact that the students were examining data which they themselves had collected.) Our students' and our own expectation that compliments would be more varied than they actually proved to be indicates that speakers think of complimenting as a creative speech activity. While it is a well-known axiom of sociolinguistics that native speakers are largely unaware of their own speech forms, it is nevertheless true that some speech acts are recognized to be formulas. It seems unlikely that educated speakers, no matter how naive with respect to linguistics, would evince much surprise if they were confronted with proof that greetings or thanks were formulaic in nature. Why then should we be surprised to discover that compliments are formulas?

Compliments differ in a number of important respects from formulas such as greetings, thanks or goodbyes. First, the formulas for these other speech acts are overtly taught, whereas compliments are not. Second, compliments have a much broader function than the other formulas mentioned since they often appear as part of, or even in place of, thanks, greetings and goodbyes. A further reason for the lack of recognition of the formulaic nature of the compliment is the fact that compliments are very often preceded or followed by framing remarks. Also, compliments, although strongly expected in certain cases, are not specifically required at any definite point within an interaction. Finally, the complexity of the rules for formulating compliments obscures their underlying regularity and even simplicity.

If our students were surprised to see that compliments are formulas it is possible that this was due, at least in part, to the fact that complimenting is not a speech act which people are usually taught explicitly. A very little thought would suffice to remind almost any native speaker that formulas such as "bye-bye" and "thank you" are among the earliest words a child learns to say. Furthermore, as everyone knows, children are constantly being reminded, as part of the socialization process, to be sure to say "hello" and "thank you," and such reminders are often given quite publicly with no embarrassment on anyone's part. This is not at all true of compliments.

Another reason why compliments are not generally recognized as formulas has to do with the fact that they frequently serve other functions within an interaction. In addition to being an independent speech act, the formulaic compliment may be used as a way of thanking or greeting. In such cases the compliment frequently, but not necessarily, occurs in conjunction with one of the conventional expressions of thanks or greeting:

(57) S: Hi, you sure look sharp today.
A: Thanks.

(58) S: Thanks a lot for your present, Jane. I'm so excited with it. It's beautiful.
A: I'm sorry I wasn't there but I wanted you to have something from me. I'm glad you like it.

(59) S: Thank you so much, darling. You really are a good kid.

(60) S: Those flowers are beautiful. Do they come from your garden.
A: Yes, I cut them. They're not my favorite color of azalea, but that's what I have.
S: It was sweet of you to bring them.

The fact that a compliment formula is being used may be obscured by its inclusion in another speech act which has its own, more conventionally recognized, formulas.

Even when the compliment functions as an independent speech act, the formula may be obscured by related remarks which frequently precede and/or follow the compliment itself. Although these remarks are part of the same exchange, they need not occur in the same utterance as the compliment. Unlike compliments, framing remarks are syntactically unrestricted. They seem to have two basic functions. Those which precede a compliment generally serve to identify and focus attention on the item to be complimented, as in the following examples:

(61) S: Did you get your hair cut?
A: Yes.
S: It looks cute.
A: Thanks.

(62) S: Did you lose weight? You look thin.
A: Yes, I was on a diet.

(63) S: Let me see your ring. Jesus Christ! It's beautiful! How many carats is it?
A: I think it's 1.18.

The framing remark which follows the compliment in example 63 serves the second basic function of such remarks; namely, it requests further information about the object complimented. Additional examples of this very common type of frame are:

(64) S: I love your sweater. It's beautiful. Where did you buy it?

(65) S: This is delicious. You have to give me the recipe.
A: It's easy to make.

The display of interest reflected in these remarks serves to intensify the compliment. Such intensification may also be effected by offering additional comments of a more specific nature:

(66) S: I really like the way you play banjo. I heard some licks there that I'd never heard before.
A: Well, they come from just sittin' and practicin'.

(67) S: Your plants certainly are pretty. You must spend a lot of time with them.
A: Thank you. Actually, I don't spend as much time as I should but they do seem to be doing well.

Because the framing remarks serve the purpose of focusing attention on the object of the compliment or of intensifying the compliment in some way, they must be seen as part of the entire discourse unit, which includes the framing remark(s) if any, the formulaic compliment and any response. A formulaic compliment is almost invariably a component of such a discourse unit. Example 61 is typical in that once the addressee responds to the question 'Did you get your hair cut?' a compliment is forthcoming. However, the fact that the central portion of such units is a formulaic compliment may be disguised by related framing remarks which follow no regular semantic or syntactic pattern.

Compliments, unlike thanks, greetings, and goodbyes, are never absolutely required at certain specifiable points within an interaction. Greetings and goodbyes, of course, are not only required in every interaction, but their position of occurrence is completely determined. Thanks are most flexible in that their position within an interaction is not entirely fixed, and they may be repeated several times within the same speech event. Nevertheless, it is important to recognize that even thanks, with their more flexible pattern of occurrence, do not exhibit the degree of freedom found in compliments. As has already been noted, compliments need not be in any way related to the subject of the conversation in which they occur. This is not to say that compliments are not, under certain circumstances, strongly expected, so much so that speakers recognize and may even comment, perhaps jokingly, on that expectation. Thus a hostess offering pastries to a guest at a party was overheard to say:

(68) S: Have one of these, I made them.
A: (Takes a cookie)
S: Now you have to tell me it's good.

Another woman elicited a compliment on her new furniture from a close friend and then commented on it:

(69) A: John wouldn't let us put a black phone here because . . . (gestures to new furniture).
S: I love these, by the way. They're very nice.
A: Thank you. I've been waiting.

As this second example shows, new furniture and indeed new clothing, jewelry or hairdos when seen for the first time, usually require a compliment. This, of course, is related to the cultural assumption mentioned earlier which places a positive value upon 'newness'. So strong is the expectation of a compliment in such cases that its absence may be perceived as a sign of disapproval. For example, a woman who wore a new dress remarked to a friend that some mutal acquaintances must not have liked the dress since they had said nothing about it.

Although compliments are, if not obligatory, at least very strongly expected in certain situations, they also occur quite frequently in situations where there is no such expectation. This aspect of their occurrence gives compliments an aura of spontaneity, which may be heightened by the use of exclamative forms. Some indication of spontaneity seems to be essential for the compliment to be perceived as more than the obligatory gesture which, in fact, it often is. That is, compliments are expected to at least **appear** spontaneous in order to be accepted as sincere expressions of approbation. The major function of complimenting is to create or reinforce solidarity by expressing appreciation or approval. In those very frequent instances where the compliment is, to all intents and purposes, required, recognition that the compliment is required and furthermore that it is nothing more than a precoded formula might well counteract the very effect which compliments are intended to create. The feeling of spontaneity can only be maintained by avoiding focusing attention on the compliment formula and directing it instead to other aspects of the speech act. That is, by offering an expected compliment in an unexpected position, by using an exclamative form and/or intonation, or by preceding or following the compliment with additional, related remarks, attention is diverted from the fact that the compliment had to occur somewhere and that it is almost certainly unoriginal in form.

In conclusion, it must be recognized that the compliment formula in American English is a very complex one with regularities existing on at least four levels. On the syntactic level we find that the majority of compliments are of three basic sentence types, with almost all the rest falling into six less common patterns. Morphologically, verbs are found almost invariably in their simple tenses and adjectives in their base forms. On the semantic level we find a very limited set of positive adjectives and verbs recurring repeatedly. The function of identifying the object or person to be complimented is typically served by one of a very small set of deictic elements. This, combined with a general rule which holds that compliments are to be addressed directly to the person being complimented, relates the speech act to the discourse and the overall interaction of which it is a part. Finally, there is a set of general cultural assumptions which are reflected in both the compliments themselves and the responses to them. We have touched on this last only briefly in this paper; analysis of the rules on this level is still in progress. The overall regularity which results from the interaction of these various patterns serves two important functions. It makes compliments identifiable no matter where in the discourse they occur or what precedes them. Even more important, it makes it possible for people of widely different backgrounds to minimize speech differences which might otherwise interfere with their attempt to create solidarity. The formulaic compliment, however, is not, like formulaic expressions of thanks or greeting, explicitly recognized by members of the speech community. The rule which permits compliments to occur in virtually any position within the speech event, the varied uses to which compliments are put, and the fact that the compliment formula itself frequently appears as part of a larger discourse unit, all serve to obscure the astonishing regularity which has been demonstrated to be a basic characteristic of compliments. We have seen that the formulaic nature of compliments is highly functional. Interestingly, the obscurity of this characteristic nature is equally functional. Thus, both the use of a formula and the lack of recognition that a formula is involved are required to successfully fulfill the **major** function of complimenting: creating or affirming solidarity.

NOTES

1. The terms **speech act, speech event** and **speech situation** are to be understood here in the technical sense proposed by Hymes (1972).
2. Our thanks to the following people for their contributions to the corpus: Emily Atlas, Barbara Beattie, Franzella Buchanan, Debra Cohen, Stephen Coleman, Sandra Cox, Dara Devaney, Luz Diaz, Bill Evans, Evelyn Fitzhugh, Arlyne Handel, Susan Hess, Marcia Jacobs, Martin Kinsey, Carolyn McCarthy, Alex May, Kathy Rowland, Aurie Schwarting, Stephanie Toteff, Polly Vanraalte, Vaughan Waters, Robin Weiss, Violet Wu, Karen Yee.
3. It may well be that the analysis presented here holds for all varieties of American English. However, since the data upon which it is based were collected by and among speakers of the standard dialect in and around Charlottesville, Virginia and Philadelphia, Pennsylvania, we would not wish to make any claims for the validity of this analysis for **all** American English speakers.
4. For reasons of privacy, all names which appear in examples have been changed.
5. In these syntactic patterns, the following conventions are observed:
   a. *Really* stands for any intensifier (*really, very, so, such,* etc.).
   b. All verbs are cited in the present tense.
   c. *Look* stands for any linking verb other than *be,* or what Cattell (1969:46) terms 'sense-verbs' (*look, seem, smell, feel,* etc.).
   d. *Like* and *love* stand for any verb of liking (*like, love, admire, enjoy,* etc.).
   e. *ADJ* stands for any semantically positive adjective.
   f. *ADV* stands for any semantically positive adverb.
   g. *NP* stands for a noun phrase which does not include a semantically positive adjective. In sentence types 29 and 30 the noun phrase typically contains a second person pronoun or a demonstrative.
   h. *PRO* stands for *you, this, that, these,* or *those.*
6. We classify *have* separately from other verbs (V), following Fillmore's (1968:47) analysis of *have* as a form which is obligatorily inserted in certain 'verbless sentences'.
7. Negative interrogative exclamations can be formed from any of the non-exclamative patterns.
8. Our thanks to Max Manes for confirmatory information on the use of this expression. [Editor's note: Cf. Matisoff's paper on "Psycho-ostensive expressions in Yiddish" as quoted by Tannen & Öztek, this volume.]
9. A more complete analysis of the cultural assumptions underlying compliments and responses to them is in progress.

JEF VERSCHUEREN

The Semantics of Forgotten Routines

ABSTRACT

This article is based on the assumption that studying the words and expressions which people have at their disposal to talk about linguistic action may indirectly yield insights into its nature. An overview is presented of a number of conversational routines for which speakers of English and Dutch do not have descriptive verbials (i.e. verbs and verb-like expressions) available. These 'lexical gaps' are explained in terms of the cognitive salience of the routines in question. The investigation leads to some interesting conclusions, for instance in connection with the status of expressives as a separate class of speech acts and with the role of expectation patterns in the conceptualization of conversational interaction.

The following paper is based on a chain of controversial assumptions which I cannot defend within the scope of this text. A full justification is to be found in *What People Say They Do With Words* (Ph.D. dissertation, University of California at Berkeley; the present article is a slightly adapted version of one chapter of this dissertation). I restrict myself to listing the assumptions here:

(i) All social actions consist of two dialectically related components: practices and concepts.
(ii) Because of the unity between practices and concepts it is impossible to understand most forms of social action without understanding the way in which the participants in the action conceptualize it.
(iii) Conceptualizations cannot be studied directly.
(iv) The lexicon of every language reflects (in an imperfect manner) the conceptual distinctions that its users habitually make.
(v) As a result, one indirect way of approaching conceptualizations of social actions consists in studying the lexical items that the participants in the action have available in their natural language for describing it.
(vi) Therefore, the study of linguistic action verbials (i.e., verbs and verb-like expressions used to talk about linguistic action) is likely to yield insights into the nature of linguistic action.

(vii) Comparative studies of linguistic action verbials could be regarded as an empirical basis for the study of universals of linguistic action.

In this article, such a lexical approach to linguistic action is used. The following conventions should be kept in mind: A stands for a linguistic action; D for a description of an act A; C stands for the condition(s) under which a certain linguistic action verbial is used appropriately in a particular D as a description of a certain A; Sa and Ha are the utterer and the addressee of an act A, respectively. A justification of the principles of lexical semantics used will also have to be looked for in the longer work mentioned. The only languages compared in this article are English and Dutch. Results of the comparison are always summarized in what I call semantic dimension comparison tables (henceforth SDC-Tables).

INTRODUCTION

We are about to enter an area of linguistic action which is marginal in some respect, but very central in another. The topic of investigation is the area of conversational routines. I am not only referring to formulaic expressions (as described by Tannen and Öztek 1977) and politeness formulas (Ferguson 1976), but also to routine utterances of a less fixed nature and with different social functions. Thus I shall not only (not even mainly) be talking about expressions such as "God bless you" (uttered when someone sneezes) which is formulaic in nature and which constitutes a form of linguistic politeness, but I shall also pay attention to a number of quite flexible, non-formulaic responses to acts of insisting, giving permission, requesting, advising, etc. which are not necessarily induced by politeness.

The centrality of conversational routines in linguistic action is beyond doubt. Without them, conversation would cease to exist. Further, the occurrence of formulaic expressions and politeness formulas appears to be a universal phenomenon, though their actual shapes vary cross-linguistically and cross-culturally. Moreover, their importance emerges from the fact that omitting them (e.g., by neglecting to greet a person one knows) or failing to acknowledge them (e.g., by not responding to a greeting) inevitably creates tensions in interpersonal relationships. These observations lead naturally towards the following question: In what sense could we say that conversational routines (including formulaic expressions and politeness formulas) are marginal?

The production of conversational routines involves a high degree of *automaticity*. Whereas lying requires a conscious messing around with the propositional content of a statement-like utterance, and whereas commanding involves a conscious act of the will, replying "You're welcome" to "Thank you" is largely automatic. Therefore, if we agree that a human action typically results from a conscious impulse of the will, we have to conclude that routine utterances are less central instances of linguistic action than, say, lies or commands or even many acts of being silent.

This observation is not meant to detract from the importance, emphasized in the previous paragraph, of routine utterances as aspects of conversational interaction. But it may help us understand why, as Ferguson (1976:137) puts it, "this universal phenomenon has been very little studied by linguists or anthropologists or other students of human behavior." It may also explain why, for a number of these routines, many languages lack descriptive verbials. If, for instance, John says "God bless you" when Jane sneezes, there is no easy way for speakers of English to describe what John *did* or, in other words, what type of linguistic act he performed. A description such as "John wished that God would bless Jane" would be hopelessly inadequate; no native speaker of English would take it seriously. The problem remains the same for the alternative and equivalent formula "Gesundheit" which could not be accounted for by claiming that "John wished Jane health." One would have to take refuge in the phrase "John said 'God bless you' " which does not yield any insight into the type of act performed because the linguistic action verb **to say** is so general that it can be prefixed to any utterance (in directly or indirectly reported speech). The automaticity with which routine acts are performed may explain why there are many gaps in the lexical frame associated with them: their being performed more or less unthinkingly diminishes their cognitive salience, which is reflected in the absence of a lexicalization.

It is the set of non-lexicalized conversational routines that I call *forgotten routines*. This chapter is an overview of some major lexical gaps in this area in English and Dutch.

The foregoing tentative explanation (in terms of the automaticity involved) of why some types of routine utterances are easily 'forgotten', however attractive it may be, still leaves us with mysteries. Indeed, it might even make some facts harder to comprehend. For instance, how is it that certain types of routines (e.g., greetings) are so salient that they get their own descriptive verbials, whereas others can hardly be described at all in a given natural language? Sometimes it will be possible to present a hypothetical answer to this question; sometimes it will not. But in all cases the question will be relevant.

There is something peculiar about a semantic discussion of lexical gaps. What I hope this chapter will lead to is a partial understanding of the types of conversational routines which are easily 'forgotten' in the sense mentioned and which, therefore, require special study. We will be skimming through a semi-conscious area of linguistic action in which some of its most fundamental properties may be hidden.

THE EXPRESSION OF EMOTIONS AND ATTITUDES

A large proportion of linguistic routine acts can be situated in the domain of what Searle (1976) called *expressives,* i.e., the class of speech acts the illocutionary point of which is that a certain psychological state, emotion or attitude is expressed. Of course this area shades off into the other traditional classes because the speech acts of which the expression of a psychological state is no prominent aspect (e.g., Searle's declarations) are rare.

In English and in Dutch, as in many other languages, there are specialized linguistic action verbials to describe the expression of some emotions. For others, there are no such lexical items. This first contrast between lexicalized and non-lexicalized linguistic actions, which is amply illustrated in the following paragraphs, will lead us to some interesting conclusions as to why expressives were made into a separate class of speech acts.

Let us first consider some of the ways in which sorrow (or regret) and pleasure can be expressed.

(A1) I am sorry that you could not come over for a visit
(A2) I regret that you could not come over for a visit
(A3) I am sorry for being so rude to you
(A4) I regret that I have been so rude to you
(A5) I am sorry that your father died
(A6) I am glad that I have gotten the fellowship
(A7) I am glad you've gotten the fellowship
(A8) (I am) glad/pleased to meet you

Descriptions (D1) to (D8) correspond to acts (A1) to (A8), in the same order.

(D1) Sa said/stated/claimed that he was sorry . . .
or: Sa expressed his regret that . . .
(D2) Sa said/stated/claimed that he regretted that . . .
(D3) Sa apologized for being rude
(D4) Sa apologized for being rude
(D5) Sa commiserated/condoled Ha's father's death
(D6) Sa said/stated/claimed that he was glad that he . . .

(D7) Sa congratulated Ha on getting . . .
(D8) Sa greeted Ha

It will be clear that the phrase "Sa said/claimed/stated . . ." could have been employed in all of the above descriptive acts. Notice, however, that this phrase, which can introduce any type of reported statement-like utterance, would not normally be used by a speaker of English who was asked to tell what Sa did when uttering (A3), (A4), (A5), (A7) and (A8). Instead, the specialized expressive linguistic action verbials **to apologize, to commiserate, to condole, to congratulate** and **to greet** would be used. Notice, moreover, that English lacks such specialized verbials for the description of (A1), (A2) and (A6). In other words, there are no verbials available for describing (A1), (A2) and (A6) *as expressions of emotions,* i.e., verbials which focus on the emotion-expressive aspect of these acts. Thus, some expressions of pscho-logical states are lexicalized whereas others are not. The discrepancy is striking because sometimes identical formulas are used for the lexicalized and the non-lexicalized expression of identical emotions. A case in point is the formula "I am sorry" which always expresses a feeling of regret but which introduces what would be described as a simple statement in (A1) whereas it triggers the descriptive verbials **to apologize** and **to commiserate** in (D3) and (D5). Similar things happen with "I regret" and "I am glad."

A completely analogous picture emerges from Dutch. The formula "I am sorry" can be replaced by the impersonal phrase "Het spijt me" (lit. 'it sorrows me') in (A1), (A3) and (A5); "I regret" can be translated as "Ik betreur" in (A2) and (A4); and "I am glad" is equivalent to "Ik ben blij." In (D1), (D2) and (D6) the phrase "Sa zei/beweerde . . ." ('Sa said/claimed . . .'), which can introduce any type of reported statement-like utterance, would be used, whereas the verbials **zich verontschuldigen** ('to apologize'), **zijn deelneming betuigen** ('to commiserate'), **gelukwensen** ('to congratulate') and **groeten** ('to greet') would be used in the remaining describing acts.

This complete parallelism shows that probably we are not dealing with one of the whimsical features of natural language. But before attempting to formulate an explanation we shall take a look at some more comparable data.

Consider the following acts in which liking and disliking is expressed.

(A9) I (don't) like working late
(A10) I like your plan very much
(A11) I don't like the way you dress

Act (A9) can be described as in (D9).

(D9) Sa said/stated/claimed that he liked (did not like) working late

Though the same statement-formula "Sa said/stated/claimed . . ." could be used to account for (A10) and (A11) in all circumstances, there is another possibility as well. Imagine that Sa is Ha's employer. Thus condition (C1) applies to (A10) and (A11).

(C1) Sa has authority over Ha (with respect to the topic of Sa's utterance)

In such circumstances we are likely to get (D10) and (D11) as descriptions.

(D10) Sa approved of Ha's plan
(D11) Sa disapproved of the way Ha dressed

Again we are confronted with linguistic actions in which identical psychological states are expressed by means of identical formulas, though for only some of them English provides us with descriptive verbials.

Once more the parallelism with Dutch is striking. The verbs **goedkeuren** (lit. 'to judge good," i.e., 'to approve') and **afkeuren** ('to disapprove') would be used in (D10) and (D11). Moreover, the distinction between (A9) on the one hand and (A10) and (A11) on the other, is reinforced by the fact that the verb **houden van** ('to like') can be replaced by **goedvinden** (lit. 'to find good'), which is ambiguous between liking and approving, in (A10) and (A11), but not in (A9).

A minor difference between English and Dutch is the following: whereas **to approve** and **to disapprove** are not necessarily linguistic action verbials (i.e. they can be used to express the attitudes rather than their expression), **goedkeuren** and **afkeuren** can *only* be used to describe the *expression* of approval and disapproval.

The divergence of human emotions and attitudes is unlimited. So is the number of their linguistic forms of expression. In this paragraph I shall offer a random selection of the remaining ones. Unlike those discussed so far, the following ones will not constitute *pairs* of lexicalized and non-lexicalized forms of expression. Yet they will present exactly the same problem in the sense that, for no obvious reason, some of them are lexicalized whereas others are not. The expression of a wish, and the expression of gratitude are two examples of lexicalized expressives. Consider (A12) and (A13).

(A12) I wish I could go
(A13) I'm truly grateful for your hospitality.

These two can be described by means of the linguistic action verbs **to wish** and **to thank** as in (D12) and (D13).

(D12) Sa wished he could go
(D13) Sa thanked Ha for his hospitality

In contrast, there are no emotion- or attitude-oriented verbials associated with the expression of a hope as in (A14), the anticipation of pleasure as in (A15), disappointment as in (A16), surprise as in (A17), and concern or worry as in (A18).

(A14) I hope he arrives on time
(A15) I am looking forward to receiving your reply
(A16) I am disappointed that he did not come after all
(A17) I am surprised that he came
(A18) I am concerned/worried that/about . . .

Both in English and in Dutch these can only be described as statements. (A12) and (A13) are also lexicalized in Dutch: the verbs **wensen** ('to wish') and **(be)danken** ('to thank') would be used in (D12) and (D13).

Notice that **to wish** (Dutch **wensen**) is a borderline case in the sense that its use as a linguistic action verbial is extremely limited. An act such as (A12) is likely to be described by means of "Sa expressed the wish that he could go" rather than by means of (D12). But in the case of (A14) through (A18) similar paraphrases are the *only* way out.

The data presented so far are summarized in SDC-Table 1 (with **to wish** and **wensen** between brackets because of their marginal character). We should now start looking for explanations.

What needs explaining is the fact that some linguistic expressions of emotions or attitudes can only be described as statements whereas others are lexicalized in such a way that they seem to take on a totally different speech act status. In other words, the problem is that some of these expressions, *as expressions of emotions or attitudes,* are simply forgotten in the conceptualization underlying the sets of linguistic action verbials in English and in Dutch. The best place to look for an explanation is in the pairs of identical formulas expressing identical emotions, which are sometimes lexicalized and sometimes not, i.e., in (A1) through (A11).

Let us take, for instance, the formula "I am sorry." What distinguishes its use in (A1) from (A3) and (A5)?

(A1) I am sorry that you could not come over for a visit

DUTCH	SEMANTIC DIMENSION	ENGLISH
ϕ	{(A1) (A2)}	ϕ
zich verontschuldigen	{(A3) (A4)}	to apologize
zijn deelneming betuigen	{(A5)}	to commiserate, to condole
ϕ	{(A6)}	ϕ
gelukwensen	{(A7)}	to congratulate
groeten	{(A8)}	to greet
ϕ	{(A9)}	ϕ
goedkeuren	{(A10)-(C1)}	to approve
afkeuren	{(A11)-(C1)}	to disapprove
wensen	{(A12)}	to wish
(be)danken	{(A13)}	to thank
ϕ	{(A14) (A15) (A16) (A17) (A18)}	ϕ

SDC-Table 1

(A3) I am sorry for being so rude to you
(A5) I am sorry that your father died

I believe that the major difference is the following. Whereas in (A1) Sa is simply conveying information about himself which may or may not interest Ha, in both (A3) and (A5) the speaker's psychological state expressed is of crucial importance to the hearer. (A3) presupposes that Sa has been rude to Ha; therefore, all further interaction between the two interlocutors depends crucially on Ha's coming to know whether Sa feels sorry about his previous behavior or whether he can expect similar behavior in the future. Similarly, (A5) presupposes that Ha's father died; whether Sa feels sorry (for Ha) about this unfortunate event partly defines Sa's attitude toward Ha, and therefore it is important for Ha to know Sa's feelings. My hypothesis is that the importance of the emotions expressed in (A3) and (A5) for the relationship between Sa and Ha and for their social interaction increases the cognitive salience of these expressions within the domain of linguistic activity to such an extent that their conceptualization and lexicalization *as expressions of emotions* became inevitable. An act such as (A1) lacks this cognitive salience and is therefore 'forgotten' in the lexicalization process, though both the emotion expressed and the formula used are identical with (A3) and (A5).

In Searle's typology of speech acts (A1) would simply be described as a statement (a representative) whereas (A3) and (A5) would be said to be expressives. Thus, if my hypothesis is correct, the distinguishing trait of expressives is not the expression of a psychological state as such but the expression of a psychological state important to the hearer. Our lexical data support the validity of the distinction between representatives and expressives while enabling us to formulate the distinction more accurately.

We still have to check the validity of our explanation for the rest of our data. The contrast between (A2) and (A4) can be put in the same terms as that between (A1) and (A3). Also the congratulation (A7) and the greeting (A8) differ from the statement (A6) in that the attitudes expressed are important to the hearer. Exactly the same holds for the difference between the approval (A10)-(C1), the disapproval (A11)-(C1) and the simple statement (A9).

But what about the non-paired examples (A12) through (A19)? The importance to Ha of the gratitude expressed in an act of thanking as in (A13) is evident. On the other hand, the hope in (A14), the disappointment in (A16), the surprise in (A17) and the concern in (A18) do not show the same kind of relevance to the hearer. This does not mean that sentences starting with "I hope . . .," etc., are always just statements. Consider (A19).

(A19) I'm giving a party tomorrow. I hope you can come.

In this case "I hope you can come" is clearly an act of inviting Ha to come to the party; an invitation is a directive speech act. The only points I want to make are that sentences starting with "I hope . . .," etc., though they clearly constitute the expression of a psychological state, cannot be described by means of a linguistic action verbial focussing on the psychological state expressed, because no such verbials are available, and that the lexical gaps in question result from the fact that the expression of the feelings expressed lacks an inherent importance for the relationship between speaker and hearer.

So far the hypothesis seems to work. There are, however, two troublesome cases, namely (A12) and (A15).

The first problematic case is (A15), which is a widely used phrase to end a letter.

(A15) I am looking forward to receiving your reply

One might want to argue that the anticipation of pleasure expressed in (A15) is important to the reader of the letter. Of course it is. But upon closer investigation the problem turns out to be imaginary. The anticipation of pleasure is only important to Ha in the same way as the hope expressed in "I hope you can come" (as in (A19)). That is, the verbalized psychological state does not matter as such. What really counts for Ha is its implication. The expression of Ha's hope that Ha would be able to come implies that Sa wants Ha to come, and therefore the sentence "I hope you can come" counts as an invitation. Similarly, Sa's looking forward to receiving Ha's reply implies that Sa wants Ha to reply, and therefore (A15) counts as a polite request to reply.

The directive overtones of (A15) and (A19) dominate so strongly that it would be surprising to get a description emphasizing the expressive aspect of these acts.

The only real problem is (A12), which can be described by means of **to wish** used as a linguistic action verbial (though, as said before, such usage is extremely marginal).

(A12) I wish I could go

What makes wishing so different from hoping that (D12), as a description of (A12), can be interpreted as an account of the *linguistic action* performed, whereas (D14), as a description of (A20), can only be regarded as an account of the *psychological state* expressed in the act?

(A20) I hope I can go
(D12) Sa wished he could go
(D14) Sa hoped he could go

In other words, what makes **to wish** into a linguistic action verbial (in one of its marginal senses), whereas **to hope** can only refer to a state of mind? Obviously, there is no difference in importance to the hearer between the expression of a wish and the expression of a hope. It is even hard to see any difference between a wish and a hope as states of mind. I want to suggest that in this case the hearer-oriented principle I formulated is overcome by a second principle which is idiosyncratic to acts of wishing. What made **to wish** into a linguistic action verb may have been the belief that a state of affairs can be created by putting one's wishes into a linguistic form (e.g., a magical formula, a prayer, etc.). As a result, the meaning of the verb **to wish** got extended from a state of mind to the linguistic expression of that state of mind.

The belief that verbalizing one's wishes may bring about the described state of affairs, and the resulting strong association of wishes (as mental acts) with their expression (as linguistic acts) and with the desired state of affairs itself (brought about by the formulation of the wish), might explain another peculiarity of the verb **to wish**. Wishing normally concerns a state of affairs which does not yet obtain, as in "wishing someone a happy New Year," which is done at the beginning of a year. However, "wishing someone a happy birthday," though not entirely synonymous with "congratulating someone on his birthday," has as its object a state of affairs which in most cases does already obtain. This extension of the meaning of **to wish** could be explained as follows. Take t1 to be the time at which a wish is uttered and t2 as the time at which the state of affairs which is the object of the wish obtains. In the paradigm case of "wishing someone a happy New Year" t2 is later in time thn t1. Now, imagine someone wishing that it would stop raining. If one believes that uttering a wish can bring about the desired state of affairs, then t1 and t2 could nearly coincide: immediately after someone's wish that it would stop raining, it might indeed stop raining. This quasi-identification of the act with its object makes it possible to understand how wishing got extended to circumstances in which its object is already present. This extension is very nicely reflected in the fact that the Dutch verb for **to congratulate**, in all its occurrences, is **gelukwensen** (lit. 'to wish happiness').

But whatever the explanation for its behavior, **to wish** remains marginal as a linguistic action verb. Due to its marginal character it does not present a real threat to our hypothesis about the lexicalization of expressions of emotions.

NEGATIVE AND POSITIVE RESPONSES

The subject matter of the previous section could be called the *expressive dimension* of forgotten routines. We discussed the types of psychological states for the linguistic expression of which languages such as English and Dutch do not provide descriptive verbials. Now we are going into the *textual dimension* of forgotten routines. We shall present an overview of the gaps in the lexical apparatus to describe *responses* to diverse types of speech acts. In this section the overview will be limited to responses to speech acts of a directive nature. All of the responses can be negative or positive. Thus, we are concerned with two types of acts, (A1) and (A2).

(A1) Sa responds positively to a speech act performed by Ha
(A2) Sa responds negatively to a speech act performed by Ha

The nature of the preceding discourse can be specified in the form of conditions on these acts. Consider (C1).

(C1) The act performed by Ha is a suggestion such as "I suggest we take the night train"

Examples of responses can be given as follows: (A3) is a response of the (A1)-(C1) type; (A4) is a response of the (A2)-(C1) type.

(A3) Let's do that
(A4) I don't feel like it

These two responses could be described as in (D1) and (D2).

(D1) Sa agreed to take the night train
(D2) Sa disagreed about taking the night train

Thus, the verb **to agree** can refer to positive responses to suggestions, whereas **to disagree** denotes, amongst other things, negative responses to suggestions. Consequently, if (C1) obtains, both types of responses are lexicalized in English. Dutch provides the verbial **akkoord gaan** ('to agree') for (A3); however, its negation **niet akkoord gaan** ('to disagree') would be rarely used for (A4); instead, the verb **afwijzen** (more or less equivalent to 'to decline') would be more likely to occur as in (D3).

(D3) Sa wees het voorstel af
(lit. 'Sa declined the suggestion')

Let us go on to a second type of preceding discourse.

(C3) The act performed by Ha is an act of insisting such as "I insist that you come home with me"

A possible (A1)-(C2) act is (A5), whereas (A6) represents the (A2)-(C2) type.

(A5) O.K. Fine with me
(A6) No, I won't

A quite natural way of describing (A5) would be to use the verb **to give in** (in Dutch **toegeven**, which is ambiguous between 'to give in' and 'to admit') as in (D4). For (A6) one might use **to refuse** (Dutch **weigeren**) as in (D5).

(D4) Sa gave in (and went home with Ha)
(D5) Sa refused (to go home with Ha)

As with suggesting, there are no lexical gaps here.

In the case of advising, an additional complication arises.

(C3) The act performed by Ha is an act of advising such as "You'd better take your medicine."

To a piece of advice two types of positive and negative responses can be given: one can either concentrate on the representative aspect of advice as in the responses (A7) and (A9), or on its directive aspect as in (A8) and (A10).

(A7) I think you're right
(A8) O.K. I will
(A9) I don't think so; it's still too early
(A10) No, I won't

The verbs **to agree** and **to disagree** can be used to account for (A7) and (A9), as in (D6) and (D7).

(D6) Sa agreed (with Ha on taking his medicine)
(D7) Sa disagreed (with Ha on taking his medicine)

The Dutch comparable verbials **akkoord gaan** ('to agree') and **niet akkoord gaan** ('to disagree') could be used. The directive-oriented negative reply (A10) can be described by means of **to refuse** (Dutch **weigeren**) as in (D8).

(D8) Sa refused (to take his medicine)

A problem arises with the directive-oriented positive response: I did not succeed in finding a linguistic action verbial (apart from the passe-partout verb **to say**) suited for the description of (A8). Here we seem to be confronted with a first gap.

Next in line is the speech act of inviting.

(C4) The act performed by Ha is an act of inviting such as "Would you like to come to my party tomorrow night?"

The positive (A1)-(C4) response could simply be (A11), and (A12) could be the negative (A2)-(C4) reply.

(A11) Yes, I would
(A12) No, I can't

To describe these two acts the verbs **to accept** (Dutch **aannemen**) and **to decline** (Dutch **afslaan**) might be used as in (D9) and (D10).

(D9) Sa accepted (Ha's invitation to come to the party)
(D10) Sa declined (Ha's invitation to come to the party)

Again, all lexical slots are filled. (Note that "No, I wouldn't" cannot be regarded as an appropriate negative response to an invitation; it would count as an insult rather than as an act of declining the invitation.)

What about responses to requests?

(C5) The act performed by Ha is an act of requesting such as "Can you possibly give me a lift?"

Acts (A13) and (A14) are adequate replies of the (A1)-(C5) and the (A2)-(C5) types, respectively.

(A13) Sure
(A14) No, I'm afraid not

The negative response (A14) can be described as a refusal (using the verb **to refuse**, Dutch **weigeren**) as in (D11).

(D11) Sa refused (to give Ha a lift)

For the positive response, however, no adequate linguistic action verbial presents itself. Thus, (A1)-(C5) is our second lexical gap. Notice that the gap cannot be filled with a phrase such as "to comply with the request;" this phrase, just like "to follow someone's advice" or "to obey someone's order," indicates a positive behavioral response, not a positive linguistic response.

Similar to requests are orders or commands. According to the traditional accounts they mainly differ from requests in that they require authority on the part of the speaker over the hearer. As far as the set of descriptive linguistic action verbials is concerned, the responses to both types of acts show an identical pattern. Consider (C6).

(C6) The act performed by Ha is an act of ordering such as "Come here, Michael!"

Acts (A15) and (A16) are possible responses of the (A1)-(C6) and the (A2)-(C6) types, respectively.

(A15) O.K.
(A16) No, I won't

(A16) could be described by means of the verb **to refuse**, Dutch **weigeren**.

Once more, no adequate linguistic action verbial presents itself for the positive reply (A15).

At least two more types of directives deserve our attention: permissions and prohibitions.

(C7) The act performed by Ha is an act of giving permission such as "You can go home now"
(C8) The act performed by Ha is an act of prohibiting such as "You mustn't leave this early"

(A17) is an appropriate positive response to the permission; (A18) is a possible negative one.

(A17) Thank you
(A18) I'm not going now

The prohibition can be replied to positively as in (A19) and negatively as in (A20).

(A19) Fine with me
(A20) I'll do it anyway

(A17) is simply an act of thanking for the description of which we have the verb **to thank**, Dutch **(be)danken**, available. As a result, (D12) is an adequate account of (A17).

(D12) Sa thanked Ha (for the permission to go home)

But for (A18) through (A20) no descriptive verbials seem to be available.

SDC-Table 2 summarizes the verbials available for the description of positive and negative responses to a number of directive speech acts. How can we explain the gaps? How can we explain the fact that some response types were 'forgotten' in the lexicalization process? I believe that a vague principle of *harmony of interaction* can show us why some responses to particular types of directives are cognitively less salient and, therefore, do not need to be lexicalized.

Acts of inviting, suggesting and even insisting leave the hearer completely free to do as he chooses. These acts clearly indicate the speaker's preference with respect to the hearer's actions. But no matter what course of action the hearer takes there is nothing disharmonious about the interaction. Therefore, both positive and negative responses can be expected with equal probability. As a result, both options got lexicalized.

The same reasoning applies to advising when its representative aspect is focussed upon. But what happens if its directive component is envisaged? It seems to me that advising is much stronger as a directive than insisting, however unlikely this may be at first sight. The reason is that advising implies some kind of authority on the part of the speaker: not the kind of 'power

DUTCH	SEMANTIC DIMENSION	ENGLISH
akkoord gaan	{ (A1)-(C1) }	to agree
afwijzen	{ (A2)-(C1) }	to disagree
toegeven	{ (A1)-(C2) }	to give in
weigeren	{ (A2)-(C2) }	to refuse
akkoord gaan	{ (A7) > (A1)-(C3) < (A7) }	to agree
ϕ	{ (A8) > (A1)-(C3) < (A8) }	ϕ
niet akkoord gaan	{ (A9) > (A2)-(C3) < (A9) }	to disagree
weigeren	{ (A10) > (A2)-(C3) < (A10) }	to refuse
aannemen	{ (A1)-(C4) }	to accept
afslaan	{ (A2)-(C4) }	to decline
ϕ	{ (A1)-(C5) }	ϕ
weigeren	{ (A2)-(C5) }	to refuse
ϕ	{ (A1)-(C6) }	ϕ
weigeren	{ (A2)-(C6) }	to refuse
(be)danken	{ (A1)-(C7) }	to thank
ϕ	{ (A2)-(C7) (A1)-(C8) (A2)-(C8) }	ϕ

SDC-Table 2

authority' needed to be able to force someone to do something, but some sort of 'knowledge authority'. It is assumed that the person giving the advice knows what the best course of action is. As a result, the hearer is expected to respond positively and not to disregard the advice. Since harmony of interaction can only be obtained if the response is positive, the positive response itself is taken for granted to such an extent that it loses its cognitive salience. This explains the absence of a verbial to describe (A8). On the other hand, the negative response is cognitively salient because it disrupts the harmony of interaction.

Completely analogous accounts can be given for the gaps in connection with requests and orders. Complying with a request and obeying an order are the harmonious reactions expected. In the case of orders the expectation results from the 'power' authority' involved. Requests are quite compelling in spite of the absence of such authority.

What about permission and prohibition? Why are the negative responses to these types of acts not lexicalized, though they no doubt disrupt interactional harmony? A possible explanation is that in the case of prohibitions negative responses are not only unexpected and disruptive but also rare because of the high degree of authority involved: a speaker who prohibits something is often in a position to actively prevent the hearer from doing what he prohibits him to do (whereas in the case of an order such active intervention is usually harder since it is much more difficult to make someone do something than to prevent him from doing it). On the other hand, permissions imply that the hearer wants to do what he is allowed to do; therefore negative responses to permissions are rare as well. The scarcity of negative responses to acts of permitting and prohibiting deprives them of the cognitive salience which they gained by being disruptive. Therefore, they are 'forgotten' in the lexicalization process.

A final question has to be answered. How come that there *is* a verbial to describe the positive response to acts of permitting, even though that response is certainly the expected and harmonious one? Since permissions imply that the hearer wants to do what he is allowed to do, and since the speaker has authority over the hearer with respect to the act in question, the positive response is, not surprisingly, an expression of gratitude. And since expressions of gratitude also occur in other contexts and are generally called acts of thanking, it is only logical that the same name is given to the expression of gratitude following a permission. (It is quite possible that in an imaginary language in which gratitude would only be expressed after obtaining a permission, there would be no word equivalent to **to thank**.)

FIXED ROUTINE RESPONSES

The responses studied in the previous section could be either positive or negative. There are also routine responses of a fixed formulaic nature which lack the negative-positive option. Some of these are easy to describe in English and in Dutch. Consider the response act (A1) uttered in the contexts specified by (C1) through (C3).

(A1) Thank you

(C1) The act performed by Ha is an act of congratulating such as "Congratulations on your birthday"

(C2) The act performed by Ha is an act of condoling such as "I'm terribly sorry that your father died"

(C3) The act performed by Ha is an act of welcoming such as "Welcome home"

In all of these contexts (A1) can be described by means of **to thank**, Dutch **(be)danken**, as in (D1).

(D1) Sa thanked Ha

Sa expresses his gratitude for Ha's kind attitude towards him. Hence (A1), in response to acts of congratulating, condoling and welcoming, is not an empty or obscure routine. Its conversational meaning coincides with the lexical meaning of the words used.

A bit more complicated are the responses to greetings. In the context specified by (C4), several replies are possible, some of which are listed as (A2) to (A4).

(C4) The act performed by Ha is an act of greeting such as "How are you?"
(A2) Very well, thank you
(A3) Fine. How are YOU?
(A4) Very well, thank you. And you?

Though in (A2) the same formula, "thank you," is used as in (A1), and though (A2) could be said to express appreciation (if not gratitude) for Ha's interest in Sa or for his polite display of recognition (which is probably the essence of every greeting), (A2) can hardly be said to be an act of thanking. Nor do we have any other linguistic action verbial at our disposal to describe the response act. Acts (A3) and (A4) are return greetings, describable by means of **to greet**, Dutch **(be)groeten**.

Finally, there are a number of fixed routine responses for which no descriptive verbials exist at all. First, consider (A5) through (A9), uttered when (C5) obtains.

(C5) The act performed by Ha is an act of apologizing such as "I am sorry for being so rude to you"
(A5) No harm done
(A6) Never mind
(A7) That's quite all right
(A8) Please don't worry
(A9) Forget it

For none of these acts do we have descriptive verbials.

Second, consider (A10) through (A14) uttered in a context in which (C6) obtains.

(C6) The act performed by Ha is an act of thanking such as "Thank you very much"
(A10) You're welcome
(A11) That's quite all right
(A12) Not at all
(A13) Forget it
(A14) Don't mention it

Again, no descriptive verbials seem to be available in English and Dutch. Just as "thank you" as a response to a certain type of greeting, "you're welcome" as a response to an act of thanking is a forgotten routine, though **to thank** and **to welcome** are linguistic action verbials. The reason is that the conversational meaning of the formulas does not coincide with the lexical meaning of the words used. Similarly, in many languages there are fixed routine responses to acts of thanking which include an equivalent of the verbs **to pray**, **to beg**, **to ask**: German *bitte,* French *je vous en prie,* Italian *prego,* Hungarian *kérem* (**bitten**, **prier** and **pregare** mean 'to pray, to beg, to ask'; **kérni** means 'to ask (for something)'). Yet these acts would never be described as acts of praying, begging or asking.

Notice that (A7) is identical with (A11) and that (A9) is identical with (A13). This is possible by virtue of the fact that both apologizing and thanking express the speaker's feeling that he owes something to the hearer. (Cf. Coulmas' account of thanks and apologies, in this volume.)

DUTCH	SEMANTIC DIMENSION	ENGLISH
(be)danken	{(A1)-(C1), (A1)-(C2), (A1)-(C3)}	to thank
ϕ	{(A2)-(C4)}	ϕ
(be)groeten	{(A3)-(C4), (A4)-(C4)}	to greet
ϕ	{(A5)-(C5), (A6)-(C5), (A7)-(C5), (A8)-(C5), (A9)-(C5)}	ϕ
ϕ	{(A10)-(C6), (A11)-(C6), (A12)-(C6), (A13)-(C6), (A14)-(C6)}	ϕ

SDC-Table 3

The material presented in this section is visualized in SDC–Table 3 which is, so to speak, filled with gaps. The acts surveyed are all responses to expressive speech acts. The high proportion of lexical gaps should not surprise us given the fixed, formulaic nature of these acts. The *automaticity* involved in their performance is extremely high, and therefore their cognitive salience can be expected to be low. It is only when the routine responses are not made with the expected accuracy and speed (as in the speech of a foreigner) that they come to mind.

The presence of a verb, **to thank**, to describe responses to acts of congratulating, condoling and welcoming is due to their formal and semantic similarity to independent (i.e. non-response) expressions of gratitude.

Responses to greetings are no less automatic than replies to apologies and thanks. But they can often be described by means of **to greet** because of the frequent reciprocity of acts of greeting.

In the previous section it was suggested that the normal, expected, harmonious responses to speech acts are cognitively less salient and are, therefore, likely to escape lexicalization. This hypothesis may explain the many gaps in the area covered by this section. The routine responses under investigation, lacking the positive-negative option, are so compelling that they form part of a strong expectation pattern of harmonious interaction. One could almost say that acts of apologizing and thanking are not complete unless an appropriate routine response follows. The responses are part of the act and hence, as separate speech acts, they tend to escape our attention.

CONCLUSIONS

This chapter is certainly no complete overview of the gaps in the lexical frame associated with linguistic action. Its purpose was to draw the attention to certain types of acts which, because of their routine character, are easily overlooked and which, therefore, require special study.

The complete parallelism between Dutch and English, which will be hard to find in other areas of linguistic action, shows that language, in particular the lexicon, does not even make forgetting into a totally whimsical activity. Such adherence to a kind of cross-linguistic systematicity lends our hypothetical explanations some strength. This is not to say that there is any universality to the findings of the extremely limited investigation presented. However, the apparent strength of the lexicalization principles involved, reflected in the complete parallelism between English and Dutch, makes the search for universals in this domain of the linguistic action verbials particularly compelling.

All the hypothetical explanations presented for the phenomena under investigation boil down to one basic principle: the gaps in the lexical frame associated with linguistic action are due to the low cognitive salience of the corresponding acts. This principle, if it is correct, proves that there is a relationship between the lexicon, or the lexicalization process, and habits of conceptualization. Hence, this chapter confirms our belief that studying and comparing the verbials available in different natural languages for the description of linguistic action may yield insights into people's language-specific and culture-specific conceptualization and experience of linguistic behavior and, therefore, into the nature of linguistic behavior itself.

PART TWO

Strategies and Action Patterns

JULIANE HOUSE and GABRIELE KASPER

Politeness Markers in English and German

ABSTRACT

This paper attempts to reveal – on the basis of a corpus of parallel German and English interactions – how different norms concerning interlocutors' interpersonal communicative strategies result in differing distributions of deference markers in the two speech communities. Although the phenomenon of deference formulas seems to be universal, their structure and use are clearly culture-specific, i.e., part of an emic system.

INTRODUCTION

Politeness seems to be a social value that occurs in all civilized societies, even though the social norms relating to what is and what is not considered polite behavior may vary across cultures. We don't know whether politeness is a universal phenomenon; therefore the following remarks are meant to hold for highly differentiated societies whose predominant cultural feature with respect to forms of interpersonal contact might be called "urbanity". The most salient characteristics of urbanity are a highly developed emotional control in the individual (see for instance, Elias 1977:45) and the social recognition of an individual's face, i.e., "the positive social value a person effectively claims for himself by the line others assume he has taken during a particular contact" (Goffman 1972:319). We understand politeness as being a specifically urbane form of emotional control serving as a means of preserving face. Goffman states with respect to face-saving that "the person will have two points of view – a defensive orientation toward saving his own face and a protective orientation toward saving the other's face" (1972:325). Both these functions – one defensive or ego-oriented, the other protective or alter-oriented – are fulfilled by politeness. We would suggest that both aspects are implied when politeness, or tact, as it is sometimes called, is defined as "strategic conflict avoidance" (Leech 1977:19) or as a device used "in order to reduce friction in personal interaction" (R. Lakoff 1975:64).

How does politeness manifest itself in verbal interaction? In analogy to Grice's conversational postulates, Robin Lakoff states the following "Rules of Politeness": "1. Don't impose. 2. Give options. 3. Make A feel good – be friendly" (1973:298). The second rule, in particular, is in agreement with the parameters Leech (1977) has set up for defining politeness in language. He distinguishes (1) the "cost/benefit scale, i.e., the scale which specifies how much the act referred to in the propositional content (*X*) of the speech act is judged to cost or benefit *s* or *a*," the "optionality scale, i.e., the scale which specifies how far the performance of *X* is at the choice of *s* or *a*" (1977:4). The higher the optionality factor and the benefit factor and the lower the cost factor is relative to the addressee, the more polite is the utterance of the speech act in question. In formulating what he calls the "Tact Maxim," Leech states that "the more tactful a directive is, the more indirect and circumlocutionary it is" (1977:19). We shall take up this idea of directness being a politeness indicator and use it as a starting point for our analysis.

The need for analyzing politeness phenomena in English and German contrastively became evident for us through the observation that the verbal behavior of German learners of English is often considered impolite by native speakers. Are such "pragmatic errors" (cf. Kasper 1979a; 1979b) due to the learners' simply not knowing the formal English equivalents of what they would say in their native language, or are there perhaps different social norms in the two speech communities which affect the linguistic behavior of native speakers in terms of its politeness? If the latter were the case, the German learners' errors might be due to what Coulmas (1978) has termed "pragmatic interference". We feel that a contrastive investigation into politeness phenomena in both languages is a necessary – though not a sufficient – condition for clarifying this issue.

The conversational data which is the basis for our analysis was elicited via role play. Pairs of German and English native speakers, all of them students, were given role descriptions of informal everyday situations and were asked to act them out verbally. We invented 24 such situations, and each of them was performed by two native speaker pairs in English and German. The role relationship of the interactants was varied along two parameters: it was characterized either by authority or by lack of authority of one interactant over the other (± authority – X<Y/X=Y) , and the interactants (X and Y) either knew each other or they didn't (± social distance). The conversations were taped, transcribed and have been analyzed under various aspects (cf. Edmondson et al. 1979).

For the present investigation, we selected 24 conversations in each language, the underlying role descriptions of which were likely to elicit the speech acts *complaint* and *request*. Our decision to subject the realizations of these two speech act categories to analysis in terms of their politeness was determined by our intuitive assumption that, because of their inherent pragmatic features, complaints and requests usually involve the use of politeness markers. By slightly modifying Leech's categorization of speech acts (1977: 16), and substituting X and Y for the 2 interlocutors, a *complaint* can be characterized as being "post-event," i.e., the "complainable" has already happened, and this event is at a cost to the speaker or "anti-X". A *request*, however, has the features "pre-event" and "anti-Y", i.e., the event – the action X wants Y to perform – is at a cost to Y and is to take place after the utterance of the speech act. The "anti-X" and "anti-Y" -properties respectively make it likely for complaints and requests to require politeness in order to avoid potential – or further! – conflict between the interlocutors. Note that we use both speech act categories in a broader sense than usual: complaints embrace other expressives sharing the features "post-event/anti-X" which may be referred to in English by such verbs as "criticize," "accuse" or "reproach"; requests include other directives characterizable as "pre-event/anti-Y", which may be referred to in English by verbs such as "order," "command," "ask" or "beg".

DIRECTNESS LEVELS

In order to be able to compare both the complain and request acts in terms of their directness in the German and English data sets, we have made use of a schema of directness levels for each act type. These schemata will now be detailed.

Complaints[1]

If a complaint is to occur, the addressee Y must have done an action P which X interprets as bad for him. Now depending on whether

1. P is mentioned implicitly or explicitly;
2. X's negative evaluation of P is expressed explicitly;
3. Y's agentive involvement is implicitly or explicitly expressed, and
4. the negative evaluation of both Y's action and Y himself are implicitly or explicitly expressed,

8 different levels of directness result, with level 1 being the most indirect, and level 8 the most direct level. On all the lower levels the addressee Y must perform an inference process on the basis of the situational context, especially the relationship holding between the interlocutors X and Y and the social norms recognized by both X and Y. Through this inference process Y is enabled to work out for himself both an adequate propositional content and

the intended illocutionary force of X's utterance. Such inference processes are very complex. In the following they will be sketched out very roughly using the situational context: "Y – who, as is well-known to X, often borrows X's things – has stained X's new blouse."

1. By performing the utterance U in the presence of Y, X implies that he knows that P has happened and he implies that Y did P
   Odd, my blouse was perfectly clean last night.
   Seltsam, gestern war meine Bluse doch noch ganz sauber.

2. By explicitly asserting that P, X implies that Y did P
   There's a stain on my blouse.
   Da ist ein Fleck auf meiner Bluse.

3. By explicitly asserting that P is bad for him, X implies that Y did P
   Terrible, this stain won't ever come off.
   Schrecklich, dieser Fleck wird wohl nie wieder rausgehn.

4. By explicitly asking Y about conditions for the execution of P or stating that Y was in some way connected with the conditions for the doing of P, X implies that Y did P
   Did you wear my blouse by any chance?
   Hast du etwa meine Bluse angehabt?

5. X explicitly asserts that Y did P
   You've stained my blouse.
   Du hast den Fleck draufgemacht.

6. By explicitly asserting that the action P for which Y is agentively responsible is bad, or explicitly stating a preference for an alternative action not chosen by Y, X implies that Y is bad/or X asserts explicitly that Y did P and that P is bad for X, thus also implying that Y is bad
   You shouldn't have taken my blouse without asking my permission/
   You have ruined my blouse.
   Du hättest die Bluse nicht ohne meine Erlaubnis nehmen sollen/
   Du hast meine ganze Bluse ruiniert.

7. X asserts explicitly that Y's doing of P is bad
   I think it's mean that you just take my things.
   Ich finde es gemein von dir, daß du einfach mein Sachen nimmst.

8. X asserts explicitly that Y is bad

You are really mean.
Du bist wirklich unverschämt.

This schema when applied to a comparison of acts of complaint in the English and German data yielded the following results:

Table 1

Directness Level COMPLAINTS	1	2	3	4	5	6	7	8	Σ
GERMAN									
number of instances	7	8	18	10	19	36	8	1	107
relative frequency	0·065	0·075	0·168	0·093	0·178	0·336	0·075	0·009	1
ENGLISH									
number of instances	11	5	14	17	15	18	–	–	80
relative frequency	0·138	0·063	0·175	0·213	0·188	0·225	–	–	1

We found that in the English data levels 7 and 8, the most direct levels, never occurred at all in a total of 80 complaints, whereas in the German data level 8 occurred once (0,9 per cent) and level 7 8 times (7,5 per cent) out of a total of 107 complaints.
For example:

(1) (level 8) (student to her friend who forgot to hand in her paper and didn't admit this)
X: Bist doch 'n Feigling

(2) (level 7) (same context as in (1) above)
X: Das find ich wirklich ne Unverschämtheit von dir.

Levels 7 and 8 in the German data occur in both + and – social distance and authority role relationships.
Level 6 is by far the most frequently used complaint level in the German data (36 instances out of a total of 107: i.e. 33,6 per cent); this level is so to speak the "standard complaint format" in our corpus, and it is used in both + and – social distance and authority relationships. In English, level 6 is used 18 times (22.5 per cent) out of a total of 80 occurring acts, most frequently in -social distance and -authority constellations. Some examples for level 6 complaints in the two data sets:

(3) (patient to doctor who prescribed wrong antibiotic)
X: das hätten Sie mir aber vielleicht vorher sagen sollen

(4) (student to friend who didn't admit having forgotten to hand in paper for him)
X: ich mein wenn de die schon vergißt dann solltest des wenigstens sagen damit ich Bescheid weiß

(5) (student to her friend)
X: don't see why you shouldn't do some work some time

(6) (librarian to student who made pencil marks in library book)
Y: a member of the public is simply just not supposed to handle them and treat them in this sort of way

In contrast to the heavy concentration of complaints on level 6 in the German data, there is a fairly even spread on levels 3, 4, 5 and 6 in the English data. Here are some examples of these levels in the English data:

(7) (level 3) (patient to doctor who is responsible for rash)
X: look it really is giving me more trouble than the tonsillitis

(8) (level 4) (student to fellow student who has taken her seat in library)
X: you must have realized somebody was here

(9) (level 5) (student to employer)
X: you must be mistaken there

Further, level 1 occurs more frequently in the English data: 11 (13,8 per cent) out of 80 complaint acts vis à vis 7 (6,5 per cent) out of 107 acts in the German data. Here is one example of level 1 from each data set:

(10) (student to fellow student who took her seat in library)
X: well honestly I left my books here and my bag

(11) (same context as (10) above)
X: du hör mal ich hab da eben grade gesessen

Taken together, these results suggest that the German students in our sample tend to select more direct complaints than their English counterparts.

Requests[2]

We distinguish again 8 levels of directness for requests, level 1 being the most indirect and level 8 the most direct type of request. In the following, the different levels will be illustrated by means of the situational context "X wants Y to close the window."

1. *Mild Hint*
   The proposition expressed in the locution is distinct from the proposition to which the illocutionary point refers, but clearly some implicational relationship must be discoverable for Y
   It's very cold in here
   Es ist sehr kalt hier drin

2. *Strong Hint*
   The proposition expressed in the locution is not identical to the proposition to which the illocutionary point refers but is related to it in that both have referential elements in common other than reference to either of the interlocutors
   Why is the window open?
   Warum ist das Fenster offen?

3. *Query-Preparatory*
   The locution queries a preparatory condition holding for the execution of the action denoted in the proposition
   Can you close the window?
   Kannst Du das Fenster zumachen?

4. *State-Preparatory*
   The locution asserts a preparatory condition holding for the execution of the action referred to in the proposition
   You can close the window
   Du kannst das Fenster zumachen

5. *Scope-Stating*
   The locution expresses X's intention, desires, or feelings vis-à-vis the proposition he expresses
   I would prefer it if you closed the window
   Mir wärs lieber, wenn du das Fenster zumachen würdest

6. *Locution-derivable*
   The illocutionary point is directly derivable from the semantic meaning of the locution

You should close the window
Du solltest das Fenster zumachen

7. (a) *Hedged-Performative*
X names the illocutionary intent he wishes his locution to be understood by Y as having, but hedges by using a modal auxiliary.
I must ask you to close the window
Ich muß dich bitten, das Fenster zuzumachen

(b) *Explicit-Performative*
X explicitly names the illocutionary intent he wishes his locution to be understood by Y as having
I ask you to close the window
Ich bitte dich, das Fenster zuzumachen

8. *Mood-derivable*
The grammatical mood of the locution conventionally determines its illocutionary point as a request
Close the window!
Mach das Fenster zu!

An application of this schema of levels of directness to our comparison of the German and English requests yielded the following results:

Table 2

Directness Level REQUESTS	1	2	3	4	5	6	7	8	Σ
GERMAN									
number of instances	3	3	14	4	4	23	4	7	62
relative frequency	0·049	0·049	0·226	0·065	0·065	0·371	0·065	0·113	1
ENGLISH									
number of instances	6	3	18	6	3	2	1	5	44
relative frequency	0·136	0·068	0·409	0·136	0·068	0·045	0·023	0·114	1

We found that while all levels are used in both the English and the German data, in the English data level 3 is by far the most frequently used level: it is used 18 times (40,9 per cent) out of a total of 44 requests. Level 3 requests are of the type:

(12) (student to fellow student in library)
Y: Could I possibly share your desk?

All the other levels are fairly evenly spread in the English situations. Level 8 is used in both + and – authority situations; however, in + authority situations it is only used by the interactant who is in possession of the authority, e.g.,

(13) (doctor to patient)
Y: just give this prescription to the nurse

Level 1, the lowest, most indirect level, occurs considerably more frequently in the English data than in the German data, i.e., 6 (13,6 per cent) out of a total of 44 requests vis-à-vis 3 (4,9 per cent) out of a total of 62. An example of a level 1 act in the English data is the following:

(14) (student to fellow student in library requesting permission to retain seat he is occupying)
Y: I've just got to read this periodical about 20 minutes that's all

Now in the German data we find that it is level 6 which is by far the most frequently used: 23 times (37,1 per cent) out of a total of 62 acts compared to only 2 (4,5 per cent) level 6 requests in the English data out of a total of 44 requests. An example of a German level 6 request is the following:

(15) (student to friend who has just borrowed some records)
Y: und da sollte auch eigentlich nichts dran kommen

The highest levels, levels 7 and 8, are used in both + and – authority situations, but much more frequently in + authority situations and in these only by the interactant in authority (as was the case in the English data). Level 7 is used 4 times (6,5 per cent) in the German data and level 8 is used 7 times (11,3 per cent) out of a total of 62 requests as compared to the English data where there is 1 (2,3 per cent) level 7 request and 5 (11,4 per cent) level 8 requests out of 44 requests. Consider the following examples of level 7 and 8 requests in the German data:

(16) (level 7) (student to fellow student in library)
X: also ich muß dich schon bitten den Platz zu verlassen und dir irgendwas andres zu suchen

(17) (level 8) (teacher to student who has form in hand)
Y: zeig mal bitte her

As in the case of complaints we have again found that the German students in our experiment tend to select on the whole more direct request levels, which – this is our hypothesis – may be an indication of differing social norms operative in the two cultural systems.

MODALITY MARKERS

If we consider requests like: *come here!/Komm her!,* which are clearly level 8 requests, and we compare them with acts like: *please come here, will you/ komm doch bitte mal her, ja,* which are, according to our present schema, also level 8, we are bound to realize that it is necessary to take a more differentiated view of the directness levels than we have so far done. We must recognize that on one and the same directness level quite different effects of "politeness" may result depending on the kind and number of what we shall call *modality markers* present in the utterance. We shall distinguish between two major kinds of modality markers: *downgraders* and *upgraders.*

Downgraders

These are markers which play down the impact X's utterance is likely to have on Y. We differentiate between 11 different types of downgraders:

1. *Politeness marker*
   Optional elements added to an act to show deference to the interlocutor and to bid for cooperative behavior, e.g. *please/bitte*

2. *Play-down*
   Syntactical devices used to tone down the perlocutionary effect an utterance is likely to have on the addressee, e.g.,
   (a) past tense: *I wondered if . . ./Ich wollte dich bitten . . .*
   (b) durative aspect marker: *I was wondering*/no German equivalent
   (c) negation: *Mightn't it be a good idea . . ./Wäre es nicht eine gute Idee . . .*
   (d) interrogative: *Mightn't it be a good idea?*
   (e) modal: *Mightn't . . .*

3. *Consultative Device*
   Optional devices by means of which X seeks to involve Y and bid for Y's cooperation; frequently these devices are ritualized formulas, e.g., *Would you mind if . . ./Hättest du was dagegen, wenn . . .*

4. *Hedge*[3]

   Adverbials – excluding sentence adverbials – by means of which X avoids a precise propositional specification thus circumventing the potential provocation such a specification might entail; X leaves the option open for Y to complete his utterance and thereby imposes his own intent less forcefully on Y.

   e.g., *kind of, sort of, somehow, and so on, and what have you, more or less, rather/und so, irgendwie, und so weiter, ziemlich*

   Could you kind of lend us some records/Könntest du uns irgendwie 'n paar Platten oder so leihen

5. *Understater*

   Adverbial modifiers by means of which X underrepresents the state of affairs denoted in the proposition.

   e.g., *a little bit, a second, not very much, just a trifle/ein wenig, eine Sekunde, nicht sehr viel, ein kleines bißchen*

   I'm a little bit disappointed in you/Ich bin ein kleines bißchen von dir enttäuscht

6. *Downtoner*[4]

   Sentence modifiers which are used by X in order to modulate the impact his utterance is likely to have on Y;

   e.g., *just, simply, possibly, perhaps, rather/ja, mal, eben, schon, wohl, einfach, denn, vielleicht*

   Couldn't you just move over a bit/Könntest du mal eben 'n bißchen rücken

7. – (*"minus"*) *Committer*

   Sentence modifiers which are used to lower the degree to which X commits himself to the state of affairs referred to in the proposition. X thus explicitly characterizes his utterance as his personal opinion

   e.g., *I think, I guess, I believe, I suppose, in my opinion/Ich glaube, ich meine, ich denke, meiner Ansicht nach*

   I think you've made a mistake/Ich glaube, Sie haben da einen Fehler gemacht

8. *Forewarn*

   A kind of anticipatory disarmament device used by X to forewarn Y and to forestall his possible negative reactions to X's act. Typically a forewarn is a metacomment about what X is about to do, a compliment paid to Y as a preliminary to a potentially offensive utterance, or an invocation of a generally accepted cooperative principle which X is about to flout.

far be it from me to belittle your efforts, but . . ., you're a nice guy, Jim, but . . ., this may be a bit boring to you, but . . ./ohne deine Leistungen schmälern zu wollen, aber . . ., du bist ein netter Kerl, Peter aber . . . vielleicht langweilt dich das ein bißchen, aber . . .

9. *Hesitator*
   Deliberately employed malformulations, used to impress on Y the fact that X has qualms about performing his ensuing act,
   e.g., *erm, er/äh*; stuttering, reduplication

10. *Scope-Stater*
    Elements in which X explicitly expresses his subjective opinion vis-à-vis the state of affairs referred to in the proposition, thus lowering the assertive force of his utterance
    I'm afraid you're in my seat; I'm a bit disappointed that you did P; I'm not happy about the fact that you did P/Ich finde es nicht so gut, daß du da auf meinem Platz sitzt; Ich bin etwas darüber enttäuscht, daß du P getan hast; Ich bin nicht sehr glücklich darüber, daß du P getan hast.

11. *Agent Avoider*
    Syntactic Devices by means of which it is possible for X not to mention either himself or his interlocutor Y as agents, thus, for instance, avoiding direct attack.
    e.g., passive, impersonal contructions using *people, they, one, you* as "neutral agents" lacking [+ definite] and [+ specific] reference.
    This is just not done, Mr Robinson/Man tut so etwas einfach nicht, Herr Schmidt

Further, the presence of other elements in an utterance, especially so-called *gambits,* i.e., optional, mostly phatic discourse-lubricants (cf. Edmondson, 1977) may be interpreted as downgrading the impact of an utterance on a given addressee. In particular two types of gambits, which Edmondson has called *cajolers* and *appealers,* function as downgraders. Cajolers are elements used to increase, establish, or restore harmony between the interlocutors. Their significance may be informally glossed as "please be in agreement with my speech act." Tokens are: *you know, you see, I mean, actually/ich meine, weißt du, eigentlich.* Appealers appeal to the hearer and function to elicit a hearer signal, an uptaker. Examples: *okay, right, yeah/ja, oder, nich.*

Apart from gambits, the presence of what we call *supportive moves* may act as downgraders. If we consider acts like "request" or "complaint" to be central acts in a discourse where the main business is X's requesting that

P be done or complaining that P has happened, then certain other moves may act to support these central moves. Supportive moves can be of three kinds:

1. *steers,* where X intends to steer the discourse in a certain direction consistent with the fulfilment of his intent (as expressed by his central move) by introducing a topic which has one or more features in common with the business conducted in the central move; e.g., (X wants to borrow Y's records) *Would you like to put a record on?*

2. *grounders,* in which X gives reasons for his intent (as expressed in his central move). Grounders may precede or follow the central move; e.g., *God, I'm thirsty. Get me a beer, will you?* (where the grounder precedes the central move).

3. *preparators*: X indicates or suggests what type of an intent he is going to make manifest without, however, specifying the nature of the proposition following the preparator; e.g., *I would like to ask you a question.*

Upgraders

These are modality markers which increase the force of the impact an utterance is likely to have on the addressee. We distinguish 6 subtypes:

1. *Overstater*
   Abverbial modifiers by means of which X overrepresents the reality denoted in the proposition in the interests of increasing the force of his utterance.
   e.g., *absolutely, purely, terribly, frightfully/absolut, rein, entsetzlich, furchtbar*
   I'm absolutely disgusted that you left the bathroom in such a state/ Ich finds absolut widerwärtig, daß Sie das Bad in so einem Zustand hinterlassen haben.

2. *Intensifier*
   Adverbial modifier used by X to intensify certain elements of the proposition of his utterance.
   e.g., *very, so, such, quite, really, just, indeed/sehr, so, solch, doch, wirklich, ausgesprochen, in der Tat*
   I'd be really pleased if you could help me/Ich würde mich wirklich freuen, wenn du mir helfen würdest

3. + (*"plus"*) *Committer*
   Sentence modifiers by means of which X indicates his heightened degree of commitment vis-à-vis the state of affairs referred to in the proposition,
   e.g., *I'm sure, certainly, obviously, really/sicherlich, gewiß, bestimmt, auf jeden Fall, doch, wirklich*
   You should certainly have informed me/Du hättest mich doch wirklich informieren sollen

4. *Lexical Intensifier*
   Lexical items which are strongly marked for their negative social attitude.
   e.g., swear words.
   That's bloody mean of you/Das ist aber verdammt unverschämt von dir

5. *Aggressive Interrogative*
   Employment by X of interrogative mood to explicitly involve Y and thus to intensify the impact of his utterance on Y.
   e.g., *Why haven't you told me before?/Warum hast du mir das nicht vorher gesagt?*

6. *Rhetorical Appeal*
   In using a rhetorical appeal, X attempts – by claiming or implying the non-possibility of not accepting that P – to debar Y from not accepting that P.
   e.g., *You must understand that, anyone can see that, it's common knowledge that/du mußt verstehen, daß; jeder weiß ja, daß; es ist doch ganz klar, daß*
   You must understand that this is public property/Sie müssen verstehen, daß es sich hier um öffentliches Eigentum handelt.

Let us first have a look at how complaints are modulated in both languages. Tables 3 and 4 show the correlation between directness levels and upgraders/downgraders in English and German (cf. page 172 and 173).

As can be seen, there is a fairly equal distribution of upgraders and downgraders in English and German on level 5. The lowest occurrence of upgraders is on level 4 in English and on level 2 in German. We were surprised to find that upgraders in German most frequently co-occur with a level as high as 7 (cf (18)).

(18) (X notices that Y did not hand in her term paper)
X: dir geht's *doch wohl* zu gut

English speakers display a similar preference: while they make less frequent use of their highest directness level, i.e., level 6, than do Germans, they tend to rather intensify than lower its illocutionary force: the highest frequency of upgraders and the lowest occurrence of downgraders is to be found on level 6 in the English data, of which (19) is an example.

(19) (Student to a co-student who is giving a party)
X: *do you realize* you're making *a hell of* a noise

It is also level 6 which tends to completely lack modality markers in English: every second complaint on that level is not modulated at all. In German, however, level 6, which is the most frequent level to be used, never occurs without a downgrader: on an average, a German complaint on level 6 contains 3 downgraders. The highest frequency of downgraders in English occurs on level 3. In sum, German speakers use more modality markers with complaints than English speakers (3:2.3); in particular, they employ twice as many upgraders.

Among the *downgraders,* the class which is used most frequently in German is the *downtoner* which accounts for about 30 per cent of the German downgraders. This class has the lowest frequency in English (3.75 per cent). German downtoners co-occur with any directness level, but most frequently with level 6 (0.97), cf. (20).

(20) (Y did not hand in X's term paper)
X: hätt ich *eigentlich* nich gedacht wenn ich dir das gebe du weißt was davon abhängt

Another downgrading device which is employed 6.4 times as often in German (0.16) as in English (0.025) is the *agent avoider,* which also usually co-occurs with level 6. There seems to be a stronger tendency for German than for English speakers to avoid directly addressing the receiver of a complaint, cf.

(21) (a librarian notices scribblings in a book which a student is returning)
Y: ich meine so läuft das wirklich nich wenn *jeder* hier reinschmiert und so weiter nä

While English speakers, on the other hand, do sometimes phrase a complaint as in (22), they usually seem to prefer the more direct expression as in (23):

(22) (as 21)
Y: *a member of the public* is simply just not supposed to handle them and treat them in this sort of way

Table 3

	Directness level									
	1	2	3	4	5	6	7	8	Σ	
COMPLAINT E	f_i $\bar{x}$	f_i $\bar{x}$	f_i $\bar{x}$	f_i $\bar{x}$	f_i $\bar{x}$	f_i $\bar{x}$	f_i $\bar{x}$	f_i $\bar{x}$	f_i $\bar{x}$	
politeness marker										
playdown									15 0·19	
hedge									7 0·09	
understater									3 0·04	
downtoner									3 0·04	
hesitator	6 0·55		13 0·93	8 0·47	6 0·4	8 0·4			41 0·51	
-committer									5 0·06	
fore-warn									8 0·1	
agent avoider									2 0·025	
scope stater									12 0·15	
+consultative										
cajoler									29 0·36	
appealer									7 0·09	
preparator									2 0·025	9 0·11
grounder									7 0·09	
steer										
Σ downgrader	15 1·36	9 1·8	40 2·86	29 1·7	24 1·6	23 1·27			140 1·75	
overstater									7 0·09	
intensifier									8 0·1	
lexical intensifier									5 0·06	
rhetorical appeal									6 0·08	
+committer	4 0·36		6 0·43			6 0·33			17 0·21	
aggressive interrogative									4 0·05	
Σ upgrader	6 0·54	3 0·6	10 0·71	6 0·35	6 0·4	16 0·88			47 0·59	
no modality markers									16 0·2	

Table 4

COMPLAINT G	Directness level 1 f_i $\bar{x}$	2 f_i $\bar{x}$	3 f_i $\bar{x}$	4 f_i $\bar{x}$	5 f_i $\bar{x}$	6 f_i $\bar{x}$	7 f_i $\bar{x}$	8 f_i $\bar{x}$	Σ f_i $\bar{x}$	
politeness marker										
playdown									11 0·1	
hedge									16 0·15	
understater									10 0·09	
downtoner	4 0·57	2 0·25	8 0·44	7 0·7	10 0·53	35 0·97	2 0·25		68 0·66	
hesitator									19 0·18	
-committer									11 0·1	
fore-warn									8 0·07	
agent avoider						13 0·31			17 0·16	
scope stater									12 0·11	
+consultative										
cajoler									24 0·22	
appealer									8 0·07	
preparator									2 0·02	6 0·06
grounder									4 0·04	
steer										
Σ downgrader	4 0·57	9 1·125	30 1·66	19 1·9	30 1·58	111 3·08	18 2·25		221 2·07	
overstater									8 0·07	
intensifier									34 0·32	
lexical intensifier									8 0·07	
rhetorical appeal									8 0·07	
+committer	3 0·43		13 0·61			21 0·58	3 0·375		40 0·37	
aggressive interrogative									12 0·11	
Σ upgrader	4 0·57	1 0·125	30 1·66	11 1·1	8 0·42	40 1·1	15 1·88	1	110 1·03	
no modality markers									6 0·06	

(23) (as 21)
Y: well you know *you* shouldn't mark library books Mr Robinson

In English, the most frequently used downgrader is the *hesitator* which accounts for 29 per cent of the English downgraders and has a relative frequency of 0.51. It shows a fairly even distribution ranging between 0.4–0.55 in levels 1, 4, 5 and 6, its highest frequency being on level 3 (0.93), cf. (24):

(24) (patient to doctor who prescribed her a medicine which produced a rash)
X: *it's er* it's spread all over my body and it's itching me like mad

While Germans sometimes use hesitators, too (0.18), they usually prefer more explicit downgrading devices.

Another downgrader which is preferred by English vis-à-vis German speakers is the *playdown* whose relative frequency is almost twice as high in English as it is in German. It most frequently co-occurs with level 4 (0.35). So while German speakers would normally prefer (25)

(25) (as 24)
X: ich glaub Sie haben mir 'n falsches Rezept gegeben

to (26)

(26) (as 24)
X: ich hab festgestellt daß also die Vorschrift die Sie mir gegeben haben falsch *sein muß*

the formal equivalent of (26) is quite frequently employed in English, cf. (27)

(27) (student complaining to employer about wrong tally sheet)
X: I think your calculation *must be* wrong

Speakers of both languages make frequent use of *cajolers,* particularly on levels 3 to 6, with a slight majority on the English side (0.36:0.22), cf. (28) and (29)

(28) (Y didn't hand in X's paper)
X: *I mean honestly* I I did trust you to give in that paper

(29) (as 28)
X: *ich mein* immerhin hab ich mir ja die ganze Arbeit gemacht und hab dich darum gebeten ob du mir den Gefallen tun könntest

As the occurrence of other downgraders is low in both languages, we shall only mention two more. One of them is the *scope stater* which is to be found with roughly the same frequency of 0.11 in German and 0.15 in English, mostly on level 6 in English and on level 7 in German, cf. (30) and (31):

(30) (X and Y are quarrelling about Y's not handing in X's paper)
Y: but I think you know *it it's just g- gets on my nerves* that it should be er should be me who's get who's getting in trouble because of you

(31) (as 30)
X: *das find ich wirklich 'ne Unverschämtheit* du hattest mir das wirklich fest versprochen

(30), by the way, is a particularly fine example of the co-occurrence of various modality markers of the same and of different classes in a single utterance.

Finally, there is the *hedge* which is employed more frequently by German than by English speakers (0.15:0.09), and mostly so on level 2; cf. (32) and its English counterpart (33):

(32) (X has left the bathroom in a mess)
Y: äh ich bin heute früh noch in die Toilette gegangen hab festgestellt daß das Bad nich *ganz* sauber war

(33) (as 32)
Y: I'd just like to *sort of* show you that I don't like *this type of thing*

Now with *upgraders*, the most frequent class in both languages is the *+committer* with a relative frequency of occurrence of 0.37 in German and 0.21 in English. It is most likely to be found on levels 1, 3 and 6 with a fairly balanced distribution of 0.43-0.61 in German and 0.33-0.43 in English, in German also occurring on level 7 with a relative frequency of 0.375. Compare (34) and (35):

(34) (Y has taken X's library seat)
X: ja aber ich war *doch wirklich* nur für einige Minuten unten in der Cafeteria

(35) (student complaining to employer about wrong tally sheet)
X: *I'm sure* I've done seven today

Overstaters, rhetorical appeals and *lexical intensifiers* have an equally low occurrence in both languages, ranging from 0.06-0.09. Compare data (36)-(40):

(36) (X has stained Y's new suede jacket)
Y: *du weißt doch* daß die Jacke neu war und die war so *unheimlich* teuer und wie soll ich den Fleck jetzt rauskriegen

(37) (X has left scribblings in a library book)
Y: the next reader I'm sure will not *terribly* appreciate your comments underlinings and underscorings and heaven knows what else you have

(38) (Y has taken X's library seat)
X: *surely you could see* it was my place

(39) (X has left the bathroom in a mess)
Y: ja die ganze Badewanne und Toilette und alles *versaut* also nein wirklich

(40) (X and Y are quarrelling about Y's not handing in X's term paper)
Y: but you don't hand it in do you you get me to hand it in every *flipping* time

Intensifiers are used over three times as frequently by German speakers (0.32: 0.1), *aggressive interrogatives* over twice as frequently (0.11:0.05), cf. (41)-(44):

(41) (X has stained Y's suede jacket)
Y: ja ich weiß ja nich ob der *überhaupt* rausgeht bei der Reinigung der Fleck

(42) (as 41)
Y: it's gonna be *pretty* hard to remove really

(43) (Y didn't hand in X's term paper)
X: ich setz mich hin mach wochenlang meine Arbeit schufte dafür und du verklüngels das *und jetz mein Schein was mach ich jetz*

(44) (as 43)
Y: *why should I hand in your work* anyway

The general tendency we may observe here on the basis of our small corpus is that German speakers display more aggressive verbal behavior in socially delicate situations.

Let us now turn to the relationship of modality markers and directness levels with requests, as represented in tables 5 and 6 (cf. page 178 und 179).

There is an overall tendency for German speakers to use *upgraders* 4.6 times as often as English speakers, who hardly use them at all with requests. Compared to their use with complaints, however, upgraders are used much less frequently with requests in both languages (German: 2.07:0.32, English: 0.59:0.07). We interpret this finding as resulting from the nature of the speech act category request: speakers of both languages – and English speakers even more so – seem to sense the social impact of a request as being stronger than that of a complaint. It is precisely the "postevent -anti-x" property which makes our speakers feel they can legitimately use upgraders widely with complaints, and the "pre-event -anti-y" property that makes them refrain from using them with requests. Given then the negligible frequency of occurrence of upgraders with *requests* we shall restrict ourselves to the discussion of downgraders.

In toto, *downgraders* are employed by English speakers 1.5 times as frequently as by German speakers (3.59:2.39), i.e., 2.7 times as often as with complaints (1.75). This is consistent with the remark we've just made about the pragmatic features of a request. Although levels 1 and 2 are so poorly represented in both languages that we can't draw any generalizations from this, it seems surprising that the lowest directness levels should display the highest relative occurrence of downgraders: 5.67 on level 1 in English and 4.33 on level 2 in German. In the more highly represented levels 3 in English (18) and German (14) and 6 in German (23), English speakers use downgraders 1.36 times as often as German speakers (3.5:2.57).

The frequency of occurrence of the various subclasses of downgraders used with requests shows a distribution similar to their use with complaints: it is again *downtoners* in German (0.73) and *hesitators* in English (0.75), which occur most frequently and both classes are again rather poorly represented in the other language in each case. Thus on level 3, you are likely to find (45) in German, its most frequent English equivalent being (46):

(45) (patient who has got an allergy to the doctor)
X: ja können Sie mir *dann vielleicht* was gegen die Allergie verschreiben

(46) (as 45)
X: well can you *er can you* prescribe anything for the allergy

Table 5

REQUEST E	Directness level 1	2	3	4	5	6	7	8	Σ	
	f_i $\bar{x}$	f_i $\bar{x}$	f_i $\bar{x}$	f_i $\bar{x}$	f_i $\bar{x}$	f_i $\bar{x}$	f_i $\bar{x}$	f_i $\bar{x}$	f_i $\bar{x}$	
politeness marker									2 0·05	
playdown			16 0·89						25 0·57	
hedge									11 0·25	
understater									2 0·05	
downtoner									2 0·05	
hesitator	9 1·5	3 1·5	7 0·39	4 0·67	3 1				33 0·75	
-committer									6 0·14	
fore-warn									6 0·14	
agent avoider									1 0·02	
scope stater									3 0·07	
+consultative			6 0·33						9 0·2	
cajoler	9 1·5		4 0·22	4 0·67					18 0·41	
appealer									2 0·05	
preparator									4 0·09	29 0·66
grounder									15 0·34	
steer									10 0·23	
Σ downgrader	34 5·67	7 3·5	63 3·5	24 4·	9 3·	9 4·5		12 2·	158 3·59	
overstater										
intensifier										
lexical intensifier										
rhetorical appeal									1 0·02	
+committer									2 0·05	
aggressive interrogative										
Σ upgrader									3 0·07	
no modality markers									5 0·11	

Table 6

REQUEST G	Directness level									
	1	2	3	4	5	6	7	8	Σ	
	f_i $\bar{x}$	f_i $\bar{x}$	f_i $\bar{x}$	f_i $\bar{x}$	f_i $\bar{x}$	f_i $\bar{x}$	f_i $\bar{x}$	f_i $\bar{x}$	f_i $\bar{x}$	
politeness marker									9 0·15	
playdown			7 0·5						17 0·27	
hedge									9 0·15	
understater									5 0·08	
downtoner		5 1·67	8 0·57		5 1·25	16 0·7	3 0·75	8 1·1	45 0·79	
hesitator									12 0·19	
-committer									7 0·1	
fore-warn									2 0·03	
agent avoider						6 0·26			8 0·13	
scope stater									1 0·02	
+consultative									2 0·03	
cajoler									7 0·1	
appealer									9 0·15	
preparator									3 0·05	21 0·39
grounder									15 0·25	
steer									3 0·05	
Σ downgrader	4 1·33	13 4·33	36 2·57	10 2·5	14 3·5	48 2·08	8 2·	15 2·14	148 2·39	
overstater										
intensifier									10 0·16	
lexical intensifier									2 0·03	
rhetorical appeal									2 0·03	
+committer						3 0·13			7 0·1	
aggressive interrogative										
Σ upgrader						8 0·38	4 1·		20 0·32	
no modality markers									5 0·08	

While downtoners in German most frequently co-occur with the most widely used directness level, i.e., level 6 (0.7), hesitators in English do *not* occur most frequently on the directness level which is used in most cases in English, i.e., level 3, but on level 1 (1.5). Compare (47):

(47) (Y has taken X's library seat)
X: well look I wouldn't otherwise but *erm* you know *I* I've got this project I've got to finish by the end of term

The downgrader which is to be found most frequently in level 3 in English is the *playdown* (0.89), a device which in English has the second highest relative frequency (0.57), following the *hesitator*, cf. (48).

(48) (X tries to cancel a baby-sitting date)
X: I'm just wondering if I *could* possibly back down on tomorrow

This shows English speakers' preference for using syntactic means as modal qualifiers, while German speakers, on the other hand, tend rather to use lexical means. When German speakers do use playdowns, however, – which they do half as often as English speakers (0.27) – they also employ them most frequently on level 3 (0.5), cf. (49):

(49) (student wants teacher to fill in a certificate for him)
X: *vielleicht* könnten Sie da eben äh einiges ausfüllen

In English, another important downgrader with requests is the *cajoler,* which is used with a relative frequency of 0.41, whereas it is of minor importance in German (0.1). While cajolers in English occur with a similar frequency with both complaints and requests, German speakers tend to employ them regularly with complaints only (0.22:0.1). For an instance of cajolers used with requests in English, see again (47).

The *appealer,* on the other hand, which is used with similarly low frequencies with complaints in both languages, is used more often by German speakers with requests, in particular on level 6, whereas it occurs only twice in the whole of the English data. Compare (50) and (51):

(50) (X has left the bathroom in a mess)
Y: ja also diese Schlamperei wollen wir nich anfangen *ne*

(51) (X and Y are quarrelling about Y's not handing in X's paper)
Y: next time just just decide what you're gonna do *right*

Agent avoiders, which are used at a relative frequency of 0.13 by German speakers and mostly co-occur with level 6, are used with requests in English only once. Compare the formal equivalents in German and English in (52) and (53) to the more usual functional equivalent in English, i.e., (54):

(52) (X has left the bathroom in a mess)
Y: ja ich will diesmal noch darüber hinwegsehn wenn das in Ordnung *gebracht wird* ja

(53) (as 52)
Y: so now that you know that I don't like this perhaps *it won't happen* any more in future

(54) (as 52)
Y: perhaps in future if *you* have left anything rather untidy perhaps *you* can just clear it up as quickly as possible

A stronger tendency for German than for English speakers to avoid addressing the other person directly seems to be confirmed here.

The downgraders with a pretty low frequency in both languages but still a higher frequency in English are the *consultative marker* and the *forewarn,* cf. (55) to (57):

(55) (X suggests to Y that a friend of X's should do the babysitting for her)
Y: well *do you think* you could kind of have a word with her

(56) (X has left some scribblings in a library book)
Y: *was halten Sie davon* wir ham hier 'n Radiergummi wenn Sie das jetz noch schnell ausradieren

(57) (as 55)
Y: you know *I feel terrible about it but* erm you know do you think we could I have a friend

Supporting moves are of minor importance with complaints where they only have a relative occurrence of 0.07 in German and 0.11 in English. With requests, however, they play a more significant role: they are used in German with a relative frequency of 0.39 and in English with one of 0.66, thus representing the modality device which is used with the second highest frequency. Among the supporting moves, the *grounder* is most common in both English and German, and is most frequent with level 3, of which (58) and (59) provide examples:

(58) (Y has taken X's library seat)
X: aber kannste jetzt vielleicht da weggehn *ich möchte jetz wieder arbeiten*

(59) (as 58)
X: well couldn't you just read it couldn't you take one of those chairs in the other place *cos I need to write while I'm doing me thesis* you see

It is not surprising that supporting moves occur more frequently with requests than with complaints, as the "anti-y" property of a request makes it more necessary for speakers to carefully prepare the ground for their speech act in order to avoid conflict.

CONCLUSION

In conclusion, we can state that our comparison of directness levels and modality markers in complaints and requests in a number of situations acted out by German and English native speakers respectively, yielded the following results: on the whole, Germans selected higher levels of directness in the case of both complaints and requests. The distribution of modality markers in the two languages varies with the speech act category as well as with the directness levels they combine with. Upgraders are rarely used with requests, and with both requests and complaints, they are used more frequently by German than by English speakers, i.e. German speakers show a stronger tendency to intensify the force of their speech act in actual or potential conflict situations.

In the case of requests, it is the relatively low level 3 that is the most frequently used level in English, and the relatively high level 6 that is by far the most frequently selected level in German. English speakers not only use lower directness levels with requests but also more downgraders than German speakers. This seems to indicate that German speakers do behave more impolitely when making requests, if we accept the "degree of effort" (Leech 1977:19) in terms of directness levels and modality markers as a measure of politeness. We shall discuss below whether this seems a reasonable conclusion in the light of our data. Further, the tendency for low directness levels to be used with a higher frequency of downgraders in both languages in the case of requests, is an interesting outcome which, if it were confirmed by a larger sample, could be interpreted as an indication of speakers' heightened awareness of the interactional consequences their speech act may entail, which induces them to "play it doubly safe."

The occurrence of directness levels in the case of complaints and their modulation presents a more complex picture. The two highest levels are never used by the English speakers but do occur in the German data, and the third highest complaint level is, in fact, by far the most frequently used "standard complaint" in the German data, whereas complaints are fairly evenly spread across the different levels in English. The complete lack of levels 7 and 8 in English, and these levels are clearly linguistically available, seems to be due to different social norms in English and German which govern the usage of these levels in interaction: attacking one's interlocutor's identity seems to be a taboo in the British cultural context, while it seems perfectly appropriate behavior for Germans under specific interactional conditions. Of course, it could be argued that this difference was due to the artificial communicative situation in which the data was elicited, and that British native speakers do not always respect their own and their interlocutor's face in natural conflict situations. This is very probable, indeed, but does not invalidate our hypothesis: if speakers behave more consciously norm-oriented under experimental than under natural conditions, the different use of directness levels in English and German rather confirms the assumption that different social norms obtain in the two speech communities.

When using level 6, however, English speakers tend to intensify it by using upgraders rather than lower its force by using downgraders. We interpret this finding as an attempt by English speakers to compensate for the social non-availaibility of levels 7 and 8 by increasing the force of level 6 through the use of upgraders and the non-use of downgraders. From this follows an interesting hypothesis to be investigated: should perhaps level 6 (+ upgraders/ – downgraders) in English be functionally equivalent to levels 7 and 8 (± downgraders) in German?

The relationship between the schemata of directness levels and the categories of modality markers seems to be very complex: there is no clear negative or positive correlation between them, rather a much more differentiated interaction of levels and markers seems to take place in native speakers' behavior. In order to make valid statements about relative degrees of politeness of utterances in the two languages, it will surely always be necessary to take both components, directness levels and modality markers into account; however, in order to establish their relative value, an empirical investigation would have to be conducted, which examines the different perlocutionary effects various combinations of levels and classes of modality markers produce on the addressee.

Further, while in the present investigation we have on the whole restricted ourselves to examining individual acts – as a first step in the comparison of politeness phenomena – it would surely be advisable for further investigations to take into account the entire discourse, in which the individual acts are embedded. The place of an individual act within the act sequences in a discourse may be another important factor to be considered in determining an act's degree of politeness; especially taking account of the addressee's responses to the speaker's speech act seems to be important, as they may be an indication of the act's perlocutionary effect.

We have earlier pointed out that, on the whole, the German speakers selected more direct levels for both complaint and request acts, and that they used fewer downgraders in requests than the English speakers. Does this now mean that the German native speakers are on the whole less polite than the English native speakers? To answer this question, a consideration of Pike's (1976:37) distinction between *emic* and *etic* standpoints for the description of behavior seems to be relevant, i.e., studying behavior relative to context and function within a system of cultural meaning (emic standpoint) vis-à-vis behavior relative to a system as seen by an "outside observer" (etic standpoint). From an etic standpoint, then, the behavior of the German speakers may well be considered impolite by reference to an English norm; however, from an emic standpoint, which is the one we would prefer here, one would simply claim that the differential behavior displayed by the German and English speakers may be a reflection of the fact that the two cultural systems are organized differently, and that, e.g., a level 6 complaint in the German culture is not necessarily comparable to a level 6 complaint in the English culture, because the value of each is derived from the value it has relative to the remaining levels, and their frequency and modality of use in the particular cultural system.

Now, in order to avoid the type of pragmatic errors that – as we have mentioned above – native speakers of German make when learning or speaking English, it seems to be most important to include the pragmatic aspects of language use in language teaching, one of them being the interpretation and use of politeness in utterances. It seems also to be advisable for the teacher to explicitly point out to the learner that politeness markers are an integral part of the foreign cultural system, and should neither be used nor interpreted by reference to the learner's native system. More effective teaching of the behavioral component may minimize native cultural interference and prevent impolite, ineffective, or otherwise inappropriate behavior on the part of the learner. One important precondition for this type of teaching is, of course, more detailed and comprehensive research than we have undertaken here.

NOTES

1. The following schema detailing the different levels of directness of complaints was established by House (1979) and has been slightly modified in the present investigation.

2. The schema classifying requests in terms of their directness level was developed in co-operation with another member of our research group, *W. J. Edmondson.* Starting point for the classification was *Wunderlich* (1976:302ff.) and *Searle's* (1975) work on indirect speech acts.
3. Our definition of a hedge is much narrower than e.g., *G. Lakoff's* (1972:196) who subsumes under "hedges" a conglomeration of "vague" or "fuzzy" phenomena, among them items like *often, especially, virtually, very, really,* elements that can, in our view, act to intensify the proposition.
4. Downtoners correspond to what is referred to as "Abtönungspartikel" in the German literature.

PEG GRIFFIN and HUGH MEHAN

Sense and Ritual in Classroom Discourse*

ABSTRACT

The main concern of this paper is with the sociolinguistic complexities of lessons. The analysis of discoursive interchanges in the classroom shows that linguistic routines in institutional settings exhibit a fine interplay between ritual and spontaneous motifs. A careful study of the language that occurs in classrooms suggests that this is so, because utterances fulfill multiple functions simultaneously. Spontaneous utterances are not viewed as *de novo,* and can thus be related to the ritual properties of speech events. The cases examined in this paper bear testimony to the polyfunctional nature of language, and to the insufficiency of a grammar that requires only that a single underlying form be related to each surface structure.

INTRODUCTION

This paper reports our retrospective consideration of our separate but compatible investigations of classroom interactions (Shuy and Griffin, 1978; Mehan, 1979). Our investigations were motivated in part by an interest to get inside the process of education left untouched by large-scale surveys and on-the-spot codings. Our videotape data base provided us the opportunity to examine teaching-learning as social process unfolding through time.

A major way to begin to see what is going on in classrooms is to look at the language that occurs there. As we looked at a number of classrooms, in widely separate geographic areas, and with considerably different compositions, we find that our conception of language were being shaped by the organization of utterances occurring there, and the work we saw them doing. Specifically, we saw utterances fulfilling multiple functions simultaneously, negotiated conventions constituting the social event called the lesson, and more than one person taking part in the accomplishment of lesson components, even single utterances.

*An earlier version of this paper was presented at the Annual Meeting of the American Education Research Association, Symposium on Discourse Processes in the Classroom, San Francisco, April 9, 1979.

One longstanding view of language is that its purpose is the representation of objects in the world. This "referential view' of language rests on the Aristotelean notion that the world is ordered previous to people's perceptions of it into categories of objects each of which is necessarily identified by name. The Aristotelean notion, which also has its roots in Augustine, and is succinctly stated in Wittgenstein's *Tractatus,* makes language not an active force in the life of people, but a passive vehicle for connecting words and objects.

The referential conception of language treats words as signs which can point to, direct attention to, report, denote, connote, signify, stand on behalf of, or otherwise indicate something else (Langer, 1944; Cassirer, 1945; Morris, 1946; Ogden and Richards, 1935). Although not always physical entities, referents can be best thought of as "objects" in the world. Referents can either be physical (in the sense of material things without life or consciousness, such as chairs, tables, pens) or, they can be such non-material aspects of the world as centaurs and unicorns. Referents can also be social objects – social in the sense that they are matters or affairs which involve humans in events or situations. Referents, in short, are anything that stands in relationship to signs.

This conception presents an overly simplified view of language. While making connection between words and objects may be important, it is mistaken to conclude that this is the only important aspect of language. Language serves a wide variety of functions beyond the referential.

Austin (1962) showed that people do many things with their words besides refer to objects. Most notably, he pointed out that words perform deeds. That is, there are certain classes of actions, like apologizing, promising, pledging, that are accomplished by the very act of speaking words. The saying of the words: "I am sorry" (under certain conditions) constitutes an apology. Austin's initial investigations into "performatives" have influenced the development of speech act theory (e.g., Searle, 1969; 1976). Studies influenced by speech act theory (notably Dore, 1977; Labov and Fanschel, 1977; Ervin-Tripp, 1976) demonstrate the value of studying language events from this larger perspective.

While communicating, a person is not only transferring information about a referent, (s)he is conveying information about his or her very existence, physical condition, or emotional state. Information communicated about, and alerting other parties to the state or condition of the speaker has been called the "emotive" or "affective" function of language (Sebeok, 1962; cf. Searle's (1976) "expressives".). When information is conveyed which signals how a denotative or referential message is to be interpreted, a "meta-communicative function" (Bateson, 1972) or "communication about communication" (Watzlawick et al., 1967) is said to be occurring. Statements like: "I am serious," or "this is an order," are examples of meta-communicative messages that are communicated verbally.

Not all meta-communicative messages are communicated verbally, however. The ways in which words are spoken, involving such features as voice set, voice quality, stress, pitch, the spacing and timing between words can communicate the emotional state of the person speaking, or inform others about how words are to be interpreted (Gumperz, 1976).

Sebeok (1962:434) says that Malinowski may have been responsible for the identification of yet another language function, which he calls "phatic communion". This is the type of speech in which ties of union are created by the exchange itself. He was talking about messages which serve to establish, prolong, or discontinue communication. The "ums," "ahs," 'uh huhs," eye contact, glances, head nods, and other "back channel" work that (Duncan, 1972) discusses are examples of actions that serve to check whether the channel connecting the speaker and the hearer is in good working order.

While alerting us to the multiple functions of language, these investigations leave the impression that any single act of speech can only serve one function at a time. There is a recognition that language as a general system can serve multiple functions, but a particular act of speech is not seen as serving more than one function at a time (Searle, 1969; Sinclair and Coulthard, 1975). If more than one function at a time is involved, different functions are assigned to different aspects of the message, or to different channels in the communicative process. So, for example, emotion is said to be conveyed non-verbally, and carried in the visual channel, while denotative meaning is conveyed linguistically, and carried in the verbal channel (Ekman, 1968).

Furthermore, there is an impression that the relationship among participants in a speech event is simply that of sender and receiver(s); a speaker formulates a message and a hearer receives it. The message is composed quite independently of the hearer, and entirely before its transmission, with no modification by the hearer, or transformation of the message as the exchange unfolds. The roles of the participants may reverse as utterances are chained together but the basic relationship between interlocutors is not, in essence, any different than the relationship between a person strolling in the forest and the proverbial tree that falls and makes a noise in that forest.

A different picture of the relationship among interlocutors and a different characterization of their utterances emerges from the work of conversational analysts. Their work shows that there is a "reflexive" relationship between utterances in the flow of discourse. This reflexive relationship binds separate acts of speech together into units of an interactional nature. Given the first part of a sequence (an initiation act, a greeting, or other first-pair part), the second part of the sequence (a reply, another greeting) is "conditionally relevant." That is, the appearance of the first part of a sequence makes the appearance of a second part prospectively possible. The actual appearance of the second part of the sequence gives meaning to the first part. This reflexive relationship is illustrated in the following example:

(1) Child: Mommy, where are you? Where *are* you?
Mother: What did you say, dear?
Child: Where are . . . oh. I want to have a cookie.

In this case, the child's question has channel problems, because the mother is outside and around the corner of the house. The mother requests a repetition, a normal sequence of conversation under such circumstances. What is conditionally relevant after a "request for repetition" is for the child to give the repetition. The child starts to give that, and then seems to realize that it simply doesn't work. The content of the child's question has been answered by her ability to locate her mother by reference to her mother's voice. Here the conditional relevance is recognized, then seen to be irrelevant and then is disestablished in the self correction by the young child – an intricate reflexive relationship.

The reflexive feature of these sequences suggests that they have more in common with "social acts" (Mead, 1934) than "speech acts" (Searle, 1969, 1976). A speech act is usually seen as complete in itself; one need not look beyond the boundaries of the speech act to determine meaning. A social act requires the cooperative completion of an activity by the participants involved. The social act begins with the action of one person. The response to that initiating act completes the social act which was begun by the initial action. The response to the completion of the social act provides meaning to the initial act which began the act (cf. Stalnaker, 1978 and Rogers, to appear). Mead (1954) talked about this process as the "emergent present". That which is going on in the present inexorably becomes the past, informing and reforming the present, while future events inform the sense of the present.

The recognition that meaning resides in the reflexive assembly of sequences of interaction emphasizes the part played by the hearer in the construction of the meaning of an utterance made by the speaker, and takes language from a psychological, or personal level, and places it on a social or interactional level. People *participate* in conversation; conversation is more encompassing than any of the parties involved. The presence of a conversation requires social activity; speaking implies hearing, and hearing implies engaging the speaker in an unfolding spiral of meaning, not the transmission and reception of information as separate and distinct acts. While studying an occasion of engagement of a sect of interlocutors, there is a need to deny that the occasion is a separate and unique act, and to come to grips with the fact that interlocutors have a history. The issue of how original an engagement is and how historical it is, brings up the general issue of ritual, and its place in everyday life.

That which transpires in classroom lessons emphasizes the complexity of language as a social act. The following three sections are embroideries on these themes.

MAKING SENSE

In our classroom data, there are many occasions where one utterance does more than one piece of work and the multiple pieces of work are not always attributable to different parts of the utterance or to different levels or sections of the language or communication system.

Before we present the cases of multiple simultaneous functioning, we need to consider three points basic to our work. First, there is a tendency to view analyses of classroom interaction as important when considering the social side of the classroom and as less important when considering the academic or cognitive side. Often, the picture is that the social aspect can alter the image of the child's academic performance for better or for worse but that it has little to do with his actual cognitive academic functioning. We wish to expressly deny that such is the case. While it may be a convenient heuristic to consider the content of a child's answer separately from its placement or mode of expression in a lesson discourse unit, it is not acceptable to reify this convenience as two categories of language or two separate parts of a speaker's competence. There is no evidence, as far as we know, that the process or structures proposed as acceptable analyses of the cognitive, academic, or content aspects of lessons would be any different than the processes or structures involved in the social aspects. With this lack of evidence, and with the evidence developed below from the multiple simultaneous functioning involved in utterances in teaching-learning sequences, we believe that a separation of the academic and the social is untenable. A child's ability to deal with the sociolinguistic complexity of lesson discourse is not frosting on the cake of the math or reading lesson or the math and reading skills involved in the lesson. The increments to a child's skills, concepts or information base that a lesson is designed to facilitate are not available for the teacher to offer, or for the child to grasp, or for the analyst to locate except as they are instantiated in the social negotiations of the speech event. If you are learning in a lesson, you are doing so by virtue of your participation in a lesson speech event. It may be possible to participate in a lesson without achieving the increments in learning that the lesson was planned to promote (McDermott, 1976), and, of course, it is possible to participate in the assembly of parts of lessons that are not involved with increments in learning (e.g. disruptions), but it is not possible to get those increments in learning from a lesson without participating in the assembly of that lesson. Our view, then, is that while some subset of the utterances of the lesson may be easier to tag as "on task" academically or cognitively than other parts, such a tag should not be taken to mean that these utterances are any less involved in the sociolinguistics of lessons than any others. This view is substantiated in the cases that follow.

A second point involves the notions "function" and "intention". Discussions which rely on an analysis of the talk exchanged in a situation must, we feel, rely on what is available in that exchange. The analysts and the participants have access to surface behaviors and to the patterned regularities of those behaviors in the exchange being studied *and* in other exchanges related to it by virtue of language and other social conventions. "Functions" and "intentions" are available to participants and analysts as they are derived from the surface behaviors. Some studies of "functions" or "intentions" appear to rely on material beyond surface behaviors and their patterns. Systems which code discourse for the sole purpose of quantification are one example. Coders seeing and hearing an event or a videotape or reading a transcript are trained to attribute functions or intentions to utterances. These attributions are "good data" to the degree that the coder shares the participants' language and other social conventions. The problem is that the degree of sharing, or "co-membership," (Erickson and Shultz, 1979) is not static. If the coder were in the interaction his contribution to it and interpretation of it may be similar to the participants in some places and different in others. In fact, co-membership is part of what is negotiated in interactions. Thus coders may at one time be accurate in attributing a function or intention to a speaker, and at another time produce false positives and at another time produce false negatives. (Cf. Ervin-Tripp, 1976.)

Quantification systems may be a useful approach to survey large bodies of data in order to determine what co-occurs with certain functions or intentions or sub-classes of them (e.g., restrictions on contexts of utterances, or on social personages who utter them). However, coders are basically "stand ins" for a participant; in the best of instances, they respond with the same intuitions that a participant does to the surface behaviors and their patterns. Coding systems cannot provide us with an explication of these intuitions and, in the worst of cases, they can mislead us if the coders (or the coding manual) have little co-membership with the participants. Analyses based on coding systems, then, cannot stand as analyses of *how* the function is derived or of *what* it is, but rather as part of an analysis of what the function correlates with.

Approaches to studying language function which begin with some set of probable functional categories (argued to be jointly exhaustive and mutually exclusive) may be used in such a way that they have the limitations of coding systems; however, such approaches may include rigid rules of evidence that require that category differences be reflected as differences in surface behaviors (cf. Sadock, 1974). In the latter case these approaches are available as analyses of how the function is derived and what it is. It doesn't matter whether the analysis proceeds from the top-down or the bottom-up. Both of these kinds of analyses depend upon the evidence available to participants in an exchange (and the evidence which participants make available for one another in an exchange) and thus are sufficiently constrained so that they can be more than just one among several possible analyst's constructs and can, instead, be argued to be participants' constructs. These analyses of what functions are or how they operate are the kind that we consider to be fully warranted analyses. Our discussion of functions are limited to those for which we can provide a warranted analysis; we are attempting to explicate the language code, not re-code it in a reduced form.

Instances of multiple simultaneous functions are systematically unavailable to some ways of doing analysis, however. If the analyst is searching a corpus for instances of a set of functions and does not attend to how the whole speech event is working, single functions may be found even when an utterance is participating in more than one piece of conversational work. If the analyst is working with a self-constructed corpus – constructed particularly to examine a possible explication of how a function is derived and what it is –, the corpus will, not surprisingly, reveal no multiple functions. In our work, we dealt with whole events of actually occurring social events – lessons – and found that the idea of multiple functions occurring simultaneously had to be given a place of central importance.

A third point, before we lay out some of these cases, concerns the sequence which we, and others (cf. Sinclair & Coulthard, (1975), Mishler (1975a b), have seen as a pervasive part of lesson discourse. Example (2) is a representation of the three part sequence which occurs

(2) T: elicitation
C: response
T: evaluation

more often than anything else in the lessons we taped. The first part, spoken by the teacher, is a question about an academic topic and an indication of who should answer it. The second part is a child's reply to the question. The third part is the teacher's expression of approval or rejection of the response to the elicitation. It is important to emphasize that the sequence is not one sentence long, but can be inclusive of three full sentences spoken by two different people. We have presented evidence elsewhere (Mehan, 1979; Griffin and Humphrey, 1978) that these units participate in still larger units. Here we will concentrate on the multiple functioning of utterances in these sequences.

Cases 3-11 form one class to be examined.

(3) T: Good, Chip. Let's see, Sally.
(4) T: Does anybody, if you do raise your hand, remember what I bought?
(5) T: What is the last thing in the top row, Lisa?
(6) T: Will everyone give this last answer?
(7) T: Does anyone know a word beginning with *B*?
(8) T: Susan, Jenny, do either of you have a watch?
(9) P: What was the example in the testing tapes?
B: It was too complicated to use.
(10) T: (*addressing the whole group of children*) The first thing is, I'm going to ask you not to touch the equipment yet.
R: O.K. (*puts down battery.*)
(11) T: Good. Susan?

Example (3) is either a case of simultaneous functions in one unit (one turn of talk) or it is a challenge to turn-at-talk as a unit. It is easy enough to show that the evaluation realized as *Good, Chip,* and the elicitation realized as *Let's see, Sally* in (3) are in fact two parts which simply happen to share a turn. We can cite evidence from intonation, from overt addressee differences, from the ordering of parts, and from the limited privileges of occurrences of this compound turn compared to the different privileges of occurrence of each part separately. Roughly speaking, these compounds are "lesson middle" – they can appear only in the interior of a larger discourse unit. By contrast, elicitations that are uttered separately can be lesson initial, but not final, and evaluations that are uttered separately can be lesson final, but not initial. Example (3) as discussed so far would not compel us to accept a notion of simultaneous function. We can, instead, merely refine our definition of a turn as a functional or formal unit.

However, hidden in (3) and more explicit in (4) is a more serious issue, discussed in detail by Mehan (1979). Here the two parts of one turn are not as easily separated into two units. The embedded amalagam, represented by '*if you do, raise your hand*' in (4), indicates how the response should occur, and prepares for a subsequent indication of who the respondent will be – the response referred to being in both cases, the elicitation represented by '*Does anybody remember what I bought?*' This is a case of an "invitation to bid' turn allocation procedure. As Mehan (1979) argues the initial part of the sequence represented in (2) includes both elicitation and turn allocation elements. In (4), these are separable utterances. In (5) and in the last part of

(3), the vocative use of the child's name may be seen as a separable part and as an example of "individual nomination" turn allocation precedures. Except for the interrelationships of the parts here, we might base a rejoinder around a claim for proper units of analysis, rather than accept the argument for the simultaneous function of these utterances.

However, example (6), an "invitation to respond' turn allocation procedure questions such a solution, as does (7), a "turn not assigned" turn allocation procedure, according to Griffin and Humphrey (1978). Either these do not have a turn allocation part, or it is inseparable from the elicitation part of the utterance. Both our analyses militate against denying the turn-allocation aspects of the elicitations in (6) and (7). The patterned regularities in the data are as strong for cases like (6) and (7) as for cases like (3), (4), and (5).

While examples so far are easily identifiable as "lessons" discourse, example (8) shows a "next speaker selection"[1] procedure (Sacks et al, 1974) with a structure similar to (5) operating in another discourse setting. The case could be made that, like (3), (4), and (5), these are realized as separable parts, and do not provide evidence for simultaneous function. Note, however, example (9). The content and the context of this utterance serve to select "B" as the next speaker. (No one else knows about those tapes.) No separate unit solution is plausible here. Similarly, in (10), in a lesson, the utterance content indicates what is to be done at the same time as it references the context and, in so doing, simultaneously functions to indicate who is to respond to the teacher's directive. Rene was the only one touching equipment.

In sum, utterances that look toward the change of speakers, whether they are the specialized turn-allocation procedures of classroom lessons, or the next-speaker selection principle of other discourse events, provide good evidence for simultaneous functions in single utterances. Example (11) shows the tail wagging the dog: the allocation procedure alone is lexically indicated. (Susan is nominated to take the next turn.) But its simultaneous function as an elicitation is clear in our data, *and* the elicitation is recoverable in all its particulars, not only by analysts, but by kindergarten children as they work with teachers and each other to assemble classroom events.

(12) T: It does start with a '*t*'.
(13) T: That's backwards.
(14) Letterwriter (on a recommendation form, when X is a candidate for a chemistry job: Mr. X has very good handwriting.

Another set of utterances, like those in (12)-(14), further support the notion of simultaneous functions. (12) and (13) occur in the third part of a sequence of the pattern given in (2). The straight forward third parts (e.g., 'good' and 'no') occur in sequences adjacent to the problem sets involving

(12) and (13); the responses that are given prior to (12) and (13) are treated like those that receive negative evaluation (i.e., they are replaced by the same student or another student, and they do not get summarized in the lesson). If we take as a heuristic that interlocutors are cooperative, then (12)-(14) are problems. The teachers in (12) and (14) are not obviously doing what they are supposed to do (i.e., the teachers aren't saying that the students are wrong), and the letter writer isn't saying that Mr. X is good or bad as a chemist. Grice (1968) considers cases like (14). Roughly speaking, Grice says: When a speaker seems to be behaving 'wrong,' his behavior can be examined for evidence that his behavior is a way of behaving 'right'. Given the circumstances of the speech event, being uncooperative may be a way of being cooperative. The letter writer of (14) seems to be wrong – irrelevant and incomplete – but his very wrongness (not commenting on X's ability as a chemist) can be noticed as wrong, and can, by a chain of reasoning, be related to a negative job recommendation of Mr. X. The circumstances that produce this circuitous recommendation are not unfamiliar to most of us. Extremely important to a Gricean analysis is that the utterance's literal meaning be taken seriously, or else the implicated meaning can not be computed. Also important are aspects of the context and of the identity of the participants in the talk exchange.

In the examples from the classroom (12) and (14), the teacher's role as the "evaluator" is important for noticing the "wrong," (i.e., the missing evaluation) as well as for understanding the implicature. In both these cases, the teacher refrains from giving an expected simple negative evaluation, and instead, gives a description; and, in so doing, succeeds in implicating a negative evaluation. Thus, the seemingly unexpected and uncooperative behavior does the work that is expected and cooperative.

This intricate kind of simultaneous function can be best understood by an examination of (12) in a larger context, as in (15):

(15) T: *writes 'tree' on paper attached to board* . . . If you know what the word says, put up your hand
R: Top
T: No, unn-uhh, put your hand up. Andre.
A: Tab
→ T: It *does* start with 't' . . . Matthew?

Like the job recommendation example (13), this can be seen as a case of "condemning with faint praise," and the implicature of negative evaluation can be reasoned out by noting that if only part of the answer is worth mentioning, then the rest is negatively valued. The arrowed utterance has several characteritics: (a) it is in a third slot in a sequence like (2) above; (b) it is spoken by the teacher; (c) it is not an overt evaluation, as would be expected given (a) and (b); (d) it is an accurate description of the written word "tree"; (e) it is "responsive" to the preceding utterance by virtue of the stressed "does," and the reference to "start with." Not just any utterance with accurate descriptive information about the word '*tree*' could fit into the discourse and the implicature. Had not a wrong answer '*Tab*' been on the floor, (12a):

(12a) T: There is a long vowel sound at the end, 'e'.

would have been as fitting a descriptive utterance. And, had the wrong answer been 'knee' (12a) but not (12) would have been appropriate to simultaneously function as an evaluation. Further, not just any utterance which responded to the child's answer, '*tab*,' could do the work of negative evaluation; for instance, (12b) would fail.

(12b) T: *Tab,* like on top of the box of crackers would fail.

Just as the utterance being what it is literally, is necessary for the implicature to be what it is, the implicature being what it is, restricts the class of possible utterances. In figuring out the circuitous cooperativeness (cf. Griffin and Humphrey, 1978) of these kinds of "third parts" in structures like (11), we see again simultaneous functions – these particularly intimate in the reflexivity of their restrictions. Previous discussions of Gricean implicatures have not discussed the simultaneous functioning involved, probably because the work has been carried out on self-constructed data sets which were sufficient to locate implicatures but which could miss the simultaneous functions. The surface utterance must "fit" in the discourse, here as a description, and at the same time not "fit," here as a violation of the expected evaluation.

(16) T: Then you put what letter?
Children: *H.*
→ T: Then what letter?

(17) T: What's the first thing in the top row, Child A?
Child A: A flag.
→ T: What's the last thing in the top row, Child B?

(18) T: Wait a second, Child A, why would there be needles?
Child A: Cause.
→ T: What are the needles there for? (*to Child A*)

(19) T: What are the needles there for? (*to Child A*)
Child A: Porcupine needles.
→ T: Why does the porcupine and the cactus have needles, Child B?

Another class of simultaneously functioning utterances both displays and manipulates the regularities of classroom language. Griffin and Humphrey (1978) discuss examples (16)-(19) as cases of "covertly accomplished evaluations". The polarity of the evaluation is exceptionlessly recoverable – that is, the arrowed utterances in cases like (16) and (17) covertly accomplish always and only positive evaluations of Child A's response, while cases like (18) and (19) are always and only negative evaluations. While the third part of the structure represented in (2) is not overtly rendered by the teacher, this exceptionless recoverability provides strong evidence for the claim that the third part is covertly accomplished. *How* it is covertly accomplished involves a recognition that the teacher's second question is simultaneously functioning as an evaluation of the child's response. By asking a new question to the same child (16) or to a new child (17), the teacher covertly accomplishes positive evaluation. By asking the same question to the same child (18) or to a new child (19) the teacher covertly accomplishes negative evaluations.

This analysis relies on several facts about lesson discourse in which covertly accomplished evaluations are found: The identity of the speaker of the utterance as the teacher, the fact that the teacher issues both elicitations and evaluations in lesson discourse, the regularity of the three-part sequence in classroom discourse, and the content of the two sequences. More important, however, is that the evaluation of one sequence is regularly issued immediately preceding the elicitation of the next sequences. (cf. (3) above.) The sequential ordering within structures like the one represented in (2) and the sequential ordering among such structures in a lesson set the stage for the simultaneous functioning of elicitations as evaluations. What looks at first glance like irregularities in classroom discourse (especially after incorrect replies) – irregularities occasioned by missing third parts to sequences like (2) – turn out instead to be grounded in those regularities by way of mechanisms involving simultaneous functions.

Other cases of simultaneous functioning occur in our data and most, like these, depend upon the regularities found in classroom discourse events. The nature of these regularities is, in itself, an interesting issue.

MAKING RITUAL

Interaction in the classroom has often been described as an automatic and repetitious ritual, composed of behavior that is highly predictable. The idea that classroom life is ritualized can be related to Lewis's (1969) description of a convention.

Lewis, describing the development of a convention, cites the process involved as colleagues establish and then maintain a regular meeting place for lunch. One colleague calls another to meet for lunch. A detailed conversation ensues, in which time, place, and date of the meeting is explicated. At the conclusion of the lunch meeting, the friends agree to meet again. During the week, telephone calls are exchanged, and date, time, and place are again established. This same pattern of information exchange is repeated for a few weeks. Then, gradually, the explicit information concerning the meeting is not exchanged, and the friends simply show up at the regular restaurant at the previously appointed time. At the time that these colleagues continue this course of action automatically, without explicit instruction, Lewis says that a convention has been established. There is a regularity in the behavior of members of a community established on the expectation that others will conform to the pattern.

Thus, in Lewis's conception, negotiation and explicit instruction are necessary at the beginning stages of the establishment of a convention. However, after the particular pattern of behavior is established, negotiation and explication drop out of the process. The course of action becomes automatic and routine. Particulars, which at first were debated, are soon merely confirmed, and eventually are not discussed at all.

Once a convention is established, then, people conduct a course of action automatically, without need for negotiation. It is at such times, Goffman (1967) would say, that a ritual has been established.

At first glance, the organization of classroom events on a particular day, and their refinement across the school year *do* seem to conform to Lewis's notion of automatic convention. The first few weeks of the year, especially in the primary grades, are given over to establishing behavior patterns. Early in the year, teachers spend considerable time describing rules, correcting mistakes, and shaping behavior. Teachers engage students in explicit tuition about expected modes of behavior, appropriate ways of self expression, the use of instructional materials, and the like. Then, as the year progresses, the amount of time and energy spent in transitions between major classroom events decreases, and the density of procedural instructions diminishes. Students and teachers move from place to place and event to event smoothly. They seem to carry out the business of learning "automatically," thereby providing support for the notion that classroom behavior is ritualized convention.

A similar progression can be seen occuring across grade levels from nursery to third grade (Shuy and Griffin, 1978). Some routines involve the whole school; others are so central to classroom operations that they are expected at each grade level. These take a lot of time, and are explicitly taught to four year olds in nursery classes but they are hardly noticable in third grade classrooms (cf. Cahir, 1978).

In a similar manner, the conduct of instruction within the interior of classroom lessons seems to support the idea that behavior is automatic and ritualized. The pattern of Teacher Initiation, Student Reply, and Teacher Evaluation seems so pervasive to be automatic. And this pattern *does* become streamlined as the year progresses (Mehan, 1979). At the outset of the school year in a primary grade, students were found to be competing with the teacher for conversational space. Students attempted to introject conversational topics into the middle of ongoing Initiation-Reply-Evaluation sequences. The teacher responded to these student initiations as intrusions, and either negatively sanctioned them, or ignored them.

As the year progressed, the students in the classroom became adept at locating the seams in lesson discourse. Instead of indiscriminantly introjecting answers and comments into the middle of instructional sequence, they introduced topics in the juncture between the completion of one instructional sequence and the beginning of another. The consequences of this modification in student behavior was that the students effectively gained control of the floor. Instead of having their ideas treated as things thrown on the floor to be swept away, their ideas were picked up by the teachers and students, incorporated in the lesson format, and in some cases, changed the direction of discouse in significant ways. Thus, by the middle of the year, classroom lessons in this classroom proceeded smoothly. There were few interruptions, even fewer sanctions, and a rhythmic flow of interaction between teacher and student was visible.

The metronomic quality of classroom lessons has led to some interpreters to conclude that discourse which proceeds smoothly is automatic and mechanical, behavior which is patterned and completely predictable. We find such interpretations to be oversimplified characterizations of life in classrooms. It seems to us that such conclusions are reached because the subtleties of cueing behavior and the interpretation of behavior that occurs as classroom interaction unfolds has not been given careful attention.

(20) (lesson where hand raising rule had been invoked earlier)
T: Give me a word beginning with a B
Many: call out "bowl," "ball," and "me"
Brian: *raises hand*
T: I like the way you are raising your hand, Brian
Many: *stop calling out; raise hands*
T: Olivia?

For instance (20) is not an uncommon classroom occurrence. Some children act as if there is a hand raising convention in effect, while others do not. We could explain these occurrences by saying that some of the children have not been adequately socialized into the community in which the convention operates. However, two pieces of evidence suggest this interpretation is wrong. First, the pupils do not act in the way we would expect if the problem was one of differential rates of socialization, i.e., there is not a consistent set of students who call out rather than raise their hands, and, individual students are not shown a consistent pattern of evaluation by the teacher. Second, there are occasions where teachers reject answers that are called out, whether or not the hand raising rule was on the floor. When the called out answers attain the uniformity of a choral response, when an unexpected individual calls out, when a valuable answer is called out, the teacher may act as if the rule is not there. Thus, a more reasonable explanation involves the rejection of a fully automated conception of convention operating in classroom lessons, and the adoption of a more improvisational conception.

That we reject the ritualized sense of classroom convention does not mean that we endorse a purely spontaneous sense of convention, a position that has been identified with certain readings of ethnomethodology. This radically contextualized position maintains that there is no need to look beyond the boundaries of the immediate situation and consider past experiences, previous biographies, structural conditions, practical and historical circumstances because participants in interaction create meanings anew upon each occasion of interaction.

Wells et al. (1978) articulate this position. They maintain that the structure of conversation can not be predicted because it is a completely free wheeling activity, and hence not governed by rules:

> . . . most adult child conversation in the home is less focused and it appears that the sequencing constraints that operate apply over very short stretches of discourse. It is only relatively rarely that tight functional and thematic links can be found over more than adjacent pairs or triples of utterances. This finding . . . suggests that *it is not appropriate to describe the sequential structure of conversation as rule governed,* except as greetings and other routine transactions . . . (Wells et al., 1978:8) (Italics added).

There *is* data from our studies that lend credence to views like these.

(21) (The teacher has been asking children to give sufficient descriptions of blocks. When they provide a size, color, and shape description, she gives them a block fitting the description. The children are seated on the floor in a circle. After a few children have taken turns:)

T: Now, that was very helpful. Alright, someone who has his hands (*children start raising hands after 'alright'*) Let's see, I'll tell you what. Let's go around the circle. Maybe that is the quickest way to do it.

Example (21) exemplifies the short-lived sequencing constraints in the classroom. A hand-raising rule is suspended and supplemented by an "automatic turn-allocation" technique (Griffin and Humphrey, 1978), where the seating plan plays a big role in the selection of which child will answer next.

Another example of a radically contextualized rule in classrooms is found in a first grade "morning circle" during discussions of the daily weather report. Sophia raises her hand; the teacher looks at her and says: "Is it about the weather?" with normal question intonation and rhythm; Sophia lowers her hand; the teacher looks at Sophia first, and then at the rest of the class and says:

(22) "Is it about the weather"

with a rhythm and intonation that are unusual for questions; another child raises his hand, the teacher calls his name, and he makes a comment about the weather. A sequencing constraint about what the next topic is has been established on the spot.

In spite of examples such as these, a radically contextualized view can not be maintained given the evidence presented above about the gradual conventionalization of classroom rules and evidence to be presented below about the improvisation of classroom rules. Note also the evidence for historic conventions inherent in the timing of the children's handraising in example (21). The children started to follow the rule before any overt reference was made to it.

Our interpretation of classroom interaction recommends a third position, which can be called "negotiated convention". This position recognizes that each piece of interaction in the classroom is constituted by a negotiated process requiring the interpretation of behavior and precise timing, while at the same time acknowledges that the pattern of action emerging from this dynamic interpretive work has historicity.

Schiffer (1972) presents a notion of convention that is similar to Lewis's (1969), but which never reaches such a level of automaticity. Specifically dealing with language conventions Schiffer, too, begins with an agreement or precedent among the members of the community, but the difference is that even after the regularity has been established, negotiation is still considered to be operating.

Just as in the beginning one party acts in a certain way such that the act will work to allow the other to infer what the act is intended to convey, so too, at the end, the party's actions are still dependent on the interpretive work by the interlocutor. What the establishment of a convention adds to the process is that each party's knowledge of it lends more certainty, and speaks to the negotiations carried on as behavior and inferences about them.

Active interpretive work is required on the part of classroom participants all the time, not just at "beginnings" – be they classroom events, school days, or school years. Students always need to know when a context occurs such that certain behavior and not other behavior is acceptable (Erickson and Shultz, 1977). They must interpret behavioral cues that contextualize behavior (Gumperz, 1976), and interpret teacher's statements that index the existence of underlying rules for classroom behavior (Griffin and Humphrey, 1978; Mehan, 1979).

Rules of classroom comportment and contextualized constitutive rules are at the center of a class of utterances which render the notion of the classroom either as automatic ritual, or as a historic spontaneity problematic.

(23) T: Uh, whose name (*raises namecard*)
J: Sabrina
C: Sabrina
T: Raise your hand, raise your hand to give other people a chance to read it
(*Children raise hand. Teacher calls a name. Named child reads Sabrina*)

(24) T: (*begins to draw J____ / S____ on board*) Um, who can think of some words? (*continues to draw*)
Many: Jelly, Jerome
T: Martin, raise your hand to give other people a chance to think. That's why I want you to raise your hand, to give other people a chance to think
Many: (*raise hands*)
T: Leola?
L: Jelly

(25) T: Raise your hand if you know where Leola's house would go on this map
Many: (*raise hands*)
T: Carolyn?
C: right there (*pointing to map*)

(26) T: OK, now raise your hand. What can you think of, first of all, whose name in this room begins with this letter. Raise your hand, any children whose name begins with this letter (*points to letter 's' which is drawn on the board*)

J: (*raises hand*)
T: Jerome?
J: Sabrina

(27) T: Give me a word beginning with B, Audrey?
A: Ball
T: Good (*writes B-A-L-L on board*) Give me another word, Bill?
B: Puff
T: No. That one begins with "Puh," P. What's a word that begins with B?
C: Ball
→ T: We have ball. David?
D: Bowl

(28) (Grant is talking with a classmate during a lesson while the teacher is asking a recyclable question to another pupil and that pupil is answering.) Then:
→ T: Grant?
G: Uh *pause*
T: Grant, what's the answer?
G: Uh *pause*
T: Grant, what question did I ask you?

First, an idea of the rules. In examples (23), (24), (25), and (26), the rule is the well known hand raising rule. In (27) the arrowed utterance indexes a "unique answer" rule which can be formulated as: "an answer that is the same as a correct answer previously given is incorrect by virtue of it being a second instance". In (28) the teacher is trading off the "recyclable rule". That is, when a student's name constitutes the whole utterance of the elicitation as it does in an utterance like the arrowed one in (28), the elicitation is retreivable as a recyclable of a prior elicitation.

Although practical, daily concerns of teachers in classrooms are social order and the exchange of academic information, the rules that are a part of this concern must be negotiated continually by the teachers and students. Statements of classroom precedures are like other rule statements in that they have a "tacit dimension" (Polanyi, 1962) i.e.. they are often not stated in so many words.

In (23)-(26) the students were not provided with information about the appropriate way to gain access to the floor explicitly. They hear statements that index the existence of classroom rules. Teacher's statements like "raise your hand" or "wait a minute, give other people a chance to think" are not the classroom rules *per se*. They are statements that index classroom rules. In these cases, the underlying rule is orderliness. As a result, students have to "go beyond the information given" (Brown, 1973) to understand classroom rules. The same holds for the non-comportment rules indexed in (27) and (28).

The classroom situation is complicated because statements that index the existence of the underlying classroom rules appear both in retrospective and prospective relation to children's behaviors. They appear retrospectively when a teacher responds to a student's action which is thereby constituted as a violation of classroom rules (23), (24), (26) and (28). On such occasions, "raise your hand" or "we have ball" serves as a retrospective evaluation of the immediate past action of the students. These statements indicate that a certain classroom procedure should have been in effect, but wasn't. The retrospective appearance of a procedural statement requires teachers and students to negotiate a sense of social structure. Students must assign meanings backwards in time in order to know what the preferred state of affairs should have been, and should be under similar circumstances in the future. These retrospective statements become historic material for subsequent negotiated conventions.

Statements like "raise your hand" also appear prospectively to indicate that a certain classroom procedure will now be in effect (25) and (26). The appearance of procedural statements with a prospective horizon also requires students to engage in interpretive work. Since the temporal parameters of such procedures are not stated, the duration of their effect must be decided from occasion by the students involved. In (20), the teacher's elicitation did not contain an explicit "invitation to bid". Indeed, some students took this as an "invitation to reply". Yet, the teacher's response to the students' replies indicates bids rather than replies were expected.

Students become adept at interpreting the temporal parameters of these rules. In cases like (27), children understand that the unique answer rule does not operate when the lesson enters a summary/review phase. In fact, only answers that are not unique, that have been previously given and accepted are appropriate for summaries or reviews.

So, what we have here are neither automatic rituals – repeated endlessly and mechanically, nor instantaneous creations, – emerging uniquely upon each occasion of interaction. These are negotiated conventions – spontaneous improvisations on basic patterns of interaction.

Verification for this view emerges from an examination of an event of peer teaching among first graders. Mark has been charged with "being the teacher" to a group of his classmates for a drill on recognizing short vowel sounds. Mark, a good reader, has been given a list of one syllable words, each with a short vowel sound, like the *a* in bag or the *u* in lunch. The ritual of elicitation-response-evaluation is established with a slight change – a child is a teacher.

Mark reads a word (the first word is *edge*); the other children write a response indicating which vowel they think is in the word ("e"); Mark then calls on one of them to say the answer; one of the other children gives an answer; Mark evaluates it, and sometimes then asks how many got it right and says 'good' or 'okay'; Mark then reads the next word (the next word is 'cat'). The structure is as in (29):

(29) Mark: elicitation
Children: write response
Mark: allocates turn to Child A
Child A: responds
Mark: Evaluates

The "round" is repeated several times. Mark is taking the teacher role in talk. Note already the elasticity of the elicitation-evaluation ritual. It adjusts to written responses and can adjust to evaluations of more than one response as needed. As the lesson goes on, some jokes occur, and Mark's peer status is clear. Then another child suggests what the next elicitation is (the next word is 'brunch'). Elicitation is Mark's job; responding is the other students' job. Mark responds to the suggestion by evaluating it negatively and calling for another suggestion. We see this as a kind of reverse leap frog. When the peer "students" appropriate the peer "teacher" role as speaker of the elicitation, the peer "teacher" acts as if there had been an elicitation (*viz.*, "what's the next elicitation?") and provides the evaluation and then he re-issues the pretended elicitation. So the structure is (29b):

(29b) Child B: Elicitation
Mark: Evaluation
Mark: Elicitation about elicitation
Child C: Response
Mark: Evaluation

Mark, making use of the ritual, improvises a "new" lesson and retains the role of teacher. Adults, even sometimes experienced teachers, talk of losing the class; Mark negotiates classroom conventions with ease, with flair, and keeps control of his mini-class. Not only is his talk contextualized, it is contextualizing.

Throughout our classroom data, students and teachers are negotiating what the rules are, when they operate, and how they are to apply to a certain context. Those who conceive of rules as automatic ritual would call such work as redundant, and recommend that pre-service teachers be trained to establish clear rules that then could be enforced with dispatch throughout the year. From our point of view, such training would poorly prepare teachers for the necessary negotiations which we have seen as an integral part of classroom interaction.

On the other hand, those who view rules as purely spontaneous would view the negotiatory work we have seen as either inadequate or as operating on mysterious principles. They would disparage any attempt to order the classroom as unfounded rationality (Anderson, 1978), and would encourage teachers to rely on intuitions to get through classroom days. The concepts we are presenting – of rules as spontaneous rituals and negotiated conventions – views the negotiation of teachers and students as necessary, and recommends to teacher training that teachers be prepared to take advantage of the historic aspect of classroom rules, while at the same time, they be prepared to negotiate with students so that the rules are made to work in varying and unexpected classroom circumstances.

MAKING SENSE

A final set of cases that we consider calls particular attention to the term "sociolinguistics". There are utterances and sequences of interaction whose operations are understandable only if we accept the notion that the accomplishment of linguistic acts is a social, i.e., multi-party endeavor.

Examine again (15) above. The child says 'tab,' in response to which, the teacher says (12), responding much as she might to an utterance like

(30) C: I think that the word written up there starts with a '*t*' '*tuh*'.

This teacher response is not so exotic as the following explication may make it seem. Almost anyone reading, listening to, or looking at (15) would agree that it is reasonable for the teacher to assume that a child who misreads *tree* as *tab* has correctly recognized the letter *t* (the child has said *tab* and not *knee*), has a correct sound correspondence for that letter (the child has said *tab* and not *thank*), knows about initial position and sidedness as a written English representation of sequentiality in the speech stream (the child has said *tab* and not *bat*).

While we can agree that this much is so, we have not dealt with the fact that the child said *tab*. For all we know or the teacher knows he may have been choosing between saying *Tab* and *Fresca*, and simply happened to have settled on "Tab" when he started to speak.

There is no way that analysts or teachers can know for sure whether the child is displaying bad sight word skills, or is considering issues related to a diet soft drink, or reporting on what was read to him that morning from the lid of a cardboard container, or has like a good decoder, emitted a /t/ derived from the written word '*tree,*' and /æ/ as a more or less random syllable. And yet, we find it not outrageous that the teacher assumes the utterance displays decoding skills, and we find it not uncommon for teachers to act on that assumption.

That is, '*Tab*' as the second part of sequences like (15) is vague – it could be a reference to a soft drink or a part of a cardboard container, or an initial consonant and a random syllable. And, like other instances of vagueness, it is useful, and like othe instances, its vagueness is specifiable in the discourse event.

The difference between it and other kinds of vagueness is that the next speaker provides the specification. That is (31) repeated from (15) above, specifies *tab* as a /t/ cued from the written word tree, and a random syllable. By contrast, (32)-(34) illustrate other possible manifestations of available specifications of the utterance *Tab*:

(31) It *does* start with T
(32) We are talking about what's in the park, not what we might bring on a picnic to the park
(33) It *is* a short word with a hump at the beginning
(34) R makes a blend with the 'tuh' not an /æ/ sound

Utterance (31) exemplifies a way of teaching reading called phonics; (32) would fit into a reading lesson developing context comprehension and prediction clues to reading; (33) would fit where sight words are what is supposed to be learned; and (34) again fits into phonics but focuses on the sound correspondence for *R*. By specifying, in fact, by reifying one of the possible interpretations of an utterance by a pupil, a teacher cooperates in the construction of that utterance as a learning of (or partial learning of, or steps toward learning) what is supposed to be learned.

Further examples of teachers and students cooperating in creating a conversation (with structures of educational consequence) are presented in (31)-(33):

(35) (*Teacher holds up a story board to a group of pre-readers in a reading circle)
T: Ok, what's the name of this story?
Ss: *no response*
T: Who remembers, what's the name, what's the story about?
Ss: *no response*
T: Is it about taking a bath?
Ss: No

T: Is it about the sunshine?
Ss: No
T: Is it about the map?
Ed: Yes
→ T: The map. That's right this says 'the map.'

In this situation, the teacher's initial question required a reading of the title, and it was not answered. As a follow-up, the teacher provides that the answer to the first question be constructed as answers to other questions. Since what a story is about and what its name is, are often the same, there is a good chance that an answer to the "about" question can be specified by the teacher as an answer to the "name" question. In fact, in (35), after presenting an "about" question, requiring that the children give a noun phrase, the teacher constructs the appropriate noun phrase with the children merely answering 'yes' or 'no.' Then, in the arrowed utterance, Edward's "yes" response is specified as an answer to the reading of the title asked for in the initial question. Thus, the child's agreement is constructed to be equivalent to the child's statement of the story title (cf. Vygotsky, 1978:79-91).

This reification process, noticable in the completion of partial answers, is also visible in the collaborative production of other aspects of classroom life:

(36) (Classroom situation: a "circle," in which the teacher is assigning classroom jobs to students. The job to be assigned is responsibility for recreation equipment at recess:)
T: *points to list of jobs*
W: We ain't got no girl's ball, no jump rope
C: (Whispers to friend next to her): I'm gonna hang up my sweater. (Outloud to teacher) I'm gonna go back there
→ T: All right, Carolyn, go see if there's a jump rope or a girl's ball
C: (leaves circle, hangs up sweater in clothes closet, gathers sunflower seeds from her purse; checks equipment closet which is next to clothes closet. Returns to circle, shaking her head 'no')
T: It's my turn to talk after Carolyn reports (Carolyn still shaking her head 'no.') Okay, then, we don't need those jobs

It is important to know that the teachers in the classroom in (33) wanted students to confine clothes changing and other movement around the classroom to breaks in between academic activities (e.g., lunch, recess). So, it seems that Carolyn's aside to her friend "I'm gonna hang up my sweater," and her statement to the teacher "I'm gonna go back there" (see arrowed utterance) are announcements that she is going to break some classroom rules. And, a student simply walking away from a classroom activity would certainly receive reproach from the teacher. Carolyn in fact does go to the clothes closet to change clothes. In the process she brings some nuts from her purse. And, she carries out this course of action in such a way that she not only escapes negative sanction, but she receives compliments from the teacher for her cooperation.

The social accomplishment of reification contributes to the assembly of this artful episode. The student's announcement to the teacher has an "open horizon of meaning" (Schutz, 1962). It doesn't report in so many words Carolyn's intention of going to the closet for the purpose of depositing her sweater. Its very vagueness provides for the possibility that Carolyn is volunteering to help the teacher get her work done, and not announcing her intention to leave the circle.

The teacher specifies Carolyn's essentially open statement. She specifies Carolyn's utterance as an offer to carry out an instruction which actually hasn't been given; she ratifies the offer by providing the supposed instruction to do what has been offered. In this way, Carolyn's leaving the circle is socially (i.e., collaboratively by the teacher and student) constructed as "helping the teacher" and not "breaking the rules".

"What's supposed to be learned" is an easy way to gloss the decision-making process that was the total work done by the analytic approach to this kind of data proposed by Griffin and Humphrey (1978). This approach attempts to specify the practical procedures the teacher uses such that the analyst would arrive at the same guess about childrens' answers that the teacher does. The algorithm involves the teacher's turns (elicitations, evaluations, and informatives) throughout the lesson, plus the objectives of the lesson, plus the sub-components entailed by the objectives. All of the pieces of information added together show that there is a derivable account for the teachers saying what they do (e.g., *It does start with a 't'*), in response to the children saying what they do (e.g., *tab*). This approach can provide a reasonable analysis of the teacher's problem solving procedure, when the problem is that an answer is on the floor. In some cases (where the task is not overtly specified, or not as easily sub-divided as are reading tasks), this kind of analysis is difficult to develop. We may be able to account for how come it is reasonable for the teacher to arrive at a particular interpretation – how come the teacher attributed certain characteristics to the particular utterance of the child, and this may be extended to cover cases like (36). But, we have not resolved the issue of what characteristics the utterance has apart from the teacher's attribution.

We now prefer an alternative approach. The approach that we now prefer admits outright that utterances like these vague ones are simply not amenable to an analysis that captures our and the teacher's intuitions about them as displays of what counts as knowledge in the classroom, i.e., they are not amenable unless more than one speaker's contribution to the utterance is considered.

This approach differs from two others. First, some coding schemes recognizes a somewhat similar phenomena when they treat answers to yes-no questions. Answers to those questions are coded as operating at a low cognitive level, thereby operationalizing the view that (1) speakers of these utterances may be merely responding to the form of the question and (2) any inference about the utterance's meaning based on the question that preceded it is unwarranted on the possibility that the answer was generated by a guess. So, (37) is distinguished from (38) on the basis of cognitive complexity and the probability of guessing.

(37) A: Did ethnomethodology originate in sociology?
B: Yes

(38) A: In what field did ethnomethodology originate?
B: Sociology

In these kinds of analyses, the 'yes' in (37) can be attributed to Speaker A as much as Speaker B, whereas this is not the case with 'sociology' in (38), or for any of the cases we have considered to be the social construction of two speakers. The approach we prefer considers not only yes-no questions, but the full range of question types to be social constructions. Furthermore, it treats the property of vagueness as an inherent part of the operation of all teacher-student sequences and when these appear in lesson sequences like (15), there is a reasonable account for their appearance as an utterance co-constructed as unambiguous and clear by the learner and the instructor as an educational method. On other occasions, outside of learning events we (and we believe the participants) would grant the full specific non-vague form of a yes-no response and expect the chance of guessing to be encoded by other possible utterances like "maybe," or "I don't know."

Second, the approach we prefer differs from previous analyses of reflexivity in conversation. While we agree that a question is a question by virtue of there being an answer present or presentable, and an answer is an answer by virtue of there having been a question present that sense of reflexivity maintains that the production of an utterance provides for its interpretation by others, and is provided for by its interpretability by others. By contrast, the sense of reflexivity that we are considering suggests that some utterances are designedly vague, and require for their construction as a contribution to the discourse, that some next turn participate in their specification. It is not merely that the contribution of the non-speaking interlocutor is to add an interpretation to the production of an utterance; it is, rather, that multi-party co-production is involved for the construction of an utterance as the utterance it turns out to have been in the first place.

The conventional wisdom about schooling includes the view that children enter school as *tabula rasa,* to be etched with the knowledge necessary not only for performance in school, but for life after school as well. This conception treats the process of education as accretion; knowledge is added to knowledge step by step until the requisite total amount of cognitive and technical skills is reached.

Our experience with the teaching-learning process in elementary schools suggests an alternative view. It seems that students come to school with a wide variety of experience and varying interpretations of the world. Schooling, having identified some forms of knowledge as correct and proper, subtracts other forms of knowledge from the student's repertoire. It is evident in the occurrence of sequences that include vague utterances like (15), (Tab), that a child brings this repertoire to school and that teachers choose among the items in the child's repertoire to accomplish with him his education. Thus, instead of making entries on a blank slate, teaching in school seems to be involved in erasing entries from a too full slate.

CONCLUSIONS

We have considered some of the sociolinguistic complexities of lessons – the simultaneity of functions of utterances, the fine play between ritual and spontaneous motifs, and the mutual accomplishment of linguistic acts. These views of what people assembling lessons are doing have consequences for views of what people must be like, and what the language code they use as a resource must be like. The people are able to construct turns at talk that do many kinds of work at once; they are able to rely on the historical ritual aspects of a speech event, and they create, modify, and manipulate those aspects as they act to maintain them from moment to moment.

As a consequence, the language code must have two kinds of properties: first, properties such that the restrictions and options that account for the construction of appropriate utterances – the grammar – have access to principles that coordinate the selection and restriction of simultaneous functions; second, properties such that spontaneous utterances are not viewed as *de novo,* and can be related to the ritual properties of speech events.

The cases examined here point out the inadequacy of linguistic evidence based on a restricted set of abstract types of utterances, rather than on classes of contextualized tokens of utterances. Furthermore, they, like G. Lakoff's amalgamated sentences, suggest the insufficiency of a grammar that requires only that a single underlying form be related to each surface structure.

A final challenge to views of the code and the people who use it is one that particularly calls attention to the term sociolinguistics. We see more and more substance to that term, as it captures the sense that language operates in *social* situations, as a *social* act.

The data also addresses central issues in education. The model of the child as an actor in the performance of education in the school is as an active participant in the construction of knowledge, not as a passive recipient of received information. We do not see students as empty vessels being filled with knowledge by teachers, but teachers and students collaboratively constructing the very vessels which provide for the possibility of knowledge.

The increased interest in social interaction and language use in classrooms has led some to the conclusion that social or interactional competence is a necessary companion or supplement to academic knowledge. While we have come to appreciate the necessity for classroom participants to be attuned to the subtleties of interactional contours, we find no justification in treating interactional competence as an entity separate from academic knowledge, nor as an entity subsidiary to it. The academic and interactional aspects of schooling seem to be involved in each other to such a degree that it is impossible to separate them; as complementary processes of a single mechanism, they seem indissociable except for heuristic purposes.

NOTE

1. We would not claim that next speaker selection procedures are the same as turn allocation procedures, because speaker selection procedures are: (1) not role restricted; (2) not as frequent; (3) not overtly taught; (4) not as overtly sanctioned; (5) there is no equivalent of the "invitation to bid" procedure.

JOCHEN REHBEIN

Announcing—On Formulating Plans

ABSTRACT

After a general discussion of preparatory activities (§1) the pattern of announcing is developed in its structure with each position of the pattern being discussed separately (§§2.1–2.3). Particular aspects of announcing and forms of its realization are looked at (§§2.4 and 2.5.). Three aspects of the purpose of announcing are pointed out, followed by an investigation of the tasks announcing fulfills in the organization of joint action (§3). In §4, a range of different elements which partition the discourse in a way similar to announcements but which are different in their communicative category is to be analyzed: pre-fixed announcements, pre-fixations, pres, connectors, stand-ins. The specific role of pre-announcements is accounted for in §4.6. Introductions are found to serve entirely different tasks than announcements (§5). Two institutionalized forms of discourse, newspaper headlines (§6) and moderating in TV-reports (§7), are dealt with as having something in common with announcements. §8 gives a summarizing chart of the phenomena discussed in the paper.

1. PREPARATORY ACTIVITIES[1]

The greater the division of labor in a society, the more disparate is the distribution of social knowledge amongst its members, thus necessitating media that provide actors with the essential knowledge for the realization of their action-potential. Should such media not have a routine form then speech actions are necessary which organize the disparate amounts of knowledge and the action-potentials of actors, or groups of actors, *for a certain period of co-operation*. It is from this need that the tasks of preparatory activities arise.

The more complex a society, however, the more frequently a contradiction arises. The knowledge about what will take place increases, but only as far as society as a whole is concerned. This knowledge is almost always unequally distributed. Some social actors have more knowledge and consequently more certainty about future events, others have less, so that, in case of joint activities, this contradiction has to be solved. In order to solve these contradictions different forms of *preparatory activities* have been developed.

Actions and occurrences which are of importance to a society and which demand the co-operation of many actors, particularly joint production under unforeseen conditions, are therefore unthinkable without preceding distribution of social knowledge. Actions and occurrences of this kind appear in different social formations according to the respective forms of division of labor.

This is why ethnolinguists are also interested in preparations for co-operation. For example, Whorf (1956) already pointed out the importance of preparatory activities and their various shapes in different societies. The example of the Indians' hunter society lead him to make the following observations:

> A characteristic of Hopi behavior is the emphasis on preparation. This includes announcing and getting ready for events well beforehand, elaborate precautions to insure persistence of desired conditions, and stress on good will as the preparer of right results . . . This Hopi preparing behavior may be roughly divided into announcing, outer preparing, inner preparing, covert participation, and persistence. Announcing, or preparative publicity, is an important function in the hands of a special official, the Crier Chief. Outer preparing is preparation involving much visible activity, not all necessarily directly useful within our understanding . . . (Whorf (1939) (1956, pp. 148-49)).

This shows: With the Hopi preparations were given an institutional form by making them the charge of certain people. The members of the tribe have to attune their activities with regard to the expected event, whereby the different conceptions of time, particularly those which stem from coping with nature, play a significant role (and which aroused Whorf's curiosity). However, preparations have not always developed into institutions.

Ethnomethodology, too, has directed its attention to preparations, namely under the aspect of a phenomenology of beginning. Proceeding from a reflection on gatherings, Turner (1972) analyzed the start of a therapeutic session. In this respect he also discusses announcements, namely with regard to their task of leading the participants towards a joint start of the session. Turner refers to Moerman (1969), who studied the beginning of negotiations amongst the Lue in Thailand, where announcements form an institutionalized transition to the substantial part of a trial.

In fact, however, Moerman deals with openings which, by means of an *explicit speech action,* mark the beginning of a court case, thereby placing all further activities up to the explicit end within a *framework* and precisely determing the *main* activity and the *side* activity of the participants (cf. op. cit. pp. 460-464).

In the aforementioned studies preparation, commencement, beginning etc. and announcements are indiscriminately dealt with together. The functional relationship between these various activities is mentioned but not worked out[2] according to its "inner mechanism".[3] What one has to do in order to find the inner mechanism is to analyze these activities in themselves, the various forms of their realizations and to contrast them with related forms of speech.

It is the aim of this paper to show that announcing represents a *pattern* of communicative action which the actors can resort to when wanting to reach an understanding about their plans. The job of announcements in a co-operative action is to make known a decision which the actor has taken entirely by himself. Thus announcements are characteristic of *non-collective decisions* whereas *co-operation* during the execution is demanded by the intended results. However, announcements are not obligatory in the course of an action but only appear if considered necessary by the announcer.

The pattern of announcement is employed differently in various settings which show a division between people competent to make plans and people not competent to make plans. It is not restricted to a specific institution but is a complete unit of interaction in itself which, as a whole, is spontaneously applicable. Its function lies in the production of a common basis for the execution of a future action (see below §3.3. p. 234f.).

In more recent studies announcements are classified as "metacommunicative speech acts" (cf. Meyer-Hermann (1978, p. 136)). This is correct to a certain extent. Yet if one takes such utterances as 'By the way, tomorrow, I'll carry some furniture into the cellar' or, 'Listen, I wanted to let you know that I'll start exercise y tomorrow' show that the announced actions ('carrying some furniture into the cellar,' 'starting exercise y') are in no way linked to a linguistic interaction in their execution. Although it is important to analyze announcements according to their referents (see Meyer-Hermann), these referents are not "objects" (Objekte) but what is referred to by the speaker are *plans for* "objects". As they include the execution of an action we look upon these "objects" as being *actions.*

2. THE STRUCTURE OF ANNOUNCING

2.1. Example and Methodological Remark

(E1) This example is taken from a school lesson. The transcribed text is reproduced in a segmentary form. The teacher starts a new topic in the middle of the lesson; she says:

(s1) Gut.
(s2) So.
(s3) Jetzt machen wir etwas ganz anderes,

(s4) was richtig Gutes.
(s5) Und zwar gehen wir'tz einkaufen ... ähm ... zum Lebensmittelhändler.
(s6) Jetzt möchte ich gern von euch hören, was ... ihr da alles einkaufen könnt, nich?

(270379/5.Kl./German/f/G)

The phenomenon we are dealing with is found in the segments (s3)-(s5): In (s3) "now" ('tz = jetzt) states a point in time which is going to follow the actual time of speech. Secondly, the speaker's intentions are mentioned, and this statement consists of the lexical elements (a) "do something completely different" (etwas ganz anderes machen) (b) "something really good" (was richtig Gutes) (c) "to the grocer's" (zum Lebensmittelhändler) "to shopping" (einkaufen gehen), whereby "now" (jetzt) is repeated once again. (s4) is a comment in relation to (s3), (s5) is an elucidation in relation to (s3); they are therefore speech actions which operate on that in (s3). All in all, we consider the text as a complex form of announcing.

This example outlines the general structure of announcements the elaboration of which makes it necessary to clarify the framework of the *basic situation* in which announcements are employed.

A basic situation contains a certain number of possible forms of action which are repetitive, in the realization of which a certain number of speech actions systematically play a part. We call a basic situation such as this a '*constellation*' (see Rehbein [1977] and Ehlich & Rehbein [1979]). The following analysis of the speech action **announcing**[4] therefore takes into consideration the underlying constellation. The significance of this analytical implication will become clear when announcing is confronted with other speech actions the constellative feature of which is to refer to future occurrences, such as **threat, prediction** etc.

Not to be dealt with here is that type of "announcement" which refers to objective circumstances from which a percipient actor can infer a future event – e.g., an "announcement" of a crisis, thunderstorm etc. In such cases one should talk of a 'sign'. We take as announcements utterances of human actors only.

2.2 Elements of Announcing

The elements of announcing analyzed below are constitutional. They were gained from an analysis of the everyday concept confronted by texts and semi-empirical examples. The procedure is as follows:

- The elements will be presented in a relatively abstract manner; most of the examples will be given in discussing phenomena closely related to announcing.
- The pattern of announcing is phased in 'prehistory', 'history' and 'post-history' and its analysis follows these lines in order to build up a 'scheme' in which the elements are summarized in their individual functions.
- The *pre-history* of announcing is mainly of a mental kind and consists of three elements: the plan (§2.2.1.), the speaker's relationship to the plan (§2.2.2.) and the unpreparedness of the hearer (§2.2.3.).

2.2.1. Plan for Future Action

We proceed from the fact that an action is to be carried out in the future. (The future action will be referred to as 'G'.) It is not taken into consideration whether the action is to be carried out by one of the actors who is present or whether it is to be delegated. In example (E1) this action is to "go shopping" (einkaufen gehen) (s5).

The formation of a plan for G is already completed before the time of the speech action and thus also the decision-making process as such, i.e., at the time of the speech action a plan for G already exists in the space of action.

Two things have to be considered: Firstly, in speaking of a plan I mean a *complete* plan not only a vague intention to act. Complete plans can be either mental or institutional (see Rehbein [1977 §5.4.3.], [1976]).

In the plan for G the realization of G is *pre-organized,* this for example is the case when the next program is announced on the radio or when a person announces what he is going to do. The pre-organization of G in the plan for G is reflected in the speaker's *knowledge of the completed process of forming a plan.*

Secondly, when a "present space of action" is referred to later on, this is relative to a *certain time space of speech,* namely to the space in a certain period of time in which the actor makes the utterance; the plan for action G is always relative to the time space of speech. The formation of a plan as such is completed, yet the realization of the action has not yet started. We have to note the following: Between the plan for and the factual occurrence of G there is a temporal "gap" and it is exactly there that announcements find their place. There is no point in announcing an action after its having become an irrevocable fact or its being already realized.

2.2.2. The Speaker's Relationship to the Plan

As a result of the complete plan the speaker (:S) has a certain relationship to the occurrence of G. This relationship is rather complex.

In order to clarify matters we have to bring to mind an analysis of the '*modal apparatus*' designed by Ehlich & Rehbein (1972, p. 329) regarding the modality of '*shall*' (werden). The basis of a 'shall' (werden) is always an 'ability' (können), in two cases also a 'want to' (wollen), and in a third case a 'have to' (müssen) instead of a 'want to' (wollen). In a similar way we can determine the relationship of the speaker to the plan for G.

On the part of the speaker, these components of modality bring about a *resolution of execution* (Ausführungsentschluß):

(a) The speaker has gained *certainty of his ability* to execute the action. It is interesting how 'ability' is acquired because it does not refer to already existing conditions of realization but to those which lie in the future. The future space of action has therefore to be *anticipated* by the speaker in order to find out whether the action is feasible or not.

While it is irrelevant whether the speaker made the plan himself or made use of already existing plans, it is important that he has certainty of the feasibility of G (see above §2.2.1.). The speaker gains certainty by means of several procedures of anticipation, one of which is the mechanism of belief, i.e., a mechanism which works on routinized procedures of anticipation.

(b) The speaker has developed a *motivation* for the action, i.e., he has created a 'want to'. This 'want to' has been especially thematised when forming the plan, or rather, when adopting the plan. The motivation can be separated and replaced by a mostly institutional necessity (as is at least partly the case in school curricula as in (E1): then there is a 'have to').

Both components, 'ability' and 'want to' (or 'have to'), when combined form an important part of the illocutionary force of the announcement, in as far as the latter contains elements of the pre-history with regard to the speaker; they constitute the resolution of execution.

According to the analysis in Rehbein (1977), I refer to a *resolution of execution* as a separate element in the process of the formation of a plan. The resolution of execution leads up to the concrete realization of the action aimed at during the speech situation of the announcement. This shows the reason why **announcements** are not simply indications of planning activity.

2.2.3. Unpreparedness of the Hearer

The *direct* pre-history of the announcement starts with the speaker's and hearer's lines of action drawing nearer to one another, without their already being involved in a joint process of action. The approach of the lines of action to one another often result from the fact that the actors have come into touch for some other reason. If for example persons assemble in a hall for a meeting, an **announcement** can be made that a collection will take place at the end of the meeting. In this case the meeting is only used as an opportunity. The lines of action followed by the actors S and H at close quarters are called A_S and A_H; they constitute a common *space of action A*.

Another condition belongs to the direct pre-history: As a result of his observation or from other sources of information, or from inference of plausibility or anticipation of the hearer's (:H) activity, the speaker has the impression, that a space of action *could* develop from the given situation in the space of action A, in which the hearer does not consider the future action G to take place, i.e., a space of action in which H will be surprised by the occurrence of G. This space of action is the *space of action G* which would take place in the "normal course of events" if the announcement did not occur, whereas the *space of action G* is the one H is prepared for because of the announcement. Now, as far as G is concerned, the hearer is *without a focus.* He may have an abstract pre-knowledge of G but he knows nothing about its planned occurrence.

The speaker will have to stop or at least *interrupt the activity in the space of action A,* in order to enable the hearer to take notice of the speech action of announcing at all. An intervention such as this comes unexpectedly to the hearer. An interruption of H's activity in the space of A is achieved by the speaker by means of specific elements, as in (E1) by the use of "all right" (so) or by means of addressing "by the way" (übrigens) etc., in short, by elements which indicate the end of an ongoing activity and the beginning of a new one, i.e., a change in the lines of action. We call such elements '*caesura-elements*'[5] according to their function, and label them with A, because they interrupt the activity A.

Announcements always occupy the first position within a sequence of action. By using the caesura-element A this first position is effected discoursively. (Another type of caesura-element will be dealt with in the discussion of the sequential closing of announcements; cf. § 2.2.6. below.)

2.2.4. Propositional Structure, Scheme Verbalization and Time Indication

In the following (§ § 2.2.4., 2.2.5.), we will enter into the *history* of announcing which covers both a speaker and a hearer section in which the actual speech action is produced and received. First of all let us discuss the propositional act, and afterwards the illocutionary function.

In announcing the speaker makes an utterance in which he discoursively relates to the plan for the future action G. This relation can be either verbal, or non-verbal (as by an "expressive smile" [vielsagendes Lächeln] etc.). The less explicit the realization of the announcing, the greater the pre-knowledge of the hearer has to be: Otherwise, it would be impossible, for example, for the speaker to announce the ommission of an action by a wave of his hand. In any case, words or signs have to be of such a kind that the hearer can figure out the future action. Thus, the utterance has the force of a *representation of the future action G* within the space of action A which is constituted by other elements.

The representation of G contains both: the relation to the plan, i.e., the '*schematized rendering*' of the plan, and the indication of that *point in time* when G is supposed to be executed. Both elements are realized in the utterance and mark its propositional structure.

Consider the following two examples:

"I won't have time *for hours*" (Stundenlang hab ich *nicht* Zeit) ((E6); p. 232f. below): The speaker states that a break-off of an envisaged appointment (action G) will be necessary after a certain span of time, without using the term "break off" nor giving a precise indication of time. In ((E3) p. 227) we find: "We shall read the real story of Robinson Crusoe" (wir werden die richtige Robinson Crusoe Geschichte lesen). Obviously, it is sufficient to mention the *name* in order to picture the activity, without developing in detail what the "real story" (richtige Geschichte) consists of.

Firstly we will discuss the schematized rendering of the plan. The speaker of the announcement uses *names, catchwords, abbreviations, key-words* etc. for the different kinds of action which he announces. Very often he uses *nominalizations* (at least in German), often *verbs* which *describe activities* and expressions which *designate speech actions.*[6] Thus he operates on the common knowledge: What he does is to categorize in advance the future action G according to the categories of knowledge which are considered to be well-known by the hearer and to belong to his everyday activities (otherwise the speaker would have to be more explicit when making a normal announcement). This categorization in advance is what I call '*scheme*' of action.[7]

It is just these schemes that form a part of the propositional content of announcing. To be precise, what is called 'scheme' here is dependent on the *form* which transfers the propositional content to the hearer. The propositional content is always a function of the speaker's knowledge about the hearer's knowledge; but it is the linguistic form which conveys this knowledge and opens the hearer's relevant domain of knowledge. As a result, in the propositional content of an announcement future actions are schematized.

Going on further, we can say that it is a characteristic of schemes that they are summaries or abbreviations of plans. It is not necessary for the plan to be rendered as a whole; in fact, this is seldom the case. Moreover, the plan for a future action is not pictured as a whole in the speaker's and hearer's space of imagination (Vorstellungsraum) before the actual moment of its realization. And in the case of announcements the realization is not yet at hand. The scheme suffices to give the hearer a rough picture of the future action. On the linguistic surface schemes often *appear* as *summarizing characterizations* of the future action. Such characterizations can have many different forms, e.g., that of a global assessment.

In this respect, Kallmeyer (1978) by the term of 'pre-elucidation' (vorgreifende Verdeutlichung) obviously refers to the scheme's force of categorizing in advance. However, in announcements one does not always meet with "elucidations" as this would imply the *elaboration* of the future act which is just being announced. Contrary to Kallmeyer, it has to be noted that the announcer verbalizes a knowledge about a *plan*. This means that the speaker does not have to know every *individual* step of the plan; this is rather a matter of the execution, in which the plan is put into concrete terms in the space of action G. "Plan" is not to be understood in a cognitive rationalistic sense only but as comprehending programs for *different* kinds of activities; in many cases, plans are acquired through socialization, the actors therefore not necessarily being aware of them. Thus schemes, as verbalizations of plans, only issue those parts of the plan that the speaker himself is conscious of.

The *indication of a point in time* is the second element in the propositional structure of announcing and covers an *entire class of expressions* such as 'soon,' 'at the end of,' 'later,' etc., by which the speaker indicates the *anchoring point* of his activity, i.e., the start of the realization of the action; he indicates the point of transformation of the execution of the plan. The indication of the point in time is the indication of the future which localizes the "*Hic-et-nunc*-point," that is the *origo* of the future action G with regard to the present time space of speech (in the space of action A). In other words, the communication of the existing plan for G is so specific that it is possible for the hearer to localize the point in time in his mentally preconstructed time axis. (*Hic-et-nunc*-point cf. Bühler (1934), Rehbein (1977), Ehlich (1979)).

2.2.5. On the Illocutionary Act of **Announcing**

In general, the illocutionary act constitutes the action-related component of a form of speech. In the present case of announcements this component is specified in two ways:

(1) *Exothesis of the Resolution of Execution*
In the illocution the speaker combines the elements of 'ability' and 'want to' or 'have to' which he gained from the pre-history and places them in a synthetical form in the space of interaction. In their purest form announcements contain an 'I will.' This 'I will' is the result of an immediate transformation of a mental "event" into a verbal expression; processes of this kind are referred to by the term 'exothesis' (cf. the analyses of the *different* processes resulting in the expression of 'shall' (werden) in Ehlich & Rehbein (1972); also Redder (1980)). In announcements, we often also find utterances of the type 'I want to do p.' If it can be concluded from the context that the speaker *can* indeed execute the action, then this utterance is also interpreted as an announcement; the same is true for 'I have to do p,' if the person *can* execute the action. 'I will,' then, contains either 'can' and 'want to' or 'can' and 'have to.'

(2) *The Mental Activity of the Hearer*
By the utterance, a relationship towards the future action is set up in the hearer which bears the following characteristic aspects:
   (a) The hearer *receives* information about a future action which will occur independantly of his own relationship towards it.
   (b) The information provides him with an orientation which makes him go beyond the existing speech situation. Thus the hearer is given a *new focus.* I call the focus towards the future action 'F_G', the existing focus towards the presently existing activity A the focus 'F_A'.

The consequences H may draw from this new focus are not specified; the only important fact is that the hearer knows something about the plan for an action now which is not yet in the actual space of action A; the receiving of the speech action has constituted a second space of action (space of action G) *within* the first space of action.

With regard to the focus formation on the part of H, a development seems to be important which to my mind has not been taken into consideration adequately so far. The focus of H stretches out beyond something which he neither sees nor perceives in any other way, but which is located outside his direct field of action. Focusses concerned with immediately perceivable objects are directly confirmed by perception; in such cases the mental process is directly controlled by reality. This is not the case here. Rather the hearer gets a focus which, as a result of the speech procedures, relates to something represented by signs only. Such a focus necessarily employs already existing elements of the hearer's knowledge and its structures of relevance. The focus as a selective instrument for guiding the attention, is steered by that part of the hearer's knowledge which is actualized by what the speaker says. This focus therefore is a '*prolonged focus*'. The prolonged focus correlates, on the part of the hearer, to the speaker's plan for action G.

It is characteristic of an announcement that a focus towards the planned action G must not previously exist on the part of the hearer; the following example (E2) demonstrates this in a negative way:

(E2)	1	B	Ich brauch äh doch Unterlagen für Kundenfahrten, nicht?
		A	Ja. Hm.
	2	B	Ja, im Februar/Februar
		A	Und wann willst du den wieder eine machen, B? Ja. Hm.
	3	B	März.
		A	Ja, aber jetzt mußt du natürlich erst das Semester zuende
	4	B	Ja, öh leider.
		A	bringen, ne?

(Texts III, p. 63)

In this case **precision** (in 2) about a project of B is requested by A. This means that the hearer A is already familiar with B's plan. A demands information about the point in time of B's planned activity (wieder eine machen). This shows that the hearer was previously focussed *before* the speaker's information "in February, March" (hence, no announcement).

In sum, the task of the illocution of an announcement is to depict a plan for a future action and to shift the hearer's attention towards it.

2.2.6. Post-history: Caesura-Element G; Point in Time of the Realization of the Planned Action

As pointed out in § 2.2.1. the action, the plan for which the speaker indicates in his announcement, must not have already taken place. This criterion is important in order to be able to differentiate **announcements** from **introductions** (see below §5). Although the point in time of the execution is not clearly marked in all announcements it is always clearly apparent during practical action. On the surface, the start of such realizations marked by a hic-et-nunc-point, a point in the line of action which makes the transformation of the planning become obvious and signalizes a caesura (segmental borderline) in the interaction. Anchoring points and realization of actions vary in their stretch of time; but we do not want to go into this, rather we want to consider the discrete separation of announcing, and the anchoring point (the start of the announced action). There is a clear segmental borderline between them which drastically separates the history from the post-history of announcing. The hearer then makes a number of preparatory activities under the new orientation of the focus F_G, which he is able to find through practical inferences anticipating G.

2.3. Summarized Scheme of the Announcement

If we summarize the individual elements of announcing with regard to pre-history, history and post-history we get the following picture of the *structural scheme*:

Pre-history

(1) Regarding a time space of speech there is a complete plan for an action G, either mentally or objectively;

(2) S has both an 'ability' and a 'want to' or a 'have to' with regard to the planned action G;

(3) S and H are involved in a common activity A (which constitutes a space of action A with-focus F_A of H);

(4) S utters an element, through which the common activity A is interrupted (caesura-element A);

History

(5) S makes an utterance in which
  (a) S verbalizes the scheme of the future action;
  (b) S indicates the point in time of the realization of the future action;
  (c) S communicates a resolution of execution, in pure form with 'I will' (exothesis);
  (d) H develops a new focus F_G (prolonged focus F_G) and anticipates the space of action G;

(6) Segmental caesura between space of action A and space of action G (caesura-element G);

Post-history

(7) Preparatory activities of H (and S) with regard to G, between space of action A and space of action G.

The different steps (1)-(7) of the structural scheme are called '*positions of the pattern*'.

2.4. Weak Announcements

In order to illustrate the abstract analysis above, we shall discuss an example taken from the material of transcripts:

(E3) During a lesson, the pupils solve problems in team work. The teacher converses with several children quietly. Suddenly she raises her voice and says:

1 L Wir reden vielleicht/Wir werden vielleicht am Ende,[8]
2 L wenn wir mit unserer Unterrichtseinheit fertig sind,
3 L mal die richtige Robinson Crusoe Geschichte lesen.
4 L Das stimmt zum Teil nicht, da habt ihr völlig recht.
S_1 Stimmt
5 S^1 alles nicht.

(181174/7/G+P/f/GS/p. 14)

In this example the different positions of the pattern of announcing are scattered throughout the text: "We shall" (wir werden) is the exothesis of the resolution of execution ((5c) in the structural scheme); the personal pronoun "we" (wir) reflects the teacher's power to dispose of the process of thematizing for which she alone makes the resolution; "at the end" (am Ende) is an adverbial clause of time which indicates the point in time of realization, whereby the temporal expansion "when we have finished our unit" (wenn wir mit unserer Unterrichtseinheit fertig sind) describes the type of common activity, in which S and H are involved (activity A). Therefore position (5b) is taken as well as position (3), whereby the point in time of realization is related to the given time space of speech. Simultaneously, the temporal specification also adopts the function of determining a caesura between the action presently being performed and the announced action G (in other words position (6)). The verbalization of the scheme (position (5a)) is given with "to read the real story of Robinson Crusoe" (die richtige Robinson Crusoe Geschichte lesen), from which the pupils can infer the entire action.

The announcement in (E3) is, however, not distinctly marked; there is a restriction by the particle "perhaps" (vielleicht). (Incidentally, the repair shows that "perhaps" (vielleicht) is fully intentional and not just coincidental). The particle refers to the *illocutionary force of the utterance*: The speaker therefore makes the execution dependent upon certain conditions. Let us recall that the pre-history of the resolution of execution must contain ability (position (2)): This ability is questioned by "perhaps" (vielleicht) and blocked to a certain extent. In this way the illocutionary force manifesting in "we shall" (wir werden) is *depotentiated*, so that we are only dealing with a weak announcement. (The procedure of depotentiating the illocutionary force is shown by Ehlich & Rehbein [1977a], [1977b], and Rehbein [1979a] on empirical grounds).

Now, where do we have the caesura-element A (position (4)), by which the activity of the speaker and hearer is interrupted in order to initiate the announcement? In the above example the caesura-element is *not lexical,* but is realized by *intonation*: It is by raising her voice that the teacher intervenes.

2.5. Realization Matrix of Announcements

We will now discuss the *utterance act* of the given pattern of action. Analytically we are dealing with the verbalization *product* (or utterance product) which comprises a number of speaker and hearer activities without their being directly recognizable. As a result of this, an interpretation which considers the linguistic surface only is in danger of becoming entangled in the jungle of different forms of realization which by themselves are non-suggestive of the underlying structure of the pattern. Nevertheless, we want to take a look at the realization forms of announcements in order not to give the impression that the analysis elaborates the abstract elements only, ignoring all facts of speech. The following elements often appear to be linguistically realized:

(1) *One of the actually acting persons in the speech situation* as 'I,' 'we;' not: 'you' sgl./pl. ('ich,' 'wir;' nicht: 'du,' 'ihr') is referred to (subject position). The addressee(s) adopt(s) the object position of the future activity (frequently but not necessarily).

(2) An element by means of which the speaker indicates the *certainty of his knowledge* about the future: The speaker believes that a state of affairs will occur. Often such a declaration is made by using the future morpheme; in German, also the present tense has such a function:[9] 'ich esse etwas' can either be translated as 'I shall eat something' ('je vais manger quelque chose'), and, in this case, may count as an **announcement**; or as 'I am eating something' ('je suis en train de manger quelque chose') in which case the utterance may count as an **assertion**, the English and the French language being more precise here. The usage of the modal 'want to' (wollen) can also refer to a future state of affairs, and the same applies to 'should' and 'have to' because these verbs express an obligation for the actor which can force him to bring about a future act. The use of the *verba dicendi* also adds to the credibility of what the speaker says: 'Peter *said* he would come' (Peter hat gesagt, daß er kommt). Verba dicendi *designating speech acts* show that the speaker

has reason to believe, as a result of an utterance made by an actor that an action will occur.

The linguistic element which indicates the certainty of knowledge simultaneously links the speaker to the existing plan via its utterance; the speaker therefore gains his certainty from his conviction of the existence of the plan. Should the speaker employ expressions such as 'perhaps' (vielleicht), 'I believe that' (ich glaube, daß) etc., he then indicates that the mechanism of belief no longer functions with him. This is the case with weak announcements (cf. § 2.4. p. 227).

(3) *Indication of the point in time,* when the execution of the action will occur ('soon,' 'in a minute,' 'now,' 'then,' 'later,' 'in two hours,' 'at the end of,' 'the day after tomorrow' etc.). The body of elements of this *class of expressions* and their usage has to be examined more closely; all we can say now is that they have to be indications of the future. *Indications of the future* do two things at a time: They indicate the point in time *when* the state of affairs (according to the speaker's knowledge) will occur (thus the *Hic-et-nunc*-point of the action in the space of action G), and they indicate the relationship to the actual time of speech. Indications of the future represent a temporal point in time of the realization of the action; they shift a future action into the hearer's domain of knowledge.

(4) *Linguistic presentation of the action* which is yet to be performed: This formulation takes place on an informative basis; on the one hand use is made of the hearer's pre-knowledge (as far as this is supposed by the speaker) and on the other hand, the action is not formulated in detail but only in catch-words etc. (cf. § 2.2.4.) which are sufficient to identify and to represent the planned action in the hearer's space of imagination. Here the *aspects* and the *nominalizations*[10] of verbs become relevant. This formulation is what was called above a 'scheme' of the future action.

(5) Direct/indirect reference to the immediately preceding and/or immediately subsequent action in which speaker and hearer are involved. This is done by *caesura indicating* elements (caesura-elements A and G) added to the beginning and the end of the announcement-discourse.

We summarize these components in the following matrix:

(A)	(a)	(b)	(c)	(d)	(e)	(G)
caesura-element A	persons in the speech situation (subject/object position)	exothesis 'shall' (werden)	indication of the future	scheme of future action G	reference to present action A	caesura-element G

With reference to this matrix we wish to discuss the example given above (E3) (p. 227):

(a) The persons of the speech situation are "we" (wir);
(b) the exothesis of resolution is "shall" (werden), whereby the teacher refers to a plan she has in mind;
(c) the indication of the future is "at the end" (am Ende), and is determined more precisely with "when we have finished the unit" (wenn wir mit der Unterrichtseinheit fertig sind);
(d) scheme of the action: "read the Robinson Crusoe story" (die Robinson Crusoe Geschichte lesen);
(e) the reference to an element of the present action is more indirect; it is contained in "the *real* . . . story" (die *richtige* . . . Geschichte), i.e., the present story which is the actual point at issue in the space of action A is only partly dealt with under certain aspects.

2.6. Incidental Announcements

In connection with the forms of realization of announcing, a further phenomenon has to be dealt with. Let us proceed from the example (E2):

(E4)			
1	B	Das macht nichts. Mir einmal nicht. Ich brauch äh doch	
2	B	Unterlagen für Kundfahrten, nicht?	
	A		Ja. Hm. Und wann willst
3	B		Ja, im Februar/Februar, März.
	A	du denn wieder eine machen, B?	

In response to B's utterance that he needs "forms" (Unterlagen) for his "tour" (Kundfahrten), A does not go into the forms but makes further enquiries about the project of going on a tour. A has obviously focussed his attention on this matter.

In example (E4) it becomes clear that the hearer A interprets the utterance of B "I do need forms for my tours" (Ich brauch doch Unterlagen für Kundfahrten) as an announcement of further tours. With this interpretation A places the focus differently from how *the speaker B sees the relevance of his utterance*; to A the relevance of the utterance lies in "forms" (Unterlagen) and not in "tours" (Kundfahrten). Phenomena of this kind, in which the hearer "spells out" an announcement from an utterance which is not in the speaker's domain of relevance, can be looked upon as '*incidental announcements*'.

Such phenomena could also be referred to as 'implications' (Andeutungen) had they not been described in an unequivocal sense by Kallmeyer (1978). Implications particularly refer to the relevant points of the utterance. The phenomenon of the 'incidental announcement' is therefore dealt with under the forms of realization because, in principle, it is valid for many realizations of speech actions; a hearer often interprets the relevance of an utterance differently from what was meant by the speaker (cf. for 'implications' below §4.6. see note 19, p. 258).

Incidental announcements are frequent because the activity of the hearer plays an important part in this linguistic pattern and produces misinterpretations. *Many utterances make passing reference to plans* which, with the pre-knowledge of the hearer on the one hand and his willingness to focus on the other, are to be interpreted as announcements.

3. PURPOSE OF ANNOUNCING

The pattern of announcing differs from related forms, among other things, in that it is not closed but aims at a future participation of the hearer in the announced action. Related forms are for example **assertions** since they can show a similar linguistic surface (see § 2.5. (2) p. 228).

As opposed to announcements **assertions** only give information about something which the hearer wishes to know: The speaker is not interested in the further processing (action-wise) of the imparted knowledge. Even if the speaker informs a hearer about a plan – which is not exactly the standard case of asserting – it is wrong to talk of an announcement if a further participation of the hearer is not desired; because **assertions** are interactionally closed (a detailed analysis of assertions can be found in Ehlich & Rehbein (1979)).

Let us discuss the function of announcing under three aspects: the *co-ordination* of the action, the *pre-construed* activity of the hearer and the *role in institutions.*

3.1. Co-ordination of Action

Announcements belong to a group of linguistic means by which the action of all participants is co-ordinated. To that extent announcements are meant to co-operatively organize the actual practice taking place in a space of action which is already institutionally pre-organized. The job of announcements is to relate the actual processes of action as far as their starting point is concerned to underlying plans which are repetitive and mostly of an institutional character; determined by underlying plans announcements *partition* the discourse.

(E5) (From a breakfast-conversation)

1	B	Mama, ich komme heute mittag nicht. Nein.
	A	Wieder nicht nach Hause.
2	B	Weißt du, warum?
	A	Ja, also, das geht doch nicht so weiter, du!
3	B	Weil mir das viel zu dumm ist, so weit zu laufen.
	A	Wär grad recht
4	B	Machst du mir jetzt zwei . . . Brote? 'N ganzen
	A	für dich, grad gesund.
5	B	Tag.
	A	Ja, aber das Gemüse fehlt ja doch.

(Texts III, p. 72/73)

The announcement "I am not going to come this afternoon" (ich komme heute mittag nicht) evokes a dispute in the course of which A has to put up with the "not coming." The announcement partitions both the preparations which have to be made, and hence the next steps which have to be taken as well as the mother's entire plans for the day with regard to her actions concerning her daughter. "Mama" is, incidentally, the caesura-element A by means of which the speaker prepares the announcement.

Occasionally, the task of announcements has been determined by their classification into the group of metacommunicative speech actions (Wiegand, Meyer-Hermann (1978)). This "metacommunicative function," however, remains to be clarified, since they refer not only to communication in general, but to an action, which can be processed both verbally and non-verbally.

(E6) (A and B are arranging an appointment)

1	A	Äh aber das muß ich dir voraussagen: studenlang hab ich nicht

2	A	Zeit, ne? Ich bin/ich bin nämlich wieder in Bedrückung äh
	B	Das begreif ich, A. Wie/was
3	A	Ja. Also In Druck, ja . . . . . Insofern, als ich öh mein
	B	heißt? In Druck? Ja, ja. Hm.
4	A	Papier für den NN-zwei fertig machen muß, und das wäre gestern
5	A	fällig gewesen, und ich hab dann gerade angefangen, ne? Aber/aber
	B	Hm.
6	A	wir können uns hier 'n bißchen unterhalten. Komm heraus!
	B	Ja.

(Texts III, p. 64)

Speaker A is pressed for time (in Bedrückung); he therefore announces the temporal limitation of the conversation to B, the break-off: "I haven't got time for hours" (stundenlang hab ich nicht Zeit). Simultaneously, the announcement comes close to a precautionary **apology** because the speaker limits his action by reference to an external force: "but I *have to* let you know in advance that . . ." (aber das *muß* ich dir vorassagen). (At the same time this is a prefixed announcement of the subsequent action of speech; incidentally, it makes use of the introductory "but" (aber). See below § 4.1.).

By delimiting the span of time available for the suggested joint action speaker A prestructures the hearer's expectancy. As opposed to this form (E6), the announcement in example (E5) partitions the activities as not to be jointly performed: The organization of action is determined by the fact that an expectancy of an action is *transformed* into an expectancy of the non-occurrence of the action. This transformation, on the part of the hearer, makes room for other activities: he reorganizes his expectations. The fact that the hearer may not approve of the non-occurrence is of no functional bearing. Regardless of how the expectancy of the hearer is structured in any case what the announcement does is to co-ordinate the future lines of action.

Further analysis shows that a number of speech actions fulfill functions in the co-ordination. Among these, **announcements** have specific functions; **warnings**, **promises**, **requests**, **admonitions**, **threats** etc. have others. Most of them are related to a common constellation in the frame of which the different speech actions represent a future action in order to affect the hearer's actual line of action.

3.2. Pre-construction by the Hearer

Recall that announcements are not continually incorporated in the actor's process of action but are discontinued and discrete. They are localized in a gap of action between planning and execution. An announcement is thus a sequential pattern which refers to later units of action in which the production of action G takes place.

Announcements have no obligatory function since the substantial action thematized in their propositional content takes place independently. By means of announcements the actors communicate their own plans and their knowledge about the plans concerned and refer to them in acting and talking. By means of announcements a speaker gives precise information as to what the hearer can expect to happen. Thus, the other actor (hearer) is not unprepared for the action, he is focussed on it.

The *focus* has an important function for the "sequencing of the lines of action".[11] This means that the focus of an actor represents the beginning of his own action; but also the co-actor, the hearer, has to be focussed on the respective action; otherwise neither co-operation nor conflict is meaningful. Now, this is a matter of constituting a focus for an action which is yet to occur. To constitute a focus means to orientate the hearer towards the plan for an action which will at some time occur in his space of action.

In forming a focus the hearer mentally pre-construes the action in some way; the pre-construction is the correlate of the schematized rendering of the plan for G. In a mental activity of focussing, the hearer works out an anticipated axis (i.e., imaginative succession) of action and orientates his further activity towards this. The anticipating orientation enables him to continue his own action under this presupposition. The speaker, on his part, assumes this to be the effect of his speech action. As a result, there is a *succession axis of actions* built up in the speaker's and hearer's space of imagination which contains as common knowledge certain fixed points in the future.

By means of an announcement, then, the speaker impresses a certain plan upon the hearer and *partitions* the hearer's and thereby his own activity *in advance.* This anticipating partitioning by announcements will be discussed more concretely in § 4 below.

3.3. The Role in Institutions

Let us discuss a statement made by Turner (1972). Turner says there are so-called "core-activities" in gatherings such as therapeutic sessions, which for the participant constitute the relevant course of the gathering. According to Turner, announcements are used to draw the participant's attention to relevances of this kind. However, I would dispute that this relevance is constituted subjectively.

Agents of an institution often use an announcement in order to subordinate the clients to certain plans of action preferred by the institution or, more generally, to the standardized courses of the institutional activities, the *course of pragmemes.*[12] From the point of view of the institution these are the essential actions which therefore belong to its basic structure and, as such, have to be performed co-operatively by the participants; they can then be referred to as "core-activities," whereby it is of no significance whether they are subjectively considered to be relevant. As was shown above, announcements are not necessarily localized at the very beginning of the entire unit of an institutional process but can occur at different stages. We give an example for this from a classroom interaction (nearly at the end of the lesson).

(E7) L: Eh . . . Hört mal! Obwohl wir die letzte Aufgabe noch nicht haben: Ich teil euch die Hefte aus.

(160176/4/Mathematics/H/M/p. 57/2-3)

The announced 'handing out of the exercise books' (Austeilen der Hefte) is a central and for the teacher also a relevant activity. By means of the announcement it is marked as the next step in the lesson, so that the pupils can prepare themselves for it. The announcement impresses a plan on the further course of the lesson.

Announcements are not always at the beginning of institutional processes; there are, however, specific speech actions similar to announcements which have their typical position at the beginning: These are **openings**[13] (of meetings, negotiations etc.) which are bound to specific *routine formulas*[14] (a well-known one is: 'I hereby open this year's exhibition'). Another one can be found in police and court interrogations: the **counsel.** At the entrance into larger processes which are strongly repetitive, we find **instructions**; e.g., when starting a new job. The beginning of an institutional process is, therefore, not unequivocally and comprehensively characterized by the occurrence of announcements. Announcements do not only have the function of "introducing" institutional processes. To a certain extent, they can be found at the beginning but do not contain all of the activities of an institutional beginning listed by Schütze (1978) (cf. his summary p. 54). Moreover, at the beginning of a major institutional stage, e.g., the beginning of a trial a whole cluster of different activities is used in order to secure the client's entry into the standardized course of the institution.[15] In my opinion, Schütze confuses announcements with beginnings in general; according to his view, announcing plays the formal role of a starting point within an institutional course of action conceived as a linear succession only. As opposed to this, it must be noted that announcements have the character of a pattern of speech action which is employed for the purpose of establishing a prolonged focus of the hearer and which can be inserted between different stages of a broader context of action. It can be used by the speaker and – in the case of *pres* (see below § 4.4.) – by the hearer, wherever co-ordination calls for it.

4. ACTIVITIES OF PARTITIONING

By means of their function, announcements touch a number of elements whose task lies in the *organization and steering of the discourse* or, more generally, of the *joint* activity of co-actors. On the one hand, these elements have a specific place in the linear course of the discourse, and, on the other hand, they guide the co-activity of the hearer. Among those which have this function and come close to announcements the following elements are to be discussed: pre-fixed announcements, pre-fixations, connectors, pres, stand-ins, pre-announcement and preceding summaries. They all have a special relationship to the *pattern* of **announcing** but, unlike announcements, *they do not have the structure of a pattern* of action; rather, they belong to a special *communicative apparatus* by means of which speaker and hearer mutually steer each other (for a discussion of this term cf. Rehbein [1979a]). Elements of this category have communicative tasks of their own, and their structure is derived from their operating on discoursive processes which in themselves are structured by different patterns of action. The elements of a communicative apparatus as the ones described in the following, therefore, are not to be regarded as full speech actions. Their particular feature lies in that they, in their inner mechanism, come very close to that of the speech action of announcing; that is why they have to be taken as *announcements in a broad sense.* Communicative apparatuses have the property of generating *formulas*; some examples of this property will be found in the following.

4.1. Pre-fixed Announcements

As discourses dealing with preparatory activities are mostly concerned with plans of the participants *themselves* which have to be realized within the discourse, it is by discoursive elements that the subjective partitioning of the space of interaction is achieved. The individual participant attempts the interaction according to his own plan.

We distinguish between two forms as follows:

(1) In the first form, the speaker refers to *propositional elements* of his subsequent talk, and thus issues a partitioning of the thematic structure

of what he wants to say. In announcing he marks a new theme or a re-thematization. Within **lectures** or at the beginning of a lengthy contribution to a talk, we often find phrases like this:

(E8) G Ich wollte noch mal auf das Regenschwarz/das Regenschirmschwarz
G und so weiter zurückkommen.

(Texts I, p. 66)

Here the speaker announces a new theme with reference to the foregoing discussion in the form of *dethematizing.* The speaker verbalizes a scheme of what is to take place propositionally in his next speech action.[16] In this respect the talk is partitioned with regard to what precedes and what follows. The discourse knowledge is linearily structured by the formation of a focus.

(2) In the second form, the speaker refers to the *illocutionary markings* of the subsequent talk, i.e., he uses speech act designating expressions. Consider the following examples:

(E9) (Report of an accident)

1 B Jetzt hab ich zunächst ma, bevor wir in die Einzelheiten einsteigen
2 B dieses Falles, ins Konkrete kommen, die Frage an Sie: Wollen Sie
3 B aussagen oder nicht? Bitte!
A Ja. Jetzt hab ich noch-'ne Frage. Ob Sie mir
4 B Nein, nein.
A sagen können, was gegen mich vorliegt?

(Texts III, p. 125)

Here we have two announcements of this sort, one from A and one from B, each of them referring to his own plan. In both cases the announced speech action is conceptually and verbally schematized as a "question".

A similar case can be found in the following example:

(E10) (Advice at a health insurace company)

1 A Guten Täg! Äh folgendes Problem/äh ich bin doch
B Guten Tag!
2 A doch hier richtig bei D., ja? Mein Name ist A, ja? Öh ich hab folgendes Problem: Ich habe mich erst vor kurzem hier bei der Krankenkasse angemeldet.

(Texts III, p. 134)

Speaker A announces a verbal action which he has already planned. He characterizes the plan as "problem". The first attempt (in (1)) is interrupted (symbol '/'), and then recommenced (in (2)). This example shows that the speaker realizes the caesura, which discoursively follows an announcement, by a further interruptive sequence ((1)-(2)). After the repetition of the announcement a caesura is realized again, which is symbolized by a colon (in (3)).

To sum up our observations on the two forms of discoursive announcements (examples (E8)-(E10)), it becomes obvious that the speaker realizes the announced action *immediately after the announcement.* This shows that the caesura which sets off the execution and is normally indicated by a caesura-element of type G, only lies here in the linear caesura setting off the subsequent segment of the talk; in other words, announcement and execution are directly adjacent to each other. Because of this the speaker often uses elements from the *class of catadeictic expressions* (cf. Ehlich [1979 § 6]) such as 'following' (folgendes), 'now' (jetzt) etc. As this is a matter of an *independent speech action,* one should not speak of a simple augmentation of the subsequent speech action in the sense of a pre-fixation. In order to do justice to both aspects, independence and pre-fixation, the term '*pre-fixed announcement*' is chosen.

4.2. Pre-fixations/Announcements of Paraphrases

In contrast to the group of partitioning activities of discourse dealt with above, the following elements of speech are not independent.

In some utterances no scheme rendering expressions are used, but only elements directly addressed to the hearer and meant to attract his attention. These utterances have an announcing character in as much as they point out to the hearer a speaker's plan of action which takes place in the next step of action. Here are two examples:

(E12) | L Paßt auf . . . Ich unterbreite euch jetzt folgenden Vorschlag:
| L Wir versuchen, weder Kamera noch diejenigen . . .

(080774/5/German/G/m)

(E13) | L Folgendes: . . . . . . eh Wer erklärt nochmal

(ibid., p. 6)

The underlined expressions and many others such as 'listen' (hört mal), 'well' (also) 'now' (jetzt) etc. are characterized position-wise in that they immediately precede the speaker's speech action: They are therefore called *'prefixations'*. They have the function of opening the hearer's focus on the immediately subsequent speech action; they are an augment of speech action and, therefore, contribute to the guiding of the hearer by the speaker.

Rath (1975) pointed out a further interesting phenomenon. He showed that a group of routine formulas such as 'in other words,' 'that means,' 'to be more precise,' 'more precisely,' 'more clearly,' 'more generally speaking' etc., are used to announce paraphrases which are made in the subsequent utterance. They have a discourse partitioning function, too, and, in my opinion, they have to be seen in the broader context of hearer steering which is discoursively done by augments of speech actions.[17] 'I repeat' and similar formulas containing a verbum dicendi that lexically signalizes the re-commencement of talk also belong to this complex of phenomena.

4.3. Connectors

Elements which have the function of inducing a co-actor to change to another line of action, such as 'so,' 'by the way' etc. are referred to as 'connectors'. Connectors are also a type of caesura-elements at the beginning of announcements. Furthermore, a number of augments, particularly addresses, assume a similar function when they induce the co-actor to break off his action, and orientate him towards the process of action desired by the speaker. Even completely developed patterns of speech action, such as **admonishing**, can adopt a task of this kind. However, connectors are segmental elements suitable for steering the discourse in a co-ordinative manner without interrupting it. They are only mentioned here – without analyzing them more closely – because they can be mistaken for announcements; more precisely: announcements can sometimes be used in their place.

4.4. Pres

The linguistic and non-linguistic elements summarized under the category 'pre' are too manyfold to be listed one by one; e.g., a **frown** can be a pre for non-comprehension, a **clearing of the throat** can be a pre for the request for a turn etc. On the whole, pres have the force of announcements. They are mostly very brief and do not take much time interactionally, but are all the more effective as signals. In general, their internal structure is in accordance with that of announcements but their sequential organization is different.

Pres are mostly signals on the part of the hearer. They are inserted in the speaker's pauses and contribute to the steering of the speaker; thus a German 'hm' serves as a signal of agreement or disagreement by means of which the hearer announces a plan to protest. Generally, such pres are attentively observed by the speaker.

Secondly, it has to be emphasized that pres operate on a kind of "shallow" or latent structure of the common discourse knowledge. Simple signals are sufficient to let the speaker know what the hearer means, what exactly he is announcing. This works because the speaker interprets the hearer's signals on the background of his own behavior as a hearer in a correlative situation. The speaker constructs a close relationship between the perceived hearer's signal and the respective future action, although he gets no explicit scheme rendering of the future action. He can do so because he makes use of routinized plans which are part of the common knowledge. Therefore, pres contribute to the co-ordinative steering of inter-actors in a common space of action, just as the other types of announcements do.

Opponent parties trying to obtain a turn often announce their **objections, replies, interjections** etc. by pres, using a variety of formulaic expressions such as:

(E14) 'Yes, just a minute, but . . . . . .'
'Wait a minute!'
'Just a minute!' etc.

Formulas of this kind used at a specific sequential point in discourse comprise two positions of the announcement: On the one hand, they have a caesura force and adopt the role of caesura-element A, and, on the other hand, they indicate a plan for a propositional content opposed to that uttered by the speaker; the plan, however, is not yet schematically specified. From the last example we can now deduce a tentative generalization: A pre is *an illocution of an announcement lacking propositional content.*

This determination makes pres appear particularly suitable for *linearly* organizing not only the discourse within a single pattern of action but also the course of several patterns of action. This becomes obvious when the actors are still involved in one pattern of action (such as a hearer during a **report**) while the planning and resolution of execution is already carried out for the next pattern (e.g., the **questioning** of the reporting actor). The linear course of the pattern of action at hand makes it impossible to already announce a full-fledged propositional content. Instead, during the execution of the pattern-of-action$_1$ a pattern-of-action$_2$ which is related to the first is announced as a meaningful subsequent action as planned by one actor.

4.5. Stand-ins

Actors can resort to announcements when they cannot immediately carry out an action and, at the same time, do not wish to reject it. In this case announcements have the role of substituting the future action and of assuring the other actor, that the plan for this action actually exists on the speaker's part. He can thus postpone the necessary action without having to fear sanctions. We call these kind of announcements '*stand-ins*'. They are often realized simply by the use of indications of the future, such as 'in a minute,' 'tomorrow,' 'in ten minutes' etc. In such cases the other actor is given a point in time as to when the action will take place and thus can orientate himself accordingly. Because of its second sequential position (cf. § 2.2.3. above) this type of "announcement" turns out to be a **promise** or an **assurance**. Anyway, stand-ins have an important function in the organization of the actors' processes of action; stand-ins *prepare* the hearer for the point in time when the respective segment of action, in which the desired action will be realized, is to be expected.

Stand-ins have a particular function when several demands are expected to be simultaneously fulfilled by one of the actors. If, for example, someone who is engaged in a telephone conversation is approached with a question he will often say 'wait a minute,' 'just a moment' etc. Sequential co-ordination problems like this are solved according to the maxime "one action at a time!". A co-ordination element of the above kind serves to work out co-ordination problems communicatively.

Let us consider another example from classroom-discourse:

(E15)
L Ach, dann lassen wer's jetz ma, bis ihr euch beruhigt habt . . .
L Christoph? Ja, da kommen
Ch Was hat das mit dem Thema Politik zu tun?
L wir gleich drauf. Leider ist die Zeit jetzt so knapp, daß wir das
L nicht mehr ganz fertig machen können.

(181174/7/G+P/GS/f)

The pupil Christoph puts a question to the teacher (a rare event); instead of giving a full answer, the teacher uses a stand-in "just a second" (gleich) which allows her to postpone the full answer and to continue the thematic progression as planned by her.

4.6. Pre-announcements

In the following, we talk about a phenomenon which is easily mistaken for explicit announcements. Beforehand we would like to point out the excellent work of A. K. Terasaki on "Pre-Announcement Sequences in Conversation;" unfortunately, a detailed discussion of the work of this advocate of "conversation analysis" is not possible here.

Speakers often have a plan for a complex of speech actions, either for a *chain* of them or even for a complete *type of discourse*. For its realization a particularly strong focus of the hearer is necessary or, more generally, a particularly intensive willingness of the co-actor to co-operate.

The necessary focus of the hearer can be achieved by verbal reference to major units of action, particularly units of discourse the instruments of which can be found in specific formulas such as:

(E16) (a) 'Do you know what I dreamt of last night?'
(b) 'Guess what I heard about her!'
(c) 'You just can't imagine what I went through at the customs!'

With these formulas the speaker refers to something the hearer does not know, but which the speaker characterizes as worth knowing. He thereby evaluates certain elements which he picks from his planned talk (in this case a narration) as being of interest to the hearer. Nevertheless such formulas at the same time are statements about the subsequent talk *as a whole*, without giving detailed information, thus establishing the hearer's focus on a long stretch of discourse. In short, with these formulas the speaker emphasizes
(a) the entirety of the unit of discourse, which he outlines as a type,
(b) its characteristic element, the "object of interest".

The object of interest, whose indication is supposed to bring about the hearer's formation of focus, is directly referred to:

(E17) (a) 'Be quiet, he's got something interesting to say'
(b) 'I've got to let you know something of importance'
(c) 'Listen, your friend, he's really great. He . . .'

Often such formulas are not explicitly used: instead the relevance of the planned unit of discourse and its being of interest is only implied and has to be interpreted by the hearer by means of an inference of relevance.

(E18) "During a drive in the Skoda 100 through Thüringer Wald, the temperature gage of the cooling water was way above 120° C."[18]

Here, the 'extraordinary thing,' the temperature gage, is obviously the characteristic which evokes a positive procedure of evaluation in the hearer with reference to the speaker's announced narration.

There are also formulaic expressions by which the speaker "anounces" something negative for the hearer:

(E19) (a) 'I heard something unpleasant about you yesterday'
(b) 'I regret to have to tell you that . . .'

In these cases, the execution of the announced discourse will affect the hearer in some way, at least it will have a negative effect on his mechanism of evaluation; but apart from this the formulas function in the same way as the positive ones.[19]

Speech actions which formulate a *negative evaluation* of the action still to be executed often also refer to **revelations** (cf. (E17)). They can schematically name the type of discourse: 'I have to make a confession to you,' for example. Nevertheless, they also refer to an **assertion** the propositional content of which will contain negative information for the hearer.[20]

What is it that the phenomena discussed above have in common and what distinguishes one from the other?

In the above example formulas are given by which the speaker wants to elicit the utterance of an "attitude," or, more precisely, an assessment from the hearer. Only in a few cases does he give a complete and explicit verbalization of the scheme of the planned action, and in even fewer cases the exothesis of the resolution of execution which characterizes a substantial part of the illocutionary force of the announcement (see above § 2.2.2.). Rather, the speaker choses the procedure of a *'pre-sequence,'*[21] in order to attract the *attention of the hearer,* which is a substantial element of announcements, too.

In many cases **pre-announcements** show the following structure:

(1) exothesis of evaluation of a future action by the speaker;
(2) assessment by the hearer;
(3) (a) announcement by the speaker/forbearance of the announcement; and/or:
(b) beginning of talk by the speaker.

The pre-announcement therefore takes place when the speaker has not made a final resolution of execution; moreover he has a *'want to'* or a *'have to,'* but he makes his *'ability'* dependent on the previous evidence of the hearer's willingness to co-operate. A pre-announcement therefore contains a demand for the hearer to give an explicit and positive point of view about the planned action and, in this way, to *enable the speaker* to make his resolution of execution.

The following is a particularly frequent case of a **pre-announcement,** namely, when a pupil wishes to get rid of a turn. In fact two pre-announcements appear in the following example:

(E20) (Extract from a lesson in "German as a foreign language")

1	L	Keine Einzahl und keine Mehrzahl. Das is einfach eine . . . unbestimmte Menge
2	L	Hm? Und damit ich das überhaupt zählen kann,
	S_1	Oh, Frau Lehmann, wir ham a/wat
3	L	muß ich also sagen: Drei Stück Käse oder fünfzehn Scheiben Käse oder
4	L	n' halbes Pfund Käse, oder sowas . . . Hm? Honig . . . ((schreibt an die
	S_2	Honig. Honig.
	S_3	Brot.
	S_1	Ich habau' einen, das's
	S_4	Marmela
5	L	Tafel)) Und so weiter. Ja? Sehr schön. Kommt gleich.
	S_1	ganz wichtig. Äh. Wasser, irgendwie sowas.

(290379/5/G/German/f)

The first **pre-announcement** of pupil S_1 (in (2)) proves to be a pre-starter, because he does not get a turn and has to break off his utterance. His second pre-announcement is introduced with "I've got one too" (ich hab au' einen) in order to tone down the character of interruption, the caesura character. "That's ever so important" (das's ganz wichtig) is a formulation which is aimed at a positive classification of relevance of the pupil's planned turn: for the assessment of his plan, S_1 makes use of the explicitness of a "maxim of conversation," namely "Say the essential things!"

The *explicit verbalization of a matter of course* such as this, however, depotentiates particularly the illocutionary force of the pre-announcement – a case which is not atypical of foreign pupils.

4.7. **Preceding Summary (abstract)** vs. **Preceding Comment**

There are two complex forms of speech by which reference to the subsequent discourse can be made and in which what the speaker is going to say is resumed beforehand: These are the **summary** and the **comment** both preceding types of discourse which consist of a chain *of speech actions,* e.g., a **lecture** or a **narrative**.

Both forms refer to the *thematic organization* of the planned discourse, but they have different functions. Firstly, an example of a **preceding summary**:

(E21) (The example if taken from the beginning of a lecture on criteria for pupils' tests; for a detailed analysis see Rehbein (1977).)

(1) Ich möchte also nach dem ersten . . ., dem Textverständ-
(2) nis,
(3) nachdem ich das vorgetragen habe,
(4) nachdem wir auch mithilfe der . . . Ihnen . . . zugesandten . . .
(5) ehm . . . Unterlagen –
(6) das sind ja . . . tatsächlich geschriebene Arbeiten mit
(7) allen Fehlern, die drin sind,
(8) manchmal hat man es schwer, es überhaupt zu *verstehen* –
(9) . . . möchte ich die Vorstellungen hier diskutieren.
(10) Und das machen wir mit dem zweiten Teil . . . ebenso.

(031076)

The text summarizes the lecture which consists of several parts indicated accordingly by the use of the key-words: "text understanding" (Textverständnis) ((1)-(3)), analysis of the "material" (Unterlagen) ((4)-(8)), "discussion" (9) and "second part" (zweiter Teil) (10).

What the speaker does here is to partition his theme in advance. He does this by verbalizing the individual elements of the planned propositional content of his theme and at the same time emphasizing their discoursive succession. At the beginnings of narratives, we often find **comments** in which the speaker makes an assessment of the propositional content without verbalizing it as a *whole.* By this linguistic procedure the expectation of the hearer is structured as far as the thematic organization of the discourse is concerned.

It is obvious that in these cases the planning process as such has not yet arrived at a definite resolution of verbalization: The speaker does *not yet know exactly how to begin.* For this we give the following example:

(E22) (The text originates from a consultation: C: counsel A: Person seeking advice)

1 C How are you?
A Oh, not too bad, thank you. Uhm tell me/I don't
2 A know how to start this but I seem to be getting constant (playing
3 A ball) from the police. I can't move . . . an inch without 'em
having to stop me an' . . . saying somethin' or the other . . . . Uhm
4 A about a month ago on the twelfth of June . . . . . . I had a ( )

(270778)

Before the person seeking advice (in (4)) begins her actual narration with "uhm about a month ago . . ." she renders her viewpoint on what has happened to her (in (2-4)). From these words it is not yet possible to gain the actual propositional content of what is going to be told. The **comment** provides a general assessment of the situation picking out some exemplary occurrences only.

We see here that the **preceding comment** formulates the particular purpose, as to why a **narrative, lecture, report** and other types of discourse consisting of chains of speech actions are delivered. Hence, the function of the preceding comment is to provide a purpose-directed embedding of the subsequent discourse.

This function of **preceding comments** explains why they cannot be classified as **announcements in a broad sense.** Rather, it is their job to produce in the functional context an anchoring point for the chain of speech actions in its entire form, i.e., to interpret in advance the **narrative** as useful for the consultation. Thereby, amazingly, **preceding comments** come into the category of **introductions** because introductions have to do with fixing the activity in the space of action itself. The preceding comment is an attempt of this sort.

5. INTRODUCTIONS

Introductions are phenomena which, when looked at superficially, come very close to announcements. Yet, announcements have entirely different tasks.

Sacks (1971) did not make a clear distinction here. When he spoke of "announcements," "story prefaces" (310), or simply "introductions" (311) he obviously referred to the same phenomenon, which he examined in the framework of the turn-taking-device. He assigned to "announcements" the function of gaining and maintaining the hearer's attention for contributions consisting of more than a single turn. "Announcements" do not only contain information about what is going to happen but also about the "conversational duration", i.e., about the expected end of the contribution. The phenomenon discussed by Sacks falls into the category of announcements in a broad sense, and therefore the above made distinctions apply here. In as far as **permission** (to speak) has to be obtained by means of such a speech act, we would speak of **pre-announcements**. If permission is not explicitly obtained, but only the hearer's *attention* is aroused for the following chain of speech actions, then it is a case of a **pre-fixed** or an **augmented announcement.** But in no case do these phenomena belong to introductions. The necessary differentiation to be made here was correctly pointed out by Meyer-Hermann (1978).

Before discussing an example, let us outline a number of characteristics of introductions:

(1) Like announcements, introductions are related to a coming action. However, in the case of an introduction, (a) the actor of the future action is the speaker himself; (b) the future action does not occur *after* the speech action, but its start is marked by the speech action.[22]

(2) Introductions are a means of expanding the beginning of the speech action in two different ways:

(a) *on the part of the speaker*:
It is often impossible to complete the formation of a plan before speaking. In other words, when he begins to talk the speaker may still be in the process of working out an appropriate plan according to the situational conditions. Hence, introductions exhibit a great number of anacoluthons, repairs, etc. which occur when the speaker "*does not yet know exactly what he wants to say*" (cf. (E24)). This is why we find in introductions many planning indicators, e.g., hesitation phenomena.

(b) *On the part of the hearer*:
The speaker tries to make use of certain elements of the hearer's knowledge. Thus, unlike announcements, introductions are not directed to the future but to the hearer in such a way as to provide him with some guidance concerning the action which is yet to occur. Furthermore, the realization of an introduction directly refers to the hearer's state of knowledge by confronting him with the action in question *in statu nascendi,* hence attracting or stimulating his attention. This is shown by many of the *formulaic expressions* which are used as introductions in everyday conversation and which have a relating or casual character such as, 'By the way,' 'What I was going to say,' 'actually' etc. These are formulas by means of which the speaker tries to connect the *beginning of the action* with the hearer's domain of knowledge, thus to its *situational scope* of knowledge.

Introductions are, therefore, not patterns or instances of pattern positions in speech activities but *discoursive procedures* which are often realized by formulaic means, as in the following example:

(E23) Es gibt auf den Philippinen eine alte Geschichte, die im Volk erzählt wird, wie die Philippinos entstanden sind. Zunächst gab es nur den Himmel und das Wasser. Es gab noch kein Land . . .

(Texts I, p. 74)

The phrase "there is . . ." (es gibt . . .) when used to introduce narratives is of formulaic character.

In the next example, many of those elements can be found which we call 'shifters;' they constitute a *captatio benevolentiae* of the hearer. The example also shows the process of the speaker's plan formation in actu:

(E24) (extract of a seminar discussion)

1	HP	Übrigens äh, es fällt mir da noch 'n Problem bei auf, . . . ne?, bei
	J	Jā.
2	HP	diesem "Wiederholen im ganzen Satz". was du da hast, ne? . . . Äh
	J	Hm̆. Das ist
3	HP	Das is 'n bi chen weiter dann, ne? . . .
	J	jetzt schon 'n bißchen weiter? Hm̆ Hm̆.
4	HP	Äh . . . und zwar . . . wo ist der jetzt? ((blättert)) Verdammt!
	J	((Räuspern))
5	HP	((blättert)) Ah ja, hier: "Say it in a sentence", diese Geschichten, ne? Ah
6	HP	Zum Beispiel dreizehn hier. "Dieser komplette Satz".
	J	Welche Seite?
7	HP	Anders is noch mit dem Beispiel auf vierzehn, da hatten wer gestern
8	HP	schon ma' darüber gesprochen. Aber . . . dä/das Komische is, daß es bei diesem
9	HP	Geschichte/bei diesem "Wiederholen im ganzen Satz" ja eindeutig um die
10	HP	Äußerungsseite geht. Insofern ist das "Wiederholen" schon äh richtig da
11	HP	angewandt, ne? Andererseitz äh ist aber nicht das "Perzipieren eins"
12	HP	gefährdet gewesen, oder so etwas. Äh. Sondern das Wiederholen erfolgt
13	HP	also auch nicht/Es ist auch kein "vorsorgliches Wiederholen", um's zu
14	HP	gewährleisten, sondern die/das Grund für diese Wiederholung liegt
15	HP	irgendwo/bedingt mehr durch den Einschätzungsapparat als durch den äh
16	HP	Perzeptionsapparat. Und das is irgendwie 'n merkwürdiger Fall, an
17	HP	dieser Stelle. find ich

(061078)

The development of the propositional content in this contribution aims at the utterance part (14-17): 'sondern die/das Grund für diese Wiederholung liegt irgendwo/bedingt mehr durch den Einschätzungsapparat als durch den äh Perzeptionsapparat. Und das is irgendwie 'n merkwürdiger Fall, find ich" (but the reason for the repetition lies somewhere/caused more by the assessment apparatus than by the uhm perception apparatus – and that's a strange case, I think) (14-17). This part of the utterance can be looked upon as being the *rheme* of what is said, therefore the core of what the speaker HP is driving at in his different starts and verbalization attempts.

Let us take a look at what introductory elements[23] can be found before the speaker arrives at the rheme, the core of the contribution: "übrigens" (by the way) (in (1)) adds additional elements of knowledge to the already existing thematized elements; "noch" (another) (in (1)) has a similar additory force of supplementing something already known; with "bei diesem Wiederholen . . ." (with this repetition) the speaker refers to a seminar text which is under discussion; "hier" (here) (in (5)) and (in (6)) has a similar function; "anders" (different) confronts two aspects of the seminar text at hand thus operating on the hearer's knowledge; "da hatten wir gestern schon ma' darüber gesprochen" (we already spoke about that yesterday) is a reminder; "aber" (but) (8) is oppositional, but also adds to what has just been thematized; "das Komische ist, daß . . ." (the strange thing is that . . .) (in (8)) is, by the way, a built-in announcement; "diesem" (this) (in (9)) is an elucidation of something known; "ja" (in (9)) actualizes the hearer's knowledge; "insofern" (to that extent) is argumentative and thereby structures the hearer's domain of knowledge; the same applies to "andererseits" (on the other hand) (in (11).

All of these partial utterances operate on what is *pre-known* to the hearer; it is either re-thematized or structured according to the speaker's speech procedures. By means of these the speaker incorporates the *theme* in the hearer's domain of knowledge, he so to speak 'shifts' the theme into the discourse.

The *rheme* of contribution is arrived at in the first "sondern" (but) (in (12)) yet not continued since the speaker inserts two negative paraphrases. It is not before the second "sondern" (14) that the rheme is restarted and then completely verbalized ((14)-(17)).

The distinction between **introductions** and **announcements** becomes more evident now:

Introductions mark the *beginning* of a longer, mostly complex action. Beginning means that the *Hic-et-nunc*-point of the action has already started in the space of interaction. Thus introductions come *after* the caesura segment by means of which the unit of action is separated as a new segment of discourse from the preceding segment. The basic task of **introductions** is reflected in one of their functional elements, the 'shifters,' which serve to anchor the theme of what is to be said in the hearer's knowledge. Their function is to conjoin elements of knowledge to give the theme and to supply the theme with the *here-and-now on the part of the hearer.* Thus introductions are marked by hearer directed origo-fixation attempts since without a correlative origo the hearer could not be certain what the whole utterance is leading up to and thus could not be prepared for what is new. In introductions, therefore, the ongoing action is adequately decomposed and spread out by the speaker in single acts and activities which appear necessary for the reception. This decomposition and spreading out of the action is, at the same time, a realization of the potentially existing plan of the speaker and a discoursive elaboration of his plan for execution..

By contrast, **announcements** only give a rough scheme of the future action of the speaker. In announcements the actual elements of knowledge remain unelaborated because the realization of the plan is separated from the announcement by a segmental caesura. The schematized description of the future action (rendering of the plan) constitutes the full-fledged propositional content of the announcement. Whereas in introductions the action is only torso-wise verbalized as the theme.

A last example should help to clarify a somewhat complicated but often occurring case:

(E25) (Asking for advice at a health insurance company)

A Und jetzt hab ich noch 'ne Frage öh die betrifft meinen Sohn. Ähm Ich hab da in diesem/in diesem äh Heft, das Sie mir zugeschickt haben/da stehen lauter so Krankenscheine drin, die man also offensichtlich.

(Texts III, pp. 139/140)

Is this an announcement or an introduction? First of all, an announcement of the planned action appears to be given with "Und jetzt hab ich noch 'ne Frage äh und die betrifft meinen Sohn" (And now I've got another question. It's about my son). The action to be performed is unequivocally schematized by "Frage" (question). But the shifters "und" and "noch" indicate a continuation of the preceding utterances. Therefore, it is a case in which the announcement is functionally integrated into the framework of an introduction. How can this be done?

According to the above analysis, **announcements** produce a focus alteration and a focus prolongation in the hearer; the new focus does not only actualize a particular knowledge but also *categorizes* it. It is this categorizing procedure that is exploited in using announcements for introducing. In being given the category of what is to be expected, the hearer's reception of the current speech will be more firmly anchored in his mind and he will be better prepared for the perception of the unfolding action of the speaker.

6. HEADLINES (a complex case)

Newspaper headlines are preparatory activities related to a specific *type of text,* i.e., newspaper articles, and as such are short forms of texts. At second glance, headlines turn out to have a *duplex illocutionary structure,* i.e., two illocutionary functions are executed by a single speech action. This duplex structure distinguishes **headlines** from **announcements**.

On the one hand, headlines summarize a chain of assertions contained in the subsequent text. A headline highlights essential parts of the subsequent text in picking out some of its main points, but – in terms of the analysis at hand – it does not outline a complete scheme of the entire text and, hence, does not reveal its plan as a whole. Rather, a headline prefigures the situation described in the text and, in this manner, effects an intense focus on the part of the reader. It approaches the **preceding comment** (cf. § 4.6. above) but lacks its character of being closed because it does not give an over-all assessment in advance. Its textual job of prefiguring the situation is reflected in specific linguistic forms, especially its lack of the copula (another case of simplified speech): "PEACE DISCUSSED AMID NICARAGUA FIGHTING," "WHALES ASHORE IN NEWFOUNDLAND" etc.

On the other hand, the second structure of a newspaper headline is due to its function of rendering past actions, events etc. Strictly speaking, a headline is a type of **report**: It reports discussions, speeches, talks, attacks, violations, acts of war, treaties etc., and, among other things, decisions, measures, revolutions etc. *which will have consequences in the future,* and in this last case what is reported can be seen as an **announcement** of the future action. If the headline contains an announcement the readers become the addressees of the announced action depending upon whether they are subjected to it or not. This matter is illustrated in the following example:

(E26) The headline refers to an article about measures under the new law of work promotion. Below, we are going to interpret the main title and the two subtitles only:

FÜR ARBEITSLOSE WIRD'S SCHWERER.
Viele müssen ihre Familien verlassen –
Frauen müssen den ganzen Tag arbeiten.

(MORE DIFFICULTIES FOR UNEMPLOYED.
Many have to leave their families –
Women have to work all day.)

(Bild, 23.11.78)

The group of addressees the headline is aimed at are the "unemployed" including those threatened by unemployment; this also is true for the first subtitle whereas the second subtitle is aimed at the subgroup of "women".

According to its textual illocutionary function the headline summarizes the main point which is concerned with (un)employment. According to its rendering illocutionary function the headline is an **announcement** of legislative measures and their consequences which directly affect the group of addressees ("leave their families," "have to work all day"). The scheme of this announcement is extended here to a presentation of the emotional effects ("more difficulties").

Thus, a change in the course of their everyday life is announced to the addressees among the readers in such a form that they themselves cannot do anything about it: "More difficulties" states an established fact; both groups "have to" do something. The reader's relationship to what is reported is therefore so determined that they have to submit to abstract powers which have made a resolution of execution concerning their future action.

By the reference to an already effective plan of action the reader is confronted with a feeling of inescapability as well as with the impossibility of making a plan of his own. From this analysis it can be concluded that "more difficulties" is an announcement of an act of sanctioning (thus a **pre-threat**) without the recipient having a chance to change his line of action. Thus, headlines containing announcements can also serve as a means to direct the actions of certain groups of readers.

7. MODERATING

Finally, let us touch on a special type of discourse by means of which **reports**, **newsreels** etc. are presented on TV. It is a type of discourse which appears in magazine programs such as "Themes News" (Tagesthemen) and in "Sports Report" (Sportschau). The television commentator gives a brief survey of what is contained in the report without informing in detail about the contents and establishes a kind of link between the preceding program and the subsequent one. This type of discourse is called 'moderating'. Because it contains more than a single speech action, it has to be seen as a discourse which, on the basis of an announcement, is enlarged to meet specific institutional purposes.

Let us again start the analysis by giving an example which, however, is not a pure case but a mixed one. Since **moderations** are extended announcements, they, like other announcements, serve to direct the hearer's focus in a purposeful and anticipatory fashion. This funcion is made use of by TV where it is particularly necessary to set up disparate pieces of information scattered in different reports in a meaningful way.

It is typical of **moderating** that it characterizes the general situation in which the subsequent report is located.

(E27) The following **moderation** was used to present a report on the steel workers' strike at the end of 1978. The report depicts the situation from the point of view of a rolling mill enterprise which needs fresh supplies of material but cannot obtain them because of the strike, and which has hence announced dismissals.

(1) Zahltag für die Stahlkocher – aber von der falschen Seite
(2) sozusagen. Zahlmeister sind diesmal die Gewerkschaften,
(3) jedenfalls was jene Stahlarbeiter angeht, die vom Arbeits-
(4) kampf betroffen sind. Aber auch da gehen viele leer aus,
(5) denn die Nichtorganisierten kriegen gar nix, und bei den
(6) andern richtet sich die Auszahlung nach der Beitragshöhe.
(7) Heute mußten die Gewerkschaftler aus der Streikkasse immer-
(8) hin fünfundsechzig Millionen Mark berappen; was Arbeitskampf
(9) und Arbeitsausfall die Unternehmer kosten, ist noch gar
(10) nicht abzusehen, aber ein ganz schöner Brocken ist es jetzt
(11) schon. Langsam stellt sich die Frage nach dem Sinn der ge-
(12) werkschaftlichen Trutzaktion, wenn man noch dazu hört, daß
(13) der Streik ausgeweitet werden soll. Die Ankündigung dieser
(14) Ausweitung war dann heute noch verbunden mit einer Erklärung
(15) zu Kompromißbereitschaft. Das ist entweder höhere Logik
(16) oder verzuckerter Rückzug, jedenfalls ein Ritual, das die
(17) Stahlarbeiter selbst trifft, auch jene, die noch nicht im
(18) Streik und Aussperrung verwickelt sind. Manchen Betrieben
(19) fehlt inzwischen Rohstahl zur Weiterverarbeitung. Deswegen
(20) brauchen sie auch die Arbeitskräfte nicht mehr und schicken
(21) sie nach Hause, wollen das jedenfalls: Ein Beitrag von
(22) Wolfgang Strüpp. –

(261278/ZDF/HEUTE, 21.00 Uhr)

The text consists of two sections: The first one lasts up to "sind" (1-18), the second one (18-22) begins with "Manchen Betrieben . . .". In the given text a moderation only appears in the last section (18ss), where the situation is described and the respective reporter introduced. Its institutional purpose requires of a moderation to give a schematical description of the general situation but not to go into the informative contents.

What happens in the first section of the transcript? First of all, there is a thematization ("Zahltag für die Stahlkocher" (payday for the steel workers)) of a very ambiguous kind: One does not know who pays. This is followed by an extended description of the actual situation which determines the *perspective* under which the reported events have to be seen and which therefore passes beyond the normative form of **moderating**. The moderator does not only build up the viewer's focus and present a rough assessment but he also channels the reception of the actual report, since, afterwards, it will be difficult for the viewer to form an evaluation of his own. This procedure can be called an '*over-all assessment in advance*:' it is applied because, obviously, different assessments *can* arise in the reception of the report, so that different, undesired evaluations could form a controversial picture of the situation.

To sum up, moderations as institutionally extended announcements can give a schematizing characterization of a report. As the announced action is focussed under a certain aspect, its realization may not create a picture in the hearer (viewer) which differs from the one already impressed upon him in the announcement.

8. SUMMARY

Let us review the aforementioned phenomena and show their systematic interrelationships by means of a chart (Fig. 1).

Announcing *in the proper sense* as elaborated by an abstract analysis (§ 2) is a *pattern* of speech. It is employed to serve special purposes within the frame of co-ordination of action (§ 3). It is interrelated with other patterns of speech like **threatening, promising, warning** etc. all of which are functionally localized *in the same constellation* of actions; this constellation underlies those forms of speech by which a particular future action is represented in an actual space of action. By its characteristic of being a pattern **announcing** in the proper sense is distinguished from similar discoursive elements all of which belong to **announcements** *in a broad sense*: pre-fixed announcements, stand-ins, pres, pre-fixations/announcements of paraphrases, connectors (§§ 4.1.-4.5.). It is significant of these discoursive elements that they are part of a categorically different functional mechanism, i.e. of the *communicative*

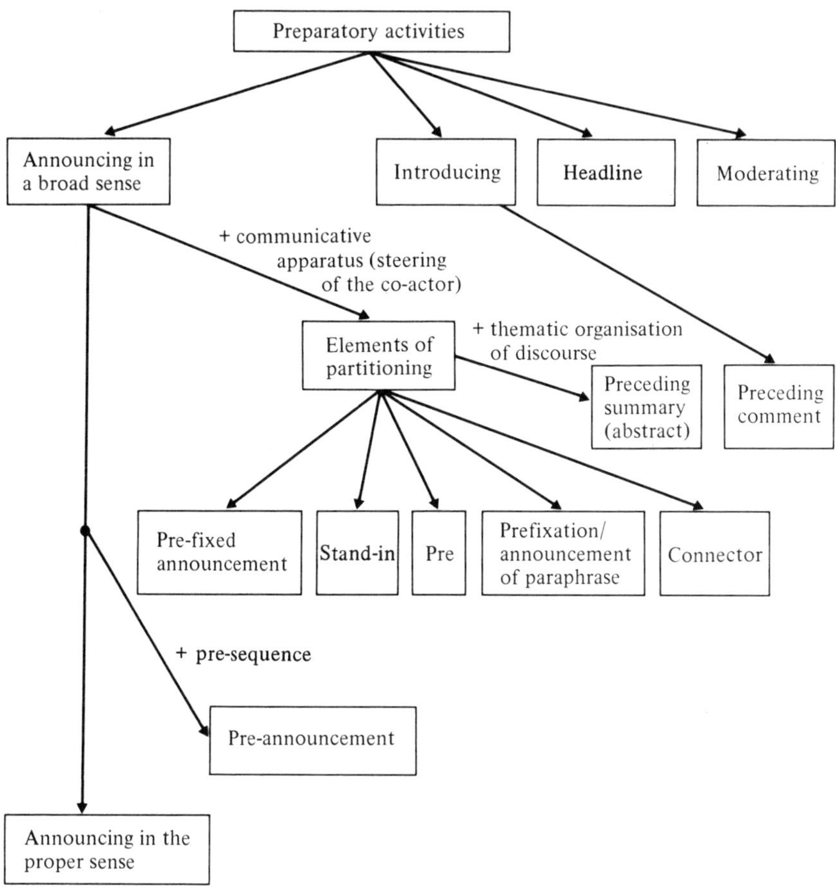

Figure 1

apparatus of 'speaker/hearer steering;' their job is to partition the discourse, and therefore they play an important part in organizing it. **Pre-announcements** check the hearer's willingness to follow a planned speech action (§ 4.6.). **Preceding summaries (abstracts)** and **preceding comments** (§ 4.7.) are separate phenomena because of their function in the *thematic* organization of discourse. Introductions (§5) are discoursive *procedures* of anchoring the theme of the following speech in the hearer's domain of knowledge; they are basically of formulaic character and should not be confused with announcements although the latter sometimes can do the work of introductions. Newspaper **headlines** (§ 6) and **moderations** on TV (§ 7) are other kinds of preparatory activities and as such come very close to announcements but have different structures according to their specific tasks in different institutional settings. **Introductions**, **announcements** *in a broad sense,* **headlines**, and **moderations** prove to be systematically related.

Not all of the phenomena concerning the preparation of activities and the organization of future actions could be discussed here. In this domain, many complex forms of social organization need further investigation. Some of them have already been examined: **programmes, advertisements, declarations, credits, forewords** etc., to name but a few. Most of them are public kinds of text. Their organizational objectives have to be studied. It is not unlikely that they turn out to have more complicated structures than announcements.

Transcripts and Text-Materials

1976 Bewertung von Abiturarbeiten in Englisch (Aufnahme Rehbein)
26111978/BILD-Düsseldorf
26121978/HEUTE/Sendung des ZDF

Texts I: Texte gesprochener deutscher Standardsprache I. Erarbeitet im Institut für deutsche Sprache. Forschungsstelle Freiburg. Redaktion der Texte: Andresen u.a. München (1971): Heuber

Texts II: Texte gesprochener deutscher Standardsprache II. Erarbeitet im Institut für deutsche Sprache. Forschungsstelle Freiburg. Ausgewählt, redigiert und eingeleitet von Charles van Os. München (1974): Hueber

Texts III: Texte gesprochener deutscher Standardsprache III. Erarbeitet im Institut für deutsche Sprache. Forschungsstelle Freiburg. Herausgegeben und eingeleitet von H. P. Fuchs und G. Schank. München (1975): Hueber

Transcripts of the project 'Kommunikation in der Schule (KidS)':
080774/5/Deutsch/m/G
071174/6b/Mathematik/f/GS
181174/7/Geschichte und Politik/f/GS
210176/6/Mathematik/f/HS
300176/8/Englisch/f/HS
290379/5/Deutsch/f/G

06101978 Seminardiskussion (Aufnahme Rehbein)
27071978 Consultation (Aufnahme Rehbein)

NOTES

1. The following analysis starts out from the everyday concept of "Ankündigen" (*to announce*) in *German*. The *English* word "announce" also means "inform". In this paper, I wish to explicitly exclude this meaning (unlike Terasaki (1976) who proceeds from this usage).

   In a variety of foregoing analyses relation to the structure of action, announcements were dealt with in Rehbein (1977) without, however, examining them in detail. In Rehbein (1976) a classification of announcements was suggested which had to be subsequently revised in order to account for new material necessitating finer and more rigorous distinctions. The next elaboration (Rehbein (1979b)) was based on the original analysis, in particular on the insight that announcements play a substantial role in social planning.

   A detailed discussion with Harrie Mazeland convinced me of some serious mistakes, thus leading to yet another revision. In the meantime I gained insight into the excellent work of Terasaki (1976) which, however, had no significant influence on the basic conception of this paper. The problem of classifying announcements still waits for an appropriate solution.
2. A more precise description is given by Humpert as far as the beginning of school lessons is concerned.
3. An example of what I mean by "inner mechanism" is given in the analysis of **effective reasoning** (Begründen) and its complex pattern (in Ehlich & Rehbein (1976a)).
4. Speech actions in bold face are discussed on a *factual level*. Terms are marked by simple inverted commas. Cited words and extracts from transcripts will be given in double inverted commas.
5. Cf. the corresponding term 'topic-change-gambit' discussed by Keller (1979) (this volume).
6. Cf. Verschueren (this volume) for an elaboration of this point.
7. In some types of discourse such as **telegrammes** ('arriving Tuesday') or **notifications** which contain announcements, the scheme is given in *abbreviated locutions*. This is characteristic of the register of "*simplified speech*" (Ferguson (1971)). It will become apparent during further discussion that announcements can generally be placed in such a register if they contain all obligatory elements. As the propositional act only calls for a rough description of the future action, also those speakers who can only speak in simple terms are often able to successfully announce. On the other hand, many utterances made by speakers in a foreign language are interpreted as only being announcements even if they are already involved in the action they verbalize ("broken language").
8. The underlining in the transcripts points out the phenomenon under discussion. The sign ,[' (Partiturzeichen) embraces those lines of utterances which have to be read simultaneously. (For further explanation of the transcript symbols, see Ehlich & Rehbein (1976).)
9. Cf. Brinkmann (1971^2), p. 330 f.
10. Cf. in detail Ullmer-Ehrich (1977).
11. Rehbein (1977, p. 152).

12. See Ehlich & Rehbein (1974) for further explanation of this term.
13. Cf. the category of 'openers' worked out by Keller (this volume).
14. See in more detail Coulmas (1979). In the following, I refer to 'routine formulas' when speaking of 'formulas'.
15. Cf. the analysis of Humpert (1975).
16. Keller (this volume) calls the procedure by which the speaker focusses the hearer upon the content of the subsequent turn 'semantic framing'.
17. 'Augments' (: tags) of speech actions are analyzed in Rehbein (1979a).
18. Isenberg (1976, p. 62). Isenberg's *textlinguistic* analysis of announcements as "right-orientated partner functions" between two subsequent sentences appears superficial and moreover tautological. It is obvious that hearer activity as an essential part of speech actions like announcement has no place in his theory.
19. Kallmeyer was the first to describe a particular form of announcement under the name of '*implications*' (Kallmeyer (1978, p. 228 ff.) but he places implications *next to* announcements and attributes a special kind of focussing to them. He is dealing with utterances in which someone announces something of importance but then says 'that's not so important' or 'that would be going too far now'. These are formulations by means of which the speaker anticipates barriers in the hearer and, according to Kallmeyer, either respects them or requests a demand to nevertheless begin his talk on what he has implicated. However, two distinctions have to be made: On the one hand, we have something like a **directed indiscretion** by which the hearer develops a strong focus; in this case implications could count as announcements. If, on the other hand, the speaker is sincere then we have a dethematization, which is the same as a *withdrawn* announcement.

    It has to be noted that many of the examples of announcements given by Kallmeyer actually prove to be pre-announcements; the same applies to the examples of implications: implications are made in order to overcome certain "barriers".
20. In Rehbein (1976) 'introductions of revelations' were looked upon as particular types of announcements. This classification no longer appears to make sense. Firstly, it is not a matter of introductions (see § 5 on the distinction introduction/announcement), secondly, they can be included in the announcements just dealt with.
21. Sacks (1976) was the first to comment on pre-sequences. Rehbein (1976, § 3.2.) gives a determination of the function of pre-sequences. Terasaki (1976) also uses the term of pre-sequence.
22. Cf. the differentiation within the category of 'openers' worked out and discussed by Drazdauskiene and Keller (both in this volume).
23. Gülich (1970) provides a detailed analysis of all kinds of opening signals in speech contributions. Lack of space prevents me from discussing her results.

BRUCE FRASER

On Apologizing*

ABSTRACT

Apologies are viewed in this paper as one type of remedial work, action taken to change what might be seen as an offensive act into an acceptable one. The act of apologizing is analyzed into its necessary properties – those which must obtain for the act to come off – and those beliefs we usually take to be true about someone who has apologized. Ten different strategies for apologizing are presented with examples to illustrate each. Finally, the results from a research effort to identify those contextual features such as severity of infraction, sex of speaker and formality of situation which might influence the choice of a particular apologizing strategy are presented and analyzed.

During the course of our everyday affairs we may offend another. An offense of this sort often arises because we violate social norms: for example, belching at the dinner table, arriving late to a doctor's office, or telephoning an acquaintance late at night. On the other hand, an offense may arise because we fail to fulfill a personal expectation held by the offended individual: for example, when the offended person anticipates a call on his birthday, or anticipates being acknowledged as having contributed to the ideas underlying a scholarly paper.

In such cases, once the offender recognizes that some infraction is perceived by another, he may attempt to put things right, thereby relieving himself of some if not all of the associated moral responsibility. To do this, the offender must undertake what Goffman (1971) has called "remedial work," work whose function is

> ... to change the meaning that otherwise might be given to an act, transforming what could be seen as offensive into what can be seen as acceptable. This change seems to be accomplished, in our Western society at least, by striking in some way at the moral responsibility otherwise imputed to the offender. (page 109)

Goffman suggests that such remediation is accomplished by three main devices: accounts, requests, and apologies.

*I would like to thank Jean Fraser and Ellen Rintell for comments on earlier versions of this paper. Neither of them offers any apologies for the errors left within.

On Goffman's analysis, an account – what in common usage is an excuse or explanation – consists of restructuring the initial response of the offended and appreciably reducing fault (responsibility) of the offender, at least among reasonable people. As he argues:

> The more an actor can argue mitigating circumstances successfully, the more he can establish that the act is not to be taken as an expression of his moral character; contrarily, the more he is held responsible for his act, the more fully it will define him for others. (page 112)

Thus the 'goodness' of an account rests on the degree to which the offender can transfer the responsibility of the offense to another party or source. Strategies for providing accounts include claiming that the act didn't really occur, admitting commission of the act but claiming ignorance of its effects, and claiming impaired competence such as drunkenness or passion. Clearly the success of an excuse or explanation will depend on the severity of the act at issue and the extent to which the account is a plausible justification of the behavior involved. Daydreaming is an acceptable account for failing to notice a friend; it fails as an account for causing an auto accident.

Requests, as Goffman has characterized them, ought really be labeled as "requests for permission to infract;" that is, instances in which a potential offender is "asking license of a potentially offended person to engage in what could be considered a violation of his rights" (112). The requester in such a case is indicating that he is fully aware of the potential offensiveness of the proposed action, but is begging sufferance, thereby exposing himself to rejection. Saying "Excuse me" before passing someone, muttering "Getting off" when leaving a subway train, or asking , "May I ask you a personal question?," are all ways of begging sufferance. In these cases, the request is made prior to the commission of the potentially offensive act, the assumption being that when the potential violation is invited, or at least countenanced by the potential victim, the action ceases to be a violation.

The third device for remedial work suggested by Goffman is the apology. Here we have the offender working after the offensive action, similar to an account though unlike a request, but with the added feature not shared by an account that the offender is expressing regret for the undesirable effect of the act upon the offended party. It is here that I want to focus my attention in this paper. I first will characterize an apology in terms of (1) what we assume to be the beliefs held by the person apologizing and (2) what must actually be conveyed for an apology to come off. Then I will examine the strategies one can employ to carry out an apology for, like requests, there are a variety of semantic formulae that can be utilized by the speaker in apologizing.

Finally, I will report on work aimed at examining how certain social factors appear to determine the choice of a strategy in a given situation.

AN APOLOGY

An apology is incontestably a type of illocutionary act, a type of speech act Austin (1962) claimed could be performed by invoking the appropriate formula under the appropriate circumstances.[1] Indeed, when the speaker utters, "I apologize for . . ." there is no question that an apology has been made, or perhaps more accurately, offered. Of course, whether or not this ought to count as a sincere apology is another issue, one we will consider below. Given that an apology is a type of speech act, what do we understand an apology to consist of?

We can analyze an apology into two different spheres: what we customarily believe to be true about the speaker who is apologizing; what must be true in order for an apology to be made.[2]

Looking first at the belief sphere, there are four assumptions we take to be true of the person who apologizes. First, we assume that the speaker believes that some act, A, has been performed prior to the time of speaking, even if only the act of *not* doing something. Note that one cannot apologize by saying "*I apologize for not having left by tomorrow" since there is, at the time of speaking, no relevant act over which to apologize.[3] Second, we assume that the speaker believes that the act personally offended the hearer. Though one can utter, "I apologize for thinking such fine thoughts about you," it is never taken to be a serious apology since the thinking could not have offended the hearer.[4] Thirdly, we assume that the speaker believes he was at least partly responsible for the offense. Here, also, though one can say, "I apologize for being born," it is used in jest, not as a serious apology, presumably because the speaker has little control over his birth. Finally, we assume that the speaker genuinely feels regret for the act he committed which offended the hearer; one finds "I apologize for stepping on your toe, but I'm not sorry" a very strange apology at best.

Before turning to the second set of conditions. I should point out that although the four speaker beliefs just articulated are customarily held by the speaker who apologizes, this need not be the case. A speaker can violate one or more of these positions and still apologize successfully, albeit insincerely. I might, for example, apologize for breaking your valuable vase which, in fact is still whole. A strange apology, but an apology nevertheless. Or, though I know you value highly the book I sent you for Christmas, I might apologize for having done so. Finally, even though I might know that

I had nothing to do with your being fired from your job, I still might apologize to you by saying "I apologize for your having been fired last week." (Such a gratuitous apology might turn on the speaker who may afterwards be viewed by the hearer as actually having played some part in his being fired.) Thus, in violating one or more of these speaker conditions, we may render the apology defective, though not null and void.[5]

Whether or not the speaker holds the three conditions just discussed, an apology may be performed just in case two basic conditions are met: first, the speaker acknowledges responsibility for having performed some act; and second, the speaker conveys regret for the offense which came about as a result of the commission of the act. Note that neither, "I apologize for Xing, but I deny that I did it" or "I apologize for Xing, but I don't regret it one bit" can be used as an apology, even an insincere one. In short, to apologize is to do two things: take responsibility for an offensive act, and express regret for the offense committed, though not necessarily for the act itself.[6]

Of course, there are cases in which an expression ordinarily used to apologize is intended quite differently. The use of "Excuse me" is one such example. On the one hand, this expression might be used as a bona-fide apology; on the other hand, it might be used as a request for sufferance in the sense discussed above. Which force is intended by the speaker must be determined by the context of utterance.[7] Similarly, the use of "I'm sorry" may have the force of an apology, or simply count as the expression of regret on the part of the speaker, with absolutely no implication of speaker responsibility intended. The use of "I'm sorry" to the relative of one just passed away comes to mind as one example of this expression not being used as an apology. The use of "Please let me pay for the damages" may be used as an apology under certain circumstances; it may also be used as a simple offer to the injured without any implication intended that the speaker is either responsible in any way for the offense or harbors any regret for the offense sustained. One need not go further to establish the point, namely, that although there are certain strategies for apologizing, some of which are better known and more frequently used than others, none can be uniquely interpreted as being used as an apology, except perhaps the performative form, though this, also, is subject to certain alternative interpretations.[8]

STRATEGIES FOR APOLOGIZING[9]

Given the analysis of apologizing just presented, how does one go about making an apology. That is, what can one say in order to apologize? Goffman took a relatively narrow view on this question when he wrote that when apologizing, "whether one runs over another's sentence, time, dog, or body, one is more or less reduced to saying some variant of 'I'm sorry.' " (page 117) Though the expression of regret on the part of the speaker is certainly one of the primary strategies – semantic formulae – for apologizing, there are a number of others which bear examination. I will list them first with some representative examples in terms of the specification of the strategy, and then comment on them.

Strategy 1: Announcing that you are apologizing
"I (hereby) apologize for . . ."

Strategy 2: Stating one's obligation to apologize
"I must apologize for . . ."

Strategy 3: Offering to apologize
"I (hereby) offer my apology for . . ."
"I would like to offer my apology to you for . . ."

Strategy 4: Requesting the hearer accept an apology
"Please accept my apology for . . ."
"Let me apologize for . . ."
"I would appreciate it if you would accept my apology for . . ."

Strategy 5: Expressing regret for the offense
"I'm (truly/very/so/terribly) sorry for . . ."
"I (truly/very much/so . . .) regret that I . . ."

Strategy 6: Requesting forgiveness for the offense
"Please excuse me for . . ."
"Pardon me for . . ."
"I beg your pardon for . . ."
"Forgive me for . . ."

Strategy 7: Acknowledging responsibility for the offending act
"That was my fault"
"Doing that was a dumb thing to do"

Strategy 8: Promising forbearance from a similar offending act
"I promise you that that will never happen again"

Strategy 9: Offering redress
"Please let me pay for the damage I've done"

The first four strategies seem to fall together since they are relatively direct: in each, the speaker mentions that an apology is at issue, though only in the first, the performative form, does he actually *say* that what he is doing is apologizing. The other three strategies – that of expressing the obligation to apologize, offering to apologize, and requesting the hearer accept an apology do not literally count as announcing that one is apologizing, but there is little likelihood that the speaker's intentions are other than to apologize in choosing one of these strategies. That one of these rather than the more formal sound performative form or one of the others listed below is chosen is an interesting question, one we examine below. Notice that in none of these four strategies does the speaker explicitly *say* that he has committed the offensive act or that he regrets the offense, though these two points are certainly contained in the meaning of the words *apology* or *apologize.*

The next five strategies are much more indirect than the first four; in these the speaker does not *say* that an apology is at issue. In strategy 5 the speaker is, however, explicitly expressing regret for the offense as well as explicitly acknowledging responsibility for the act itself. Of course, in using the more abbreviated form of "I'm sorry" or just "Sorry," the speaker must assume that the identity of the offending act is shared by both parties. The inclusion of *very, so, terribly,* and the like do not convert this strategy into another, but rather, intensify the sense of regret expressed by the speaker. Whether or not such intensity is truly felt is, of course, another question.

In requesting forgiveness for the offense, strategy 6, the speaker is again explicitly acknowledging responsibility for the offending act, but not explicitly expressing regret. By saying "Please excuse me for stepping on your toe" I have not specifically *said* that I have any regret for having offended you, though there is certainly an entailment that I feel it; why else would I be seeking your forgiveness? The same point holds for strategy 7 in which the speaker is expressing responsibility for the offending act ("that was my fault") – but here regret is only implied, not entailed. Whereas the seeking of forgiveness or seeking to be excused from the consequences of some prior act does indeed linguistically entail regret for having brought about those unfavorable consequences, this does not hold for simply admitting that one previously did something. In both strategies the speaker expresses responsibility for the offensive action, but in the first case, there is a strong (entailed) connection to the requirement of regret necessary for an apology, while in the second, only what we can call a conversational implication.

In choosing the 8th strategy, the speaker expresses neither responsibility for having performed the act nor regret for the offense committed. Both of these apology conditions must be inferred by the hearer from the context of speaking and knowledge of what had previously occurred. A similar situation holds for the 9th strategy in which the speaker offers to make redress for the offense. In saying "What can I do to make amends" or "How can I ever repay you" the speaker is certainly implying that he has some responsibility and feels regret, but this does not necessarily follow. One can easily imagine hearing from a wealthy father whose son had just broken a neighbor's picture window, "Let me pay you for the damages," not because he felt any regret for the damage (he might be secretly delighted at the inconvenience caused to the neighbor whom he didn't like) nor any responsibility for the act (his son was over 16 years old and accountable under the law) but because he felt it easier to offer to pay the damages at that point and be done with it rather than wait until later.

A final strategy is that of recantation. Frankly, I am relatively unfamiliar with this mode of apologizing though I'm told that it is used to renounce one's erroneous political orientation in totalitarian states. Since this form of apologizing is not frequent in English language countries, it is probably not worth examining further here.

As I mentioned earlier, though any of the 9 strategies above might be used to make an apology, it is often the case that they are not used alone but are combined. It is not unusual to hear some variation, "I'm sorry. Please excuse me; that was a dumb thing to do. It won't happen again.", a combination of four of the ten strategies just presented. Similarly, one hears combinations such as, "I apologize for knocking that over; what can I do to make it up to you?" Which one or ones are chosen in any given instance appears to depend on the particular circumstance under which the apology is required, a topic we turn to in a moment.

Before doing so, however, it is worth noting that there are strategies for responding to an apology just as there are strategies for making one. One can reject the need for apologizing, for example, by saying "You didn't have to apologize; I certainly understand." Or one can deny offense, for example by saying, "I wasn't really upset." Another acceptable response is to express appreciation for the concern of the speaker "Thanks for your concern," while yet a fourth response is to reject speaker responsibility for the action, for example, by saying, "Well, you really couldn't help it." What the hearer cannot do, or at least cannot do under most circumstances, is *accept* the apology, even if the strategy for making it is to request acceptance. Thus, if the speaker has apologized, even by saying "Please accept my apology," the response cannot be "I accept your apology" unless, of course, one wants to maintain a social distance that is very great and suggests, though does not require, that the hearer is not about to accept the attempt at remedial work.[10]

FACTORS INFLUENCING THE CHOICE OF APOLOGIZING STRATEGY

In considering how various factors influence the choice of an apologizing strategy, one must immediately ask: Why was it that people even chose to apologize? The first answer is the obvious one, namely, that the individual feels genuinely regretful for his actions and wants to set things right by taking responsibility and expressing regret. This is surely the case of a mother, who in talking to her children about an impending divorce, said, "I'm sorry. I know how much it hurts you. I just have to do it and you've got to try to understand. Daddy will still be your father."

However, there appears to be another motivation other than genuine concern, what we might class as a ritual apology.[11] In these cases the speaker is simply fulfilling what is expected of him. This is surely the case of the salesman in Filene's Basement, a large bargain basement store, who routinely utters "Pardon me" or "Sorry" as he carries a huge armful of clothes through the throngs of shoppers, whether or not he touches them, never looking right or left to see the extent of any injury, if any. Similarly, the airline clerk on the telephone who returns after a considerable delay and begins by saying, "I'm sorry you had to wait so long; thank you for waiting." Both of us knew it wasn't her fault.

This ritual motivation for apologizing can be viewed as a facilitating move, wherein the person apologizing does so primarily to get on about the business at hand, whether or not there is any genuine concern or if an apology is expected under the circumstances. One instance of this occurred when the shopping cart of a middle aged woman shopping in a large grocery store was bumped into by another shopper. The first woman turned, and without hesitation said, "Excuse me," then turned around again and continued her shopping. Most of these ritual cases appear to resemble the use of "Sorry about that Chief," heard so frequently from one Maxwell Smart, the incompetent superspy on the now-defunct TV show, "Get Smart."

Clearly, it is very difficult to differentiate between the genuine and ritual apology in many cases; in fact, an apology may often be motivated from both perspectives. Our major interest in examining the use of apologies, however, was to determine if factors such as the nature of the offense, the severity of the offense, the situation of the interaction, the familiarity of the individuals involved, and the sex of the individual plays any systematic and significant role in the choice of apology strategy. To examine these questions, C. Harvey and K. Oleskey, graduate students at Boston University, and the author collected several hundred examples of apologizing through personal experience, participant observation, responses of role playing, and from reports provided by friends and colleagues. In all cases we attempted to obtain as much information as seemed relevant so that any conclusions we drew would have a reasonable foundation. We were well aware, as is anyone who has attempted this type of work, that the data we obtained would be suggestive at best. Thus, what is presented here are what appear to be clear trends, though I do not provide any statistical support for the conclusions.

The first factor we considered was the nature of the infraction: Was it a social or personal norm that was offended? We were initially led to examine this aspect from the work of Borkin and Rinehart (1978) who discussed the forms "Excuse me" and "I'm sorry" and made some interesting and what seem to be quite accurate suggestions. They claimed that the use of "Excuse me" is more appropriate when a social rule has been broken, while "I'm sorry" is more appropriate when someone has suffered some personal injury. As such, the former is more formal and provides for more social distance between the conversational participants. They argue, for example, that to say, "Excuse me, what did you say?" would be more appropriate than "I'm sorry, what did you say"? in a formal setting, while to say "I'm sorry for stepping on your sore toe" would hold sway over the "Excuse me" strategy where some personal injury was evident. One can imagine the incongruity if the divorcing mother in the example above were to have said, to her children, "Excuse me, I know how much it hurts you . . ." Borkin and Rinehart point out that there are many situations in which these two areas overlap – where rule breaking and personal injury co-exist – and in such cases, either the "Excuse me" or the "I'm sorry" may be appropriate.

That their observations seem to be quite accurate hardly needs elaboration. Suffice it to say that we seldom found an "Excuse me" when there was any trace of a personal injury; there was almost always an "I'm sorry" in some form (shades of Goffman) when there was a personal injury, and where we would judge that either might have been appropriate, the "sorry" form clearly dominated. It was almost as if the apologizer wasn't about to take any chances and adopted the view, when in doubt, cover yourself by using a strategy expressing regret for some injury.

The second area we considered was how the severity of the infraction determined the choice of strategy. Not only is the range of social violations much narrower and less severe than those of personal injury, we did not find any cases of extreme rule breaking; for example, where someone stumbled upon a couple in the throes of love-making or where someone lost his dinner at the table, or when someone suffered from flatulence during a moment of silence for a loved one. Thus, our social violations consisted mostly of slight bumps, people causing a slight inconvenience to another, someone entering the wrong room, and the like. Nearly all these cases resulted in an "Excuse me," with a few "I'm sorry." However, in many of these cases of social violation and certainly in the more serious personal the simple apology was followed by another apologizing strategy and often by some account which sought to provide an explanation or excuse for why the infraction happened in the first place. A waitress came over to our table after we had been waiting for nearly half an hour for service and said, "I'm terribly sorry. Two of the staff are sick today." Not just an apology, but an account as well. We weren't any less hungry but somewhat less annoyed at the lack of service. One finds similar combinations of apologies and accounts in many varied places; for example, in doctor's offices where "emergencies" are the rule rather than exception, with building contractors and workmen where "unforeseen" extras abound, even in the face of promises to the contrary, and with the telephone company when complaining about faulty service, where they are constantly installing new, better equipment, but for some reason, always on my line, and always after 6 p.m. In short, one finds many many cases of apologies for personal injury accompanied by accounts, particularly the more serious cases.

However, for the cases where there was some significant injury or inconvenience, there appeared to be a change from an apology with an account to an apology with an offer of redress. This was illustrated when the author was bumped into at the supermarket, causing an armful of groceries to tumble to the floor. The perpetrator of this infraction began with "Excuse me," went on to "Oh my, I'm so sorry" when she saw the problem, and then followed with "Here, let me help you pick them up." C. Harvey asked respondents to a role play situation to indicate what they would say after they had just run over the neighbor's puppy with their car. Almost always they followed the apology with some form of offering to help take the dog to the vets, pay for the dog, buy a new dog, and the like. The one exception was a male who claimed he would have said "That's a stupid dog you have there." We can speculate though we have no data on what would be said by someone who had in fact seriously injured another. Perhaps nothing; perhaps only an "I'm sorry." with no account, since any account might be irrelevant under the circumstances.

The third factor we considered was the situation in which the infraction occurred. These ranged from the most formal, for example the faux pas of interrupting the President of the University while he was speaking to another person, to the most intimate, for example, stepping on a spouse's toes in the shower. The former provoked an "Excuse me, I'm sorry for interrupting you" while the latter received only an "Oops." We frequently heard the more 'formal sounding' "I apologize . . ." or "Please accept my apologies for . . ." in business and professional situations but never once the form "I *hereby* apologize for . . ." The best conclusion we can draw in this area, particularly since we had only very few cases at either end of the range, is that the more formal the situation, the longer and more elaborate the apology. Even when all participants were aware of the facts, the apologies in formal situations indicated that the speaker felt a need to play out his role.

The next factor we considered was the relative familiarity between the interactants. Similar to the factor of situational formality, familiarity ranges from two people who have never encountered one another previously to those who share the same home. The former case is best examplified by the cases of apologizing observed in stores and places of commerce but, because of the limited severity and type of activity, the type of strategy used was nearly always limited to "Excuse me" or "I'm sorry," sometimes followed by a brief account. The interaction between people unfamiliar with each other tends to be limited to formal situations. (There are some obvious exceptions to this, for example, the interaction between a prostitute and her client. We tried but were unable to gain any examples from such situations.) It does seem clear that as the degree of familiarity increases between the interactants, the need (or at least the perceived need) to provide elaborate apologies decreases. Husbands and wives reported apologies frequently taking the form of "Oops," "No good," "I'm an idiot" and the like, where the utterance does not even specifically refer to the act in question nor mentioned acknowledging explicitly responsibility for the act or express explicitly regret. It appears that under such familiar circumstances, each works on the assumption that the other will "fill in" the missing parts. That this filling in could certainly be done in the more formal or more unfamiliar situation is clear; that people do not expect others to do this, or do not expect that one should expect others to do this is an interesting and unexamined aspect of remedial work.

The last factor we considered was the sex of the apologizer: Do men or women tend to apologize more? Contrary to popular stereotype, we did not find women offering more apologies than men. In all the variations of situations we recorded – formal and intimate; alien and familiar; trivial and severe; social and personal – we found that both men and women would sometimes apologize, sometimes not, with no apparent systematic or predictable frequency. The fact that we have one case of a woman apologizing to a tree stump which she had just tripped over is surely offset by the case of a man apologizing to his reflection in a glass door. On the other hand, there was one case of a woman who had just bumped into another's car who got out and said not one word of an apology; she just glared at the occupant of the other car. Matched with this is the man who pushed into the line waiting to buy tickets to a local movie theater who said not a word, didn't even make eye contact with those commenting on this who were standing nearby. In short, we found that there are those that do apologize and those that do not, and this does not seem to lie with one sex over the other.

It should be evident from the foregoing that we have not provided the last word on apologizing. One must question whether there are really only 8 or 9 basic strategies, as suggested, rather than a larger variety of subtypes. In fact, it is unclear whether it makes sense to try to fit strategies such as these into a taxonomy at all. And, while we found some trends in what strategy would be chosen in terms of the conversational circumstances, there were far more questions raised than answered. Finally, as one pursues the use of apologies in ordinary conversation, it becomes apparent that to research this area of language use is still in its painful adolescence.

NOTES

1. A more recent account of speech acts can be found in Bach and Harnish (1980) and Fraser (1980).
2. Goffman suggests that the apology in its fullest form has the following elements:

   > expression of embarrassment and chagrin; clarification that one knows what conduct had been expected and sympathies with the application of negative sanction; verbal rejection, repudiation, and disavowal of the wrong way of behaving along with vilification of the self that so behaved; espousal of the right way and an avowal henceforth to pursue that course; performance of penance and the volunteering of restitution. (page 113)

   Frankly, I do not believe that the above factors are part of a full apology, however, that ought to be defined. To be sure, they all may be part of an elaborate apology, as may many other factors such as the fact that this was the first time such an action had happened, that the offender couldn't have predicted that this would have happened, and so forth. However, Goffman's presentation does not get at the basic notion of what it is to apologize.
3. Performative verbs such as *requests, apologize, promise* and the like usually impose a tense restriction on the complement sentence which reflects certain time constraints on the act in question. Thus, "I request you leave tomorrow" but "*I request you leave yesterday."
4. One can, of course, construct contexts in which the conventions of usage are radically altered. Borodin, the composer, is said to have composed only when ill, pursuing his medical scholarship when well. Hence, his music-loving friends were heard to greet him warmly with "I hope you're feeling poorly today."
5. Austin used the term "felicitous" to refer to unimpaired speech acts, "infelicitous" to refer to those with some defect.
6. The reason for this caveat is simply to cover the case where the speaker intended to perform some act but did not or could not anticipate it offending another. In fact, the speaker might intend to perform the act again, although sincerely apologizing to the offended person for whatever offense was effected.
7. The term force, coined by Austin, should be taken to mean the name of the act having been performed. For example, the utterance of "It's cold in here" may have the force of a complaint about the temperature, the force of a request to turn up the heat or simply a report about the status of the room. Contextual factors such as the situation, the roles of the speaker and hearers, the past conversational history and the manner of speaking all must be considered in reaching a conclusion about what was intended by the speaker. Various papers have approached these issues; for example, Bach and Harnish, 1980, Fraser, 1975, 1980, and Searle, 1975.
8. Though the use of the sentence form "I apologize for . . ." is usually taken as an apology, it can be used as a statement of habitual behavior, as a reply to the question "How do you continue to get away with that nonsense?" Only the presence of "hereby" as in "I hereby apologize for . . ." forces the apology interpretation albeit in a stiff and formal way.

9. I am using the term "strategy" here to refer not to a particular sentence token nor even a sentence type, but rather to a set of sentences, each of which meets certain semantic criteria and any of which can be used to perform the act in question because of this semantic specification, although the appropriateness in a given context will vary. One strategy for requesting, for example, is that of "Expressing desire that the hearer perform the act." Sentences such as "I would like you to . . ." "It would please me if you would . . .," "I would appreciate it if you would . . .," and "It would make me very happy for you to . . ." are examples of this strategy.
10. It has been brought to my attention that in a formal situation for example, where a superior has criticized a subordinate only to have the charges successfully rejected, the superior's "I apologize for my comments" might well evoke the response, "Accepted."
11 See Coulmas, 1979, for a discussion of ritualized formulae.

WILLIS J. EDMONDSON

On Saying You're Sorry

ABSTRACT

Some different senses in which we may talk of conversational "routine" are distinguished, and a discourse model in which these distinctions are made is sketched. A communicative act is claimed to have a locutionary, an illocutionary and an interactional significance. Apologies are described as a type of illocutionary act, and in investigating the communicative acts which have this illocutionary value, the relations between locution and illocution, and between the illocution and various different interactional moves are discussed. In this discussion, communication rules, conversational strategies, and social maxims are distinguished and exemplified.

INTRODUCTION

There is a sense in which most, if not all, of everyday conversational activity can be described as 'routinal' or 'conventionalized'. This follows from the notion of discourse structure, the notion that "the moment a conversation is started whatever is said is a determining factor for what in any reasonable expectation may follow" (Firth 1964, p. 94). We may indeed go further and suggest that given a situational context, social members have strong expectations as to what types of conversation may occur in such a context, and how such conversations may be started. (See here Hasan 1978, and the notions of a "structural formula" and "contextual configuration," specifying the behavioral options for participants in classes of social events.) Thus it it perfectly feasible to chart behavioral possibilities both for the case in which a conversational goal is determined by a specific type of conversational opening (for example the case of asking for route directions – Klein 1977, Rehbein 1977), and for the case in which a specific situation limits severely the types of transaction that may licitly occur in that situation. For example to join a queue in front of a box-office, or to take a seat in a restaurant is to commit oneself in advance to specific types of conversational behavior with the ticket-seller or waitress (on the latter situation see for example Ehlich and Rehbein 1972). Consider here Halliday's remark that "From a sociological point of view, a text is meaningful not so much because we do not know what the speaker is going to say, as in a mathematical model of communication, as because we do know" (Halliday 1975, p. 129).

In order to interpret such remarks, and begin to discuss some different types of routine in discourse,[1] I wish initially to make two centrally relevant distinctions: firstly, between what conversationalists may be said to "know" as opposed to what they actually *do*, which I shall link with a distinction between communicative and social competence, and secondly, between what is *said* in an ongoing conversational encounter, and what is *done* thereby (Labov 1972). In the light of these distinctions, and inside the discourse framework which I shall sketch in making them, I shall investigate some aspects of the use of apologies in conversational English. Communicative acts to be termed "apologies" will be viewed as locutions, illocutions, and interactional acts or moves, and I shall attempt to relate these three perspectives concerning a communicative act in non-arbitrary ways.

SOME DISTINCTIONS RELEVANT TO THE ANALYSIS OF DISCOURSE

Widdowson (1979) makes a distinction between "rules" and "procedures" in discourse, remarking that "a good deal of what we do, linguistically or otherwise, seems not to conform exactly to rules, seems indeed to be a manipulation of rules to suit particular occasions," (p. 141) I wish to interpret this distinction as underpinning that between "communicative" and "social" competence (see also here Edmondson 1978). Communicative competence may be represented as a series of rules concerning the encoding, decoding and sequencing of central communicative acts. In the actual business of conversation such rules are used or manipulated by members in order to achieve communicative goals and maintain or restore social harmony. The use to which communicative competence is put therefore reflects an individual's social competence. Some of us are "better" at this than others. The evaluation of social behavior is in part determined by empirically ascertainable norms of social behavior which operate for a particular community or group of social members. (See for example Leech's "tact principle," Leech 1977, pp. 19 et seq.). To give a crude exemplification, given that I am 'greeted' at the beginning of an encounter, I cannot escape the choice of returning or acknowledging this greeting, or of not doing so. This is entailed by the nature of communication. However whether I actually *do* return or acknowledge the 'greeting,' and if so, *how* I do so, is determined by my social status as an individual. I may be "friendly," "rude," "witty," "original" and so on. This does not reflect my communicative competence as a member of the relevant speech community, or sub-group thereof, but my social competence as an individual social member.[2]

This distinction is clearly not a totally sharp one, but seems important in that any notion of "conversational routine" needs to take account of what status such routines have in conversational behavior. "Routines," we may say informally, are convenient, but need not be followed. We may distinguish then between communicative rules, and actual observed conversational behavior in which the use to which the former are put may be evaluated in the light of social notions of what is 'acceptable' behavior. The central point is that in ongoing conversations the significance of the "unexpected" or "original" utterance is derived from hearer expectations which may be said to encapsulate our notions of the "expected" or "conventional". It is in the light of our knowledge of what an interlocutor *can* say or do that we interpret what he *actually* says and does. In this sense we may claim that all (interpretable) conversational behavior is based on routine, if we can relate procedures to rules, i.e., explicitly relate conversational strategy both to rules which encapsulate our notion of communicative competence, and to conventions or norms which describe a community's concept of what is and what is not socially acceptable behavior.

In approaching the notion of routine in conversation we clearly need to distinguish between what is said in an ongoing conversation, and what is done thereby. For example we may distinguish between the predictability of the use of a particular linguistic expression to perform a particular communicative act, and the predictability that a particular communicative act will be performed in particular circumstances. That a particular "fixed expression" has an associated recognizable 'function' in discourse does not mean that the communicative or other act realizing that function has a predictable distribution, nor that *any* realization of that communicative "function" will necessarily involve the use of the "fixed expression," as opposed to the use of some other linguistic (or para-linguistic) token. There are grounds for confusion here as there is an observable tendency for what we may loosely call fixed expressions to be used in predictable ways and in predictable circumstances: this is precisely why such expressions have become standardized.

In attempting to distinguish what is done from what is said in a discourse it seems to me useful and necessary to distinguish three perspectives concerning communicative acts: the locutionary, the illocutionary and the interactional.[3] The locutionary act we may crudely equate with the utterance made, its logical sense, and *locutionary* force as determined by grammatical mood. The illocutionary significance of an utterance concerns its significance as communicating the speaker's attitudes, feelings or beliefs vis à vis some event or state of affairs explicitly or implicitly referred to in that utterance. The shift from locutionary to illocutionary force has been explored in the theory of speech acts. The interactional act concerns the significance of the utterance as a contribution to the ongoing discourse of which it forms a structural part. It is in interactional terms that a discourse is structured, sequences of interactional acts constituting interactional moves, and so on (cf. Sinclair and Coulthard). Thus an utterance of the form *okay* might be said informally to constitute a "promise" as an illocution, and a "satisfy", "resolve" or "comply" as an interactional act or move, if it appeared in a (fabricated) sequence such as

– Promise me you'll come
– Okay[4]

A communicative act is then to be seen as an illocutionary act (in turn derivable via various types of convention from a locutionary act) which realizes a 'slot' in an interactional structure.[5] We may then now suggest that what we understand as routine in conversation may involve the links between a communicative act and a situation, a communicative act and some other communicative act, a locutionary and an illocutionary act, or an illocutionary act and an interactional act or move, where in the latter two cases the same utterance is involved.

Before investigating some of these aspects of conversational behavior with respect to apologies however two further distinctions may be noted.

Firstly, some illocutions may be said to be discourse-internal, in that the event or state of affairs therein referred to is a discourse-internal event, i.e., a preceding or possibly subsequent communicative act which is or will be part of the structure of the ongoing discourse. Consider the case of "thanks," which we may take to be a category of illocutionary act:

A – Hello how are you
B – Fine thanks
A – You're looking very well
B – Thank you (fabricated)

The thankable is clearly the interlocutor's preceding communicative act in such cases. Compare however:

(1) – I've brought your washing in Mrs Smith ∧
it's raining
– oh thank you

(2) – It's raining Mrs Smith
– oh thank you (fabricated)

The thankable in the first sequence is an event referred to in the preceding communicative act; in the second sequence, the thankable is the preceding communicative act itself.

Secondly, we may distinguish between discourse-internal illocutions, which by definition have an interactional function inside the structure of the discourse they occur in, and interactional lubricants, which are realized in verbal behavior, but do not have illocutionary significance, as their interactional significance pertains to the modality (in the sense of House and Kasper, this volume) of a temporally contiguous communicative act performed by the same speaker. Such interactional lubricants, which one may term "gambits," (cf. Beneke 1975, Edmondson 1977, Keller, this volume) are therefore not communicative acts in the technical sense meant here. Consider the following:

Y: yeah even on the other occasions he's been er something of a bore
hasn't he you know [I mean
X: yeah] but ^ well he's not a bad bloke now is he I mean . . .

(2C12)[6]

The expression *you know, I mean,* and *well* are here used as gambits. Firstly the speaker is not *saying* that something or other is "known" to the hearer, or is "meant" by himself, or is done "well". Secondly these expressions are not syntactic constituents of some contiguous locution. Thirdly, they cannot be claimed in themselves to have illocutionary significance, and fourthly, if occurring alone as a turn to talk, they could not be deemed to constitute a communicative act, as the structure of the discourse would not be affected by their occurrence. As apologies are not gambits, but a category of illocutions, I shall not investigate such devices in this paper, but it is necessary to distinguish such communicative devices from discourse-internal illocutions.[7]

APOLOGIES IN DISCOURSE

Having given a sketch of a framework inside which some aspects of conversational routine may be viewed, I wish to look in some detail at the ritual or strategic use of apologetic illocutions.

The APOLOGY[8] is an illocution Searle assigns to the paradigms of his Expressive category, for which "the truth of the proposition is presupposed"

(Searle 1976, pp. 12 et seq.). Other paradigms given by Searle are "thanks," "congratulate," "condole," "deplore," and "welcome". It is not my purpose here to discuss the appropriateness of Searle's classification, but to get at the nature of the APOLOGY by comparing this illocution with some other members of this class. Let us confine our attention to THANKS and APOLOGIES on the one hand, and "deplores" or as I prefer to say COMPLAINS on the other.

All three have a "pre-history" in the sense of Rehbein and Ehlich (1976, pp. 314 et seq.), i.e., something is "presupposed" to be the case when such an illocution occurs. The following are approximations:

APOLOGIZE S did P, P bad for H
THANK H did P, P good for S
COMPLAIN H did P, P bad for S
(S = speaker, H = hearer)

We note that in the case of the APOLOGY and the COMPLAIN, the same event P might be involved, such that what from one conversationalist's viewpoint constitutes a ground for a COMPLAIN constitutes a ground for an APOLOGY for his interlocutor. This accounts for our intuition (which may be substantiated empirically – see below) that COMPLAINS and APOLOGIES may co-occur as sequentially relevant communicative acts inside a segment of discourse (I shall use the term Exchange to denote a sequence of communicative acts in which an issue of substance raised in the initiation is resolved – see below). However, if we change the perspective on the type of subjectively-perceived event which may constitute a ground for a THANKS, giving us S did P, P good for H, it is not intuitively apparent what category or categories of illocution – expressive or otherwise – seems appropriate. "Boast" is a possible candidate, but is surely marked behavior socially, as revealed by the fact that we can say of someone that he is a boaster, but scarcely that he is a 'thanker,' a 'complainer,' or an 'apologizer'. We may then ask why there appears to be no readily available term in English to refer to the illocutionary work conducted in referring to this particular constellation of situational features.

Further, we note that with the possible exception of Searle's "deplore," there is no overt performative with which one may perform a COMPLAIN. Other things being equal, merely to say "You did P" will be interpreted as constituting a COMPLAIN, and will lead to possible countering or remedial work on the part of the Complainee. With THANKS and APOLOGIES however, the reverse is the case: it is not easy to find or imagine locutions which could be used to perform these illocutions, other than locutions containing a small set of lexical items which includes *Thank, Apologize, Sorry,* and *Grateful.*

Would we be prepared to say of utterances such as

– Oh you've washed up darling, how nice!
– I'm glad you've done the washing-up
– It was nice of you to do the washing-up
– Oh you shouldn't have done the washing-up

that they may readily constitute THANKING illocutions? Or given utterances such as

– I've gone and broken your record-player
– I wish I hadn't been so careless with your record-player
– It was really bad of me to break it

(Data fabricated)

that an APOLOGY has been made? Rhetorical questions are appropriate here, rather than negative assertions, as it is ultimately how one chooses to define a particular illocutionary act which determines whether or not a particular utterance constitutes an instance of that illocutionary category: however, definitions which run counter to members' intuitions and behavior require justification.

What these observations suggest is that "indirectness"[9] is appropriate and conventional with respect to COMPLAINING illocutions while with THANKS and APOLOGIES this is not the case. On the contrary, *gushing* is socially acceptable here ("I'm most terribly sorry, I really am," "Thanks awfully"). We need to ask why this is so, and the answer clearly involves social norms of "politeness". Leech's "Tact principle" (Leech 1977, pp. 19 et seq.) may be reformulated as an "H-Support" maxim of the form

Support your hearer's costs and benefits!

with the rider

Suppress your own!

A COMPLAIN, or an utterance referring to the case in which

S did P, P good for H

are non-H supportive behavior modes, and are thus ripe candidates for "indirectness," just as the "request" is clearly non-H supportive, and thus offers in English rich scope for indirectness (see e.g., Searle 1975, Gordon & Lakoff

1975). However with APOLOGIES and THANKS there is no cause for *not* being explicit, as such illocutions are consistent with the H-Support maxim which may be claimed to underpin social interaction.

The APOLOGY is then an instance in which illocutionary force may be derived from locutionary force (directly ascertainable for a speaker of the language) with a minimum of potential negotiation. An APOLOGY is an instance of socially-sanctioned H-Supportive behavior.[10]

Having attempted to characterize a particular type of illocution – the APOLOGY – and to account for the limited locutionary forms available in English for performing this illocutionary act, we may now investigate what speakers actually do with such illocutions in interactions terms, i.e., we may consider where APOLOGIES occur in terms of the ongoing discourse. Here I shall introduce some routinized elements of discourse structure, both sequences which illustrate communication rules, and behavior resulting from strategic ploys commonly used in conversational discourse.

In the light of the above characterization of the APOLOGY, the most predictable function of this illocution in discourse is that it counts as an attempt on the part of the speaker to cause the hearer to withdraw a preceding COMPLAIN: it is an attempt to restore social harmony. In the case that the APOLOGY is accepted (I propose the term *Satisfy* as the relevant interactional move), then the COMPLAIN is no longer a valid focus for talk- the exchange initiated by the COMPLAIN is 'closed' by the illocution by means of which the APOLOGY is accepted or Satisfied.[11] This illocution will thus be what I shall call a FORGIVE. Thus a possible three-element exchange might be as follows:

Speaker	– X	Y	X
Interactional Move	– Proffer	Contra	Satisfy
Illocutions	– Complain	Apology	Forgive

An interesting feature of the Complain is that it cannot itself be Satisfied, i.e., there is no corresponding "right-pair-part" such that together with a Complain appearing as the left-pair part a 'happy outcome' is arrived at. This follows from the fact that, in Austinian terms, the "perlocutionary intent" of a Complain is a negotiable: a hearer cannot be said to recognize by convention what behavior will Satisfy that COMPLAIN. Clearly members have strong expectations here in particular circumstances: the man who utters an APOLOGY following a COMPLAIN of the form

"You're standing on my foot"

without taking any steps to remove his offending member is behaving in a peculiar way, to say the least, but we cannot claim that in such cases the removal of the Complainable itself Satisfies the COMPLAIN – this Contra has itself to be Satisfied before the Exchange initiated by the COMPLAIN is resolved. Some instances in which an APOLOGY occurs as a Contra to a Proffered COMPLAIN may be cited:

(X notices a paper of hers in Y's possession, when she had given it to him to hand in for her as a matter of some urgency)

X: here ^ what's that
Y: [it's er

X: that's] my paper

Y: yeah I'm sorry

(3C11)

(X returns to her library seat to find it occupied by Y)

X: excuse me but I think you're in my place

Y: oh I'm ever so sorry but I'm in this terrible rush . . .

(3D21)

Apologies occur more frequently in the corpus used as Disarming moves in discourse.[12] A Disarmer is the result of using a particular anticipatory strategy derived from a social maxim formulated by Barker as

Call your own violations!

(Barker 1975, p. 37)

Crudely the strategy consists in anticipating a possible COMPLAIN on the part of a Hearer, where the Complainable is in fact a communicative act or move on the part of the user of the Disarming strategy.[13] For example given that my turning down of your request is a potential Complainable, I may APOLOGIZE prior to turning down that request, thereby effectively precluding your possible subsequent COMPLAIN. Consider the following examples:

(X is employed on a piece-rate basis on Y's farm. They disagree as to how many baskets of fruit X has picked):

X: no ^ you're wrong Mr Knox I'm sorry ^ you made the same mistake the other day remember

(3A21)

(Later in the same conversation)

Y: ah uh er well I'm sorry but there's no principle it's a fact

(3A24)

(X returns to her library seat to find it occupied by Y)

X: well er ^ (embarrassed laugh) I'm terribly sorry but er ^ I'm afraid you're in my seat

(3D11)

We have characterized an APOLOGY as having a pre-history in which S did P, P bad for Y. It does not make sense therefore to claim here that such disarming APOLOGIES in the case that they precede in time the Complainable, i.e., the communicative act which is viewed as a potential ground for a COMPLAIN – are directed towards a non-existent event.[14] Rather it makes sense to claim that in such instances a speaker is apologizing for having formulated the *intention* of performing a particular communicative act. *This* potential Complainable is of course a non-observable for the hearer until such time as the intentional state which the APOLOGY addresses find its expression in the temporarily sequent communicative act which the APOLOGY supports.

We may go a step further and suggest that not only do speakers employ communicative strategies in using supportive moves such as the Disarmer, but hearers clearly also use interpretative strategies, also based on their anticipatory powers, derived from their communicative competence and knowledge of social norms. Thus it is possible for a locution which could have functioned as a pre-posed Disarming APOLOGY to be interpreted as having the illocutionary and interactional significance of that head (i.e., non-supportive) move it could have supported. The predictability of the "following" head move follows from the fact that it is non-H-supportive behavior which is likely to constitute a potential Complainable: it is therefore non-H-supportive communicative activity which is likely to be supported by a Disarming APOLOGY. Thus the status of a responding move which is prefaced by a disarming

APOLOGY is highly predictable, i.e., it is more likely to be a "non-Satisfy" than a Satisfy. Hence the APOLOGY itself can serve to communicate that which it would or could support as a Disarming move. Given a request of the form

– Can you lend me ten pounds
utterances such as
– I hate to let you down John, but . . .
– Well I would normally John
– I don't like to sound mean John
– Sorry John

(fabricated data)

will be interpreted as constituting turndowns of that REQUEST: what might have been a Disarming supportive move functions as that which it might have supported.[15]

We can get a little more mileage out of the notion of Disarming APOLOGIES. The data here is fabricated once more, but consider the following:

– Sorry ^ I didn't quite get that
– Sorry ^ could you speak up a little
– Sorry the line seems to be bad here

Let us assume that the illocutions following the Disarming APOLOGIES may be characterized as "Requests for Repair." The speaker is not apologizing for the fact that he *intends* to make such a request for repair, but for the fact that he *needs* to do so. He is admitting to non-H-supportive behavior in the context of the ongoing conversation in that he has not heard or understood, or for some other reason is unable to interpret what his interlocutor has said.[16] Note that once again the Disarming APOLOGY may itself function as the Request for a Repair it could have supported, via interpretative strategy, but in this case intonational features mark its illocutionary value. Thus

– P

– { Sorry ^ what did you say
  Sorry. }

The function of intonation in discourse is a highly complex issue, such that I do not feel competent to go into this phenomenon in any detail. We may note however that following the argumentation above, an utterance of the form *sorry* may now constitute either a non-Satisfy to an initiating Proffer, or itself initiate an embedded Repair-exchange:

– John can you lend me ten pounds

– { Sorry
  Sorry[17] }

The distinctive intonation in the latter case therefore removes this potential ambiguity of discourse function.

Finally, I wish breifly to consider APOLIGIES appearing in what I shall call ritual Firming exchanges. These follow Business exchanges, and serve to confirm or check on the outcome of a business exchange, which we may consider for our purposes here as an exchange in which a discourse-external matter of substance is negotiated. After such negotiation, conversationalists often ratify their social standing with each other via ritual firming exchanges. There is some similarity between ritual firming exchanges and the Pre-Closes of the ethnomethodologists,[18] as in checking a negotiated outcome, the interactants are also checking that neither has more to say, and thus firming exchanges commonly follow a Business exchange, and directly precede a Closing exchange. Consider the following simple example:

Y: look there's no point in talking any more let's go
let's go and do this now
X: yes okay
Y: good
X fine
(They move off)

(2B12)

A plan of action has been negotiated here as a business. Two exchanges occur in the above extract, each having a Proffer-Satisfy structure. The second exchange is a ritual firming one, as its only outcome is a re-affirmation of the outcome of the first.

Two complementary tendencies may be observed with respect to the occurrence of APOLOGIES in ritual firming exchanges. Firstly, given a Business occasioned by a Complainable, the speaker who has been undertaking remedial face-work in negotiating that Business may ritually (re-) Proffer an APOLOGY in a firming exchange:

(X has called on Y to say she cannot keep a baby-sitting appointment. After considerable negotiation, a satisfactory solution is found, and face is restored)

X: oh ^ yes allright fine well I'll bring her round tonight

Y: yeah

X: we'll get together and erm you know ^ it should be okay then ^ I'm sure we'll come to some agreement then

Y: yes

X: and once again I'm terribly sorry about that

Y: well ^ okay okay then [Susan

X: see you] later then then shall we . . .

(1B15)

(Y had taken X's library seat, but after due negotiation, has vacated it following Y's return. The confrontation has already been resolved: the encounter ends as follows:)

Y: okay ^ er oh I'm sorry about that ^ bout that I just ^ I'm just so desperate

X: that's okay you know no hassle

(3D21)

Secondly however an APOLOGY may be Proferred in a firming exchange as a ritual *reciprocal* gesture on the part of a Complainer, who, now that the Complainable has been negotiated to a happy outcome, APOLOGIZES for having initiated the concluded business, i.e., for having issued a COMPLAIN.

(Y has forgotten to hand in a paper for X, though he had undertaken to do so. After negotiation, however, an alternative solution to the problem this poses for X has been found, and face restored.)

Y: are you sure that's okay

X: yeah that's allright ∧'s allright I'm sorry I got angry
[it's just that

Y: no you're] right I should have handed it in

X: [I mean a few hours

Y: er just had so much] on my mind ∧∧ in this ∧ physics

X: yeah I'm sorry I mean it was my own fault ∧ I ought to have done it myself

Y: yeah

(3C13)

SUMMARY

Various different senses in which we may consider conversational behavior to be 'routinal' have been distinguished, and a partial discourse analytic framework has been sketched inside which conversational rules, communicative strategies, and social maxims have been set up, largely by reference to the occurrence of illocutionary acts of APOLOGIZING. While I have concentrated in this paper on the case of the APOLOGY, I would like to think that much of the apparatus developed here for the investigation of this particular class of illocutionary acts has a much more general application to, and relevance for, the investigation of how people succeed in conversing one with another.

NOTES

1. "Discourse" is used to denote observed or observable social activity in which utterances significantly feature. "Conversation" is thus a specific type of spoken discourse, and will be my main concern. The term "routine" will be used non-technically throughout.
2. It is in the light of the distinction between communicative and social competence that I would interpret Firth's distinction between "nature" and "nurture" (Firth 1957, pp. 185 et seq.).
3. The position sketched here is also put forward in Edmondson 1978. Some parallels with Sinclair and Coulthard's "grammatical", "situational" and "discourse" categories is evident (Sinclair & Coulthard 1975, pp. 29 et seq.).
4. The terms "promise," "satisfy" and so on are used totally informally here. In the cited sequence, which is fabricated data, the utterance *okay* might constitute a commitment to "come," or a commitment to give a commitment to "come". Brazil (1975) suggests intonation will distinguish these two possibilities.
5. Cf. Klammer 1973.
6. The provenance of the empirical data used in this paper is described in Edmondson et al. 1979. The transciption used involves the following conventions: Intonation is marked selectively only, primary stress being shown by a double slash above the line, and rising or falling pitch, or combination thereof, being also shown above the line. Arrowheads indicate pauses, and square brackets enclosing segments of speech by two speakers indicate overlap – the segments so contained occur within the same time-span. When fabricated data is used in this paper it will always be stated to be such.
7. In an earlier exploration of linguistic expressions of this kind (Edmondson 1977), I used the term "gambits" to cover a wider range of phenomena, including for example turn-initial Uptakers (instances are *yeah* and *yeah but* in the extract above). I now consider it more appropriate to interpret Uptakers as discourse-internal illocutions which are elements of discourse structure.
8. It is essential, of course, to distinguish between illocutionary acts and illocutionary verbs. Names of illocutions will be capitalized, non-technical terms – possibly identical in form – will not be marked graphically. Where in discussion the status of an item is unclear, the term will be given in inverted commas.
9. "Indirectness' is relative: given the locutionary force/illocutionary force distinction, I do not accept Searle's distinction between "direct" and "indirect" illocutionary force (see here Leech 1977, pp. 3 et seq.).
10. Children are taught to act according to the H-Support maxim via instructions such as "Say you're sorry," "Say thank you," "Say hello/goodbye to your aunty." Instructions to perform REQUESTING or COMPLAINING illocutionary acts seem to be less common. Note further that expressions such as *say hellow, say thank you* and *say you're sorry* arguably constitute distinct lexical items of English: thus it is possible to say hello to someone without in fact saying "Hello" to that person, i.e., via the use of some other locution.
11. The discourse model underpinning this analysis can only be presented very incompletely here. A move consists of one or more communicative acts, being the next higher element of discourse structure above that of the interactional act (cf. Sinclair and Coulthard 1975). It is at the level of the move that turn-changing operates. Moves combine in sequences to form exchanges. The notion of an exchange used here is not precisely that of Sinclair and Coulthard however, nor is it

to be equated with the tied-pair of the ethnomethodologists (See e.g., Schegloff 1978, pp. 84–5), as an exchange as I use the term is resolved only when the business raised by the initiating Proffer has been resolved. Thus some tied-pairs may be exchanges, other will be elements of structure in non-terminated exchanges.

12. Though the corpus is small, I would hazard the opinion that the relative frequencies obtained here might well be reflected in a larger sample of conversation.
13. Some other types of anticipatory strategy are sketched in Edmondson 1978.
14. Here of course, P's non-occurrence is not itself an event. The non-occurrence of a particular act can itself be a significant event of course, in discourse and elsewhere. See e.g., Watzlawick, Beavin & Jackson 1967, p. 48, von Wright 1963, pp. 42 et seq.
15. This interpretive procedure is very common. Possibly the most frequent case is that in which a Grounding supportive move is conventionally interpreted as constituting that move it could support. Consider an example from Widdowson 1973, p. 72

    – Can you fly to Edinburgh tomorrow?
    – BEA are on strike

    In referring here to an 'interpretive' procedure, I am assuming of course that speakers also anticipate such interpretive strategies in encoding their communicative intentions.
16. Conversational co-operation is a two-sided affair, of course. Thus a requested "Repair" may itself be preceded by a Disarming APOLOGY:

    – P
    – Sorry ∧ I didn't quite get that
    – oh sorry ∧ I said that P

    The Repairer is apologising for not having made himself understood initially.
17. Compare here:

    – Eventually I plucked up courage and asked him
    – {What did you say / What did you say}

18. See Schegloff & Sacks 1973.

JOHN LAVER

Linguistic Routines and Politeness in Greeting and Parting

ABSTRACT

The purpose of this chapter is to demonstrate the importance of linguistic routines in negotiating social relationships. The course of conversational interaction develops in a continual tension between two general communicative needs: the need to communicate as efficiently as possible and the need to be polite. Linguistic routines are shown to be a tool of polite behavior. They serve as a means of reducing the risk of face threats. It is argued that the use of routines is guided by a polite norm. Deviation from the norm implicates an attempt at negotiating the social relationship between participants. The focus of the analysis is on three types of routines found in the marginal phase of conversational interaction: terms of direct address, formulaic phrases of greeting and parting, and utterances of phatic communion.

The chief function of much of the routine linguistic material of everyday conversations is a ceremonial, ritual function. This at least is the view of Raymond Firth, in his essay on verbal and bodily rituals of greeting and parting, where he writes that:

> Greeting and parting is often treated as if it were the spontaneous emotional reaction to the coming together or separation of people, carrying overtly its own social message. But sociological observation suggests . . . that for the most part it is highly conventionalized . . . In a broad sense greeting and parting behavior may be termed RITUAL since it follows PATTERNED ROUTINES; it is a system of SIGNS that convey other than overt messages; . . . and it has ADAPTIVE VALUE in facilitating social relations (Firth 1972: 29–30).

Firth characterizes his use of "ritual" here as concerning "formal procedures of a communicative but arbitrary kind, having the effect of controlling or regularizing a social situation" (Firth 1972:3). Espousing Firth's view, the purpose of this chapter is to discuss the communicative linguistic patterns of the small-scale routine ceremonies of greeting and parting, and to consider the adaptive, 'other than overt' messages exchanged by participants in these marginal phases of conversational interaction by means of which social relationships are negotiated and controlled.

To set the scene for the functional analysis to be proposed, it may be helpful briefly to discuss the rationale for the existence of a *routine* element in the linguistic patterns of conversation. In the sense to be adopted here, routine behavior is *polite* behavior. The linguistic behavior of conversational routines, including greetings and partings, as well as pleas, thanks, excuses, apologies and small-talk, is part of the linguistic repertoire of politeness. The function of such linguistic routines may therefore be illuminated by the type of analysis that Brown and Levinson (1978) have recently applied to politeness phenomena in conversation generally.

A central concept in the work of Brown and Levinson is that of 'face,' a concept derived partly from Goffman (1967). They distinguish two components of face:

negative face : the want of every "competent adult member" that his actions be unimpeded by others.

positive face : the want of every member that his wants be desirable to at least some others (Brown and Levinson 1978:67).

There are very many aspects of conversational interaction where face, in the above definition, is at risk. It may be the hearer's face that is threatened, or the speaker's; and it may be either the negative or the positive aspect of face that is concerned. But if the strategic ends of speakers in conversational interaction are to be achieved, then to cause overt loss of face is usually counter-productive. The risk to face must therefore be minimized, and this is managed by the use of appropriate polite behavior. Brown and Levinson distinguished between 'positive politeness,' which is "redress directed to the addressee's positive face" (op cit. p. 106), and 'negative politeness,' which is 'redressive action addressed to the addressee's negative face' (op. cit. p. 134).

The greater the degree of risk to face, the more constrained the options of mitigatory polite behavior become. Conversely, we can propose that interactions in which there is least choice open to the speaker of conventionally-appropriate linguistic behavior are interactions containing the highest risk to face. In other words, *maximum risk leads to maximum routine,* and conversely, *maximum routine reflects highest risk.*

An example of a conversational interaction where the linguistic choices open to the speaker are very constrained is one where an introduction is being performed. In many cultures, the conventions of polite society are almost totally prescriptive in this area, both in terms of the phrases expected of the third party performing the introduction, and often even more strongly of the phrases permitted to the two parties being introduced. In less formal circumstances, the constraints are usually less severe, which indicates a link between formality, politeness, risk and face.

A second example of a highly constrained linguistic routine is constituted by church services of baptism, marriage and burial. On such occasions, nearly all the linguistic material is explicitly prescribed by the conventions of the religious denomination concerned.

One might ask in what way is face at risk in these two examples; What do social introductions and life-crisis ceremonies in church have in common that might justify their parallel treatment? In both cases, social identify is in question. In both cases, a specially-qualified mediator is ratifying the social identify of one or more participants.

If we consider first the situation of a social introduction being performed, then it is clear that this process normally involves the mediation of a third party, known to both the unacquainted participants, in an intricate social negotiation. Ostensibly, the introducer is merely imparting information about the nominal identity of each of the participants to the other. Tacitly, however, in accepting the role of introducer he also accepts the social responsibility of standing as guarantor of the social integrity and worth of each of the participants. He affirms, in effect, that in his view acquaintance with both the participants is worthwhile. He thus tacitly addresses himself to the positive face of each of the persons he is introducing. Negative face is also involved, in that the introducer's opening remark is often made in the form of a request "May I introduce . . . ." The threat to the addressee's wish for his actions to be unimpeded by the actions of others is mitigated by the use of the polite formula 'May I . . . .'

Introductions can be seen as moments of potentially high tension. To refuse to accept a properly-offered introduction is a drastic insult to the positive face of the person being introduced and of the introducer alike. The refusal of an introduction is extremely rare: but the severity of the insult is revealing. The social worth of each of the triad of participants hangs momentarily in the balance, and the tension and risk of such occasions are made all the more acute by the fact that the tacit negotiation of social worth is accompanied by a public announcement of one's name. However, the acceptance of an introduction has benefits commensurate with the risks of refusal. After introduction, the interactants are now to some degree partners in an extended network of solidary acquaintance, with a correspondingly changed set of rights and obligations.

If we turn now to consider the linguistic routines of church ceremonies of baptism, marriage and burial, then many aspects of these interacttions are not dissimilar to the process of social introduction, in the terms just discussed. Taking the celebration of a marriage ceremony as representative of ritual, life-crisis ceremonies, then this can be seen as an occasion where individuals are in a momentary state of transition from one social identity to another. Their acquisition of a changed status is by the consent of the society within whose framework that status is set, and the change of status has to be conventionally ratified, on behalf of society, by a qualified agent, – in this case by a priest. Both positive and negative face is involved. The congregation present at a wedding thereby signal their approval of the couple's desire to be married. That there is also a potential threat to the couple's negative face is equally clear from the explicit convention that exists in a number of marriage services that the officiating priest should ask if anyone knows of any impediment to the legality of the marriage. A successful marriage ceremony has the function of ratifying social identity, and affirms common membership for the married couple and the congregation in a solidary social network, with the implication of shared rights and obligations.

It is not necessary to urge the functional parallels between introduction and marriage as social ceremonies more strongly than this: it is argued here that these two situations are both examples of interactions characterized by a high degree of linguistic routine. Both involve a potentially high degree of risk to face for the participants, and both concern the negotiation of aspects of social identity. In particular, both are concerned with changes in relationship: in the process of introduction, the participants change from a non-solidary to a solidary relationship, and in the case of a marriage ceremony, the standing of the married couple changes within the context of their solidary society.

The general principle that is being drawn here, in the choice of these examples of routine linguistic behavior, is that when such routine is observed, it is not unreasonable to suspect that face is potentially at risk, and that the negotiations that are being tacitly conducted are possibly negotiations of social relationship between the participants. This general principle will be taken to underlie the discussion in the main part of this chapter, which will be concerned with three types of routine linguistic behavior found in the greeting and parting phrases of conversation. These three types are formulaic phrases of greeting and parting, such as 'Good morning' and 'Goodbye;' terms of direct address, such as 'Mr Smith,' 'Robert' and 'Bob;' and small-talk, or 'phatic communion,' such as 'Nice day for the time of year.' In the marginal phases of conversation, where the use of such linguistic routines is most dense, participants conduct their social negotiations about respective status and role partly by means of their choices of formulaic phrase, address-term and type of phatic communion.

The strategies of negotiation of status and role in the marginal phases of conversation can profitably be discussed not only in terms of Brown and Levinson's analysis of politeness phenomena, but also within the framework of conversational logic proposed by Grice (1975). In considering the suitability of individual moves in conversation, Grice formulates a 'rough general principle which participants will be expected ... to observe,' as follows:

Make your conversational contribution such as is required, at the stage at which it occurs, by the accepted purpose or direction of the talk exchange in which you are engaged. Onc might label this the COOPERATIVE PRINCIPLE.

On the assumption that some such general principle as this is acceptable, one may perhaps distinguish four categories under one or another of which will fall certain more specific maxims, the following of which will, in general, yield results in accordance with the Cooperative Principle. Echoing Kant, I call these categories Quantity, Quality, Relation, and Manner (Grice 1975:45).

Gricean maxims (which have not failed to attract a degree of criticism) can breifly be characterized in the following way:

Quantity	:	Be as informative as necessary
Quality	:	Be truthful
Relation	:	Be relevant
Manner	:	Be clear, concise and unambiguous

Grice formulated these maxims on the specific assumption that the purpose of conversation was a 'maximally effective exchange of information.' As we shall see, when conversation has a different purpose, different maxims need to be postulated.

Grice points out that speakers may well flout, or apparently flout, a given maxim. Given that the hearer is entitled to assume that the speaker is not trying to mislead him, the hearer is faced with a problem:

How can (the speaker's) saying what he did say be reconciled with the supposition that he is observing the overall Cooperative Principle? This situation is one that characteristically gives rise to a conversational implicature (Grice 1975:49).

The meaning of 'a conversational implicature' can be understood from the following example offered by Grice:

A is standing by an obviously immobilized car and is approached by B; the following exchange takes place:

A: "I am out of petrol."

B: "There is a garage round the corner". (Gloss: B would be infringing the maxim 'Be relevant' unless he thinks, or thinks it possible, that the garage is open, and has petrol to sell; so he implicates that the garage is, or at least may be open, etc.) . . . the speaker (thus) implicates that which he must be assumed to believe in order to preserve the assumption that he is observing the maxim of relation (Grice 1975:51).

Brown and Levinson make Grice's concept of conversational implicature into a valuable tool for the analysis of polite behavior:

(Grice's) Maxims define for us the basic set of assumptions underlying every talk exchange. But this does not imply that utterances in general, or even reasonably frequently, must meet these conditions, as critics of Grice have sometimes thought. Indeed, the majority of natural conversations do not proceed in such a brusque fashion at all. The whole thrust of this paper is that one powerful and pervasive motive for *not* talking Maxim-wise is the desire to give some attention to face . . . Politeness is then a major source of deviation from such rational efficiency, and is communicated precisely by that deviation. But even in such departures from the Maxims, they remain in operation at a deeper level. It is only because they are still assumed to be in operation that addressees are forced to do the inferential work that establishes the underlying message and the (polite or other) source of the departure – in short, to find an implicature, i.e. an inference generated by precisely this assumption. Otherwise the polite strategies . . . would simply be heard as mumbo-jumbo. There is a basic assumption in talk that there is underlying method in the madness (Brown and Levinson 1978:100).

Brown and Levinson give a very large number of examples of different politeness strategies in English, Tamil and Tzeltal in their monograph-length article, which is warmly commended to the reader. Two selected examples may give an indication of their general approach. Both examples, by apparently flouting Grice's maxims, carry the conversational implicature that the speaker wishes to signal his desire to attend to aspects of the hearer's face.

The first example concerns positive politeness, which was described above as directed to the addressee's positive face, or, as Brown and Levinson put it,

his perennial desire that his wants (or the actions/acquisitions/values resulting from them) should be thought of as desirable. Redress consists in partially satisfying that desire by communicating that one's own wants (or some of them) are in some respects similar to the addressee's wants (op. cit. p. 106).

Postive politeness is characterized by an element of exaggeration, with a consequent flouting of the maxim of quality. Brown and Levinson suggest that this

serves as a marker of the face-redress aspect of positive-politeness expression by indication that even if S can't with total sincerity say "I want your wants", he can at least sincerely indicate "I want your positive face to be satisfied". Thus the element of insincerity in exaggerated expressions of approval or interest ("How absolutely marvellous! I simply can't imagine how you manage to keep your roses so exquisite, Mrs B!") is compensated for by the implication that the speaker really sincerely wants Mrs B's positive face to be enhanced (op. cit. pp. 106–108).

The second example concerns negative politeness. This was described above as directed to the addressee's negative face, or

his want to have his freedom of action unhindered and his attention unimpeded. It is the heart of respect behaviour . . . Where positive politeness is free-ranging, negative politeness is specific and focused; it performs the function of minimizing the particular imposition that the Face Threatening Action unavoidably effects. When we think of politeness in Western cultures, it is negative-politeness behaviour that springs to mind. In our culture, negative politeness is the most elaborate and the most conventionalized set of linguistic strategies of FTA redress; it is the stuff that fills the etiquette books . . . Its linguistic realizations – conventional indirectnesses, hedges on illocutionary force, polite pessimism (about the success of requests, etc.), the emphasis on H's relative power – are very familiar . . . (op. cit. pp. 134–135).

One example that Brown and Levinson cite of a conventionally pessimistic request of this sort is:

There wouldn't I suppose be any chance of your being able to lend me your car for just a few minutes, would there? (op. cit. p. 147).

There are of course very many occasions in conversation where the need for maximum efficiency of communication over-rides the need to be polite. Emergency situations demand urgent action, and imperative verb forms are characteristic, in examples like 'Help!,' or 'Don't burn your hand!' Brown and Levinson suggest that urgency of this sort may be metaphorically exploited in formulaic entreaties, such as 'Excuse me,' 'Forgive me,' 'Pardon me,' and 'Accept my thanks' (op. cit. p. 101). They go on to suggest, interestingly for the purpose of this chapter, that the usage of imperative verb forms for actions 'directly in H's interest' give rise to 'a host of cliché farewell formulae, as in the English "advice" delivered to those departing on a trip.' They give the examples 'Take care of/Treat/Enjoy yourself, be good, have fun,' and 'Don't take any wooden nickels' (op. cit. p. 103).

It should be clear from the discussion above that the process of conversation displays a continual tension between two general communicative needs – the need to communicate as efficiently as possible and the need to be polite. Grice himself acknowledges this. He recognizes that, in addition to the maxims he suggests, based on the need for a 'maximally effective exchange of information,'

There are, of course, all sorts of other maxims (aesthetic, social or moral in character), such as "Be polite", that are also normally observed by participants in talk exchanges, and these may also generate unconventional implicatures (Grice 1975:47).

The four maxims that Grice based on the effective exchange of information are strictly applicable only to those parts of conversation that have a definable propositional content. In the marginal phases of conversation, only the utterances of phatic communion have any discernible content of this sort. Address-terms and formulaic phrases of greeting and farewell such as 'Hello' and 'Goodbye' have no such structure, and are therefore not susceptible of a standard Gricean analysis. We can therefore gain a broader perspective of conversation if, as well as Grice's four propositionally-relevant maxims, we adopt his 'social' maxim noted above, which enjoins speakers to 'Be polite.' We can then see the three phases of conversation – the initial, medial and final phases – as reflecting obedience to a varying interplay between the propositionally-based and the socially-based maxims. In the medial phase, where the main business of the interaction is usually achieved, it may be that the propositionally-relevant maxims exercise their major influence, with social factors of politeness playing a less dominant part. In the marginal phases, where greeting and parting are negotiated, social factors will loom largest, with propositional mechanisms being subordinated to a social purpose.

Armed with the notions of conversational implicature, politeness and positive and negative face, we can now turn to the more detailed analysis of the routine linguistic behavior that characterizes the marginal phases of conversational interaction.

An important aspect of positive face is the hearer's need for his social identity to be acceptable to the speaker. A speaker can obey the social maxim 'Be polite,' and attend to this aspect of the hearer's face, by using linguistic routines that acknowledge his identity either explicitly or tacitly. The choice of linguistic routine has to be consistent with the relative social status of the hearer, with the degree of acquaintance that exists between the speaker and the hearer, and with situational factors such as the degree of formality imposed by the occasion of conversation or by the special nature of the setting in which the conversation is taking place. The plan of the remainder of this chapter will be to discuss the linguistic routines that constitute the polite norm, where the linguistic forms chosen are consistent with the three factors of social status, degree of acquaintance and nature of the situation, and then to discuss the implicature signalled by deviations from the polite norm, for each of three areas. These areas will be, in turn, terms of direct address, formulaic phrases of greeting and parting, and finally utterances of phatic communion.

TERMS OF DIRECT ADDRESS

For a detailed analysis of terms of direct address, the reader is referred to two seminal articles, Brown and Ford (1961) and Ervin-Tripp (1969). The analysis presented here is for address in British English, and is based on the flow-chart approach of Ervin-Tripp. The analysis is initial, merely suggesting the rule structure that underlies usage in this area: further empirical work is needed to ratify the suggestions.

Figure 1 summarizes the factors that constrain the polite choice of address terms in British English. The suggested network is classificatory, and not a

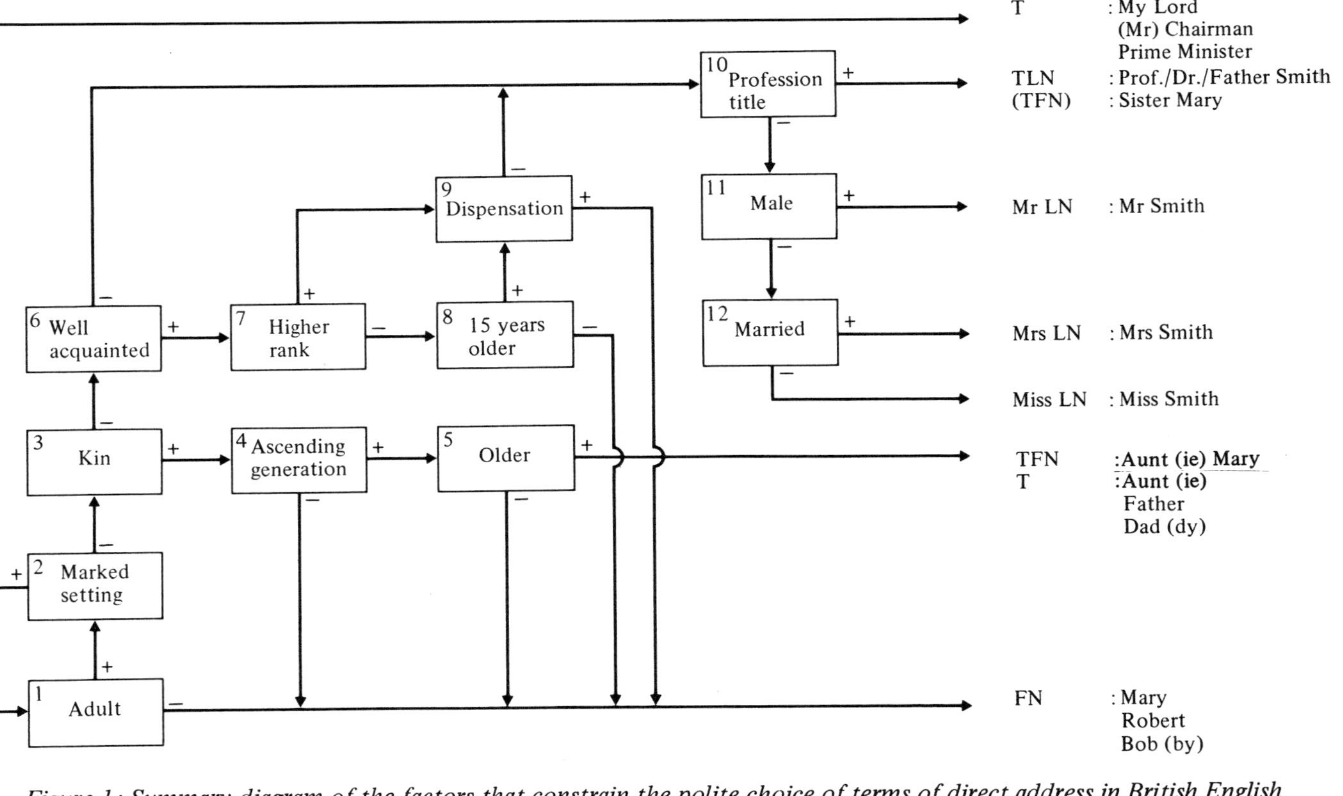

Figure 1: Summary diagram of the factors that constrain the polite choice of terms of direct address in British English

model of some decision process in the speaker's mind. Some options have been omitted. For example, in certain relationships, no term of direct address is used at all. This choice has been left out of this rather simplified diagram.

It may be helpful to comment on some of the details of the diagram, which is based on characteristics of the addressee, who must be at least slightly known to the speaker. The first analytic decision to be taken is represented by Box 1, where the addressee is classified as 'adult' or 'not adult'. The direction of flow of classificatory decisions is indicated by arrows, and a plus sign at the exit to a box signifies a positive classification, a minus sign a negative classification. Thus if the addressee is a child, no further classificatory decisions are necessary, and FN (first name) will be the polite norm.

In Box 2, a 'marked setting' is one where special address-conventions apply, in which addressees gain their relevant identity through their official and not their personal identity. Examples would be a court of law, a formal meeting, or Parliament. Box 9 reflects the social fact that acquaintances of higher rank or greater age are not addressed by FN unless they have specifically encouraged the speaker to do so by an explicit dispensation, with a phrase such as 'Let's not be formal, – please call me Robert.' Without dispensation, TLN (title – either occupational, such as Dr. or sex-specific, such as Mr, Mrs, with last name) is the norm.

As with nearly all linguistic routines concerned with the statement of social relationships, address usage is reciprocal between equals and non-reciprocal between participants of unequal status. Thus an office junior may call the manager 'Mr Smith' but receive 'Charles' in return.

To depart from the polite norm is to trigger a conversational implicature. As Ervin-Tripp comments (1969:102), 'When there is agreement about the normal address form to alters of specific statuses, then any deviation is a message.' We can illustrate this briefly with two examples. The first is where an adult addresses a well-acquainted child not with FN as the polite norm prescribes, but with FNLN 'Bobby Smith.' In such circumstances, even though children seem to learn linguistic routines very slowly, the child usually understands the implicature of reproof. The second example is where equals enjoying a growing acquaintance move from TLN to FN, thereby acknowledging the growth of their intimacy.

FORMULAIC PHRASES OF GREETING AND PARTING

A similar model can be used to summarize the factors that underlie the polite norm in choice of formulaic terms of greeting and parting. Figure 2 shows the network of addressee-characteristics that gives rise to different formulaic usages in British English such as 'Good morning,' 'Morning,' 'Hello,' 'Goodbye,'

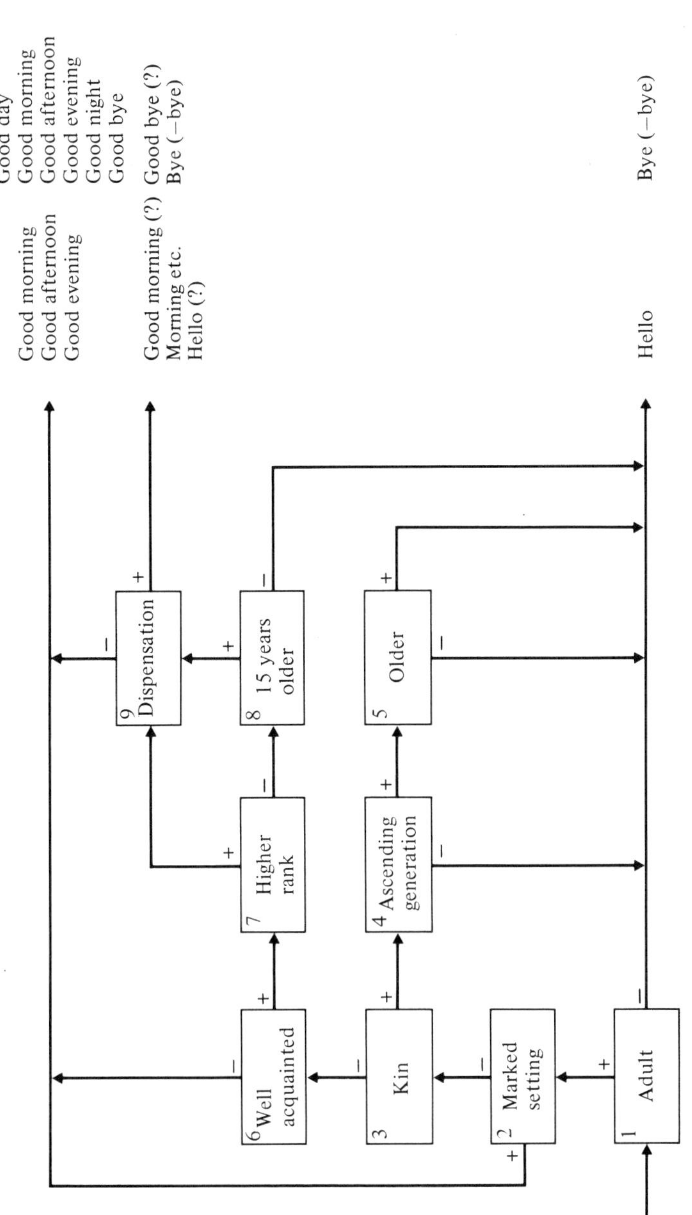

Figure 2: Summary diagram of the factors that constrain the polite choice of formulaic phrases of greeting and parting in British English

and 'Bye.' Once again, the analysis is initial, needing further empirical work to amplify the conclusions.

At first sight, the structure of the descriptive model seems simpler than in the case of terms of direct address. But in fact there are some complicating factors, left out of this simplified diagram. One of these is that the choice of formulaic terms often depends almost as much on the characteristics of the speaker as on those of the listener. For example, the formulaic parting phrases 'Cheerio' and 'Cheers' seem to be used almost only by male speakers. 'Hi' and 'Ciao' tend to be used only by young speakers, and 'Wotcher' only by speakers who are both young and male. Factors of social class are also influential, in that particular phrases are not used freely by members of all social classes. 'How do you do' is largely restricted to middle and upper class speakers, and 'How do' and 'Howdy' to working class speakers.

As with terms of direct address, a marked setting constrains the choice of formulaic phrases of greeting and parting to the formal usages 'Good morning/afternoon/evening' and 'Good day/morning/afternoon/evening/night' respectively, together with 'Goodbye.' As phrases of maximum formality and maximum distance, these are also the phrases used to acquaintances of higher rank or greater age who have not offered a dispensation to the speaker to progress to a less formal style.

As a general observation, it is striking that relatives and well-acquainted equals or inferiors are treated with the same informality of formulaic phrase as children. In between the two extremes represented by 'Good morning' and 'Hello,' however, further research is necessary to clarify less obvious usage. The abbreviated phrase 'Morning,' and its equivalents, can certainly be used to superior or older acquaintances who have offered a dispensation, as can the abbreviated 'Bye.' But whether there is a progression of informality from 'Morning' to 'Hello,' and whether 'Goodbye' can also be used legitimately to this category of listener, is not able to be stated with confidence without more evidence. Similarly, the descriptive model offered here does not handle the case of slightly acquainted equals, who have the option of using 'Morning' and its equivalents as well as 'Good morning' etc., but who do not progress to 'Hello' until acquaintance is more established.

Polite usage in this area, as with terms of direct address, is reciprocal between equals and non-reciprocal between participants of unequal status. To depart from the polite norm is to signal by implicature that a change in social relation is being negotiated. To move from 'Good day' to 'Bye' is a large social step; to move from 'Bye' to 'Good day' is an almost irrevocable act of social distancing.

UTTERANCES OF PHATIC COMMUNION

The argument that a speaker can signal his perception of the formality of a situation, and of his acquaintance and social relationship with a listener, by his choice of address-term and formulaic phrase of greeting or parting, is reasonably acceptable on the basis of common experience. The argument that similar information can be signalled by a speaker's choice of small-talk, or phatic communion, is perhaps less obvious. The argument is set out in more detail in Laver (1975), and discussion here is limited to a re-analysis, in terms of politeness theory, of some of the data presented in that article.

The small-talk of phatic communion, involving supremely obvious comments about the weather or benevolent admonitions such as 'Take care,' are largely limited to the initial and final phases of conversational interactions, and it will be convenient to treat phatic communion in these two phases separately.

In brief summary, the linguistic routines of phatic communion in the initial phase of conversation seem to have three social functions. The first of these is to defuse "the potential hostility of silence in situations where speech is conventionally anticipated" (Laver 1975:220). Secondly, it "has an initiatory function, in that it allows the participants to cooperate in getting the interaction comfortably under way, using emotionally uncontroversial ... material, and demonstrating by signals of cordiality and tentative social solidarity their mutual acceptance of the possibility of an interaction taking place" (op. cit. p. 221). Thirdly, and most relevantly for present purposes, phatic communion has an exploratory function, "in that it allows the participants to feel their way towards the working consensus of their interaction" (op. cit. p. 221), partly by revealing their perception of their relative social status. It is this third function which will be discussed here.

The basic position is that a certain pattern of phatic communion constitutes the polite norm, and that the use of this pattern serves as an acknowledgement of the social relationship that exists between the participants. Any deviation from that pattern then triggers the implicature that the speaker is thereby re-negotiating the relationship. The mechanisms of acknowledgement and re-negotiation work in the following way, it is suggested. There are three broad categories of phrases that are typically used as utterances of phatic communion. The first category is made up of phrases about factors common to both speaker and listener, most often about the weather. The syntactic structure of the phrases is typically abbreviated, which helps participants to recognize their phatic communion function. Characteristic phrases are: 'Nice day,' 'What weather,' 'Frost tonight,' 'Nice party,' 'About time the trains were cleaned.' We can call this category the *neutral* category.

The second category is made up of phrases that comment on factors personal to the speaker, which we can call the *self-oriented* category. Phrases in this category would include: 'Hot work, this,' 'I do like a breath of fresh air,' 'My legs weren't made for these hills.' The third category contains phrases that refer to factors specific to the listener, such as 'How's life/business/the wife/the family?,' 'That looks like hard work,' 'Do you come here often?,' which we can call the *other-oriented* category.

The pattern of choice of category that constitutes the polite norm is one where the speakers who are well-acquainted can freely choose any category, but where non-acquainted speakers obey a constraint which depends on relative social status. The neutral category is available to speakers of any social status, but other-oriented phrases are politely available only to speakers of relatively higher status, and self-oriented phrases only to speakers of relatively lower status. Thus, in an encounter between a country gentleman out for a walk and a hedger-and-ditcher clearing nettles from a ditch, polite options include either speaker saying 'Nice day,' the country gentleman saying 'That looks like hard work,' or the hedger-and-ditcher saying 'Hard work, this.'

The effect of violations of the polite norm is often to negotiate a greater solidarity between participants. For the country gentleman to use a self-oriented phrase such as 'I do like a breath of fresh air,' or for the hedger-and-ditcher to use an other-oriented phrase such as 'Out for a breath of fresh air, are you then?' has the effect in both cases of inviting the listener to a momentary solidarity in which the status differential between the two participants, which may be obvious from visible information such as dress, is thereby asserted as irrelevant (Laver 1975:224–225).

Considerations of face in the three categories of phrases are more problematic. Clearly, use of the neutral category threatens non-one's face. But the use of either of the other two categories may concern both positive and negative face. For example, to use an other-oriented phrase such as 'How's the wife?' could be thought to threaten the listener's negative face in that such an enquiry invades his family life; but it also attends to his positive face in an obvious way, as would 'Nice tie,' etc. To use a self-oriented phrase might be thought to threaten one's own negative face, by being revealing about oneself and thus in some sense giving the listener power through information; but it also attends to one's own positive face, in that it takes an opportunity to present onself as potentially interesting to the listener.

Where ceremonial behavior in the initial phase of conversation is often rather brief, the linguistic routines of phatic communion in the closing phase of conversation are often highly elaborate, suggesting a very high degree of risk to face. That participants are vulnerable to threat is clear if we consider the two principal functions that phatic communion serves in the closing phase:

> Firstly, it allows the participants to achieve a cooperative parting, in which any feeling of rejection by the person being left can be assuaged by appropriate reassurance from the person leaving. Secondly, it serves to consolidate the relationship between the two participants, by means of behaviour which emphasizes the enjoyable quality of the encounter, the mutual esteem in which the participants hold each other, the promise of a continuation of the relationship, the assertion of mutual solidarity, and the announcement of a continuing consensus for the shape of encounters in the future (Laver 1975: 231).

We can refer to the two major types of function being served by phatic communion in the closing phase as *mitigation* and *consolidation.* The use of these terms highlights the attention that the participants typically apply to the care of their relationship in this fragile phase: nearly all the actual utterances are examples of self-oriented and other-oriented phrases, and neutral comments seem to be used rather seldom. The polite norm in the closing phase, between participants who do not meet often, seems to be to use at least one mitigatory or consolidatory phrase, together with some appropriate formulaic phrase of parting. To omit such reparatory acts entirely is rare, and triggers a somewhat extreme implicature of rejection.

Mitigatory comments are usually addressed to the negative aspect of face, often setting the reason for terminating the encounter in a compulsion external to the speaker. Typical comments are: 'I'm sorry, I have to go, I have to give a lecture,' 'I'm afraid I must be off, I have to relieve the babysitter.' Such comments attend to the negative face of the speaker. A particularly interesting sub-category of mitigatory comment is where 'deference is expressed to the needs of the listener himself, as the compelling external authority' (Laver 1975:230). Examples of this type of attention to the listener's negative face are 'Well, I musn't keep you,' and 'I guess you have to get on, I'll be going.'

Consolidatory comments are addressed to the positive aspect of face. Esteem for the other participant is implied, in comments such as 'It was nice seeing you,' 'I do enjoy our little talks' and 'How nice to see you again.' Consolidatory caring for the other participant is shown in comments on future welfare, such as 'Hope your cold gets better soon,' benevolent admonitions like 'Watch how you go' and benedictions such as 'God bless' (Laver 1975: 230). Other consolidatory comments mention arrangements for the continuation of the relationship, as in 'See you next Saturday,' or 'Don't be such a stranger, come again soon.' Consolidation in a wider network of common acquaintances also occurs, in comments such as 'Say hello to Anne for me' or 'Remember me to Bob.'

CONCLUSION

This chapter has explored three types of linguistic routines found in the marginal phases of conversations, in the small-scale ritual ceremonies of greeting and parting. It was suggested that a polite norm exists in the choice of such linguistic routines, such that obedience to the norm has the effect of acknowledging the social identity of the listener, in terms of his relative social status, and of the degree of acquaintance between the participants. Violating the polite norm, by using other choices of greeting or parting behavior, carries the conversational implicature of negotiating a change in the relationship between the participants, usually towards greater intimacy or greater distancing. It was also suggested that a fundamental motive for polite behavior of the sort described is to pay attention to the 'face' of either or both of the participants.

Linguistic routines of greeting and parting, far from being relatively meaningless and mechanical social behavior, can thus be understood as extremely important strategies for the negotiation and control of social identity and social relationships between participants in conversation.

Bibliography

Abbs, B., Cook, V. (1970). Realistic English. London: OUP.

Abercrombie, David (1963). Conversation and Spoken Prose, *English Language Teaching,* XVIII, 1 October 1963.

Akmanova, O., Idzelis, R. F. (1978). *What is the English We use?* Moscow: Moscow University Press.

Alexander, L. G. (1972). *New Concept English.* London: Longmans.

Albert, Ethel (1968). Value Systems. In *The International Encyclopedie of the Social Sciences* 16. New York: Macmillan.

(1972). Culture Patterning of Speech Behavior in Burundi. In Gumperz & Hymes, eds., 1972 (First publ. 1964).

Altmann, G. and Riska, A. (1966). Towards a typology of courtesy in language. *Anthropological Linguistics* 8 (1): 1-10.

Anderson, Digby (1978). "Curricula as Implicative Descriptions of Classrooms." University of Nottingham: *Health Education Research papers.*

Apte, M. L. 'Thank you' and South Asian languages: a comparative sociolinguistic study. *International Journal of the Sociology of Language* 3:67-89.

Ardener, E., ed. (1971). *Social Anthropology and Language.* London, Tavistock Publications.

Arewa, E. O., Dundes, A. (1964). "Proverbs and the Ethnography of Speaking Folklore." In Gumperz & Hymes, eds., 1964, pp. 70-85.

Argyle, M., ed. (1973). *Social encounters. Readings in social interaction.* Harmondsworth: Penguin Books.

Arnold, I. V. (1973). Set expressions. Chapter 7 of *The English Word.* Moscow, pp. 140-163.

Austin, John L. (1956). "A Plea for Excuses." In *Philosophical Papers,* ed. J. O. Urmson/G. J. Warnock, 1962. London: Oxford University Press.

(1962). *How to do things with words.* New York: Oxford University Press.

(1962a). *Philosophical Papers.* London: Oxford University Press.

Bach, K. and R. Harnish (in press). *A theory of speech acts.* MIT Press.

Banfield, A. W. & Macintyre, J. L. (1915). *A grammar of the Nupe language.* London: SPCK.

Barker, G., C. Adamas and H. Sorhus (1974). *Fixed Expressions in the Canadian Context, a Dictionary-Handbook.* Ottawa: Government of Canada, Public Service Commission, Staff Development Branch, Directorate of Studies, Research Division.

Barker, C. (1975). "This is just a first approximation, but . . .", in *CLS* 11: 37-47.

Bates, Elizabeth (1976). *Language and Context. The Acquisition of Pragmatics* New York, etc.: Academic Press.

Bateson, Gregory (1972). *Steps to an Ecology of Mind.* New York: Ballantine Books.

Baumann, R. and Sherzer, J., eds. (1974). *Explorations in the Ethnography of Speaking.* New York, London: Cambridge University Press.

Becker, J. (1975). The phrasal Lexicon. In R. Schank and B. Nash-Webber, eds., *Theoretical Issues in Natural Language Processing.* Boston: Bolt Beranek and Newman, pp. m60–63.

Beneke, J. (1975). "Verstehen und Mißverstehen im Englischunterricht." In *Praxis* 22: 351–362.

Berkowitz, L., ed. (1967). *Advances in Experimental Social Psychology* 4. New York: Academic Press.

Blom, Jan-Petter and John J. Gumperz (1972). Social meaning in linguistic structures: code-switching in Norway. In Gumperz and Hymes, eds., 1972: 407–434.

Bloomfield, Leonard (1944). Secondary and tertiary responses to language. *Language* 20: 45–55.

Bloomfield, M., Haugen, E., eds. (1974). *Language as a Human Problem.* New York.

Bolinger, D. (1968). *Aspects of Language.* New York.

(1976). Meaning and Memory. *Forum Linguisticum* 1(1): 1–14.

(1977). Idioms have relations. *Forum Linguisticum* 2: 157–169.

Brazil, D. C. (1975). *Discourse Intonation.* Discourse Analysis Monographs 1, Birmingham: English Language Research.

Borkin, A. and S. Rinhart (1978). "Excuse me and I'm sorry." *TESOL Quarterly.* 12(1).

Brend, R. M. (1973). *Advances in Tagmemies.* Amsterdam.

(1978). Politeness *IRAL* 16 (3), August 1978.

Brinkmann, H. (1971).[2] *Die deutsche Sprache. Gestalt und Leistung.* Düsseldorf: Schwann.

Brown, P. (1975). Women are more polite: sex roles and women's speech in a Mayan community. Paper presented at the 74th annual meeting of the American Anthropological Association, San Francisco, December.

(1976). Women and politeness: a new perspective on language and society. *Reviews in Anthropology* 3 (3): 240–9.

In preparation. *The position of women in a Mayan society: evidence from verbal interaction.* Unpublished Ph.D. dissertation. Dept. of Anthropology, University of California, Berkeley.

Brown, P. & Levinson, S. (1978). Universals in language usage: Politeness phenomena. In E. N. Goody, ed. 1978: 56–310.

Brown, Roger (1973). *Beyond the Information Given.* New York: W. W. Norton.

Brown, R. and Ford, M. (1961). 'Address in American English,' *Journal of Abnormal and Social Psychology* 62: 375–385.

Brown, R. and Gilman, A. (1960). The pronouns of power and solidarity. In *Style in language,* ed., T. A. Sebeok, Cambridge, Mass., 1960: 253–276.

Bühler, K. (1934). *Sprachtheorie.* Jena: Gustav Fischer.

Burger, Harald (1973). *Idiomatik des Deutschen.* Tübingen: Niemeyer.

Bugarski, Ranko (1968). On the interrelatedness of grammar and lexis in the structure of English. *Lingua* 19: 233–263.

Burke, K. (1968). Interaction, Dramatism. In *International Encyclopedia of the Social Sciences* 7. London/New York.

Bynon, J. (1968). Berber nursery language. *Transaction of the Philological Society* 1968.

Cahir, Stephen, R. (1978). "Activity Between and Within Activities." Transition Center for Applied Linguistics, Arlington, Va.

Callan, H. (1970). *Ethology and society: towards an anthropological view,* Oxford:

Clarendon Press, pp. 104–24.

Carroll, J. B. und R. O. Freedle, eds. (1972). *Language Comprehension and the Acquisition of Knowledge.* Washington, D.C.: Winston.

Carswell, E. A. & Rommetveit, R. (1971). *Social Contexts of Messages.* London/New York.

Cassirer, Ernst (1944). *An Essay of Man.* New Haven: Yale University Press.

Cattell, N. R. (1969). *The new English grammar: a descriptive introduction.* Cambridge, Mass.: MIT Press.

Cazden, C., V. John, D. Hymes, eds. (1972). *Functions of Language in the Classroom.* New York: Teachers College Press.

Chafe, W. L. (1968). "Idiomaticity as an anomaly in the Chomskyan paradigm." *Foundations of Language* 4: 109–127.

(1970). *Meaning and the Structure of Language.* Chicago: University of Chicago Press.

(1973). Language & Memory. *Language* 49: 462–485.

Chao, Yuen Ren (1968). *Language and Symbolic Systems.* London: Cambridge University Press.

Chomsky, N. (1965). *Aspects of the Theory of Syntax.* Cambridge, MIT.

Cicourel, A. V. (1973). *Cognitive Sociology. Language and Meaning in Social Interaction.* Harmondsworth: Penguin.

Clark, Ruth (1973). Performing without competence. *Journal of Child Language* 1: 1–10.

Clyne, Michael (1978). "Communicative Competence in Contact: A Progress Report. Ms. (Monash University).

Cole, P. & J. L. Morgan, eds. (1975). *Syntax and Semantics* 3: *Speech Acts,* New York: Academic Press.

Coles, M. and Lord, B. (1970). *Colloquial English.* London.

Colson, Elizabeth (1973). "Tranquility for the Decision-Maker" in Nader/Maretzki eds. *Cultural Illness and Health.* Washington D.C.: American Anthropological Association.

Cooper, W. E. and J. R. Ross (1975). World order. *Chicago Linguistic Society, Parasession on Functionalism.*

Cormack, J. G. (1935). *Everyday Customs in China.* Edinburgh: Moray Press.

Coulmas, Florian (1977a). *Rezeptives Sprachverhalten. Eine theoretische Studie über Faktoren des sprachlichen Verstehensprozesses.* Hamburg: Buske.

(1977b). "Concerning the Range of Pragmatics." *Journal of Pragmatics* 1 (3): 299–307.

(1978a). Routineformeln und pragmatische Interferenzen, in *Kongreßberichte de 8. Jahrestagung der Gesellschaft für Angewandte Linguistik GAL e.V. Mainz 1977,* Stuttgart: Hochschul Verlag, pp. 31–40.

(1978b). Sequenzierungsbedingungen in präfigurierter Rede. In W. Vanderweghe and M. Van de Velde, Bedeutung, Sprechakte und Texte. Tübingen: Max Neimeyer.

(1979a). "Pragmatic Interferences in the use of Routine Formulae. Their role in acculturation." To appear in J. Regan, ed., *Discourse Analysis Systems.*

(1979b). "On the Sociolinguistic Relevance of Routine Formulae." *Journal of Pragmatics* 3 (3/4).

(1979c). Idiomaticity as a problem of pragmatics. unpub.

Couthard, R. M. (1977). *An Introduction to Discourse Analysis.* London: Longman.

Crawford, J. M. (1970). Cocopa baby talk: *International Journal of American Linguistics* 36: 9–13.

Crick, Malcom (1976). *Explorations in Language & Meaning. Towards a Semantic Anthropology*. London: Malaby Press.
Crothers, E. J. (1972). Memory structure and the recall of discourse. In Carroll & Freedle, eds., 1972.
Davidson, D., G. Harman (1972). *Semantics of Natural Language*. Dordrecht: Reidel.
Davison, A. (1975). "Indirect speech acts and what to do with them." In Cole and Morgan, eds., 1975: 143-185.
Denison, N. (1975). Culture in Language. *Grazer Linguistische Studien* 1: 5-23.
De Silva, M. W. Sugathapala (1976). Verbal Aspects of Politeness Expressions in Sinhalese with Reference to Asking, Telling, Requesting, and Ordering. *Anthropological Linguistics* 18, 8 November: 360-370.
Dickinson, L., Mackin, R. (1969). *Varieties of Spoken English*. London: OUP.
Doi, Takeo (1973). *The anatomy of dependence*. Tokyo: Kodansha.
Dore, John (1977). "Children's Illocutionary Acts." In Roy O. Freedle, ed., *Discourse Production and Comprehension*, Norwood. J.N.: Ablex Publishing Corporation.
(1978). Outline of the conversational-act system of discourse analysis. *Symposium on discourse analysis. Fifth International Congress of Applied Linguistics. Montreal, August 1978.*
Downs, T. W. (1929). Maori Etiquette. *Journal of Polynesian Society* 38: 148-68.
Drazdauskiene, M. L. (1979). Cliché as Vice and Virtue (forthcoming).
Dundes, Alan (1975). On the structure of the proverb. *Analytic Essays in Folklore*. The Hague: Mouton, pp. 103-118.
Edmondson, Willis (1977). "Gambits in Foreign Language Teaching." In H. Christ and H. E. Piepho, eds., *Kongreßdokumentation der 7. Arbeitstagung der Fremdsprachendidaktiker*, Gießen 1976, Limburg: Frankonius, pp. 45-48.
(1978). "Worlds within Worlds – Problems in the Description of Teacher-Learner Interaction," paper presented at the 5th AILA Congress, Montreal 1978. (To appear in Congress documentation).
Edmondson, Willis; House, Juliane; Kasper, Gabriele; McKeown, John (1977). *Kommunikative Kompetenz als realisierbares Lernziel*, mimeo: Ruhr-Universität Bochum.
(1979). *Sprachliche Interaktion in lernzielrelevanten Situationen*, L.A.U.T. paper 51, Series B, Linguistic Agency: Trier. Universität Bochum.
Ehlich, Konrad & Rehbein, Jochen (1972). "Zur Konstitution pragmatischer Einheiten in einer Institution: Das Speiserestaurant." In Wunderlich, D., ed., 1972, pp. 209-254.
(1972a). Einige Interrelationen von Modalverben. In Wunderlich, D., ed., 1972, pp. 318-340.
(1976). Halbinterpretative Arbeitstranskriptionen (HIAT). *Linguistiche Berichte* 45: 21-41.
(1977a). Wissen, kommunikatives Handeln und die Schule. In Goeppert, H., ed., *Sprachverhalten im Unterricht*. München: Fink.
(1977b). Batterien sprachlicher Handlungen. In *Journal of Pragmatics* 1 (4): 393-406.
(1979). Sprachliche Handlungsmuster. Erscheint in: Soeffner, H. G. 1979. *Reader zur Sprachsoziologie*. Stuttgart: Metzler.
Eibl-Eibesfelt, I. (1968). Zur Ethologie des menschlichen Grussverhaltens, Beobachtungen an Balinesen, Papuas und Samoanern. *Zeitschrift für Tierpsychologie* 25: 727-44.
Ekman, Paul and Wallace V. Friessen (1968). "Non-verbal Behavior in Psychotype of

Research." In John Shlien, ed., *Research in Psychotherapy* 3, A.P.A.: 179-216.

Elias, Norbert (1977). *Über den Prozeß der Zivilisation.* Frankfurt: Suhrkamp.

Erickson, Frederick and Jeffrey Schultz (1977). "When is a Context?" *ICHD Newsletter* 1 (2): 5-10.

(1979). *Talking to the Man: Social an Cultural Organisation of Communication in Counselling Interviews,* New York: Academic Press.

Ervin-Tripp, S. (1964). An analysis of the interaction of language, topic and listener. In Grumperz and Hymes, eds., 1964, pp. 86-102.

(1972). On sociolinguistic rules: alternation and co-occurrence. In Gumperz and Hymes, eds., 1972, pp. 213-50.

(1976). "Is Sybil There? The Structure of American English Directives," *Language in Society* 5: 27-76.

(1977). "Wait for me, roller skate." In S. Ervin-Tripp/C. Mitchell-Kernan, eds., 1977, pp. 165-188.

Ervin-Tripp, S./C. Mitchell-Kernan, eds. (1977). *Child Discourse.* New York: Academic Press.

Farb, P. (1974). *Word Play.* London: Bantam.

Ferguson, C. A. (1964). Baby talk in six languages. In J. J. Gumperz and D. Hymes, eds., Ethnography of Communication. *American Anthropogist* 66(6), pt 2.

(1967). Root-echo responses in Syrian Arabic politeness formulas. In D. S. Stuart, ed., *Linguistic Studies in Memory of Richard Slade Harrell,* Georgetown University Press, pp. 35-45.

(1971). Absence of Copula and the Notion of Simplicity. In Hymes, D., ed. *Pidginization and Creolization of Languages.* Cambridge: University Press.

(1974). Sociolinguistic research and practical applications. In Verdoot, A., ed., *Applied Sociolinguistics.* Heidelberg: Julius Groos Verlag, pp. 266-82.

(1976). The structure and use of politeness formulas. *Language and Society* 5: 137-51.

Ferguson, C. A. & Farwell, C. B. (1975). Words and sounds in early language acquisition. *Language* 51: 419-39.

Fillmore, Charles J. (1968). The case for case. *Universals in linguistic theory,* ed., by Emmon Bach and Robert T. Harms, pp. 1-88. New York: Holt, Rinehart and Winston.

(1971). Types of lexical information. In Steinberg & Jakobovits, eds., 1971: 370-392.

(1972). May we come in. In D. M. Smith & R. W. Shuy, eds., *Sociolinguistics in crosscultural perspective.* Washington.

(1976). "Pragmatics and the description of discourse." In S. J. Schmidt, ed., *Pragmatik/Pragmatics 2.* München: Fink.

(1978). On the Organization of Semantic Information in the Lexicon. *Mimeo,* 26 pp.

(1979). Innocence: a second idealization for linguistics. *Berkeley Linguistic Society* 5.

Firth, J. R. (1957). *Papers in Linguistics 1934-1951,* London: Oxford University Press.

(1964). *'The Tongues of Men' and 'Speech,'* London: Oxford University Press (first published 1937 and 1930 respectively).

(1969). Posture and Gestures of Respect. In Maranda, P. and Pouillon J. eds., *Exchange and Communication: Mélanges Lévi-Strauss,* pp. 230-54. Hague: Mouton.

(1972). Verbal and bodily rituals of greeting and parting. In J. S. La Fontaine, ed., *Interpretation of ritual.* London: Tavistock, pp. 1-38.

Fishman, Joshua A., ed. (1968). *Readings in the sociology of language.* The Hague, Paris: Mouton.

Fraser, Bruce (1970). Idioms within transformational grammar. *Foundations of Language* 6:·22–42.

(1975). "Hedged Performatives." In Cole and Morgan, eds., 1975, pp. 187–210.

(1980). *On requesting: An essay in pragmatics.* Ditto, Boston University.

Garfinkel, Harold (1967). *Studies in Ethnomethodology.* New York: Prentice-Hall.

Garvey, Catherine (1977). Play with language and Speech. In S. Ervin–Tripp and C. Mitchell–Kernan, eds., 1977, pp. 27–47.

Garvin, Paul, L. and Riesenberg, S. H. (1952). Respect Behavior on Ponape: An Ethnolinguistic Study. *American Anthropologist* 54: 201–220.

Gleason, H. A. jr. (1968). Contrastive Analysis in Discourse Structure. In *Report of the nineteenth annual round table meeting on linguistics and language studies,* J. E. Alatis, ed., Georgetown University Press, 1968, pp. 39–63.

Gleason, J. V. & Weintraub, S. (1976). The acquisition of routines in child language. *Language in Society* 5.

Gluckman, M., ed. (1962). *Essays on the ritual of social relations.* Manchester: Manchester University Press.

Goffman, Erving (1956). The nature of deference and demeanor. *American Anthropoligist* 58: 473–502.

(1963). *Behavior in Public Places.* New York: The Free Press.

(1967). *Interaction ritual: essays on face to face behavior.* Garden City, New York: Anchor Books.

(1971). *Relations in public: Microstudies of the public order.* Harmondsworth: Penguin.

(1972). "On Face-Work: an Analysis of Ritual Elements in Social Interaction." In John Laver and Sandy Hutcheson, eds., *Communication in Face-to-Face Interaction.* Harmondsworth: Penguin, 319–346.

(1974). *Frame analysis.* Cambridge, Mass. New York: Harper & Row.

(1976). Replies and Responses. *Language in Society.* December 1976, pp. 257–313.

Goldberg, J. (1976). *The syntax, semantics, pragmatics, and sociolinguistics of some conventionalized parenthetical clauses in English: you know and I mean.* Diploma dissertation, Dept of Lingusitics, University of Cambridge.

Goldman–Eisler, F. (1968). *Psycholinguistics-Experiments in Spontaneous Speech.* London: Academic Press.

Goodall, J. van L. (1971). *In the shadow of man.* Glasgow: Collins.

Goodenough, W. H. (1956a). Componential Analysis and the study of meaning. *Language,* pp. 195–216.

(1956b). Residence Rules. *South-Western Journal of Anthropology* 12: 22–37.

Goody, E. (1972). 'Greeting,' 'begging,' and the presentation of respect. In J. S. La Fontaine, ed., *Interpretation of ritual.* London: Tavistock, pp. 39–72.

ed. (1978). *Questions and Politeness.* London etc.: Cambridge University Press.

Gordon, D. & G. Lakoff (1975). "Conversational Postulates." In Cole and Morgan, eds., pp. 83–106.

Grice, H. Paul (1963). "Logic and Conversation," Portion published in Peter Cole and Jerry Morgan, eds., 1975: 41–58.

Griffin, Peg and Frank Humphrey (1978). "Task and Talk," In Shuy and Griffin, eds., 1978.

Gülich, E. (1970). *Makrosyntax der Gliederungssignale im gesprochenen Französisch.*

München: Fink.

Gülich, E. (1978). "*Was sein muß, muß sein.*" *Überlegungen zum Gemeinplatz und seiner Verwendung.* Bielefelder Papiere zur Linguistik 7.

Gumperz, John J. (1976). "Language, Communication, and Public Negotiation," In P. R. Sanday, ed., *Anthropology and the Public Interest,* New York: Academic Press.

Gumperz, John J. and Hymes, D., eds. (1972). *Directions in sociolinguistics: the ethnography of communication.* New York: Holt, Rinehart & Winston.

Hakuta, Kenji (1974). Prefabricated Patterns and the Emergence of Structure in Second Language Acquisition. *Language Learning* 24 (2): 287–297.

(1975). Becoming bilingual at age five: the story of Uguisu. (B.A. honors thesis, Harvard University, Department of Psychology and Social Relations, pp. 25–44.)

Halliday, M. A. K. (1975). *Learning How to Mean,* London: Edward Arnold.

Harada, S. J. (1976). Honorifics. In Shibatani, M. 1976, ed., *Syntax & Semantics* 5, *Japanese Generative Grammar.* Academic Press.

Hasan, R. (1978). "Text in the Systemic-Functional Model." In Dressler, W. U., ed., *Current Trends in Textlinguistics,* Berlin: de Gruyter, pp. 228-246.

Hawes, L. C. (1973). Interpersonal Communication: The Enactment of Routines. In *Explorations in Speech Communication,* J. J. Makay, ed., 1973, Ohio: O. E. Merrill Publ. Columbs, pp. 71–90.

Hill, T. (1958). Institutional Linguistics. In *Orbis* 7: 441–455.

Hockett, C. F. (1975). *Where the Tongue Slips, there Slip I. – Speech Errors as Linguistic Evidence,* ed., by V. Fromkin. The Hague, Mouton.

House, Juliane (1978). "Interaktionsnormen in deutschen und englischen Alltagsdialogen," paper presented at the annual conference of the German Association of Applied Linguistics (GAL), Mainz 1977, to appear in *Linguistische Berichte.*

Humpert, M. (1975). *Linguistische Analyse von Kommunikationsanfängen.* Düsseldorf: Staatsarbeit.

Huxley, J. S., ed. (1966). *Ritualization of behaviour in animals and men.* (Philosophical Transactions of The Royal Society of London, Series B, 251 (772.)

Hymes, Dell H. (1961). Functions of speech: an evolutionary approach. In *Anthropology and education,* Frederick C. Gruber, ed., Philadelphia University of Pennsylvania Press.

(1962). The ethnography of speaking. In *Anthropology and human behavior.* Thomas Gladwin and Willian C. Sturtevant, eds., Washington, D.C., Anthropological Society of Washington, pp. 13–53.

(1964). *Language in culture and society: a reader in linguistics and anthropology.* New York, Harper and Row.

(1964a). Introduction: toward ethnographies of communication. In *The ethnography of communication,* eds., J. J. Gumperz and D. Hymes, pp. 1–34. (Special publication, *American Anthropologist* 66 (6), part 2.) Washington, D.C.: American Anthropological Association.

(1966). Two Types of Linguistic Relativity (With Examples From American Ethnography) in W. Bright, ed., *Sociolinguistics,* The Hague, Paris: Mouton.

(1967). Models of the interaction of language and social setting. (Problems of bilingualism, ed., J. Macnamara.) *Journal of social issues* 23 (2): 8–28.

(1968). The ethnography of speaking. In J. A. Fishman, ed., *Readings in the sociology of Language,* The Hague: Mouton, pp. 99–138.

(1971). Sociolinguistics and the Ethnography of Speaking. In E. Ardener, ed., 1971.

(1972). Models of the interaction of language and social life. *Directions in sociolinguistics,* ed. by John J. Gumperz and Dell Hymes, pp. 35–71. New York: Holt, Rinehart and Winston.

Hymes, Dell H. (1974). "Ways of Speaking." In R. Bauman/J. Sherzer, eds., 1974, 433–451.

(1974a). *Foundations in sociolinguistics: an ethnographic approach.* Philadelphia.

Ingram, D. (Forthcoming). *Phonological disability in children.* London: Edward Arnold.

Irvine, Judith T. (1974). "Strategies of Status Manipulation in the Wolof Greeting." In Baumann & Sherzer, eds., 1974, pp. 167–191.

Isenberg, H. (1976). Einige Grundbegriffe für eine linguistische Texttheorie. In Danes, F. & Viehweger, D. (Hgs.) *Probleme der Textgrammatik* (studia grammatica XI), pp. 47–145.

Jespersen, O. (1922). *Language, its nature, development and origin.* London: Allen & Unwin.

(1922). Formulas and free expressions. The Philosophy of Grammar. Norton Library Edition, pp. 18–24.

Kallmeyer, W. (1978). Fokuswechsel und Fokussierungen als Aktivitäten der Gesprächskonstitution. In Meyer-Herman, R. (Hsg) *Sprechen-Handeln-Interaktion.* Tübingen: Niemeyer.

Kasper, Gabriele (1978). "Pragmatische Defizite im Englisch deutscher Lerner," in *Kongreß berichte der 8. Jahrestagung der Gesellschaft für Angewandte Linguistik GAL e.V. Mainz 1977.* Stuttgart: Hochschul Verlag 1978, pp. 41–54.

(1978a). "Errors in Speech Act Realization and Use of Gambits." *The Canadian Modern Language Review* 35 (1979).

Keenan, E. O. (1976). The universality of conversational implicature. *Language in Society* 5: 67–80.

Keller, E. (1977). A creative approach to conversational competence: gambits. Creativity, new ideas in language teaching 26. Sao Paulo, Brazil: Yazigi. (Available on microfilm from Sociological Abstracts P.O. Box 22206, San Diego, CA 92122.)

Keller, E. and S. Taba-Warner (1976); (1977); (1978). *Gambits 1, openers; Gambits 2, Links; Gambits 3, Responders, Closers and Inventory. A series of three modules.* Ottawa, Canada: Government of Canada. (Available from Printing and Publishing, Supply and Services Canada, Ottawa, Canada K1A OS9.)

Kendon, A. & Ferber, A. (1973). A description of some human greetings. In R. P. Michael & J. H. Crook, eds., *Comparative ecology and behavior of primates,* London: Academic Press, pp. 591–668.

Kendon, A., R. M. Harris, M. R. Key, eds. (1975). *Organization of Behavior in Face-to-Face Interaction.* The Hague, Paris: Mouton.

Kenyon, J. S. (1948). Cultural Levels and Functional Varieties of English. *College English* 10: 31–36.

Kiparsky, Paul (1976). Oral poetry: some linguistic and typological considerations. In B. A. Stolz and R. S. Shannon, eds., *Oral Literature and the Formula,* Ann Arbor: University of Michigan Center for the Coordination of Ancient and Modern Studies, pp. 73–106.

Kirschenblatt-Gimblett, B., ed. (1976). *Speech Play. Research and Resources for Studying Linguistic Creativity.* University of Pennsylvania Press.

Klammer, T. P. (1973). "Foundations for a Theory of Dialogue Structure." In *Poetics* 9, pp. 27–64.

Klein, W. (1977). "Wegauskünfte". Max-Planck-Institut, Nijmegen. (To appear, *Zeitschrift für Literaturwissenschaft und Linguistik.*)

Krashen, Stephen and Robin Scarcella (1978). On routines and patterns in language acquisition and performance. *Language Learning* 28: 283-300.

Labov, William (1972a). *Sociolinguistics patterns.* Philadelphia: University of Pennsylvania Press.

Labov, William (1972b). The logic of nonstandard English. In *Language in the inner city: studies in the Black English vernacular,* pp. 201-240. Philadelphia.

(1972c). "Rules for ritual insults." In Sudnow, D., ed., *Studies in Social Interaction,* New York: Free Press, pp. 120-169.

Labov, William and David Fanschel (1977). *Therapeutic Discourse: Psychotherapy as Conversation.* New York: Academic Press.

La Fontaine, J. S., ed. (1972). *The Interpretation of Ritual. Essays in Honour of A. J. Richards.* London: Tavistock.

Lakoff, George (1972). "Hedges: A Study of Meaning Criteria and the Logic of Fuzzy Concepts." In P. M. Peranteau et al., eds., *Papers from the Eighth Regional Meeting of the Chicago Linguistic Society,* Chicago: Chicago Linguistic Society, pp. 183-228.

(1974). Syntactic amalgans. In *Papers from the tenth regional meeting of the Chicago Linguistic Society,* pp. 321-344. Chicago.

Lakoff, Robin (1973). "The Logic of Politeness; or, Minding Your P's and O's." In C. Corum et al., eds., *Papers from the Ninth Regional Meeting of the Chicago Linguistic Society,* Chicago: Chicago Linguistic Society, pp. 292-305.

(1974a). What you can do with words: politeness, pragmatics and performatives. In *Berkeley studies in syntax and semantics* 1 (16): 1-55. Institute of Human Learning. Univ. of California Berkeley.

(1975). *Language and Woman's Place.* New York etc.: Harper & Row.

Langer, Susanne K. (1942). *Philosophy in a New Key.* Cambridge: Harvard University Press.

Lantis, M. (1960). Vernacular Culture. *American Anthropologists* 62: 202-216.

Laver, John (1975). "Communicative Functions of Phatic Communion." In Kendon et al., eds., 1975, pp. 215-38.

Laver, John & S. Hutcheson, eds. (1972). *Communication in face to face interaction.* Harmondsworth: Penguin.

Leach, E. R. (1966). Ritualization in man in relation to conceptual and social development. In Huxley, Sir Julian, ed., *A Discussion on Ritualization of Behavior in Animals and Man.* Philosophical Transactions of the Royal Society, Series B, 251: 249-526.

(1976). *Culture and communication.* Cambridge.

Lebra, Takie Sugiyama (1976). *Japanese Patterns of Behavior.* Honolulu: The University Press of Hawaii.

Leech, G. N. (1977). Language and Tact. *L.A.U.T. paper* 46, Trier.

Lévi-Strauss, Claude (1958). *Anthropologie structurale.* Paris. Librairie Plon. Translated as *Structural Anthropology,* New York, Basic Books, 1963.

Lewis, David (1969). *Convention.* Cambridge, Mass.: Harvard University Press.

(1972). General semantics. In Davidson and Harman, eds., 1972, pp. 169-218.

Lloyd, D. J. (1968). Our National Mania for Correctness, Language and Culture: A reader (ed., Patrick Gleeson and Nancy Wakefield), 1968, Ohio: Merrill Publishing Company.

Lorenz, K. Z. (1937). The companion in the bird's world. *Auk* 54: 245-73.

Makkai, Adam (1972). *Idiom Structure in English.* The Hague: Mouton.

(1975). Stratificational Solutions to unbridgeable gaps in the Transformational-generative paradig: translation, idiomaticity, and multiple coding. In Koerner, ed.,

Amsterdam Studies in the Theory of Linguistic Science 4, 1975.

(1978). "Idiomaticity as a Language Universal." In J. H. Greenberg, ed., *Universals of Human Language* 3, Stanford: Stanford University Press, pp. 401–448.

Malinowski, Bronislaw (1923). The Problem of Meaning in Primitives Languages. In C. K. Odgen & I. A. Richards, 1923, *The meaning of meaning,* London: Routledge and Kegan Paul, pp. 451–510.

(1935). *Coral gardens and their magic* 2. London, Allen and Unwin.

(1937). The dilemma of contemporary linguistics. (Review of M. M. Lewis, Infant Speech.) *Nature* (London) 140: 172–173.

Malkiel, Yakov (1959). Studies in irreversible binomials. Lingua 8. 113–160.

Matisoff, James A. (1979). "Psycho-ostensive Expressions in Yiddish." Philadelphia: ISHI Publications.

McDermott, R. P. (1976). "*Kids Make Sense*." Unpublished Ph.D. Dissertation, Stanford University.

McDermott, R. P. and David R. Roth (1979). The Social Organization of Behavior: Interactional Approaches. *Annual Review of Anthropology.*

Maclay, H. and Osgood, C. E. (1959). Hesitation Phenomena in Spontaneous English Speech. *Word* 15: 19–44.

McLuhan, M., with Watson, W. (1971). *From Cliché to Archetype.* New York: Pocket Books.

Mead, George Herbert (1934). *Mind, Self, and Society.* Chicago: University of Chicago Press.

(1954). *The Philosophy of the Present.* Chicago: Open Court Publishing Co.

Mehan, Hugh (1978). "Structuring School Structure." *Harvard Educational Review* 45 (1): 311–38.

(1979). *Learning Lessons.* Cambridge, Massachusetts: Harvard University Press.

Meyer–Hermann, R. (1978). Aspekte der Analyse metakommunikativer Interaktionen. In. Meyer-Hermann, R., ed. (1978).

ed. (1978). *Sprechen-Handeln-Interaktion.* Tübingen: Niemeyer.

Miller, G. A., P. N. Johnson–Laird (1976). *Language and Perception.* Cambridge, Mass.: Harvard University Press.

Mishler, E. G. (1975a). "Studies in Dialogue and Discourse: An exponential law of successive questioning." *Language in Society* 4: 31–52.

(1975b). "Studies in Dialogue and Discourse II: Types of Discourse Initiated by and Sustained through Questioning." *Psycholinguistic Research Journal* 4: 99–121.

Moerman, M. (1969). A Little Knowledge. In Tyler, ed., *Cognitive Anthropology,* New York: Holt, Rinehart & Winston, pp. 449–469.

Morgan, Jerry L. (1978). Two types of conventions in indirect speech acts. In *Syntax and Semantics* 9: *Pragmatics,* New York: Academic Press, pp. 261–280.

Morris, Charles W. (1946). *Signs, Language and Behavior.* New York: Prentice-Hall, Inc.

Morris, D. (1967). *The naked ape.* London: Jonathan Cape.

Nakane, C. (1970). *Japanese society.* Harmondsworth: Penguin.

Neisser, Ulric (1962). Cultural and cognitive discontinuity. In *Anthropology and Human Behavior,* Thomas Gladwin and William C. Sturtevant, eds., Washington, Anthropological Society of Washington.

Neustupný, J. V. (1968). Politeness patterns in the system of communication. In *Proceedings of the eighth international congress of anthropological and ethnological sciences,* pp. 412–19. Tokyo and Kyoto.

Ogden, C. K. and I. A. Richards (1923). *The Meaning of Meaning.* New York: Harcourt and Brace.

Olson, David R. (1976). "From Utterance to Text: The Bias of Language in Speech and Writing," In Fisher/Diez-Gurerro, eds., *Language and Logic in Personality and Society*, New York.

Ono, S. (1976). Fragile Blossom, Fragile Superpower. A New Interpretation. *Japan Quarterly* 23:12-27.

Oswalt, R. L. (forthcoming). Baby talk and the genesis of some basic Porno words. To appear in *International Journal of American Linguistics.*

Pawley, Andres and Frances Syder (1976). Creativity vs. memorization in spontaneous discourse: the role of institutionalized sentences. Unpubl. ms.

Peters, Ann (1979). Units of acquisition. Unpubl. ms., Univ. of Hawaii.

Philips, S. (1972). Participant structures and communicative competence. In Cazden et al., eds., 1972.

(1974). *The invisible culture.* Ph.D. Dissertation. The University of Pennsylvania.

(1976). Some Sources of cultural variables in the regulation of talk. *Language in Society* 5: 81-96.

Pike, Kenneth L. (1967). *Language in Relation to a Unified Theory of the Structure of Human Behavior.* The Hague: Mouton.

Polanyi, Michael (1962). *The Tacit Dimension.* New York: Harper and Row.

Pomerantz, Anita (1978). Compliment responses: notes on the cooperation of multiple constraints. *Studies in the organization of conversational interaction,* ed by Jim Schenkein, New York: Academic Press, pp. 79-112.

Quirk, R. (1968). *The Use of English.* London, Longmans.

Quirk, R., S. Greenbaum, G. Leech (1972). *A Grammar of Contemporary English* Seminar Press.

Rath, R. (1975). Kommunikative Paraphrasen. *Linguistik und Didatik* 22: 103-118.

Redder, A. (1980). "Ich wollte sagen." *Akten des 14. Linguistischen Kolloquium 3 Bochum 1979, Band 2*: 117-126. Tübingen: Niemeyer.

Rehbein, Jochen (1972). "Entschuldigungen und Rechtfertigungen." In D. Wunderlich, ed., 1972, pp. 288-317.

(1976). Planen II: Planbildung in Sprechhandlungssequenzen. L.A.U.T.: Universität Trier.

(1977). *Komplexes Handeln.* Stuttgart: Metzler.

(1979a). Sprechhandlungsaugmente. Zur Organisation der Hörersteuerung. In Weydt, H., ed., *Partikeln der deutschen Sprache.* Berlin usw. De Gruyter.

(1979b). Ankündigungen. In Germanistische Linguistik (Jahresbericht 1978). Hildesheim: Olms.

Rehbein, J. & K. Ehlich (1976). "On Effective Reasoning," in Nickel, G. (ed.). *Proceedings of the Fourth International Congress of Applied Linguistics,* Stuttgart: Hochschul Verlag, pp. 313-338.

Roberts, B. (1940). Breeding behavior of penguins. *British Grahamsland Expedition Scientific Report* I, pp. 195-254.

Rothkegel, A. (1973). *Feste Syntagmen. Grundlagen, Strukturbeschreibung und automatische Analyse.* Tübingen.

Ruhl, Charles (1977a). Two forms of Reductionism. In M. Paradis, ed., *The Fourth LACUS Forum,* Columbia, So. Carolina: Hornbeam Press, pp. 370-383.

(1977b). Idioms and data. In R. J. DiPietro et al., eds., *The Third LACUS Form.*

Sacks, H. (1971). Das Erzählen von Geschichten innerhalb von Unterhaltungen. In Kjolseth, R./Sack, R., ed., 1971a. *Zur Soziologie der Sprache, Kölner Zeitschrift für Soziologie und Sozialpsychologie, Sonderheft 15.*

(1972). On the analysability of stories by children. In J. J. Gumperz & D. Hymed, eds., 1972, pp. 329–45.

(1976). Paradoxes, Pre-Sequences and Pronouns. Cambridge Pragmatics Micofiche.

Sacks, H., Schegloff, E. A. and Jefferson, G. (1974). A simplest systematics for the organization of turn-taking for conversation. *Language 50*: 696–735.

Sadock, J. (1972). Speech act idioms. *In Papers from the eighth regional meeting of the Chicago Linguistic Society*, pp. 329–39. Chicago.

Sadock, J. (1974). *Towards a linguistic theory of speech acts.* New York: Academic Press.

Salomond, Anne (1974). Rituals of Encounter among the Maori: Sociolinguistic Study of a Scene. In Bauman/Sherzer, eds., 1974, pp. 192–212.

Sanches, M. and B. G. Blount, eds. (1975). *Sociocultural Dimensions of Language Use.* New York etc.: Academic Press.

Sapir, E. (1931). Communication. *Encyclopedia of the Social Sciences* 4: 78–81.

Schegloff, E. (1968). Sequencing in conversational openings. *American Anthropologist* 70: 1075–1095.

(1978). "On Some Questions and Ambiguities in *Conversation*." In Dressler W. U., ed., *Current Trends* in Textlinguistics, Berlin: de Gruyter, pp. 81–102.

Schegloff, E. & H. Sacks (1973). "Opening up Closings." In *Semiotica* 8: 289–327.

Schiffer, Steven R. (1972). *Meaning.* London: Oxford University Press.

Schlauch, M. (1945). *The Gift of Tongues.* New York.

Schütz, Alfred (1960). *Der sinnhafte Aufbau der Sozialen Welt. Eine Einleitung in die verstehende Soziologie.* Vienna: Springer.

(1962). *Collected Papers I: The Problem of Social Reality.* The Hague: Martinus Nijhoff.

Schütze, F. (1978). Strategische Interaktion im Verwaltungsgericht – eine soziologische Analyse zum Kommunikationsverlauf im Verfahren zur Anerkennung als Wehrdienstverweigerer. In Hoffmann-Riem, W. u.a., *Interaktion vor Gericht.* Baden-Baden: Nomos.

Searle, John R. (1969). *Speech Acts: An Essay in the Philosophy of Language.* London: Cambridge University Press.

(1971). What is A Speech Act? *The Philosophy of Language.* J. R. Searle, ed., 1971, pp. 39–53.

(1975). "Indirect Speech Acts." In P. Cole and J. L. Morgan, eds., pp. 59–82.

(1975a), "Speech acts and recent Linguistics." *Annals of the New York Academy of Sciences* 263: 27–38. Developmental psycho-linguistics and communication disorders, eds., D. Aaronson and R. Reiber.

(1976). "A classification if illocutionary acts." *Language in Society* 5: 1.1–23.

Sebeok, Thomas A. (1962). "Coding in the evolution of signalling behavior." *Behavioral Science* 7 (4): 430–42.

Sherzer, Dina (1975). "Saying in inventing: Gnomic expressions in Molloy." In Kirchenblatt-Gimblett, B., 1975, pp. 163–171.

Shields, M. M. (1978). "Some communicational skills of young children – a study of dialogue in the nursery school." In R. N. Campbell and P. T. Smith, eds., *Recent Advances in the Psychology of Language,* Plenum Publishing Corporartion, pp. 313–335.

Shuy, Roger and Peg Griffin, eds. (1978). *The Study of Children's Functional Language and Education in the Early Years.* Final Report to the Carnegie Corporation of New York, Arlington, Va.: Center for Applied Linguistics.

Sinclair, J. McH., J. J. Forsyth, R. M. Coulthard, and M. Ashby (1972). *The English used by teachers and pupils.* Report to Social Science Research Council of Great Britain from the University of Birmingham. Mimeographed.

Sinclair, J. M. and R. M. Coulthard (1975). *Toward an Analysis of Discourse.* New York: Oxford University Press.

Sivertsen, E. (1960). *Cockney Phonology.* Oslo: Oslo University Press.

Smith, M. C. (1957). The social functions and meaning of Hausa praise-singing. *Africa* 27: 26–44.

Sorhus, Helen B. (1977). To Hear Ourselves – Implications for Teaching English as a Second Language. *English Language Teaching Journal* 31 (3) April 1977: 211-221.

Spitzbardt, H. (1962). *Lebendiges Englisch.* Halle.

Stalnaker, Robert C. (1978). "Assertion" in Peter Cole ed. *Syntax and Semantics* IX. *Pragmatics.* New York: Academic Press, 315-332.

Stone, G. W. ed. (1961). *Issues, Problems and Approaches in the Teaching of English.* New York.

Tannen, Deborah and Piyale Öztek (1977). Health to our mouths: formulaic expressions in Turkish and Greek. *Papers from the Third Meeting of the Berkeley Linguistic Society.*

Tannen, D. (1978). The Effect of Expectations on Conversation. *Discourse Processes* 1: 205-209.

Terasaki, A. K. (1976). Pre-Announcement Sequences in Conversation. *Social Sciences Working Paper* 99. Irvine: School of Social Sciences, University of California.

Turner, R. (1972/9176). Einige formale Eigenschaften des therapeutischen Gesprächs. In: Auwärter/Kirsch/Schröter, eds., *Seminar: Kommunikation Interaktion Identität.* Frankfurt: Suhrkamp.

Turner, V. J. (1969). *The ritual process: Structure and anti structure.* Chicago: Aldine.

Ullmer-Ehrich, V. (1977). *Zur Syntax und Semantik von Substantivierungen im Deutschen.* Kronenberg/Ts.: Scriptor.

Underwood, M. (1975). *Listen to This!* London, OUP.

van Dijk, T. A. (1977). Context and Cognition: Knowledge Frames and Speech Act Comprehension. *Journal of Pragmatics* 1 (3): 211-231.

Van Lancker, Diana (1974). *Heterogeneity in Language and Speech.* UCLA Ph.D. dissertation.

Vonnegut Jr., Kurt (1974). *Breakfast of Champions.* Frogmore: Panther Books.

(1977). *Slapstick or lone so me no more!* Frogmore: Panther Books.

Vygotsky, L. S. (1978). *Mind in Society.* Cambridge, Mass.: Harvard University Press.

Warner, A. (1964). *A Short Guide to English Style.* London.

Watson, Karen A. (1975). Transferable communicative routines: strategies and group identity in two speech events. *Language in Society* 4: 53-72.

Watzlawick, P., J. H. Beavin & D. D. Jackson (1967). *Pragmatics of Human Communication,* New York: Norton.

Weinreich, Uriel (1969). Problems in the analysis of idioms. In J. Puhvel, ed., *Substance and Structure of Language.* Berkeley and Los Angeles: University of California Press.

Wells, G., M. Montgomery and M. MacLure (1978). Discourse and the development of language. Symposium on Discourse Analysis. Fifth International Congress of Applied Linguistics. Montreal, August 1978.

Whorf, B. L. (1956). *Language, Thought, and Reality.* Selected Writings of Benjamin Lee Whorf. J. B. Carroll, ed., Cambridge, Mass.: M.I.T. Press.

Widdowson, H. G. (1973). "Directions in the Teaching of Discourse." In Corder, S. P. &

E. Roulet, eds., *Theoretical Linguistic Models in Applied Linguistics*, Brussels: AIMAV/Paris: Didier, pp. 65–76.

Widdowson, H. G. (1979). Rules and Procedures in Discourse Analysis. In Widdowson, H. G., ed., *Explorations in Applied Linguistics.* Oxford: O.U.P., pp. 141–149.

Wittgenstein, Ludwig (1968). *Philosophical Investigations.* Oxford: Blackwell.

Wolfson, Nessa (1976). Speech events and natural speech: some implications for sociolinguistic methodology. *Language in Society* 5: 189-209.

(1978). A feature of performed narrative: the conversational historical present. *Language in Society* 7: 215–237.

Wolfson, Nessa and Joan Manes. In press. Don't dear me. *Language and women's lives,* ed. by Ruth Borker, Nelly Furman and Sally McConell-Ginet.

Wong-Fillmore, Lily (1976). *The Second Time Around.* Stanford University Ph.D. dissertation.

(1979). Individual differences in second language acquisition. In C. Fillmore et al., eds., *Individual Differences in Language Abilities and Linguistic Behavior*, 1979, New York: Academic Press.

Wright, G. H. von (1963). *Norm and Action.* London: Routledge & Kegan Paul.

Wunderlich, Dieter, ed. (1972). *Linguistische Pragmatik.* Frankfurt/M.: Athenäum.

(1976). *Studien zur Sprechakttheorie.* Frankfurt: Suhrkamp.

(1978). "Wie analysiert man Gespräche? Beispiel Wegauskünfte." In *Linguistische Berichte* 58: 41–76.

Yamanashi, Masa-aki (1974). On Minding your p's and q's in Japanese: a case study from honorifics. In *Papers from the tenth regional meeting of the Chicago Linguistic Society,* pp. 760–71. Chicago.

Youssouf, I. A., Grimshaw, A. D. & Bird, C. S. (MS.) (1975). Greetings in the desert. Indiana University.

Zimmer, Karl (1958). "Situational Formulas," ms. Department of Linguistics, University of California, Berkeley.

Zwicky, A. M. (1974). Hey Whatsyourname! In *Papers from the tenth regional meeting of the Chicago Linguistic Society* pp. 787-801.

Драздаускене М.-Л.А. (1970). Контактоустанавливающая функция речи. Кандидатская диссертация. Москва.

Драздаускене М.-Л.А. (1974). Лексические особенности речи в конуактоустанавливающей функции. – Вестник Московското Унивета, серия филология 5: 56–64.

Формановская, Н.И. (1977). Русский речевой этикет в коммента- риях. София. "Наука и искусство."

Халеева, И. И. (1977). Обучение диалогической речи в языковом вузе на основе использования звукозаписи/на материале устных климе немецкого языка/.Автореферат кандидатской диссертации. Москва.

Шведова, Н.Ю. (1960). Очерки по синтаксису русской разговорной речи. Москва, АН СССР.

Biographical Notes

Florian Coulmas is a research fellow at the Linguistics Department of Düsseldorf University. He has taught at the universities of Hiroshima, Japan, and Bielefeld, the institution from which he received his doctorate. His publications include a book on language understanding and articles concerning sociocultural conditions of language use and the philosophy of language. He is also the editor of *The Festschrift for Native Speaker*. The Hague: Mouton.

Maria-Liudvika Drazdauskiene is a professor at the English Department of Vilnius University, the institution from which she graduated as a B.A. She became a Candidate of Philology (M.A.) at Mascow University in 1970 and subsequently returned to Vilnius to teach at the English Department. She is the author of a book on the phatic function of speech, and numerous articles on a variety of subjects such as terminology, poetry and semantics. Her present research interest is in verbal stereotypes.

Willis J. Edmondson works at the Seminar für Sprachlehrforschung of the Ruhr-Universität Bochum, and is currently interested in theories and applications of discourse analysis.

Charles A. Ferguson is Professor of Linguistics at Stanford University. He has directed numerous research projects in language universals, psycholinguistics, and language planning. Educated at the University of Pennsylvania in Oriental Studies, he has taught at the universities of Georgetown, Michigan, Washington, Indiana and Pennsylvania. Among his many publications are books and articles on various problems of Arabic languages, contrastive linguistics, language acquisition, and sociolinguistics.

Bruce Fraser is professor of Linguistics at Boston University, Boston, U.S.A. His numerous publications include books and articles on problems of language structure and use, idiomaticity, metaphor, performatives and verbal politeness. He has also directed research projects into the intricate area of utterance meaning and pragmatics.

Peg Griffin is a research fellow at the Institute for Comparative Human Development of the University of California, San Diego conducting a research project on communication in the classroom. She has done field work in the Philippines, where she was also an English teacher. After having been engaged in a research project on "Children's Functional Language Use and Education in the Early Years" at the Center for Applied Linguistics in Washington D.C. she was an Assistent Professor at the English Department of the University of Southern California in Los Angeles.

Juliane House (Ph.D., University of Toronto) studied Applied Linguistics at the Modern Language Center, Ontario Institute for Studies in Education. She has been working at the Seminar für Sprachlehrforschung of Ruhr-Universität Bochum, FRG, since 1974. She was first involved in work on a pedagogic grammar of English, and is currently working on a project on communicative competence in English Language Teaching. Her main interests are in translation theory, contrastive analysis, and pragmatics.

Gabriele Kasper studied Sprachlehrforschung and English and German linguistics and literature. Since 1973 she has been working at the Seminar für Sprachlehrforschung of Ruhr-Universität Bochum, FRG, where she was previously engaged in a project on pedagogic grammar. She is now a "Wissenschaftliche Assistentin" and a team member on a project on communicative competence in English Language Teaching. Her publications include work on error analysis, contrastive analysis and interlanguage studies. Her current interests focus on the pragmatic dimension of interlanguages.

Eric Keller is professor of Linguistics at the University of Quebec at Montreal. He was educated at the universities of Michigan, Utrecht, and Toronto, where he received his Ph.D. in Linguistics. In 1976-77 he held a post-doctoral fellowship from the Medical Research Council of Canada at the Department of Neurophysiology at the University of Ulm. His main research interest is in a psycholinguistic theory of speech production. Among his publications are also works on neurolinguistics and conversational strategies.

John David Michael Henry Laver is Senior Lecturer and head of the Phonetics Laboratory of the University of Edinburgh. He received an M.A. in French Language and Literature in 1966, a Diploma in Phonetics three years thereafter, and his Ph.D. in 1975, all from the same institution. From 1963 until 1966, he was a Lecturer in Phonetics at the University of Ibadan, Nigeria. In 1971, he held a visiting post in the Department of Linguistics of the University of California at Los Angeles. His research interests include experimental phonetics, neurolinguistics, sociolinguistics and semiotics. Among his book publications are *Communication in Face to Face Interaction* (1972), with his wife Sandy Hutcheson, *Phonetics in Linguistics* (1973), and *The Phonetic Description of Voice Quality* (1980).

Joan Manes received her Ph.D. in linguistics from the University of Pennsylvania in 1976, and has been Assistant Professor in the Department of Anthropology of the University of Virginia since 1974. She has worked on folk definitions, combining an interest in semantics with a concern for ethnography of speaking and, in general, for a sociolinguistic approach to the study of language. Her research with Professor Nessa Wolfson of the University of Pennsylvania on American English terms of address and, currently, on the use of compliments in social interactions unites this concern with an interest in discourse analysis.

Hugh Mehan received his Ph.D. from the University of California, Santa Barbara, in 1971. He taught at the Department of Sociology of the University of California, San Diego, where he is presently director of the teacher education program. His publications include articles and books on ethnomethodology (together with Houston Wood), the sociology of language, classroom interaction, and socialization. The methodological approach Mehan advocates, "constitutive ethnography," would give equal attention to the process as well as the outcomes of structuring activities in social interaction.

Piyale Cömert Öztek received a B.A. from Bogazici University in Istanbul. Currently, she is at the University of California, Berkeley, the institution from which she has an M.A.

Jochen Rehbein is professor of the Sociology of Language with special reference to the acquisition of FL at the Seminar für Sprachlehrforschung of the Ruhr-Universität Bochum. He was trained at the universities of Berlin and Paris. He received his doctorate from the Freie Universität Berlin. From 1973 until 1978 he was an Assistant Professor at the Linguistics Department of Düsseldorf University. He worked on linguistic pragmatics, theory of action, discourse analysis, and classroom interaction, the topics on which he has written a book and numerous articles.

Deborah Tannen is an Assistant Professor of Linguistics of the Department of Linguistics of Georgetown University. As a graduate student, she was a Danforth Fellow. She received her Ph.D. from the University of California, Berkeley. Among her publications is a monograph about modern Greek literature, as well as numerous articles in the areas of discourse analysis, frame theory, and conversational strategies. In several of them constrasts between modern Greek and American English are investigated.

Jef Verschueren is a research fellow of the Belgian National Science Foundation at the University of Antwerp, the institution of which he received his degree of licentiate in Germanic Philology, and where he was an Assistant for English in 1974-75. From 1975 until 1978 he was a Harkness Fellow at the University of California, Berkeley, where he received his M.A. in 1976 and his Ph.D. in 1979. He is the author of an annotated bibliography on Pragmatics, and of articles in this field. He is also review editor of the *Journal of Pragmatics* and co-editor of *Pragmatics and Beyond.*

Nessa Wolfson received her PhD from the Department of Linguistics at the University of Pennsylvania in 1976. She taught at the University of Pennsylvania English Program for Foreign Students from 1967 through 1976 and served as Associate Director of the Program during the academic year 1976-1977. Since 1976 she has been Director of the Program in Educational Linguistics at the Graduate School of Education of the University of Pennsylvania. Professor Wolfson's range of interests include sociolinguistics, discourse analysis and TESL. She has united these interests in her research on the use of the conversational historical present and in her work with Professor Joan Manes of the University of Virginia on rules of speaking in American English, specifically forms of address and complimenting as a social strategy.

Index of Names

Index of Subjects